MAKE WORLD

Newton Phillip

A sinful world

europe books

© 2023 **Europe Books**| London
www.europebooks.co.uk | info@europebooks.co.uk

ISBN 9791220144582
First edition: November 2023

CONTENTS
A sinful world

Now read this book and be inspired
Humans' reputation is on trial

HUMAN DEVELOPMENT

The universe was formed and life developed billions of years ago.

That is the conclusion of science, proven to be true.

Humans were not the first, and maybe they will not be the last of the many creatures that came and went, some gone forever in extinction.

And yes, there is no need to guess, humans have been here for a very long time, in years counted by the thousands.

Two millennia after Christ came, and the rest, well, it's anyone's guess, nothing short of a few more thousands of years.

So yes indeed, one may pop the question. How old is humans' existence?

This question has baffled science with different opinions, and with different numbers as the answer.

Some said that humans existed for about ten thousand years, some said that it could be even much more than that, about fifty thousand years, and perhaps even many more, no one is quite sure.

Yes, that's how long it has been assumed that mankind has walked upon this earth before and after Christ.

And during such a very long time, their numbers have been steadily on the rise.

And what humans have done during all those years?

Years of darkness and years of light: years with problems day and night, years that made mankind tremble with fright, indeed, years that were very difficult just to survive, years in which superstitions instead of knowledge was the light.

And yes, it is true, and indeed very sad too that during all those years humans have created a very sinful world instead of an earthly paradise.

9

And that they did, no one knows why, and so it had been right through their lives.

And yet they agreed that it was not necessary, a paradise humans could have developed quite easily, with mankind living together peacefully, without wars, injustice, and destitute poverty.

Oh yes indeed, and most certainly if only mankind had really tried, the world could have been a paradise. It could have been a peaceful place with more kindness and less wickedness.

But instead, humans developed to be hostile and corrupt, deceitful and treacherous.

And this is why the world has always been in a mess, despite the many changes in development and progress.
Humans are always trying to escape the consequences for the wrongs they did, doing them again and again, always accusing and pointing fingers at someone else to blame.

Yes, unfortunately their weaknesses often took control of them, and that's the moment when they commit their sins.

Bold enough to do wrong things, but never prepared to accept blame, much less to face the consequences, they shield themselves with their cowardice.

Sins which were often inhumane, sins that were the cause of a great deal of suffering; sins that even claimed lives, for trivial causes people were persecuted and even murdered.

Yes, regretfully that's how humans were developing, from generation to generation they passed on their sins.

But why had this turned out to be so? Why was it that the world was developing to be so sinful?

Why was it in darkness the people chose to live? When they could have made the world a much brighter place? Why was their choice so inhumane? Creating a world with a lot of suffering.

Indeed, quite often human suffering was self-inflicted, with no other cause but himself to blame.

So again, the answers to those questions were the same: with no one able to explain, instead, fingers were always pointing at someone else to blame, that's how it was, and still it remains.

And this is what they said were the reasons for sin, 'the people were illiterate, they had no knowledge, so in superstitions they were engaged.'

Yes, regretfully that's how humans were developing, superstitions and pleasures were what they were indulged in.

Their minds were empty, their appetites hungry, so to sin was a means of nourishment for their enervated body.

It made them feel good the way they should, and the foundation was laid for a sinful world.

Yes indeed, to sin was pleasure, and to humans that's what mattered.

And that was the cause of most of their problems, piling one on top of the other.

Problems that were difficult to solve, few were ever resolved, so the piles kept on getting bigger. But there were others with a different opinion, they believed too fearful were humans.

Yes indeed, they believed that fear was the cause, and especially fear of superstitions.

People did things they believed in whether or not they were sins.

Yes, they did them inspired by fear, and the evil they did, they didn't even care.
And so it had been a reality and not a dream, that whatever humans reaped, that was what they sowed.

Passing it on to the next generation, whatever they had achieved right or wrong made no difference, both were together inherited by new generations, the past often entered the present, stayed for a moment, and then onwards to the future some went.

And that's how life went on for century after century, that was the norm in every country.

Passing progress to new generations, in a package with all sorts of problems.

Problems that were destructive, problems that created the mess the world was in, problems that seem never to end, passing all the time from one generation to the next.

So now, together we shall travel through time, from the origin of human beings to this point they have climbed.

To see exactly what humans have done, during the many years from the first day they were born.

So in this book you have a good look, and to you it shall reveal the glories, the sorrows, the tears, and the dreams.

What humans have done during their long stretch of time: how they have spent their years.

And as you continue to read this book, don't for one moment be deceived.

For this is a book about you, it is about everything that is a human being, what humans did, what they do and believe in, it is about their thoughts and their dreams, it is about their capabilities.

So yes indeed, this is a book of facts not fiction, it is about humans' development with facts of the past and the present, as seen through wise observing eyes, facts which are revealed to you as you read this book right through.

With some of the things humans have done, things they have done during their existence, things that were right as well as wrong, things outstanding as well as disgusting.

Yes indeed, they are all truths, truths collected on humans' journey towards the future, and passed from generation to generation one after the other, truths which they could not destroy nor conceal, and may even be very hard to believe.

Truths indeed which will make your hairs curl, and may even intimidate your soul.

Yes indeed, truths that are real, things that human beings have done, truths that may even swell your tongue, when with spoken words you try to pronounce.

Truths that may even traumatize your brain, making you feel proud as well as disgusted and ashamed, knowing the things humans did.

Yes indeed, truths that are very real, so don't for one moment be deceived as you continue to read.

And despite the barbarity of their deeds, humans never for one moment believed that they were wrong, barbarity was very common.

So truths continue, mean and horrible, truths that seemed impossible.

Many that were a credit to humans' existence, some things indeed exceeded excellence, and still they have not yet reached to the peak of humans' intelligence.

So yes, there were many things human beings have done during their lifetime over the centuries, and that included things they did to be right when they were wrong, and to each generation they passed them on.

And for a very long time they were common, wrongs committed as the norm, wrongs that were savagely brutal, and yet taken for granted as something normal.

Committing them time and time again, for centuries new generations did the same.

Oh yes indeed, it's all about truths you shall read, and when you have finished reading this book, refreshed, and very much younger you will look.

And if you don't, then read it again, but this time make certain that you don't miss anything.

So yes indeed, some things humans did were beyond belief, some in this book you will read, both right and wrong.

In fact, whatever was ruthless and savage, humans' hands were engaged.

Especially from the horrors of their beliefs, savagely executed in sacrificial deeds.

And it is true, no need to argue, many things human beings did were extremely ruthless and savage, impossible to forgive; luckily today they are not doing them still.

But unfortunately, human beings are still causing grief, with one another they can't live in peace.

And this is after centuries of humans' development, a cure for their malevolence is not yet found, they don't know where to look above the ground, not even among the stars nothing is found.

And as the evil of humans' ways gets entangled with their rage, there was nothing too wicked nor horrid for humans to ignore, left forgotten, left neglected, left to be blown away in the wind.

In fact, the more gruesome was their barbarity, the more they were involved, and the greater was their pleasure, indeed, they felt better.

Yes indeed, cruelty was a means of pleasure, and it was the same in every culture.

Humans did some horrid things, and often they did them to entertain.

And that justified their involvement in sin, so the horrors of their ways were repeated again whenever the occasions came.

Yes, they were repeated many times again, especially in rituals and ceremonies.

Horrors that became the norm, and were taken for granted; horrors committed in human sacrifices.

That was something no one would miss, not even if they were very sick.

So, what can we say about humans today, as compared with our early ancestors?

How much have humans changed with the progress they have made, after so many thousands of years in existence?

A great deal no doubt, with the many changes that came about, leaving much of the past to perish behind.

And this had been particularly so, in humans' quest for knowledge and their desire to know the reality of everything.

Hence, human beings have moved constantly forwards, although sometimes slipping backwards.

Moving with and without the times, taking what they needed, and leaving the rest behind. Blinded by their determination to succeed and progress, mankind continued in a direction that was not always the best.

But it was always in a direction heading towards the future, a journey that was bent and twisted with obstacles everywhere, bumpy and rugged was the pathway, yet humans traveled night and day. Traveling from one point in time, to reach to the future they had to climb.

And that they did courageously, because reaching to the future was where they wanted to be.

Yes indeed, human beings were very keen and determined, to get to the future was always their aim, and to get there they would not stop for anything.

And although it was a journey full of danger, exposed to tragedies from the forces of nature.

Still mankind pushed forwards straight ahead, doing whatever had to be done and nothing else. Doing whatever it was, right or wrong, bad or good, and whether or not they should.

And that humans did, despite their difficulties, their lack of knowledge, skills., and the uncertainties.

Humans kept on going, building and destroying, doing whatever they had to do pushing their way through.

And what they did was most daring and bold, and with determination to achieve their goals.

Although they were never quite sure of what they were doing, nor exactly where they were heading. Humans did whatever they had to do, that was the rhythm in which life continued.

Day after day getting things done, and it didn't really matter if they were right or wrong, both were a challenge to get things done, it meant progressive development.

Yes, that was what was real and certain, it was the reality of living, it was the reality of getting things done, survival favoured only the strong.

Nothing was ever given to human beings; they always had to choose and create whatever they wanted, gaining experience from making mistakes, and sometimes with severe consequences. Yes, they had to make and develop their own pathway, and it was never easy from day to day. So, the choice they made, well, it led to this way, to the development of the world as it is today. Indeed, the world has always been as it is in whatever way, from yesterday's developments that were made.

Successes and failures patched together; those were the pillars that kept the world from tumbling over.

Those were the pillars which kept the world upright, whether or not they were wrong or right.

Those were the pillars the world depended upon, to keep upright and maintain its balance.

Pillars built with efforts of success and failures, and of course with slave labourers.

So yes indeed, that was the choice taken, and perhaps with some consideration for both the present and future generations.

Yet still it was a path which led through darkness into light, still today it is not very bright.

But at least today people are more knowledgeable, creative and more adaptable.

And perhaps too much addicted to their technologies, which may one day bring them down on their knees.

And as human beings, always struggling in search of survival and peace, they were able to stay on the same pathway, despite their problems with difficulties.

And they kept on going, pushing and shoving, not always sure where they were heading.

They just followed their footsteps wherever they led, with some hope that at least it would not be through the doors of hell.

And so, it had been an exhausting journey, through a dark and troubled past.

Into the brightness of a glimmer of hope that never seems to ever last.

A journey that had been lengthy and hazardous, with constant fear of the superstitious.

Superstitious forces that humans feared, believing they were from the gods above, or perhaps from demons from hell.

Forces they dread, confused with superstitions that fill their heads.

Forces that were very real, invisible in the wind, and fetish when blowing.

Indeed, forces which brought destruction, hidden within them were demons.

Causing damage and claiming lives as humans continued on their journey mile after mile. Indeed, it was a journey that was very unpredictable, to foretell anything, not even a sorcerer was able to do.

So, driven by the forces of their ambitions and courage, early humans never lost confidence on their voyage.

They knew that they had a future to reach, and to get there, they had to be discreet.

So it was to their gods they offered sacrifices to beseeched the safety which they needed.

And troubled with that on their minds all the time, reaching to the future was an exhausting climb. A climb the people made bit by bit, some tumbled over as they slipped and tripped.

Some with a sprained ankle, or a broken arm, they carried on enduring no further harm.

Continuing forwards straight ahead, to the future they wanted to reach before they were dead; that was their worry, the noise in their heads which kept them going straight ahead. So through the dangers and the horrors of a rugged path, and through the darkness and the light, mankind tread courageously in direction straight ahead.

Right from the beginning the journey was daunting, and yet straight ahead humans kept on going.

There was never anything that was able to stop them from traveling, despite the difficulties which followed them.

Doing so with courage and a determination that they must carry on, with whatever they had they just kept on going in the same direction.

Not very sure exactly where they were heading, step after step mankind just kept on going.

But everyone knew of course that they were heading towards the future, because there was nowhere else to go whatsoever, except of course six feet under.

But what they did not know was that they still had a very long way to go, and on their journey anything was possible.

And as they were often ill-prepared for the difficulties and the troubles which ambushed them ahead.

Very often many got sick, some got wounded and ended up dead, cures at those times were very scarce, it was either blackmagic or prayers.

And that was mainly because humans had little knowledge of medicines for cures, and they were still without the necessary know-how to treat injuries and illnesses.

Indeed, humans were still without the courage and the skill to invade nature's vast encyclopedic sea of knowledge; knowledge which was theirs as nature's heirs.

So for centuries human beings remain irrational and superstitious, uneasy and cantankerous.

Without the knowledge of medicines for cures, they relied upon the stars, goddesses and gods.

Surrendering to their ignorance and fears, indeed human beings were gullible to superstitions for many long years.

Superstitions that kept them away from the light, not really knowing what's wrong and what's right. Superstitions that claimed many youthful lives, once you were ill; recovery turned a blind eye, it was time to kiss your life good-bye; the angel of death had arrived.

And that was because of the wrongs they believed were right, wrongs that were only superstitions and could not save lives.

But that never stopped humans from their adventurous drive, despite the perils they suffered under the skies.

So they drifted and settled upon new lands, expanding in numbers, in tribes and in clans.

And as the lands expanded with more and more settlers, populations kept growing unfettered.

And that's how it became that barren lands were inhabited, populated, and became the home of adventurous tribes.

Indeed, humans lived together in groups of tribes on scattered lands before the formation of nations. This is where their origin lies long before humans were civilized.

Out from the jungle humans appeared, not sudden but cautious and gradual.

And with their different cultures that were weird, especially beliefs and ceremonial rituals.

Yet indeed, everywhere human beings were developing, and after centuries although still in a primitive stage, they were progressing from age to age.

Yes it is true, very slowly it was happening, and that was because they still lacked knowledge.

But with homes, families, friends, and neighbors together, they created a structure of order within the line of borders.

And with everyone integrated socially together, subjected to the rules written and unwritten as the norm in their culture.

And with spoken words in language different from the other, mankind was now divided and maybe forever.

And so it eventually happened, the world drifted into a notable divide, kin from kin in groups of tribes.

Yes, that's what had given birth to nations, the increased populations upon settled lands.

And as settlers in places bonded together, it became necessary to communicate with one another. And that's how it was, the necessity to communicate had forged the creation of language, which, although it had taken years to be comprehensively perfect, humans' greatest achievement must be language, and still today it is.

But it was not just the spoken word that was the holy grail of language.

Language was never properly completed without grammar, rules in writing, which regulated reading to the concept of understanding.

And that humans did brilliantly, it was indeed an achievement of ingenuity.

An art in language mankind wisely created, it was one of the best things he ever did.

And as the people settled and developed the lands of their own, doing things together upon the lands they called home.

Each land with a culture and a language of their own, nations born, were now fully grown.

And that became legally established as a recognised mark of identity, with the difference of language especially, which did promote a sense of belonging with protection and security the common aim.

Having a homeland as rightfully one's own, and to have and behold that final word 'Nationality', which divided human beings permanently.

And which eventually became with great pride and glee, as a unique symbol of identity.

And the indisputable proof of belonging to a homeland, and to the broader family of an established nation.

Creating a feeling of security, with the knowledge of belonging to a land identified by everyone as their homeland, their country, their place of abode with security.

So yes indeed, that had created the birth of nations, fortuitous and unpredictable.

It came about without a plan, yet still it was unavoidable, it was like a destiny unstoppable.

It took the form of dividing mankind, with the hopes of being invincible.

It was the beginning of the shaping of the world, a reality of the many things to come.

It was the beginning of civilization with problematic difficulties, pros and cons.
And although the people never knew exactly what they were doing, unconsciously it was the future of the world they were shaping.

Creating divisions in a hostile world, which were never in the predictions of the things foretold.

It was never in the predictions of a sorcerer, no one was able to tell that humans as nations will be divided forever.

And yet still that was what was happening, right under the edge of human noses.

Divisions were occurring everywhere, with the birth of new nations here and there.

The world was now divided, and that everyone knew.

But what were to be the consequences? That was the question to which no one had a clue.

And that was very much a predicament, the outcome mankind never knew.

Not even a voodoo priest, a sorcerer, nor an oracle, no one was able to predict the truth.

So, humans simply and steadily just kept on going, doing whatever they had to do.

Going in the direction towards the future, hoping it will be bright all the way through.

And that they did with confidence, with determination and courage too.

They trotted along towards the future because they had nowhere else to go.

The only other way led to six feet under, but that direction no one wanted to know.

So into the future together was where they went, and always with fear of superstitions.

Drifting unsteady from beginning to end, without light it was very dangerous and frightening.

Yet still despite the obstacles, the hidden dangers, the many difficulties, exhaustion, and the regular natural turbulence.

Humans still carried on in the direction of their pursuits, aided with the strength of their determination, and grasping at whatever they can, towards the future they headed straight on, guided by their natural sense of direction.

And with the feeling that they had nothing to lose, they ventured boldly with no excuse.

Heading still in the same direction, destroying, developing, and progressing, those were the pursuits of their ambition, no obstacle was to be a hindrance.

Building the world for the present and the future, indeed, more often with slave labour.
So problems were indeed in large numbers, piling one on top of the other.

With heaps of problems getting bigger, progressive development was taking longer.

Taking more time that was needed, because of lack of knowledge and difficulties.

And as nations developed throughout the world, over a lengthy period of time.

Slow but certain they came into being, and during a period that was very unkind.

Yes, unkind with hostility, unkind especially to those who were of a different nationality.

With each nation creating their own methods to survive, the unkindness was a response to the human divide, with many new problems coming alive.

Indeed, that's what the people did, they created a world with mankind divided.

Not really knowing what the hell they were doing, it came about purely just by chance.

As mankind drifted and settled around the world, each taking their problems to different lands.

But that was just the beginning of the many unsavoury things to come.

It was just the beginning of human problems created from land to land.

Problems that would bring wars with destruction, and horrible deaths and suffering.

Problems that would bring intimidation, and threats of human annihilation.

Problems that will bring selfishness, in the disguise of self-interest.

And of course, problems that will bring weapons of mass destruction to eliminate entire nations, and to submerge the world in sin, into the perils of a hell that was of humans' own making.

Indeed, problems that would bring distrust and suspicions, with nations' aggressive imperial ambitions.

As mankind settled in divisions, it would never be the same again.

All trust is lost to hostility and wars, with divisions the cause.

And that's what led to the development of weapons, with nations threatening nations.

Which was exactly what had been happening, in a suspicious world, hostile and divided.

Yet still despite all of this, humans went straight ahead, although they were not exactly certain of where indeed their ambitions will lead.

They just kept on going in the same direction, not bothered for one single moment.

Taking steps both forwards and backwards, and sometimes to nowhere.

Taking steps in the darkness, and in the light, sometimes bold and courageous, sometimes timorous and cautious.

While creating a world divided and disunited, and with problems on the rise; the world was creating its suicidal demise, it was grave digging for its burial.

But that was never done with deliberate intentions, to create a divided world.

It was not with intent, ambition or purpose, but by chance it simply developed.

In fact, it simply developed naturally from an instinct of human urge, and from whatever did compulsively guide humans to such a destiny, on their journey towards their goals.

So then as it came about, perhaps that's how things were meant to be, a world divided was human's destiny, a troubled world without unity.

Creeping up in time, there was no avoidance, as mankind settled upon different lands.

So no one perhaps could have prevented the human divisions from falling into place.

It was something to which they had no control, neither were they able to predict the problems that were to unfold.

Eradicating the people's faith in trust, to the creation of a world that was very suspicious.

Sowing seeds of solidarity, confined to each nation for their security.

And with their warring intentions always on the ready, the divided world was heading to be, something dreadful, something sorry.

Taking shape as a divided corrupted world, and with consequences ruthlessly awful.

That was the path human beings had taken, as they scattered and settled upon different lands.

It was a regrettable loss of unity, and the beginning of hostility circulating among divisions.

Divisions that gave rise to crimes of inhumanity, as one division viewed the other with suspicions and disparity.

Suspicions that open the doors to wars and misery, and with very bad intentions.

And that was what created the hate and bigotry which was evident from land to land.

Warring with one another frequently, that was the curse of humans' divisions.

And that was what had invited insecurity, and often with hostile ambitions.

And so it was among the human divide, man with man was always in a fight for whatever the cause, wrong or right; a peaceful settlement was never in sight.

Death in slaughter was the wrong that became right, survival was never without a fight.

And so it was in that direction, mankind was laying the foundations for the future generations. With every nation in separation, pursuing their own interest.

Yet still that was just the beginning, with a very long way to go.

With the future still a very long distance away, and mankind progressing very slow.

Some were troubled with uncertainty and doubts, whether they would ever get to the future. That was what they were worried about, how much longer it would take them to get there.

Yes, that was what had troubled them the most, as nations jostled and bustled to get their first. But that was a very poignant question, there was no straight answer as a yes or no.

So each nation just carried on, still heading towards the future, and that they did with determination, regardless of the weather.

And that was because they hoped things would be better, and also because they had nowhere else to go.

The only alternative was six feet under, beneath the ground in darkness, deep down below.

But that had raised even more questions. What kind of a world human beings were developing?

What were the contributions to the future generations medieval humans were making?

What were their intentions and ambitions? How far into the future were they able to see?

Was it a world of superstitions, of voodoo and sorcery, or was it going to be a world of knowledge, of science and technology?

What kind of a world was it going to be? No one was certain, it was too dark and too far to see.

It was still too early to know, but the people were certain that they still had a very long way to go. So no one was able to guess with an answer to any question.

They scratched their heads in search of an answer, some gazed among the stars, but no answer was there.

Some said, "It was too dark and too far to see, even to estimate the distance with a little bit of accuracy." But others disagreed in arguments with confusing opinions which were far too many.

Opinions without an agreement, opinions with no legs to stand on, drifting away from an answer to the question.

So as time dragged along from millennium to millennium, moving from the past into the present.

The journey was rough, very tough, and it was exhausting at every moment.

So progressive development was slow, indeed very slow, there was always a great need for human conveniences, a need for things to be better still.

Indeed, there was a great need for the many things that are in the world today and taken for granted.

A world that is very much better than yesterday, and tomorrow it may be much better still.

But that of course is for humans to develop, no one can predict how it will end up.

But it certainly will develop just as mankind wants it to be, and regretfully it could still be as it is today, a world which is not certain if it is going the right way.

Yes indeed, that is not a dream, nor is it wishful thinking, or just guessing, but indeed something certain; it is very true, predicted or not, it will come through, from the passages of this book you will get a clear view.

And that is because of humans' propensity, it is the attitude they developed over many centuries.

And as mankind continues drifting from pillar to pillar, from dusk to dawn, and from corner to corner.

Still developing the world brick by brick, despite the encounters that were catastrophic.

Building for the present and for the future too, lots of time humans wasted not knowing exactly what to do, just gazing around at whatever was in view, and with a consciousness of development replacing the old with what was new.

Yes it is true, human beings wasted a lot of time doing nothing, they wasted time in wars fighting; they wasted time, cannot make-up their minds, so it was in arguing they wasted more time.

And with little knowledge for hope and guidance that they may continue in the right direction; they beseeched the unknown for deliverance.

Fearing the challenges in the darkness of their path, nervous and timid, human beings did what they did. Cautious were their efforts as they tried their best, and yet they kept doing many things that had no useful purpose.

And because humans were fearful during those primitive times, it made a big difference to their progressive development.

Fearing that the darkness was threatening with demons on the loose, for their sluggish progressive development, that was a good excuse.

But for their failures that was something else, their lack of knowledge they blamed instead.

And yes indeed, that's what humans feared, demons hidden in the darkness; that's what they believed during those years.

29

So without knowledge it was never easy, there were scores of problems with difficulties.

Problems mankind created one after the other, making mistakes and starting all over.

And since acquiring knowledge was still at a disadvantage, the answers to problems were sought in the heavens.

Yes they were sought after among the stars, by voodoo priests and sorcerers.

Indeed, superstitions took its toll, it was where people looked for answers, enriching high priests and sorcerers.

So grasping at the unknown for deliverance and hope to be unfurled, mankind stepped conscientiously but cautiously into the mystified superstitious world.

Into the world of spirits, gods, and demons, and the world of the moon and stars up in the heavens, was where the answers to problems often came from.

Yes indeed, from the unknown world of superstitions, humans sought the answers to their questions, and that they did from the day they were born, growing up in a world that was blighted with superstitions.

And right through their lives, never ever for a moment did they realise that the truths in the wonders of creation were right there before their eyes.

And yet still despite their blindness, the world was developing and progressing sometimes chaotically effervescing.

With humans severely disabled and handicapped by their lack of knowledge and courage.

Nature remained silent and secretive, with an abundance of knowledge hidden in storage. Knowledge silently just waiting to be discovered by humans, hence removing the blight of superstitions.

But until then, human beings believed in all sorts of things, since they had very little knowledge, very little was known about the reality of anything.

Whatever was said about the living and the dead, superstitions were often in the words spoken. Hence, superstitions became an unavoided influence in every aspect of human life.

It was indeed everywhere to be seen, asylum it took, in and out of one's mind.

Everyone saw it and felt it, like a voodoo's curse of black magic, and it was always present. People talked about it, they dreamt about it, in health and in sickness, in whatever business, superstitions were there in conversations everywhere; it was really something to fear.

In conversations about spirits, about demons, ghosts, gods and goddesses, about hell and heaven; the conversations continued as though there was no end.

Yes, superstitions were there everywhere, in every dream wet or dry, they were with you as you slept each night, and in most things humans tried, indeed, from superstitions there was no place to hide.

And when they were there, there was no escape, one simply had to live with the spirits.

So yes indeed, it was the very dark ages, ages that were even darker than darkness.

Human beings were constantly fighting with one another, as if they were cursed, or from something they suffered that was even much worse.

It was indeed the ultimate evil rooted deep in traditions, and translated into deeds that were horrible, and all justified by superstitions, no rational explanation.

Superstitions that ruined many lives, with accusations that were lies, destroying good homes and families.

Yet, it was in that state of mind that humans were developing all the time, creating their own difficulties with tragic consequences in tragedies.

Which indeed could have been avoided, if only humans had the knowledge.

Creating a world although progressive, it was very unsteady and aggressive, both in its shape and form, and especially in cultures which became the norm.

But then again, that was the world humans were developing on their journey towards the future where they were heading.

With all the pros and cons, the ups and downs, and all the problems they created from their superstitions. Into the future they passed them onto the young, from generation to generation.

So superstitions indeed lasted very long, with humans believing in gods and demons, beliefs that were passed on from the old to the young, beliefs that were very strong.

Beliefs that were held for an awful long time, until hopefully they took a gradual decline.

And because the world was still with little knowledge, and superstitions the only alternative, living in fear was a daily norm, fearing for a child the moment he was born.

Fearing that he or she may be possessed, or that the womb would remain empty, despite trying its best.
Yes indeed, that was how humans lived, always troubled with fear was how they existed.

Always in fear of some sort of danger, not knowing when it would appear, how, and where.

So, superstitions became faith, a sort of superstitious knowledge, a guidance in man's search for right and wrong.

Whether or not he was a Pagan or a Christian, or any other religion to which he belonged.

It was his passage to a paradise that had no entry while he was alive.

So, it was religion that humans depended upon, for a better life after they were dead and gone.

A life in some sort of paradise, for those who had lived a righteous life. So yes, it was with religion that our species had relied upon both for direction and guidance. It had given their life some meaning with faith, hope, and a purpose for living.

It guided them through their lives' journey, with the feeling of spiritual security.

It was the light to brighten their life, from the darkness of a troubled existence.

Without it, human beings had nothing else, since knowledge was scarce, and very slow to spread.

So whenever and wherever the seeds of religion were sown, rapidly they rooted and flourished; like a wild shrub scattered densely in the darkness of a wild forest.

No door was shut tightly enough, to prevent the religious spread.

It was with you wherever you went whether you were active or sick in bed, or whether or not you were alive or dead.

The religious spread was very spirited, it was always awake in everyone's head, and in deeds committed it was very brutal.

So yes indeed, wherever you were in any society, conformity was a must.

As long as you were a part of a community, you followed the local faith with trust.

Yes, that's how it was, that's how the world was developing during the darkness of medieval times. Religion and superstitions were one and the same thing, and they had their hands in bloody crimes.

From year to year and from century to century, mankind witnessed a spread in sorcery.

And with it there was debauchery brimming on the edge of insanity.

Indeed it was a very corrupt world, that's how it was developing, and with the world divided, that made things even worse still.

And that gave rise to hostility against those who were different, divisions had brought hostility and wars, with or without a justified cause.

And they had brought death, pain, and a great measure of suffering.

And they also brought more hate than love, so much so that it had appeared as if humans were cursed from the heavens above.

And that was not only among nations, but divisions among religions as well.

Which had given rise to internal fighting, with nations fighting among themselves.

Yes, religions also fought with religions, they captured, and then tortured for conversions.

It was indeed years of misery, a world that was washed with problems, and the cause was nothing more than human divisions.

And sadly, after many centuries it is still so today, in a world divided, come what may.

And what has come it is sad to say, the price is quite heavy for mankind to pay.

But that's how the world was developing throughout its existence, not only was it divided, but overwhelmed with everyday problems, difficulties, and mayhem.

And as religion further divided nations, it unlocked doors releasing the fury of hell.

Accusing, arresting, torturing and murdering, kinsman against kinsman.

And what was the cause of such a hostile force? It was just a difference in religion.

And so it had been, as the world kept on drifting in a pathway of darkness towards the future. Stumbling there and stumbling here, each step taken made a little difference, to the future mankind was getting nearer, with a burden of problems which were getting heavier.

Taking with them their religion and superstitions, and many habits developed that became the norm. Some good some bad it didn't really matter at all, they were all taken and given to the young of the future generations.

Yes, given to them as their inheritance, were the beliefs, knowledge, and achievements of their ancestors; as a part of the inheritance of the incoming future generations, for a better start in their life than what their ancestors had.

So yes, that was how the world was developing, during every age of time.

During those primitive years of BC, and AD, it was never easy to survive. And after several millennia, in a world still with little knowledge.

Superstitions were still widely practiced; those were the seeds that were sown.

It was a world in conflict with progressive development, arising from problems created by humans.

Problems passed on from generation to generation, most with roots in the soil of divisions, divisions into groups established as nations.

Divisions by culture, language and religion, and by skin colour, sex and social station.

With rich and poor the final straw, in divisions that created affluence and squalor.

Affluence for the rich and squalor for the poor, it was a reason for resentment, that's for sure.

Yet still that's the way it was, with no change in sight; that's the way the world was developing whether it was wrong or right.

And that was true upon every land where humans had settled upon.

They were always ready and prepared, either to live or be dead, so it was to battle where they were led, against another nation or religion.

And so was the world as a divided place, battles frequently raged.

With divisions as nations fighting each other, to kill, capture and enslave.

And where superstitions flourished wild, as evil freely elevated.

And where justice was not yet known, it was not yet introduced in every home, so injustice was the daily norm affecting lives from the day they were born.

And like an illness things got worse and worse, spreading everywhere like a sorcerer's curse.

Injustice was really the blight of nations, affecting the past, present and future generations.

It was like a virus spreading rapidly everywhere, with injustice on the spread, nothing was fair. So from place to place there was injustice, rooted firmly, and ruthlessly executed.

Yet still the world was developing, indeed it was progressing, that everyone knew and took for granted.

That was a purpose of surviving, you did whatever you had to do, you did what was expected of you.

So the world developed not in the best way it could, nor as it should, but with vices that were in most cases, very offensive, intimidating, and inhumanely disgusting and degrading.

So much so, that blood in horror from deeds of terror were a part of classic entertainment.

The greater was the savagery, the greater were the thrills, humans got really excited.

And that was so especially, when blood in death was not just a threat, but the reality of the terror of a kill.

Humans were amused and excited; the sheer horror of a slaughter had them thrilled.

The more gruesome it was, the more excitement of course, and that's when everyone roared, their hearts were brimming with joy.

They roared with laughter and with great pleasure, the excitement was a part of daily leisure.

Oh yes indeed blood was real, and the more that was spilled in any kill, emotions were overwhelmed, but the crowd could never have their fill.

They were always shouting for more and more, thrilled with pleasure from death in horror.

It was as if they were bamboozled, the excitement of horror made them feel really good.

It was indeed hilarious, exceptionally fabulous, horror indeed was glamorous to watch, the excitement was more than stupendous.

So yes, man fought with man often to the death, and sometimes with a much greater threat, a hungry and vicious wild beast.

And that he did to entertain large gatherings on the days of feasting and celebrating.

Those were days of joy, just great to be a part of the crowd to watch the savage slaughters.

To watch the horrors of a kill, from jaws with teeth that frightens death, and savage in their nature ripping off flesh.

Oh yes indeed, human beings were always very pleased, they gasped with joy and applauded very loud, to see the slaughter of either man or beast.

And as blood gushed out, the louder was their shout, until death had claimed the deceased.

So yes indeed, human beings were very happy with every bloody occasion of entertainment, it gave their lives fulfillment.

The horrors in death they loved to see, so they gathered in crowds with vim and glee.

That's what they did unfortunately, they were thrilled by horror and agony.

So they often gathered in crowds in large numbers, to watch the inhumane punishments which were allowed.

Be it hangings, burnings, crucifixions, a flogging, stoning, or the guillotine.

People came from all directions gathering in large numbers just to watch the horror from their curious eyes, and with the excitement they were satisfied.

Yes, they watched the inhumanity with curiosity, as if it was something delightful to see.

And then after the horror was done, as if they were troubled by their conscience, they scattered in silence as if they were in search of appeasement, or perhaps from the shock of the barbarity they were making a recovery.

Only to return again on another day, to be amused by the torments on display.

Can't keep away from the horrors of the day, the thrills and excitement were healthy entertainment, it was the best on offer in those days of terror.

So yes it was in that direction mankind was developing, brutality and horror was a stimulant to their unwitting inactive senses.

Killing in ways that were abominable and perverse, in ways that were savage and even worse, yet still humans found pleasure in brutalising one another.

So yes, in those days humans were punished in barbaric ways, where the rule of law was ruthlessly implemented, it was nothing less than savage.

That too, was how the world was developing, in ways that were merciless, ruthless and sinful; but perhaps maybe, not realizing what they were doing, so again and again humans did the same things, savagery was delightful entertainment, large crowds gathered at every event.

They gathered to be entertained with death in barbarity, and as ruthless and bloody as it could be.

And as the world was becoming more and more a hostile place, with little knowledge and learning.

Still humans pushed ahead, often sometimes they feared, and with the worry maybe, it was in the wrong direction they were heading.

So yes, sometimes the people were a bit concerned, as bad as things were then, sometimes it troubled them, asking themselves the same question. 'Could the future be any worse as things were then?'

That was a question pondering in their mind, and the answer still, no one could ever find.

So sometimes looking back behind them, they cogitated in their minds that they still had a few hills to climb, and they continued their journey in silence.

With troublesome thoughts in their minds, and the shadow of fear in front and behind, with step after step, upwards they climb.

And by now after many centuries gone threading along, several nations were formed, each on their own bandwagon heading in the same direction, to the future they were bound. And with each separated in a national bond, just like a family together secured and fond.

Ready to defend or to attack, whenever it was necessary.

Attacking those who were different, different in the words they speak, and of course in any other way, especially in their religious beliefs.

And because mankind's unity was abated, a lot more problems were created.

And this the people consciously knew that the future of the world wasn't looking too good.

It was a future without unity, without trust and honesty, and without those, the bickering followed, and quite often out of control.

Which very often, and for no good reason, invited suspicions, and threats that often led to death. Claiming lives unnecessarily, bringing grief and ruin upon families.

And the same continued for many centuries, after the establishment of faiths and nations.

Man fought with man for no other reason, but just because the other was different.

And to loot from the other all they had got, after capture and enslavement.

Or to lie dead in a grave and there to rot, slaughtered with an arrow, a sword, a spear, or an axe, and for just being different.

And that was just how things were in a progressively divided and ruthless world.

Throughout the ages that was how the world was developing, day by day, year by year, century after century; it was the same everywhere, unity and trust were nations despair.

Indeed, progress and development were not without hostility against those who were different especially.

Things were either the same or they got a little better, as mankind moved on with time towards the future.

But were the people really aware or unaware? Did they at any moment really care about how the world was developing?

Were they concerned, or preferred to be left alone in whatever way they were shaping the world?

Or, were they naive as well as foolish? In believing that they were not to be blamed for the state in which the world was developing.

Building a world with rejected bricks, upon rugged foundations that were unsafe.

And passing it on to future generations, as a developed world, despite the problems.

Fortunately for everybody the world did not stand still, it was still developing, with improved skills and knowledge.

And that had brought along frequent changes which inspired mankind to be productive whilst still holding on to their religion, for security, hope and courage.

But what the people got, it was not expected, surprise it did not engender.

It was just what religion had to offer, a simple life in fear, and spiritual surrender.

And of course, a constant reminder of hell's brimstones and show of fiery penitence, should death claim the soul without preparation, hence without a confession and repentance.

So yes indeed it is very easy to believe that medieval times were hard, very hard, hard enough to drive one mad.

And mankind's efforts just to survive, was as big a problem as was to stay alive.

But that was often how things were everywhere in the world, during the medieval years things were never as they should.

And that was because they were years of little knowledge, years of superstitions, years that kept humans in the darkness of a dungeon, years of taboos and of myths, years that brought death to many who were still in their young age.

And that was because there was no medicine to heal the sick, voodoo and sorcery did not always do the trick.

And yes it was those years that were passed unto the present, and then onwards unto the future where the problems of the world gathered together, each year increasing in number. Making the world even more intimidating, and a more hostile place to live in.

But however was the world humans still had to live, and despite their problems that's what they did. Because there was nothing else they were able to do, but to confront their problems all the way through.

There was no escape, no passage to a gate, problems had to be dealt with, and the sooner the better, never late.

And that was how the world took its form and shape, divided, superstitious, ruthless, unjust and corrupt.

Those were the building blocks, and with doors without locks, leading directly into hell, there were quite a few, and the crowds did swell.

And by now human beings were fully engaged with everything evil and everything wicked.

They were now on a path that was very crooked; the developing world was in danger of ruins, it was in danger of collapsing.

Yet still, despite the danger, it was on that pathway where mankind remained, for centuries doing the same wrong things again and again.

But why was it those dismal choices humans made, for what was their purpose, what was there for them to gain?

What did human beings hoped to gain from a troubled world deep in sin?

When they had religion as a cogent influence, and yet not much good resulted from its guidance. Leaving a future for mankind to reach, which looked ever so doom-laden, dark and bleak. A future perhaps without a future, nor with anything good whatsoever.

But still humans never gave up hope, believing that the future couldn't be anything worse.

Things were already very bad, anything worse, was to be mad.

So what was it that human beings did? They decided to pray, but not for a better world. That they were able to achieve long before today, if only their prayers were heard and understood. So life just continued as it must, with everything taking its course.

Moving onwards progressively, whilst taking a few steps backwards unnecessarily.

And as humans continued to develop the world, fitting the pieces together whenever they could. Not certain what tomorrow would bring, human beings were always prepared for anything, whether it was going to be worse or better, they were often prepared for whatever.

And that was good, it was wise, it prevented things from getting even worse otherwise.

And because the world was insecure, as much as it was a divided corrupted place.

Hostility developed everywhere, especially among divisions in religions and races.

The problems of mankind were only getting worse, some were too difficult to face.

There was for instance, always a battle to fight, regardless of whether it was wrong or right. Whether in attack or in defense, it's the same way it always ends.

To be slaughtered or to slaughter, and then to be tormented with dreams of horror.

Or just can't sleep during the night, both before and after a bloody fight.

Or the angel of death may pay a visit, after a demon strikes with a deadly sickness.

Just don't know what was wrong or right, whether a son or a daughter, or to sacrifice both together. Just don't know who must die; no one could advise what was right, not even with an answer from the stars at night.

Yes indeed, those were some headaches, and heart beats as though it was in a race.

And when you had them you could hardly sleep, and when you did, you were tormented with dreams.

And yes even with more problems still, problems, problems everywhere, one after the other no one cared.

Humans never stop creating them, without problems they are as good as dead.

And during their existence over thousands of years, with their destiny in their control.

They scattered and created many divisions, divisions into different nations and religions.

And that they did in every part of the world in a culture of divide and rule.

And that today as it was yesterday, it brought with it a heavy price to pay.

And as time moved on, waiting for no one, with more nations developed here and there. Each with a ruler, a Chief, a Pharaoh, a King, an Emperor, or a Dictator.

It was the beginning of a new era.

An era that was unpredictable, the beginning of a new progressive age.

After thousands of years of darkness in the wilderness, human beings were adapting new ways. They had already created many new things, including nations divided and separated.

And each with their own culture and language, security was now a real headache.

And that was how it was with every nation, each with their own set of rules and rulers. Always on course in the opposite direction, galloping on horses with speed to reach the other. Only to clash with weapons of annihilation, killing and wounding one another.

The building of the world meant the building of nations, so the strong set upon the weak.

They attacked and took over with intentions to build an Empire, and that they did with those they conquered.

Yes indeed, that's how it was among divided human beings, always fighting each other.

Upon their lands they remained separated, with each drawn close together as different races.

And drawn together in unity, every race as a family, drawn together in solidarity, cementing their bond with a common identity.

To defend or attack wherever it may be, and whenever it was necessary.

And that was the inheritance of each generation, a backpack of problems from yesterday. A world divided with problems created, with pros and cons, rights and wrongs, whatever the problems, they were linked to divisions.

And as the world continued developing, with constant introduction of progressive change.

With the people moving on in the future direction, divisions were always there with problems to greet them.

And although the divisions may or may not have been planned, nor were they deliberately intended. There was perhaps some sort of way in which they could have been prevented.

But instead, and straight ahead, the divisions all led to the doors of hell.

Man attacked man, demented with intention only to invade, kill, capture, and enslave.

To burn, to plunder, and to rape; to defeat the other, and from them everything to take.

One nation colonized the other, taking advantage because they were stronger.

Indeed, that was how the world was developing, during the centuries mankind existed. Centuries that rolled over one after the other, and yet human beings could not put the pieces together to create a world that was much better.

They put them instead haphazardly, as if they were in a hurry, creating a world full of tragedies with no cure, no remedies.

A world with problems stacked one on top of the other, with mankind divided, and no one trusting the other.

Always sowing seeds of disunity, just to reap in battle as a victory.

Men, women and children indiscriminately killed, one on top of the other, they lie very early in a grave. Robbed of their longevity, with the sword of insanity, robbed of everything in a manner ruthlessly.

And that was the result of a divided world with nations scattered everywhere. A world with problems of every kind, very unjust, very unfair.

And always too, very suspicious, not knowing who to trust, whether a friend, or a neighbour, an enemy, or even someone in the family.

Everyone feared the silence of the dead, treachery could be in its head.

One always had to be very careful, better not, if you were doubtful.

And those who ruled were very much confused, so their iron fist was very severe.

Passing their crown from father to son, in an absurdity of tradition.
And with continued draconian rule, so too was the reign of terror.

And that was so even though the son was still a minor.

Those around him were not there in vain, they did whatever was necessary.

And that included even murder, to replace a king by his brother, an uncle, a cousin, or whoever.

Indeed, it is very true, kings were often murdered by a family member, anxious to wear the crown.

That's how it was, so it had been, kings were murdered by their own family.

Those heads that wore the crown, they could not trust anyone, betrayal was often somewhere hidden, but not too far away from its treason.

And whenever it came, it came swift and deadly, and that was because it was well planned already.

Yes, that could have been the reason why kings ruled with an iron fist, to be certain that their reign was secured and safe.

And to guard against plots in treason, but that perhaps was not the only reason. Believing that the greater the fear the safer the crown, so the best way to rule was to be strong, regardless whether they were right or wrong, kings answered to no one.

And that's how it was everywhere with kingdoms here and there.

47

That's how the world was developing with kingdoms scattered around the world, each with the ambition and the urge to conquer, to capture and dominate, creating a world of masters and slaves. And that led often to frequent battles, in ruthless, fearsome and bloody struggles.

To conquer, capture and unite together, in the forming of an empire.

And so it was in the developing world, man fought with man to unite the world as one, and to keep it divided as well.

People killed and wounded on the battlefront, having no idea what they really want, whether it be heaven or be it hell.

And as the world kept on developing, progressing and destroying time and time again. Proceeding in a direction that was uncertain, and led by kings, and Emperors who were ruthless and cunning.

Waging battles wherever they went, causing death, destruction and mayhem.

And with the capture of foreign kings, killed and stripped of everything.

The world did look as if it was becoming a place of torment, death, and suffering.

That was how it was developing, that was how from a distance it was looking.

That was the view, and without any doubt, it did look certain that it would come about.

But yet still, no one was quite sure, no one was able to tell, not even after so many years, where indeed human beings were really heading, but it did look a bit certain that it was towards hell if anything.

So what was it that human beings really wanted? What was the purpose of the constant fighting? What justified the loss of lives? Was it to unite all the divides?

Or was it just a reality of the human divide, a reality of disunity?

With the same torments, day after day, many battles fought, lives lost. And for what?

What was the purpose, what was the good cause for so many lives lost?

Pride in victory to have slaughtered the enemy, that was the good cause maybe.

No one can see what has been achieved if anything at all, apart from the many unsavoury deaths, with pain and grief upon families.

And yet still, and without really knowing, human beings packed their bags and off they went. Heading still in the same direction, to the future or wherever their footsteps led.

Heading yes, via the battlefield, towards the future or an early grave.

That was the choice, and it was a gamble, to reach the future or in a grave to stumble.

To die young or to live long, reaching the future healthy and strong.

But was the future to be a Utopia, a purgatory, or a hell with brimstones and fire?

Or was it to be a place pleasant and safe, fit enough for the human race?

What kind of a world was mankind creating? This same question popped up again and again. The same question was asked many times on mankind's journey towards the future, and still at no time did anyone have an answer.

No one was certain, no one could tell, "It's hard to predict," that's what they all said.

And as the problems in the world continued multiplying, so too was the frequent fighting. Creating a world that was not only divided, but very hostile as well.

And with the belief that there was no one to trust, especially the ones you knew.

49

It was better to be silent, snitching was rampant, one had to be careful with whatever was said, because walls had mouths as well as ears, and whatever was said, to the gallows it could lead to a hanging by the neck until dead, or under the guillotine to slice off a head.

And yet still despite all of this, the cruelty and the injustice; all that was not, and all that was said.

Despite the unfairness, the hate, suspicions, fear, and the ruthlessness.

The world was still progressing slowly with regular development and cycles of change. Change that started from the beginning, and provided humans with clothing to cover their nakedness, as they drifted out from the rainforest. Change that gave mankind an identity in the form of a nationality, as they settled on lands together raising families, with the right to belong to a country.

And with a culture, a language, and a religion that gave them faith, hope, courage and strength.

Not forgetting human's knowledge and skills, that came about together bringing more change. And of course the many inventions too, that changed many things from old to new.

Moving with change from age to age, that's what humans did as they made progress at every stage.

So yes indeed, that's how human beings were developing, making progress with frequent change.

Making things just a little better all the time, change was very slow, not much in a lifetime.

But indeed, change was very important in the pursuit of humans' development.

Humans were always on the move forwards, although sometimes they took a few steps backwards.

But change was always continuous, from one thing to another it was obvious.

Some things were better and some were worse, with the changes whenever they occurred.

Into the future was where they went, passed on from the present.

And as the world continued to change, with the creation of new things, some which were strange.

So too was the system of bartering, which eventually was replaced by something that was common in exchange for anything.

And which eventually created an avaricious age which had given rise to the divisions of masters and slaves.

Which of course was a division of wealth and poverty, which depended upon the value of one's property, those who were lucky to have any.

So gradually it came into being, circulating and familiarizing.
It was indeed very appealing, the idea that it could be exchanged for anything.

And as it was getting to be commonly known by its Christian name, which became known everywhere in the world.

A name that had gained worldwide popularity, forcing a disclosure of its identity, not to one, but to everybody, it was a simple Christian name; 'Money'.

A name that was repeated thousands of times daily, and by any Tom, Dick, or Harry.

Either in quarrels, or in fixing prices, indeed money was mentioned in all sorts of things especially when it came to bargaining.

And as it got circulated in the beginning, it turned out to be quite challenging, quite startling and confusing, right from the very start.

And although it was exchanged for anything, to put a value on something, you really needed to be like a fox, very cunning, or at least to be smart.

So money was not that easily accepted in its early stages, no one could be trusted, because its value was not yet clearly decided; it was confusing when deciding how much to pay for something.

But the idea of its use, it really seemed good, but how to trade with it still needed to be well understood, confusion was no delusion.

And so it came about gradually, the importance and the usefulness of money.

But not only was it important and useful, but very much more than that.

Everybody was crazily in love with money, for them there was no looking back.

So minted as coins in silver, copper, bronze, or gold, they were circulated gradually.

And as it became more common in its daily use, anything was exchanged for money.

Yes indeed, so it was, everything had a measure of value which could be exchanged for a coin minted in copper, silver, gold or bronze.

The problem was how best to bargain, and get a good price for everything, a price especially in gold. Money was indeed circulating very quickly, becoming useful and desired by everybody, it was a very good common denominator with usefulness that couldn't be better.

It was exchanged for anything, whether it was something material, a service, or pleasure.

And as it became increasingly popular on our rock under the sun, to have plenty of it was everyone's desire, so a scramble for it had begun.

And because it was scarce, it had great value, you gave so much and got very little, everybody was holding on to it, it was like a leech on a rabbit.

And that had an effect in societies everywhere, the importance of money and the need to be fair. That was something causing resentment and despair because many people felt cheated, which was very unfair.

And as things completely switched from bartering to the selling and buying with coins.

A new world order was creeping in, into the forming of a new system.

No one knew of the problems it would bring, they were beyond imagination.

Problems that no one was able to predict, nor even to foresee in the light of brightness.

Everyone just did whatever everyone else was doing, often inspired by temptations.

No one was able to predict that it would lead to either hell or heaven, in the form of poverty or prosperity, the haves and have nots in societies, with problems up everyone's sleeves.

But that was exactly what it did with the problems that came with it, problems that were the cause of financial disasters, problems that were the cause of headaches.

Problems that were the cause of hunger and even sickness, as a result of empty pockets.

With everyone full of excuses blaming the system, for whatever were their problems.

There was where they always pointed their finger, furious in rage and anger.

Yes, pointing their fingers at the system, blaming it for their problems.

It was a system created from the use of money, which developed accidentally.

And it was described accurately, from the eyes of curiosity, as a system of cannibalism.

And which came to be known by everyone, right from the top to the bottom, as 'Dog eats Dog'.

Its association with cannibalism was just a stigmatized definition of what humans would do to better their position; to trample each other right to the ground as an easy solution.

But that was indeed a true description, because many things that were new in this transition had started in ways corrupted, everyone had the same intention, making money was their ambition: and so they did in all sorts of ways, especially in ways of exploitation.

And when asked why, the answers were the same. 'The system was to blame, it is very corrupted, to survive you just can't close your eyes, even in muddy waters you have to thrive, and do things you would not have done otherwise.

Yes indeed, everyone believed that the system offered a chance to get rich quick, even by breaking the law or just bending it.

Doing so in whatever way they had chosen, especially when they had nothing to lose.

It had something in it for everybody, even criminals survived financially.

And even murderers too, well, they will do the job for you, for whatever price was agreed too.

So yes it is true that even crimes had a price, there was always someone willing to pay, and someone to collect at the end of the day.

And likewise most crimes of yesterday, they are still happening today, and they will happen tomorrow still causing trouble.

Not forgetting the avaricious crime of kings, nobles, and those in high up places. "Corruption". It could always be found in the crevices of both dark and bright places, and even where it is not wanted.

Yes indeed, wherever there was plenty of money, there was corruption like seeds so many, there was where it could be found like a flourishing shrub of weeds rooted in the ground.

For instance, in the pulpits of religion, and within the secretive dark passages of governments.

In the palaces of kings, in banks, and within the corridors of businesses, in fact corruption has been everywhere, wherever it could hide, wherever there was a haven, it will find.

And yes indeed, it has always been afraid of transparency, light has been its enemy.

And it has often been in the company among those in high places, among them is where it feels comfortable, in the comfort of nobles exchanging bribes for privileges.

Doing so illegally, doing so fraudulently, doing so in whatever way, bribes for privileges were unofficial but okay.

So usually corruption was done secretly, covering its tracks with lies, concealing it vigilantly, so it was never that easy to expose to the light.

And it often travelled in one direction, crawling from the top downwards to the bottom.

Never did it travel from the bottom to the top, at the bottom, it doesn't have the strength to get up. And often too, it has been used as a shield and a cover, protecting those abusing their power. Opening up doors to a flood of crimes, affecting the law into decline.

Oh yes indeed, unfortunately corruption had embraced the abuse of power, as loyal partners together they flowered.

So it must be something worth having, to be at the top so popular.

Although it has always been an obstacle to progress, and a fatal blow from achieving the best for the greater good to humanity.

Yet still, one may be tempted to say that corruption today is not as bad as it was yesterday.

But is that really so? What is the truth? no one seemed to know, people just took it for granted. And as bad as it is, as long as humans live, corruption may never be eliminated.

Indeed it has always been there in societies everywhere creating resentment and despair.

And that is because of the inadequate laws, laws with loopholes and flaws.

Ineffective laws that have no claws, so whatever were the problems, corruption was the cause.

Indeed, those were just a few examples of the side effects of corruption within the order of societies.

Effects that were always a source of trouble, especially as a hindrance to human progressive development.

Yet still despite that hitch, there was always a tempting chance to get rich quick through the passages of corrupted influences.

It has always been a shortcut to one's dream which could not have been achieved coming clean.

And which served many people very well, to get out of hell and stand on their feet with someone beneath.

Yes indeed, they make use of opportunities, corrupted as they may be, as long as they could make money, that was their priority.

Yes, this brand-new system I have been describing upon, in a few lines above.

It only came into existence after the introduction of the distribution and the use of money.

And although it had a nature of cannibalism, which branded it with the nickname 'Dog-eats-Dog', it was baptized with the christian name Capitalism, despite its gravitation always to exploit.

Indeed, it was introduced into societies, by the rapacious use of money which, as it became more popular, capitalism spread further and further, as a system unique and fit for the survival of humans, providing opportunities for them to survive.

And that's what capitalism did serving everyone, providing opportunities to get along, without it being a master nor a servant.

Indeed, it was there for anybody to make use of it, using the system for their benefit, and it mattered not if they got poor or they got rich.

And it was there at any time, at the service of humans, with whatever they had in mind.

Indeed the opportunity was provided, and you were left to get on with it.

So yes indeed, that is the system known as capitalism, that's how it operates.

It was a new stage of progressive development at which point humans had reached.

It was often a risky challenge, getting used to the system, a swarm of vultures it had unleashed, ferociously in search of opportunities.

Indeed, it became established as the system people lived by for their survival, and it was the same for everyone, despite their nationality, their culture, or religion; capitalism provided plenty of opportunities for everyone to choose from.

It was a system which was very kind, funny and friendly too; making you happy wherever you go, and indeed, capitalism although not a servant, plenty of opportunities it offered to everyone.

But at the same time, it could be an enemy as well, leaving you in hell to dwell, with your purse empty without a penny, and of course too, destitute and hungry.

Yes indeed, capitalism has always been an agent of heaven and hell, you make your choice, and there you dwell.

And this was something too that people knew, wherever they went it was true that capitalism was never fair, neither did it care.

You can have more than enough, or not even a penny and be very hungry; capitalism doesn't care a damn, it has no compassion.

And it is even much worse than that, when you think that you were doing very well, betrayed by the system, you could be cast into hell, in destitution and without a bed, and not even with a slice of bread.

And that was because capitalism was man made, and it developed to be as it is, hardhearted.

To provide only opportunities and not favours, opportunities for humans' survival, but only through their labours, capitalism hates idlers.

So yes it was left entirely up to you, in whatever you wanted to do, capitalism was always there, but that did not mean that it cared to share.

And it matters not in which direction you chose to go, this is something else that everyone should know.

Capitalism was the only system provided by mankind, to assist him through the passages of survival.

So the decisions humans made were always theirs, how to get past the locked doors to the opportunities and the advantages capitalism offers.

They either make it or break it one way or the other, opportunities were never easy to acquire. But whatever humans did, there was always one thing to remember.

Capitalism may be a friend but never a brother, and of course you must remember this too; it never does favours, not even for you.

And if for some reason capitalism was an enemy, then that was something one had to take seriously.

Because it could leave you stranded and banished in poverty, forgotten by your friends and family. But not entirely forgotten by capitalism, although you may be exposed to many disadvantages, capitalism will always give you a chance of escape through your skills and knowledge.

But if that chance you did not take, then your life would be impoverished, one you would hate. Because your life would be a living hell; with nothing to eat, nor a comfortable bed to rest in peace your troubled head.

And as you are left stranded in the gutters of poverty, despised by capitalism without mercy.

You will simply be regarded as a nobody, and stripped of your dignity, by the unwritten laws of society.

So yes, those were just a few of the truths of the reality within the harsh domain of a capitalist society.

Created by humans accidentally, it has developed to be a two way motorway on man's daily journey to or from hell or heaven.

Yes it has existed during times most corrupted, alongside socialism, fascism, totalitarianism, communism, and it has outlived them all.

Providing opportunities and challenges for everyone; capitalism had been adapted by all nations.

Pursuing their ambitions of development, within the structures of capitalism.

And although not always playing by the rules, capitalism even provided opportunities to be a sex slaver, a murderer, a blackmailer, or just a plain drug mule, or whatever suited your character the opportunities were always there.

Yes indeed it provided opportunities for everything, a Drug Kingpin, a pimp, a boxer in the ring, whatever humans needed to make a living.

And so the world was moving on, steadily in the capitalist direction, whether or not it was right or wrong, whether or not it was a good system.

But moving towards what? it knew not where, and at the same time no one seemed to care.

But it was to the future where it was fated, with the many things mankind had created.

The creation of divisions in groups as nations, with their own culture, language, currency, and religion. And now added to this mix was capitalism with a new flavour, which created even more social divisions, this time in labour.

So yes it was certain that truth was inevitable, humans were on a path unpredictable, not certain of anything upon which they may stumble; not certain of anything intimidating or humble.

And after centuries of human development, for the benefit of human survival, capitalism was the pathway taken, it was the road to hell or heaven, to destitution or affluence.

And so it did get squeezed within the systems, releasing more opportunities from its procuring bosom.

But hidden among them was insecurity; yes indeed, hidden securely it was difficult to see.

And when it was released, sometimes devastating, that's when you lost your job, then everything.

But there was one thing in capitalism that was the most striking among them all, and that was the opportunities which rewarded incentives to toil.

So yes, capitalism has given rise to small and large businesses through incentives with opportunities it created.

And to criminal activities, although hard to believe, there were even very good opportunities.

Creating jobs and opportunities of all sorts, to make a living was everyone's aim.

Opportunities that lead to gigantic rewards, whether or not you break the laws.

So everyone carried on in the pathway of capitalism, developing their world in shape and form. Developing rapidly and progressively as they acquired lots of money.

Yes developing and prospering, making a good living, capitalism was seen as a very good thing.

But yet still, despite all of this progressiveness with opportunities to be a capitalist, the world was still in a dismal state.

It was still very much corrupt, very unfair and unjust, in fact it had appeared that was the way it would develop.

And that was because capitalism with all its incentives, opportunities, and rewards; it was still very difficult to survive, much less to stay alive.

Looking bleak, unsteady, and very wobbly, the capitalist world was a world very problematic and uneasy.

In reality it was never secured, you prospered today, and tomorrow you lose it all.

Indeed, it was never entirely a golden opportunity with guaranteed privileges and security.

It was always a gamble, as the system was unstable, but you always had one of two places to go, hell or heaven, no one was ever left in the open.

Yes for sure, the opportunities were always there, to heaven or to hell, wherever you wanted to dwell.

But then, during that moment in time, during that period of humans' development, they were still with little knowledge, little confidence, zeal and courage.

It was still a period of superstitions and fear, that is how it was upon lands everywhere.

And because mankind had already existed for many long centuries, the progress that was made was very disappointing, because a lot more was still needed.

And as humans continued on their journey towards the future, cautiously stepping with fear of danger.

Straight ahead humans kept on going, 'things will be better in the future,' that's what they were thinking, that's what they were hoping, that's what they were saying, that's what kept them forwards still going.

For that indeed, they were always hoping, because the present was not to their liking.

Stumbling upon obstacles in their path, they just kept on going when it was raining, and even when it was dark.

Hoping that one day they would reach the light, and human beings would be less superstitious, more courageous, and doing only what was right.

And as knowledge remained quietly untapped, still hidden in darkness somewhere, no one could find it anywhere.

Everyone was still very deeply engrossed, still looking for answers among the stars.

And capitalism, despite the many criticisms, was still moving steadily on the rise.

There was nowhere in the world where anyone could search for something that did not have a price. Everything and anything, it mattered not what it was; there was a price one had to pay even for hate or for love.

There was nothing that could not be bought or sold, regardless of how new or old.

Even the forgiveness of sins, by the clergy it was sold; nothing was left that was free, everything had a price in money.

Yes indeed, that was the capitalist system steadily on the rise, taking a tight grip in cultures, pushing old traditions into demise.

It was a world that was still developing, indeed it never stopped.

Onwards to the future it was always heading, and so too it was constantly changing; sometimes in ways that were better, and sometimes in ways that were worse; change came both ways, bringing blessings or a curse.

And when it was better things spilled over, and when it was worse you had an empty purse.

Yet still capitalism provided opportunities, some with difficulties, both within and outside the law. Hence making money did much sooner, to a flood of crimes it opened the door, inviting cupidity, in fact inviting any-body, anyone who wanted easy money.

So to commit sin became indispensable, in order to make ends meet.

And the social structure became indefensible, with everyday crimes on and off the streets.

So this blend of sin and crime being a part of the side effects of capitalism.

It was creeping up steadily on the rise as humans struggled to survive.

And it did create an atmosphere of hate, which sometimes exploded in rage.

And it seldom had a good ending, as some people were arrested and put in jail.
So yes indeed, this expedient system of opportunities and difficulties locked in arms together as one, famous with the name capitalism.

It led to a path of ravenous greed, to which human beings became too accustomed.

And it also unleashed without discreet, an unprecedented flood of crimes.

Crimes were committed to make a living, and that involved doing anything.

Yes, the need for money became so necessary, that evil for many became a necessity in their daily struggle to survive.

And as capitalism continued to develop and thrive, it became even more difficult not just to survive, but even to stay alive.

And as there was nowhere else to go to escape the hardships of today and tomorrow.

Humans' only choice, as hard as it was, was to pull themselves together and get out from the mud.

But getting out was never easy, often with difficulty, and you only made it if you were lucky.

That was the true face of capitalism, it was the true face of the survival system recognized by everyone in countries everywhere, the same problems they endure.

It was a face not only with disgrace, but with a smile that was with pride, so impressive it couldn't hide.

Yes, it could be said that capitalism was a two-faced system, one leading into hell, and the other into heaven.

And that is how it had spread its wings, it was vital for survival whenever people needed things.

And for those who were wise, it always had a smile, using the system to better their lives.

And it mattered not wherever you went, capitalism had many friends, despite it being unfair.

But then it was still very young, rapidly developing and getting strong, providing opportunities all along. Opportunities to take you from hell up to heaven, and even from heaven down to hell; wherever you wanted to dwell.

Whatever was the choice someone made, there were always opportunities provided.

Yes indeed, there were opportunities to take you anywhere, capitalism really didn't care.

It provided the opportunities for you, and you did whatever you wanted to do.

And as humans continued on the road to progress, advancing from one age to the next, doing what they could, doing their best, and often with exhausting efforts.

Divided into kingdoms everywhere, living with uncertainty and in fear.

Life for human beings was a constant battle, always fighting with each other wherever they traveled.

And with corrupted rulers as Emperors, and kings, their despotic rule was devastating.

So nations were invaded, people killed, some wounded, captured and enslaved.

Yet still in the same direction, and with the same intention, mankind kept on going, tired and exhausted, trotting along daily in a rat race.

Developing the world to be hostile and aggressive, divided between masters and slaves.

And even religion too, they did what they always do, body and soul they enslaved, bonded together in chains.

And after many thousands of years, with numerous battles fought.

The destruction caused, the many lives lost, still there was no end to the hostility and wars.

New generations came and soon they were engaged in wars that stole their youthful lives.

Yes indeed, the young and strong, those who, just a few years they were born; even the angel of death was surprised to cast away such youthful lives.

Yes, it was wars that stole their longevity, robbing them of a family life, and prosperity, robbing them of all that were most precious, yes, that's what wars do; and for what?

Forcing upon them a brutal end which was not natural, nor was it in any hurry, so their death was slow, bloody, and with agony.

And for what did they lose their lives? What was so important, their lives to sacrifice?

No one could answer the question with an explanation that was wise.

'Their country was at war, invaded, so they had to fight.' That was the one and only answer given to justify that they were right.

So yes indeed, unfortunately, human beings continued to fight again and again, each year and each century it was the same, killing and destroying as if they were insane.

And yes it went on with fingers pointing at someone else to blame, no one was responsible for the unnecessary killings, so the battles continued just the same, year after year graves were filled.

Thousands upon thousands of men, women, and children, slaughtered in war, both soldiers and civilians.

And for what was the purpose, what was the cause? What was the reason for the bloody wars?

Was it to create a heaven or a hell? No one was able to tell, they just all went to battle wherever they were led.

Whether or not it had any purpose at all, perhaps it was for survival, as dog eats dog.

And that's the way the world was developing, for centuries it has been the same, as reckless and as sinful as it could be.

Going right back from humans' origin, during their development there were always tragedies.

Tragedies created by humans, as they persisted in committing wrongs.

And passing them over from one to the other, many wrongs got embedded in traditions as culture. And they became the norm in daily life, until they were changed at some point in time. And that could have been for many centuries, with the same wrongs committed frequently.

And as time rolled on from century to century, with constant changes as were necessary. Yet still the world remained in captivity; and so it did for many centuries.

Yes, captured by Satan and all that was sin, that was the reality from the beginning, it was in that direction the world was drifting, despite the many religious teachings.

And that was true and very certain, the world was drifting into becoming a hostile and dangerous place to live in.

Yes, very hostile and dangerous, not knowing who to trust.

And to add some meaning to this prediction, they came into being yet more divisions with problems brought into the system by the liberal spread of capitalism.

Yes they were problems of all sorts, and division was mainly the cause.

It was the division of rich and poor, and other divisions quite a few more, and even gender division that's for sure.

And with it came new problems and many more, including racism, discrimination, exploitation, and even a stigma upon the poor.

Yes, that was the world, the real world, the world which human beings had been developing during the many centuries they had been progressing.

Indeed they have been doing a very good job, promoting evil of every sort, even within the laws.

But they were not always the choices humans made, by chance some came about falling into place, within the progressive stages of humans' development.

Yes, it was without doubt that some changes came about and fit into the systems without directly being created by humans.

And they fitted perfectly well, and became the norm in daily life lasting for generations.

Creating environments with a measure of responsibility, and a life of stability in conformity with the rules of society.

So what was it that the people had achieved during their many centuries of existence, from their beginning to the end of BC years?

Years of torment, superstitions and fears, fear to wake up, and even to go to bed.

Yes, fear of darkness and daylight, of thunder and lightning, and even of what was wrong and what was right.

Indeed with so much fear, how much knowledge did humans acquire?

What was the measure of their skills and their experiences during those troubled years?

An existence counted to be thousands of years. So what were the achievements of our ancestral peers?

Yes indeed, things got a little better from century to century, but the long time it took, much more could have been achieved.

And yet still the world remained a dismal place with too many wrongs printed on its surface.

And with human beings still fighting with each other, with many sent to early graves.

Creating and destroying repeatedly in a world advancing progressively, and yet without unity and equality, but more with divided classes, more with disparity and injustice.

Yes, that is how the world was developing as time was disappearing, as centuries came and went.

It was the same everywhere, despite the progressive development here and there.

Indeed, things were gradually changing in ways that no one was able to predict nor to prevent. Very slowly humans were making progress, with constant hindrance from corruption and superstitions radiating from religion and governments.

Yet still doing so bit by bit, humans were determined to progress, sometimes very slow, sometimes in hast with regrets, but whatever was the timetable, it was a period of success.

Putting together in every corner, whatever little bit that fits to make the world a better place. Yes, putting together in every corner the little pieces that matter.

Yet still despite this, despite human beings' worthy efforts, it was a world where all things bad, although sad, were challenging and exciting, and it was towards that frame humans were attracted.

Yes they were attracted towards the forces of evil, there was where excitement was in the open.

And from excitement of course, there was no divorce; that's what made their life worth living.

It was a world where love and care were truly rare, superstitions and fear were more inviting.

It was so vile, and yet our forebears took pride in the type of world they were developing.

Perhaps not realizing the consequences they were stockpiling.

Yes indeed, eventually it had to be, it could not be delayed or prevented any further, mankind could not wait any longer.

The direction in which mankind was heading, the predictions were, it was full of danger, full of uncertainty with so much to fear.

Indeed things were bad, people were behaving as if they were mad, so Jesus came much sooner.

Yes Jesus came to save the world from tumbling into hell, and there to remain in excruciating pain without an end to the suffering.

Guiding humans away from the edge, before they slip right through the hedge into the eternal flames.

But mankind as humans they were born to be; preferring excitement than safety.

Jesus was arrested, tortured and murdered for attempting to save the world from its sinful pleasures.

No one was safe in those days of debauchery; no one was safe from the threats of cruelty, torture before death was a frequent penalty, the laws were nothing less than brutality.

And so it was, Jesus was murdered by the barbarity of authority, both state and religion, in this dilemma they both shook hands.

So Jesus was arrested, whipped and tortured, they said he was a threat to the establishment.

And that was what Jesus had suffered, he was mocked and brutally tortured; and for the sins of the world, he was finally murdered.

Yes indeed in agony, a slow and painful death Jesus suffered, nailed to a cross by his tormentors.

That's how cruel things were as the world was developing centuries ago during medieval times.

That's how it was as the world was progressing, horror was a form of pleasure, it was a common sight, used for intimidating as much as it was for entertaining.

So yes indeed, man brutalized man mercilessly, and often just for triviality, and in a manner that could never be right.

Shaping the world to serve his needs with little wisdom, knowledge and understanding.

Things got better and sometimes worse, but that was the norm in the struggle to survive.

And so life continued just the same, passing from generation to generation yet again.

After Jesus was murdered nothing changed, just as things were, they continued the same.

Shaping the world for the future, with whatever the past and the present had to offer.

Whether they brought joy or sorrow, they were the legacy of tomorrow.

And so the world continued to develop to be as it is, and by human beings' efforts to achieve bit by bit, day after day the world was taking shape in the form that it is today.

And yet no one knew that it would turn out to be like this, no one had a clue, so they just continued with their mischief.

Shaping the world hoping for the best, when most of the time it was in a mess.

Doing whatever had to be done, whether or not it was right or wrong.

And whenever seeds were sown to reap in the future, the past was what the future reaped.
And if the past was anything evil, then the future always weeps.

And this is true in the divisions of human beings, with each different in some way.

And that was enough to fight with the other, once you were different you were a suspicious stranger; who just could not be trusted in any way or the other, always a threat sooner or later. So the fighting continued right into the future, that even today it is not yet over, and no one knows for how much longer.

And as the fighting increased even more regularly, with heated tempers to annihilate one-another completely.

Weapons became a surreptitious skill, each time they were designed, many more people were killed.

From the deadly weapons of poisonous bows and arrows, spears, swords, axes and guns; to the development of a bomb with the destructive peril of many suns.

Heading in direction of total destruction; fear kept the peace and held the lid tightly on.

But the peace was often broken up into smaller pieces; mankind never stopped, so the fighting increased.

And as the world looked set to collapse upon itself, mankind always found a way to get out of hell, but only again to repeat the same, and then pointing fingers at someone else to blame.

That was the real world human beings were living in at every age of time.

That was how it was developing; to be sinful, hostile, and unkind.

Fear was a constant irritating companion of humans, it was with them most of the time, both during rain and sunshine, and especially during the darkness of the nights, fear was their companion in and out of sight.

Yes indeed, that is how the world was developing to be, a world aggressive and hostile with constant problems and difficulties all the time.

And as the years went by with things still changing, as humans continued to try again.

Unfortunately, it was the journey they had taken, leaving death on every footstep, buried in the mud left behind.

It was the same world they kept on developing and destroying again and again, while at the same time it was progressing.

And that was because despite the superstitions, the fears, threats, and suspicious divisions; despite the warring factors, humans were always able to keep a good sense of their missions, fulfilling their ambitions, doing their best with efforts often without regrets, yes, doing their best to acquire success, it was themselves they had to impress.

So yes, mankind continued still heading towards the future, but the distance never seems to get any nearer.

Generations came, and generations went, and yet the distance to the future always seemed to be still the same.

So bewildered and troubled humans everywhere began to wonder; scratching their heads they quietly asked themselves. Is there really a future? And still deep in thoughts as though they were completely lost, they said to themselves after a little pause. "Then how the hell do we get there?" And upon their faces doubt scattered everywhere.

Troubled with those thoughts, they suddenly disappeared, somewhere they went, no one cared, so everyone continued on their journey just as they did

73

before, leaving their thoughts behind, so they couldn't be troubled any more.

And so they continued traveling every day regardless of the weather, humans' greatest fear was lightning and thunder.

But where was the future ever to be found? Which way was the right direction?

The answer to that question everyone was always asking, but no one knew, no one had a clue, they were always guessing, that's the only thing they were able to do.

So still without an answer humans carried on, hoping they were going in the right direction.

And forwards still they kept on going, often looking ahead then backwards again.

And that was because they were determined, and wanted to be certain that they were always on the right track, they always feared they may have to go back, having taken the wrong track.

Yes indeed, upon the right track towards the future, humans always wanted to be certain that they were there, and not on a track leading elsewhere, where things may be worse instead of better.

Yes it was confusing, no one was sure that the direction taken was to the future.

But with their sense of direction and good judgement they continued wherever their legs led them, believing that they were on the same track which was taken by their ancestors.

And as human beings still desperate for knowledge, to give them a boost to their wavering courage. And to stand as a bulwark against ignorance and superstitions too.

As human beings they were always deeply concerned, "What should they do?" Deep in thought, they couldn't unravel a clue.

So things continued almost the same, day after day, over and over again.

Changes came and changes went, making things only a little different.

And that's how life continued with some things changed, and some remained the same year after year again and again.

Things that brought both bad and better times, with some changes that made things worse than those that were left behind.

Pushing some old habits to take a hitch on the wind, to go with it wherever it was blowing.

And after thousands of years before Jesus came, plus several centuries after he left.

Regardless of all the changes made by mankind, and still making many more changes yet again. The world was always in a state of a mess without peace and justice; and that was so wherever you go, despite humans attempts doing their very best to develop with progress.

Indeed, the masses were never satisfied, and it was never difficult to understand why.

Yes, it was a world that was divided, by humans that's how it was created, and may never again be united, that opportunity looked discarded, lost forever in the wilderness.

And that was because divisions were by now well established into nations, offering security in a country, and belonging to a larger family all with the same nationality.

But that had created some worried heads restless on their beds, because of the problems caused by divisions.

Indeed, problems were real, instigated from suspicions and accusations.

Divisions into nations had created a world, where problems with hostility regularly occurred.

Yet still despite all the difficulties, getting to the future was still everyone's priority.

But because there was no urgency, and no one was really at any time in a hurry, they trotted along cautiously, and sometimes even carelessly.

Moving very much slower than time, often they feared they may be left behind, so they doubled their efforts to catch up with time, and even sometimes leaving time behind.

Not forgetting the system for human survival, the one they developed after its arrival. Baptized with the name "Capitalism," it had never been a very good Christian.

Yes indeed, this you could believe, capitalism created many opportunities, but that has been its purpose, and it also created the most challenging of all races, the marathon rat-race, from which there was no escape, to survive you had to be in it.

Yes it was a race created by capitalism, everyone joined in racing along, not quite sure what they were running from.

And with all its advantages and disadvantages, opening up doors to criminal privileges.

Indeed, capitalism with all its good intentions, was still associated with bad-mouthed mentions. Giving credibility to serfdom and slavery, with the masses chained to poverty.

Giving credibility to exploitation, and to make money however one can.

Exploiting the workers with wages hand to mouth, so that they remain destitute all their life with very little or without.

So eventually after existing for many centuries, with more and more people drifting into poverty, capitalism was judged to be, not as a friend, but as an oppressive enemy.

So it was considered to be more on the side of the rich, leaving the workers on their arses in a ditch.

While the rich continued in the same direction, riding in luxury on the bandwagon of capitalism.

It was the direction they took from the beginning, even before capitalism was well established.

And when they did realize, to their surprise, it was still towards the future where they were heading. The best thing for them was to keep on going, and that was just what they did.

Hoping that the opportunities would even be better, as they headed towards the future.

Hoping that it will be some sort of paradise, that's what they wanted, not to be wise.

So not taking anything for granted, they sometimes had a feeling that left them worrying, with doubts whether things will ever work out.

And although they were not sure of anything, not sure of their own feelings, yet still onwards to the future they kept on going.

So pushing forwards straight ahead, regardless of wherever it led; although sometimes with a little concern, humans did a little thinking by themselves alone, to decide whether or not they should, the future spurn.

Whether they should continue to bother heading towards the future, or just stay in the present paying rent.

Shaping the world bit by bit, and even with rejected bricks.

Shaping it in the form of capitalism, creating unsocial divisions.

A division of wealth and poverty, but still with opportunities for everybody.

And the opportunity to choose one or the other, because no one was allowed to have both together. No one was allowed to be rich and poor at the very same time together.

That was one of the unwritten rules of capitalism, created not by humans, but by the forces within the system.

And the reason for that no one understood, but everyone thought that the idea was good.

So this system of capitalism, functioning to the survival of mankind, opened up doors to both hell and heaven.

With opportunities, advantages and disadvantages too, the path you took it was up to you.

But its main function was the distribution of money, so you did what you could to earn plenty. And when you did, you made a lot of friends and a few enemies, and only because you had a lot of money people were often very friendly.

But whether or not capitalism was a good system, that was something else.

It was still passed on from generation to generation as the only system for humans' survival, the only system for them to live by, the only system which they could try.

And so capitalism remains to this day, and still functioning in much the same way.

With the capitalist system thriving from day to day, offering opportunities to human beings to make a living, some of the old ones disappeared, as people made use of the new opportunities instead.

And as money and capitalism stood side by side, in a union never broken nor even bent, apart from when Marx and Lenin said, 'no-one should never be paying rent.'

And the two together like any family member bonded inseparable for life.

So they adopted humans as their agent, honoring them as capitalists.

And offering them opportunities with incentives so attractive, no one could afford to miss.

And as nations developed separately, each crazily in love with capitalism and money.

This secret became known among everyone and all, that with the capitalist system you can rise and fall.

And the higher you rise, the harder the fall, the things you've got, you could lose them all.

And that was often when you were in debt, and failed to realize the financial threat.

So you get tangled up in its net, until squeezed into financial death.

So yes it is very important to be careful at every step, to avoid slipping and falling into financial death.

Because that's when you may break your neck, depending upon how much you are in debt.

And that is also when you can no longer sleep at night, because the worries you have, the weight is not light.

And just because you were in financial debt, you are now a victim receiving threats; can't close your eyes for a good night's rest.

You may lose your house, your business, and whatever next, that's the reality when you are in debt, you can lose everything, that's often the threat.

So it was, as a part of the system, and it is still so today, one of the perquisites of capitalism, getting into debt is a bad option, there is no altruism.

An option that can rob you of your sleep and dignity, but for all that was said, debt also provides some very good rewarding opportunities.

Yes, debt can lift you off your feet, it can lift you out of hell, but only when it is spent very well.

For as heartless capitalism may seem to be, it provides opportunities to get out of debt and poverty. And it is the same for everybody, even for criminals to make money.

And as the world kept on developing after the peaceful death of bartering.

Capitalism was now well established as the only means for making a living.

It had been established as a monopoly, creating opportunities with difficulties.

Difficulties and hardships that spread widely, with unbearable financial responsibilities.

And yes, as the weight became too heavy to bear, breaking backs here and there, and with everything appearing to be very unfair.

Humans were considering how they could end capitalism forever, how to get rid of this financial slaver.

How they could replace it with something else which was fairer in distributing wealth.

Some sort of a system, anything that was better than capitalism.

Something else humans can try, something that would make everyone smile.

And so capitalism eventually at some point in time, its monopoly was stolen by an opposition. And yet still, after centuries in existence, bombarded with criticisms, it was still creating opportunities that led either to hell, or to heaven, it always fulfilled its commission.

It was still creating opportunities for everybody, even those who were in poverty.

But that was its function, that was what it did and was doing so still, in providing opportunities it never failed.

So grasping at the comforts of luxury, or at the shackles of poverty, both doors were open for anybody. Those with or without the ability, to the appropriate door they were given the key.

Indeed, there was a place for everybody in society, either in affluence or in poverty, no one was left forsaken.

So yes, capitalism had existed for a very long time during which it got very strong.

And it built its strength gradually without any concern for right or wrong, or any concern for anyone. And all that time it had no competition, and yet it was struggling to keep its head well above ground, struggling to satisfy everyone.

Struggling to keep everybody happy, whilst more and more people were sliding into poverty, into destitution and insecurity, and even into starvation with bellies empty.

Yes indeed human beings were fed-up, despite the opportunities they couldn't get out from the rot, with prices always going up, and wages somewhere they got stuck.

Until finally, after years squeezed under the pressure of destitute poverty, a new idea was circulating, and those in poverty were very interested.

Indeed, it gave them hope, it gave them confidence, that soon one day they could have a better life for their children.

Yes indeed, capitalism had met with its first deadly threat, which was very aggressive and without respect.

And as people were developing and progressing, with their dedicated hard efforts.

Yet still it was impossible for them to make a decent living regardless of how hard they were trying. There was no escape, no doors, windows, or gates; in destitution they were trapped, poverty weighed heavily upon their backs.

So yes, capitalism was accused as the enemy; and it was hated very much by those in poverty, which in any society they were the majority.

And yes it was always blamed as the culprit, and was seen as a system by which the workers were taken for granted, exploited, and paid very low wages.

Long hours, no sick, nor paid holidays, no pay rises or bonuses.

And that had inspired the creation of a new system, one to replace capitalism.

One that would be fair with rights for the workers, one with the government as the employers.

And yes that idea was developing here and there in certain parts of the world, and eventually, suddenly people with the idea took control.

Pushing capitalism out, and implementing the new system with muscle and clout.

Indeed, there was no introduction when the new system met with capitalism, they disliked each other from the very beginning, it was a fight to the death in or out the ring.

Yes they had chosen to be enemies instead of friends, with each system keeping its distance.

And with ambition to turn things around, the new system was building its strength.

But so too was capitalism; its roots were already very deep in the ground, and it had no desire to be pushed around, it was standing very firm all along.

So the new system, without any doubt, eventually came about as a result of the intolerable oppressive disadvantages, and the bullying exploitation of the working classes.

And that was happening for century after century, capitalism was becoming less a friend and more as an enemy, with more and more people drifting into poverty, with their children bare feet and going hungry.

Yes indeed, a very intolerable situation, unbearable to families, men, women, and children.

Families unable to make ends meet, can't pay their bills, and not even for a pill when they were ill. Indeed, capitalism was becoming very much like an autocrat, very oppressive, enslaving the masses with hand to mouth wages, no holidays, no days off, not even when one was sick, no work no pay, that was the anthem of the day.

Yes indeed, that's how it was, the workers were exploited by those taking advantage, sinking them deeper in the gutter, with no respect whatsoever.

And it mattered not how hard they work, fear of the sack kept them on the go.

That was worse than the little they earned, at least they got something for them to take home.

Yes, those were the circumstances, the difficult situations created by the corrupted forces within the capitalist system, forces without a conscience of love and compassion, nor even fairness and justice.

Forces which had no respect for workers, believing that their only purpose was to make good use of their hours on the factory floors.

Forces that imprisoned them within the system, slave labour was the norm.

Forces which exploited even their children, and not for a moment did they care a damn; knowing that the workers depended on them.

And yes, it was indeed iniquitous, oppressive and invidious.

Controlling the masses with oppressive forces of exploitation; in the forms of slavery, serfdom, hand to mouth wages, and other subjugated iterations.

So, the new system with the name communism, was ready and determined to crush capitalism.

To crush and bury it deep in the ground, banished completely from its existence, removing every trace of it from the world, long before it has grown to be old.

Indeed, communism was with very good intentions, to eradicate the shackles of poverty, human indignity, destitution, and misery.

To destroy capitalism completely, and restore human dignity and self-respect, without destitution posing anyone a threat.

By smashing poverty and burying it deep in the ground, while communism grew very strong.

Hence, creating societies with greater fairness and equality, resulting in a decent living standard as a social norm and a right to everybody.

Yes indeed the ideology was good, very good, the problem was how to get it to work.

How to implement communist policies into the system? When the established capitalist order was already rooted deep, and overwhelmed with forces of corruption that kept it strong firm on the ground, standing high on its feet.

Indeed, capitalism was no easy push over; corruption had made it as strong as ever, with its many opportunities and freedoms, it had indeed many influential friends.

And that was a gigantic stumbling block that prevented communism from rising up.

Neither was communism ever baptized, and worse still, and sad to say, it was never implemented by those who were wise.

Not at any moment, not at any time was communism operating as it had intended to be kind.

And that had given rise to very aggressive enemies, so it pursued its policies even more ruthlessly.

Ignoring the fact that as an ideology, it was failing in its duty to serve the people, and not for the people to serve the ideology.

That was as foolish as it was impossible, as it was certainly to cause the system to crumble.

And given time, that was what had happened, communism into pieces it disintegrated.

Yes, it fell off the shelf, and scattered into pieces it was as good as dead.

Yes indeed it was unfortunate, communism was a system which had created another human divide, and with effects which were more foolish than wise.

With problems that had posed a very serious threat, with each system racing to produce the best deadly weapons of mass destruction.

And that was very real and a troubling political question, particularly among the advanced nations.

And it was because both sides had acquired devastating deadly weapons, and with the madness to create human annihilation.

Competing with each other all the time, there was a real fear that it may slip out of hand into the abyss of cataclysm.

Yes indeed, the two ideologies were in very strong opposition, and with a determination to inflict upon the other total annihilation which was their mission.

Both created more and more dangerous weapons, in a race to guarantee the enemy's obliteration.

Yes, the obliteration of one or the other, or even both together, it didn't really matter.

And although communism had the best intentions for, not only to cure, but to prevent destitution among the poor; hence banishing unemployment within a zero structure.

Still, despite this, it was never accepted, nor was it supported by the capitalist upper classes.

In fact, many were outraged, preferring to go to an early grave, rather than to be a part of the communist developmental stages.

And that perhaps was unfortunate, or just maybe a blessing in disguise.

Whatever it was, for mankind's sake, there were many people who wanted communism to be buried dead or alive.

And it was because it had unleashed a reign of terror, oppression with brutality were the everyday norm during the communist takeover.

It was indeed very brutal and ruthless, second to the Nazi threat.

And indeed laced with corruption from the top to bottom, with constant shortages of food and domestic conveniences, indeed, the people were fed-up with the everyday shortages.

Queuing for that and queuing for this, and when you get it, you are not sure what it is.

So yes indeed, it was a very intolerable regime, with frustration beyond the extreme.

Suppressing basic human rights; freedom of speech disappeared overnight.

In fact there was no sense of freedom, the reality was, it had disappeared and gone.

And societies became police states, with arrests, state murders and beatings commonplace.

Yes, one had to be careful whatever one did; one bad move, and you were arrested.

Not forgetting one slip of the tongue, you were locked-up in jail where they say you belong.

Yes indeed, despite the good intentions of communism, the birth of communism was the birth of a demon that came directly from hell.

And it came about during a period of chaos, discontentment and revolt.

Which had led to a catastrophe, everything was going so badly wrong, brutality was never scaled down, so the atrocities simply carried on.

Indeed the corruption, the stealing from the system, the shortages and the brutality, the loss of freedoms and the misery, it was indeed too much for anybody.

Disregarding the good intentions of communism, the best of healthcare and education, and the best of transport, and whatever good it took, within the system to promote.

Instead, the people were brutalized, they were terrified, in fear was how they lived their lives.

Always on the edge, even when they went to bed, fearing a knock on the door, which often meant that someone would be sent off to jail in Siberia.

And that for them meant to be cast off into hell, jails in Siberia were no place to dwell.

And as bad as things were during capitalism, it was now many times worse with communism.

The system was indeed threading along in the wrong direction; it took the wrong road from the beginning, doing all the wrong things.

Threading along ruthlessly, in the formation of a Dictatorial and draconian society.

Threading along without freedom, and betrayed by the forces of corruption, communism was given a death sentence.

And yet it was all totally unnecessary, communism could have been implemented properly, indeed, it could have been implemented wisely, in the interest of everybody.

Yes it could have proved itself to be a better system, just as it had intended to be.

Taking the people into prosperity, through equal remuneration and giving, hence extinguishing the degrading conditions of living.

Burying the stench of human destitution, with poverty no longer a human living condition.

Yes, the people could have been given the benefits of communism; the reality of its intentions, if only it was able to root out despotism, and crack the bad eggs in the system.

But then why did it not happen? Why was it so ruthless in implementing bad policies which were not communist ideologies?

Why were there so many wrongs executed in the name of communism?

Maybe it was too badly planned, with fear everywhere throughout the lands, so it was doomed by its own imperfections.

It was embraced by a ruthless dictator who silenced every tongue that spoke words in opposition.

But that still created oppositions that were disruptive, because life was indeed becoming very fearful as much as it was becoming woeful.

So communism had to go one way or the other, it could not be tolerated any longer, those were the spoken words which everyone understood, silent as they were.

Yes the words were silent, they had to be, but they were understood by everybody.

But when will be the end? No one knew, so the oppression continued.

Enhancing the rage, intensifying the hate, communism had to go before it was too late, it was becoming too hard to tolerate.

And that's what led, from the very beginning, to the collapse of communism into ruins.

It was only held ruthlessly together by a Dictator with the name Stalin, who grabbed hold of absolute power, murdering opponents one after the other.

And like all Dictators everywhere, he ruled with an iron fist that was very severe.

His policies were ruthless and unforgiving, many peoples' lives were brought to ruins, just for criticizing what was happening.

So the system was already doomed to fail, its legs were weakening as it dug its own grave.

And so it failed eventually despite the change of leaders with new policies.

Their policies were never good enough, so communism had to go no matter what.

And that it did after lasting for only a few years; which unfortunately cut short its longevity, which was only twenty-five years short of a century.

Not even enough time for the system to be well established, putting all its good intentions into practical uses, with trial and error shaping its future, each time for the better.

Instead, communism fell, it crumbled into pieces, and in chaos the people celebrated, not knowing exactly what the alternative would be; but no one cared, all that mattered was that communism was dead, and with freedom they could live their lives once again without fear, intimidation, or the reality of a jail sentence.

And after the hash brutality of communism now dead and gone.

The threat of human annihilation, by the use of nuclear weapons, remained something that was still troubling, because the threat was still existing.

So yes indeed, the collapse of communism did seem inevitable, its trial period was too oppressive, it was abominable, it took too many precious freedoms away from the people, and enforced oppression as an example.

Implementing policies that were causing grief to families, both physical and mental.

Repressing the people with the rule of an iron fist, which was ruthless and without justice.

And the changes that came were not all for the better, instead some were worse than ever.

With communism enforced by a ruthless Dictator, it was surely on its way towards disaster.

And with the people living daily in fear, to challenge the system was not easy to dare.

But that's what they did eventually, and brought communism crashing down, because it was not implemented properly, freedom was lost completely.

Instead, it was a system the people dread, for their families they feared, nothing appeared to be going well. Using tyranny to oppress society, indeed that was never communism's policy.

A policy that was nothing less than dangerous, and with frustration that made everyone vex.

And yet those were the policies implemented, despite the hostile discontentment infuriating the masses.

Policies that were a very bad impression, not reflecting the altruism of communism, not the good intentions that the masses expected.

So the discontentment had to explode, the pressure was too great, it was too heavy a weight.

And when it exploded it was done in hate, anger, and full of rage.

With all three components tangled together, scattering everywhere all over.

It was indeed very chaotic, the masses were rejoicing, communism was not as the masses expected, so indeed eventually it failed.

Yes indeed, communism had created a great deal of enemies during the years it was implemented.

With freedoms lost and no sense of direction, all that was left was to bring communism to its end.

And so the idea was held by many people who were very anxious for opportunities to drag communism crawling on its knees, unto its miserable end.

And to restore capitalism once again as the only system for the people to make a living.

And with all its rights and all its wrongs, its freedoms and opportunities to get along.

Its advantages and disadvantages, and with all that makes it what it is.

And so this prediction came to pass, communism for one century did not even last.

So once again as the only survival system, capitalism had regained its place and strength within the functional structure of all nations.

So the system continued once again onwards ahead, unopposed right into the future.

Opening up doors to new opportunities, and with all the ups and downs as before.

And as it continues to function daily alongside the norms of societies, capitalism may be here to stay; or for at least many more centuries providing it remains okay.

Until the people in their wisdom find another way, to make a living day after day, and in a way success will pay, and freedoms will always stay.

So it is indeed very clear that capitalism is not yet going to disappear.

It is right here, and here to stay, doing its bit everyday; providing the opportunities for the people to survive in the security of a good life.

But it is also true that it is up to you, capitalism provides opportunities and nothing else, that's the way it helps.

It is not a servant, it is not a master, opportunities are all it has to offer, giving you a chance to be an entrepreneur.

Unfortunately, it could be seen that the threat of communism is on the rise again, it is here with us today, with threats to be taken seriously.

Yes indeed, a communist country is likely to be, it is on its way to becoming the world's biggest economy.

But this is not just an idle threat to be ignored or be taken lightly, it is a serious possibility, and to that event communism could succeed, so the rest of the world must hope that it is peaceful, and not to antagonize with threats that are unwise, threats which could bring many lives to their demise.

Yes indeed, the reality of a nuclear catastrophe is not something humans want to see.

Unfortunately, at present the dangers are too many with Armageddon a possibility.

Therefore, and be very sure nations must reason together and choose their own future.

Living peacefully together should still be human beings' priority, and not to put the world in jeopardy with threats of annihilation in the horrors of cataclysm.

Not wars, not elimination, not even threats of sanctions, indeed, they are all deadly provocations that may unlock the forces of extinction.

So yes indeed, that's how it should be, living together in peace, and not in broken up pieces.

Because broken pieces could inflict injuries, awakening forces with deadly consequences.

So yes, living together in peace is better, each with their differences, that is how it will have to be as long as the world is divided.

And if communism as well as capitalism are both with us to stay; then the two ideologies, like good neighbours, although different in their ways.

They must learn to live together or face the dangers of the consequences that they themselves would have created.

Consequences of the most devastating nature devouring both sides together.

So much so for ideologies, capitalism and communism; now I must give language my attention. It is an art which humans have so wisely created as they have done with so many of their inventions.

And it could never be discarded or forgotten, it is much more important than capitalism and communism.

So it still is in use today, and it will be so for every other day; because to communicate there is no other way.

There is no competition nor an opposition, language is unique in its form.

And likewise the usefulness of money, language is even more useful and necessary.

And although it has given rise to divisions, it is without a doubt, and cannot be ruled out; that language is something humans cannot do without.

So extremely important is how it is, language will always be useful for as long as humans live.

And of all the things human beings created as you look back into the past, during their years of progressive development.

There is but one very troubling question; 'Why mankind created divided nations? For what was their purpose? Why did this come about endangering man's progressive development with an endless flow of accusations and disagreements?' Both were the cause of wars, unnecessarily many lives were lost.

So deep in thought, with something to think about. Was there a need for human divisions?

Or did it just happen purely by chance?

Something humans could not prevent during the course of their progressive development.

Indeed, they scattered here and there, so divisions were unavoidable.

And as they appeared and settled on lands everywhere, each with a bundle of trouble.

Divisions were never intended, it was never planned, humans scattered and so it happened.

That's how nations were formed, and without any justified importance.

In fact, there are more consequences resulting from border skirmishes; spying, accusations, and suspicions, with a need for nations' protection.

All are the result of a lack of trust with suspicions creating aggression.

Indeed, there has been very little or nothing good that came out from divisions, instead there has been but more selfishness with a scramble towards self-interest; with nothing for the common good, but double standards persisting whenever it could.

So what good is nationhood today when so many separations persist?' Preparing for war, spending millions and what for, only to prove who is stronger, with deadly weapons threatening each other.

Whilst living with fear and suspicions, no one can trust the other, not for a moment.

Each doing the same things differently, different values are held in accordance with traditions.

So what is right in one, the same is wrong in another; it is as if the people don't know one from the other.

There is no global conformity, nor unity; and despite the formation of the United Nations; still they are unable to solve world problems, existing no more than a house of corruption, where double standards are the norm.

Yes indeed, they are never able to negotiate global peace, everyone seeking their own interest, to say the least, and with profound arguments, they hardly ever reach agreements.

So disunity and self-interest remain paramount, with the result of bad decisions.

And the whole idea of a United Nations working together for peaceful international solutions.

That appears to be doomed, wounded with elements of corruption, as it had been with communism.

And now after many centuries of human existence, mankind still cannot yet work together for the benefit of one another, so the world remains no better; the United Nations' dream is a failure.

It never prevents wars, its policies are flawed, in fact, its existence is a fraud.

So what was man's reason for creating a world divided, could it not be prevented?

What was wrong for humans to stay united with all for one as families live, and speak in only one language? Eliminating confusion, suspicion, and hate, eliminating the divide created with the difference in language.

Creating a world with much fewer problems, understanding each and every one wherever you went because they all speak in the same tongue; like one global family, all for one.

Instead of divided and bickering, always in one's own interest, and to the advantage of the strongest, those whose weapons are the deadliest.

And yes, harboring fears and suspicions, always entangled in arguments, can't trust the other, no agreements.

Indeed, what is wrong is wrong everywhere, and it is the same for what is right regardless of culture.

Human beings wherever they are, they should be wise enough to know that wrong is wrong, and right is right, that is not something that culture decides, nor even might.

And passing bad decisions unto the future, as a legacy from one generation to the other.

Passing from generation to generation, like the habits inherited from one's parents.

No wonder it seems continuous as well as endless, with problems an everyday challenge to humans.

Problems which influence mankind's efforts to create a better world, making their efforts more useless than useful.

Leaving everyone to scramble along, always competing, threatening and fighting right or wrong, and doing so with weapons of mass destruction.

But that is the world, the real world mankind has been developing year after year, the world in which people live in fear.

The world as it is, with its rough and smoothed edges, it took human beings centuries to develop into this form and shape, with its advantages, and disadvantages, with everything just as it is.

And despite the tremendous progress that humans made, the world has turned out to be this way as it is, and not as it should be expected.

Leaving some of yesterday's problems behind, as humans trotted forwards to keep up with time. Taking with them other problems, which they passed on from the past to the present, problems of all sorts, problems of every kind, problems which were there most of the time.

Problems that were the cause of wars, and consequences of all sorts.

The superstitions, the corruption, the injustices, not much of those were forgotten and left behind.

Neither was the world divided, that too the present had inherited, instead of a world that was peaceful and amalgamated.

That's what our ancestors have willed to us, a world brimming with problems never too much.

A world in which mankind has always been searching for knowledge, with fear a condition in which people constantly live.

And although with hopes for a better tomorrow, yet still piling trouble upon trouble.

And passing them on from yesterday to tomorrow, with consequences deep in sorrow.

Yes indeed, that's how things were in the past, and throughout the ages they have lasted right into this modern day and age.

Through the thunderstorms of yesterday, hinged with difficulties and hindrances of all sorts, humans persisted, progressed, and advanced.

Yes, as it is written on the pages of history, humans have made outstanding progress, all of yesterday was not just wasted, but through the years of development, some things moved on with time through passages unwind, from BC into AD.

Encroaching upon the patience of mankind, as his rightful deserving legacy.

And as new generations seized upon their inheritance, from an innovative and a woeful past.

They simply kept on going, to the future was where they were heading, and still searching for knowledge all the time.

Yes indeed, searching in the darkness and in the light, humans needed knowledge to improve their sight; they needed knowledge to be progressive, knowledge was the key to their successes.

So forwards they pushed straight ahead, with anxiety to acquire knowledge, thundering in their heads.

Yes indeed, in their search for knowledge humans were stubborn and determined, a better world was what they wanted, and that was always their aim, that was what bothered them, that was what they wanted more than anything.

And although they were not always very certain, whatever they did they always had that feeling that they were doing the right thing, and that was a driving incentive, indeed it was their motive.

So in the same direction they kept on going, even when they were exhausted and tiring.

Their search for knowledge was never ending; that even today they are still searching.

A search that has been going on right through the ages, homo-sapiens never stopped searching the book of knowledge's pages.

And they never stopped heading towards the future either, although sometimes when exhausted, that's when they got the feeling that they shouldn't bother.

Tired, confused, and not sure of anything; humans still pulled themselves together, and continued on their journey towards the future.

And that was because they had nowhere else to go, nowhere to search for a better tomorrow.

But not all was tarnished with disappointments and hopelessness, there was still some measure of cerebral finesse.

Human's journey towards the future was not all with peril and in darkness.

There was as they hoped, a glimmer of light with sufficient brightness through the telescope and Galileo's sharpness.

The future was there for humans to reach, and they always felt that one day they would breach, so that kept them going on their feet, trampling the ground beneath.

But how much further they had to go? That was always an intrusive part of their disappointment, causing worry sometimes, as anxiety erupted in their minds with mischievous thoughts of all kinds, not sure whether or not they were going in the right direction, not sure whether or not that they had forgotten something important.

And because they were overwhelmed with anxiety, at that moment in time, it made them very angry to scurry.

So, what was it that early moderns did in their desperate search for knowledge as they journeyed towards the future?

Indeed, it has been very interesting to know what they did, as well as how they managed.

Yes indeed, what they did was very interesting, they kept on going, trying to maintain their courage in jubilant spirits, trying to overcome their weaknesses, trying to control themselves as anxiety ruptured in their heads.

Knowing quite well that in their search for knowledge they needed to be brave.

So they kept on going, they kept on searching, most of the time that's what they did.

To acquire knowledge they were determined, humans had no desire to remain still in ignorance and in superstitious darkness.

They knew that they couldn't give up, that was something in which they had no doubt, and they were very certain about.

So they had to go and keep on searching for knowledge; because some-where it was there, somewhere it was hidden, they had no doubt, they were very certain.

And that they did, they kept searching for knowledge day after day, year after year, very tired and exhausted, but they didn't care.

Generations came and they went, each searching for knowledge all the time.

So yes, they kept on searching until it was rewarding, until knowledge was within their grasp, until it was found, wherever it was hidden, humans were determined to continue.

And that they did until it was real, accidentally they stumbled upon just what they needed, a stack of knowledge surreptitiously hidden.

It was a vast treasure of natural knowledge, humans' search for the moment had now ended; they were nature's sole beneficiary, a package of knowledge was their shining jewelry.

Yes indeed, their find put smiles on their faces, they were now in possession of some knowledge, but it came with questions disturbing their minds.

How best to use such a valuable find? How best to use it without wastage and mismanagement? How best to use the knowledge to the benefit of man-kind?

Yes it was knowledge, and knowledge was what human beings needed to secure a better world. A world without superstitions, without fear, terror and ignorance.

A world without horror, and perhaps without crimes, because life will get better with changes all the time.

Indeed, that was the dream, it was the prediction on everyone's mind.

Eradicating the darkness of the past, with the possibility of creating a better developed and progressive world, that was something mankind could now see unfurled.

Indeed, that was our forebears' ambition, that was their intention, that was their dream, it was their mission.

So it was always the same with every generation that came, a better world was always their aim.

But it was never going to be easy, in times that were dangerous, superstitious and sleazy.

There were those, and among them were many, who held on tight to their beliefs as a necessity. Their superstitions to them were very real, not something to discard that easily.

Their beliefs will not be threatened by knowledge that perhaps came from the devil.

Indeed, their beliefs were rooted deep, and not easily plough from beneath.

So knowledge was a very risky thing to seek; to be certain that knowledge was not spreading, scholars were accused, leading to tortures, beheadings, or garrote.

They were never left alone, with agents in and out of their homes, seizing their books to be burnt. And in some cases, when scholars were arrested, they were punished in public places just for all to see the seriousness of the felony.

And that was intended to send a message, that the spreading of knowledge was not accepted.

So knowledge was disregarded, it was ignored, it was considered blasphemous to the gods.

And as the opposition of knowledge was very strong, with intimidating forces all around.

Scholars were driven underground, in fear, despair and in secrecy.

Their freedom was often stolen with threats to their family, so their silence was golden, their safety important; the threat of spreading knowledge was taken very seriously by the pillars of authority, and by religion especially.

Indeed, the authorities felt threatened by the spread of knowledge, so an iron fist was kept on the lid.

And the lid was secured with the wrath of torture, and the threat of death in the flames of a fire. Yes indeed, knowledge was heresy, so it was dealt with severely.

It was dealt with both by church and state, and they had no mercy for the accused culprit.

So yes indeed that's just how it had been, and without a good reason, that was how life went on, with many horrors that were wrong, and in every culture in medieval BC and AD.

Life was still a foreboding predicament, and it was the same wherever you went.

It was the same everywhere, life was a heavy burden to bear.

Those were really dangerous times, punishments often outweighed the crimes, which for many were false accusations with no opportunity of proving innocence.

Indeed, surviving was intimidating and brutal, to acquire knowledge was fatal, especially when it was contrary to the doctrines of the holy sea.

And from century to century with little change, despite humans' efforts developing.

Building and destroying again and again, and often with new ideas re-starting from the beginning.

It was indeed a vicious cycle, in times that needed a miracle.

Times when fear was always there, because it had nowhere else to go.

Times that were dangerous, very superstitious, and worse still, suspicious,.

Yes, times that just raced along, when you looked back it was already gone.

Times that had no time for humans at all, not even to answer when nature called.

Times that never for a moment stopped, preferring only to slow down.

But only when your back was already broken, trapped in discomfort under a rock, and in darkness deep under the ground.

Times that left humans with all the time in the world, to do whatever they could bad or good.

To slaughter one another, or to develop the world, and to do so however they could.

Or even to waste as much time as they could, until it was time to do what they should.

Time to stop or carry on, either to live or be dead and gone; whatever was the time it was never wrong, not by a minute or even a second.

And during all that time what the people really needed most, it was knowledge they needed to displace superstition's ghost.

To free themselves from the wrath of their predicaments, their anxieties, their iniquities, and all their corrupted involvements.

And to save themselves from a life of a perpetual curse, and the many other things that could be worse.

So despite the threats to their welfare and being, to acquire knowledge scholars did through seeing. And that was what they did, quite often secretive, they plunged into the vaults of nature's treasures.

Grasping at knowledge to their surprise and delight, which eventually in time was on the rise.

Bringing with it a catalog of changes, to a world that was desperate for both knowledge, and conveniences.

And as humans kept on developing, doing their best, century after century still making progress.

The progress they were making, sometimes it was tough, sometimes rough, and yes very slow, but there was success.

And they did so very discreetly, to avoid suspicion, arrest and persecution, even to their parents and their children often held as ransom.

So with their ambitions to make the world a better place, that was never easy, always risky, so their attempts to acquire knowledge failed in many cases.

So for many decades and even for centuries, life on earth had been blighted by the lack of knowledge, with the result of unpredictable consequences.

Consequences of all sorts, from unnecessary deaths to very serious disasters.

And one after the other they came and went, despite humans' attempts to prevent them.

Yes indeed disasters were frequent, they were common occurrences during humans' development, there were tragedies happening frequently, progressive development wasn't easy.

Humans struggled in their attempts, and very often under threats and intimidation.

Still, despite the difficulties, despite the problems with threats and intimidation, it was a world taking shape and form, in the blueprint of humans' imaginations.

With their efforts brick by brick, they were building the world in the best way they could, with new inventions all the time.

Indeed, the world was developing step by step, entering a new age of progress, and passing it on from generation to generation, as stages of humans' development.

And with many wrongs considered to be right, and taken for granted in daily life.

Wrongs that made life unbearable with intimidation and fear incomprehensible.

And even worse than that, it was a world still very superstitious, prejudicially divided, biased, unjust, discriminatory and very corrupt, those were the world's building blocks.

And drawn frequently into quarrels and battles by ingenious kings, Emperors, and Dictators, with the ambition to build and rule Empires.

And for no other purpose but to gratify their urge, to conquer, oppress, and enslave the world. And to debase the masses into submission, as slaves to the rules of oppression.

Indeed it was a world in a state of insanity, that's how it had been for many centuries.

Fear was a constant daily threat, with torment in dreams when you slept, and when you woke up, greeted in your breath, was the smell of the wrath of death.

And it affected many lives, draconian rule was the authority; torture before death was customary, or anything worse that could have been imagine, to inflict pain was the aim.

It was a world where the rule of law was often nothing more than hostile brutality.

With false accusations and arrests, then thrown into jail for years and nothing less.

Where people were inhumanely tortured, they were either slaves or prisoners.

Prisoners to the systems that impounded their lives with oppression.

And that they suffered for many years, arrested and imprisoned even though being innocent, an accusation was enough to warrant a jail sentence, often followed with torture for a confession.

But then again, however you look at it, that's how things were done in the past.

Humans were developing to be ruthless and aggressive, love and compassion were signs of weakness.

Believing that it was necessary to guarantee peace and security, indeed, ruthlessness was the only means of correctness.

Yet still, despite the severity of the ruthlessness, the forebears had never given up, nor had they lost a single measure of hope, fear and intimidation were not going to work.

They did whatever they could with determination, doing their very best trying to cope.

Pursuing knowledge from wherever it may be, be it from the skies, the forest, or from the bottom of the sea.

Pursuing knowledge from their experiments in whatever way they can.

For knowledge indeed was very necessary, and very vital to the improvement of mankind's skills and his ability, indeed, it was the only cure for ignorance and idiocy, a brain disease which had captured almost everybody.

And for his longevity too, indeed, there was where knowledge was desperately needed, for without it, sickness was a one-way ticket, and in one direction towards a grave, life in those days was short lived.

So yes indeed, during those medieval times unfortunately, things were never easy, the spreading of knowledge was a crime with a heavy penalty, even death was a threat, and with excruciating torment, it was slow and painful to the end.

Yes, the spreading of knowledge in several cases was considered to be an ominous sin of heresy, and it was even considered blasphemous, especially when it was contrary to the established spiritual religious orders.

And as state and church power were two evils that wedded each other.

With state and church as partners together, they frequently and ruthlessly abused their powers.

Committing atrocities in God's name, time and time again it was the same.

Implementing the death penalty as a deterrent, and often after a brutal torture to extract a confession. And then to suffer in the flames of hell, burnt alive until dead.

And that was to be a threat as well as a warning, to anyone accused of disobeying, or blaspheming.

Indeed, truth in knowledge was a serious threat to the establishment of the day.

It was to be hidden, completely forbidden, with a penalty very severe to pay.

And since human beings were still very superstitious, and suspicious, it was really a problem knowing who to trust, those were days you kept your mouth shut.

Indeed, fear was the engine generating discipline, and with a force so strong it was very intimidating.

Torture until death was the obvious threat: to halt the spread of knowledge, which was regarded as a source negative, nothing more than tricks and voodoo blackmagic.

'It was from the devil, so it must be evil', that was the general opinion.

And that opinion was the same from wherever it came, especially whenever it came from religion; the uncompassionate mother of superstitions.

But time never stopped, nor did the people give up; and knowledge on the surface was quietly and gradually spreading.

Indeed it was spreading secretly, driven by the forces of curiosity, spreading among those who for knowledge were very hungry.

Yes, time and time again knowledge was spreading, like a snail crawling up a hill, to its future it was heading.

True to say, knowledge like the snail was very slow in its movement, but it got there in the end.

Whenever knowledge knocked on a door, it was opened for sure, regardless of whatever for.

And yes it is also true, some slammed their door shut in its face, they were very much afraid, they wanted nothing to do with knowledge.

Since the acquisition of knowledge was still a threat, with the consequences of a painful death; fear and superstitions had a tight grip upon the masses, and they kept them firm in their places.

Indeed, they were not even allowed to write or read, the basics for the understanding of knowledge.

So for a very long time still the world remained with disruptive consequences, as a place with little knowledge; where corruption, ignorance, and superstitions flourished.

So for centuries still knowledge remained in its hiding place untouched somewhere quietly.

And dangerous to pursue because everyone knew, obtaining knowledge was a felony, it was a crime with a painful death penalty.

And that was how the world was developing and progressing, with the same problems again and again, and for centuries it remained the same, passing from generation to generation, not with knowledge, but with superstitions.

No knowledge, no learning, no understanding of so many natural things.

Yes indeed it was for centuries the masses were denied knowledge, even the basics to write and read were seen as a threat to society.

So they were kept in idiocy, and in ignorance, exploited for the benefit of the elite classes.

And they were nothing more than serfs, slaves, prisoners or servants, all with no need of an education.

No need for rights, for knowledge, or anything, when wrongs will do just the same, keeping them where they belong, keeping them in their place far behind in the rat race.

Yes, they were all considered as useless good-for-nothing, common labourers with a birthright to serve their masters.

And that's the way it had been, not for years but for centuries.

And that has been the reality of things in a world which was progressively developing.

It was indeed the everyday norm, which was considered to be right instead of wrong.

So yes, the problems of yesterday became the problems of tomorrow, that's how things were a long time ago, regretfully today many things are still so.

That was the cycle of development and progress, during the dark ages of BC and AD.

Things changed but not always for the best, passing on from one century to the next.

Passing from generation to generation, whatever were the norms, coupled with old and new inventions.

Indeed, human beings had already existed for a very long time, during which, century after century came and went.

But the knowledge they had acquired was very little to admire, and scholarly life was like a pariah.

Moving forwards yes, and progressively, but with changes occurring very slowly.

It was a world in self-captivity, hostile to humanity, and towards those who were different especially.

It was a world governed by forces of evil interwoven, dark and slippery was the pathway of entry.

It was as if the people were agents of the devil, that even religion too was a force of evil.

With fires lit daily, lives were claimed in God's name, and in the horrors of flames, exposed to the public as a warning.

And with screams so loud they reached up to the clouds, yet still, rain never came down to put the flames out, and that some said was a sign of guilt, because the heavens never opened to put out the flames.

Indeed superstitions were alive and kicking in everything, nothing existed without it in those days.

So yes indeed, that's just how it was during the long stretch of the dark days of misery, days that witnessed inhumanity, days which stained the good books of history.

To be burnt to death from living flesh to ashes was a common punishment executed, and that was done on a regular basis, to be accused of a wrong was all that was needed.

Yes, religion had claimed many lives in pain, those who were accused were burnt alive or strangled in hanging.

Accused yes, as devil worshippers, as witches, wizards, heretics, scholars, or sorcerers.

Or whatever were the accusations, torture was applied to force confessions.

Then it was death that came in the horror of flames, to signal a warning.

Yes indeed, that was the horrors of the ups and downs, exposed for all to see under the sun, a common norm during mediaeval civilisations.

It was the reality of living under the sun, during those mediaeval times life was always about superstitions, knowledge was still hidden beyond.

Superstitions indeed were always awake, and that was so with every faith.

Yet still each generation was making some progress, slow as it was; they were doing their best.

And with their focus up above, and their feet on the ground, into the future humans were moving on, they had no intention of just hanging around with their flat feet stuck in the mud on the ground.

But their pace was indeed cautious and slow; and what humans did not know was that they still had a very long way to go.

The future was not anywhere near, so they kept on traveling year after year.

Yes, traveling indeed with little knowledge, despite the many years they had been searching.

Until one day at last, and with astonishing surprise, unexpectedly they stumbled as they arrived.

Indeed, they were at the door of nature's secrets, they were about to get rich, with their inheritance of knowledge.

It was where nature's secrets were stacked from the floor to the ceiling above.

It was a view that astonished the crowd, the future of mankind could now be something proud, that was something no one had any doubt about.

111

So yes indeed, and without any asking, humans were driven by forces unyielding.

Despite the threats, torture, and painful deaths, to acquire knowledge they could not resist.

And that was because knowledge meant development and progress, knowledge meant the burial of ignorance, knowledge meant learning, it meant understanding, and it meant developing a good sense of reasoning, it meant a great deal of things, for a better life it meant everything.

So humans continued their search very cautiously indeed, hoping one day to succeed.

And that they did eventually as they stumbled upon nature's hidden treasure, which was theirs to take as nature's heirs.

Which was for several millennia in waiting for humans to uncover, to look at with awe, and understand what they have discovered.

So no sooner had humans unlocked the door of the vault of nature's valuable secrets, humans' treasure which was kept by nature awaiting discovery.

Possessed with a flow of good and bad ideas rampaging confusion in their heads.

Knowledge discovered was transformed into new discoveries and inventions after the experience of some weird experiments.

And with this in hand, humans did whatever they can, to make the world a much better place especially with the inventions of domestic conveniences.

Creating new things all the time, to improve the wretched livelihood of mankind.

So what was it that was done with the knowledge acquired by early humans to create a better world?

What was it humans did with the knowledge they had acquired, the knowledge at their disposal?

The knowledge nature bequeathed to humans. How did they use it for their benefit, progressively acquiring domestic conveniences?

It was all amazing as much as it was surprisingly inspiring, what human beings were able to do with their newfound knowledge, brand new.

It was a new world they were creating; the beginning was really exciting, the old was indeed disappearing.

It was magical, really fantastic, although it was true, it was unimaginable, people couldn't believe it, they were so impressed to know that it was something humans could do.

Indeed, knowledge was beautiful, mysterious yes, and extremely useful.

Yes indeed, they saw right in front of their eyes what they can do with knowledge, staring at it as though they were terrified, mystified, or perhaps just mesmerized; they couldn't even decide whether they were either foolish or wise; still with doubt, amazed and somewhat petrified.

It was indeed the equivalent of nothing less than a miracle, and by a god it was sent, through the innovation of an oracle.

Indeed it was really unbelievable, that it had many people thinking very deeply and cautiously that it may indeed be some trick of the devil, it really had them in a puzzle.

A trick of the devil to entice humans to the excitement of sin from the things they didn't understand, a means of attracting their attention, and then grab hold of their souls without redemption.

So what was it mankind invented that was so exciting, incredulous, and yet real?

What were the tricks they accomplished that outwitted sorcery and blackmagic?

What was it that bamboozled sorcerers, and confused witch doctors, making them all look like fraudsters?

Indeed, what human beings did, they changed darkness into light, with just the click of a switch and it was very bright.

And it happened so very fast, as swift as lightning there was light.

It was indeed an astonishing piece of magic, many believed that it was nothing more than a good voodoo trick.

It had to be a trick of the devil, for any human being to do such a thing was just impossible.

Yes indeed, that was the general opinion, especially from the think tank of religion.

And it was generated from a source they created and called a battery; without really fully understanding how amazingly useful it could be.

It was so bright, the light which was coming from something they made with glass and called it a bulb, which was connected to two pieces of wires from the battery to the bulb for the invisible electricity to travel in and out; one taking it into the bulb, and the other wire for it to travel out, back into the battery, circulating in a ring continuously.

Electricity always travels separately, one wire taking it in, and another taking it out from the battery.

And amazingly it is even able to start a fire, that's what they said about the electricity quietly and secretly traveling inside the wire.

Indeed, the magic was just fantastic, above the understanding of reality; many people saw it, and they still couldn't believe it, that brightness came just from wires connected from a battery to a bulb, and it mattered not how far the distance was.

But as bright as it was, it was still not that easy to brighten the minds of everybody with the amazing brightness from electricity.

There were those who were still not convinced, still believing it was some voodoo trick, preferring to remain in their superstitious darkness.

Indeed, they were stuck deeply in their curiosity with no outlet from their entry, asking themselves again and again, what kind of sorcery is this thing?

That was the ambivalent question restless in their heads as they stared at the brightness of the bulb with their curious eyes opened wide, and their thoughts circulating in a state of confusion causing inundation in their minds. What kind of magic could be so bright? In their silence they repeatedly asked.

How could that be possible with just wires? Deep in thought, the brightness they admire.

Staring at the bulb as if they were dazed, or hypnotized by its brightness.

It was really something fantastic indeed, just amazing to see, it had astonished everybody; brightness appeared so swiftly from something they called electricity, which was invisible, impossible to see.

And worse still, it didn't even have a christian name, so it must be from the devil where it came, traveling with speed much faster than lightning, and that's why it's impossible to see, so a trick from the devil it had to be, that's what many people had still believed.

And with this invisible electricity, humans did numerous things; that looked like magic at the beginning. It was compelling, invisible, and yet so useful.

And not yet realizing nor even fully understanding the practical use of knowledge.

Nor the very wide scope of their discovery of that invisible thing they called electricity.

There were those who still strongly believed without any doubt that it was either sorcery, voodoo, or some sort of black magic or trickery, it was from the devil, most certainly.

And they were convinced when someone got hurt, whenever the voltage was not properly earthed. It was indeed a trick of the devil, only with Satan such things were possible.

So quick, so swift and deadly, was the effect of a piece of wire with invisible traveling electricity.

So yes indeed it was very hard to believe, in a very thin piece of wire electricity can travel, and with speed even faster than lightning, and yet the wire never shakes, bends or breaks, or anything.

It remained silent, it remained still, it remained as dead as anyone will.

Yes indeed, many people just couldn't believe what they were seeing, the power of electricity was just too amazing, it was beyond their reasoning, so for them, it had to be a trick of Satan, that magic was very far beyond the reach of humans.

Indeed, 'Humans have not yet reached that far.' So said a sorcerer.

So still confused they just wouldn't let go, and between superstitions and knowledge they were trapped in the middle.

Holding them back in the darkness of their superstitions, in that environment was where they looked for answers.

And yes, even among the stars high up above, confused sorcerers searched for answers.

And as human beings overwhelmed with anxiety, their new discoveries inspired their ability with greater confidence and zeal.

They used their new-found knowledge somewhat sparingly for whatever it was that was necessary.

Creating new things for a better world, for today, tomorrow, and for as long as they could.

And as they made use of the knowledge they gathered at hand, death came eventually upon some superstitions that were no longer able to stand; and that was because their legs got broken.

Making mankind's journey a lot safer ahead, indeed, people were now able to boldly tread.

With some superstitions out of their heads, they were no longer afraid to go to bed.

No longer afraid of the dead, no longer afraid of the darkness and demons from hell.

No longer afraid of vampires, who drank human's blood as wine.

No longer afraid of ghosts and spirits, because humans now had a weapon, they had knowledge.

So people were drifting from darkness into light, electricity indeed was very bright.

So with their newfound knowledge and discoveries, indeed, human beings had less worries.

And with superstitions out of their head, they were able to get the sick much sooner out of bed. And with man-made machines doing many jobs, powered by electricity.

It was really magic directly from above, which the gods sent down to make humans' life easy; that's what some people believed, still refusing to accept the simplicity of the reality of electricity.

So yes indeed, those were both exciting and difficult times, humans were about to discard their long-held companion, ignorance was to be left behind.

And with the discovery of electricity, the future for mankind was now looking healthy.

Humans were making rapid progress as they trotted along cautiously on their journey, hoping for even more success.

And yes, their lifestyle was changing for the best, and even the style in which they dressed.

Indeed, with this new discovery called electricity, life was getting better, and living much easier, machines were doing things much quicker.

So human beings were drifting from sorcery to reality, cautious yes, but certainly they were advancing each day a bit closer, getting nearer towards a better future.

And as far as they were able to see, with their focus stretched deep into reality.

No more sorcery, voodoo, or black magic, nor ancestors with useless magical powers taking care of the sick.

No more gods to claim lives in the horrors of a bloody sacrifice, because knowledge was now the key to prolonging life.

Restoring the sick from the jaws of death, and from upon a painful bed that had no rest.

Oh yes indeed, in knowledge there is reality, no more room for uncertainty in the supernatural world of black magic or sorcery.

No more devilish tricks or voodoo mischief, knowledge is the key to reality, it is the key to humans' ingenuity, and to sensible thinking in the understanding of the complex nature of things.

And yes with knowledge it did seem that human beings were now shifting from the jaws of superstitions, but they were not yet out of its grip.

Superstitions were still the cause of many problems, and they may be so for a long time still.

So in the meantime humans were doing the best they could, embracing reality as something good.

Realizing that if they don't, they may live to regret that their superstitions were nothing more than a useless daunting threat.

So yes indeed, full of confidence, pride, and brimming with zeal, this is exactly what humans did with their knowledge and their skills.

They prolonged life, swiftly changed darkness into light, that lit up the future which did seem bright.

Giving hope for a better world, a world of knowledge, where all things could then be understood. Taking the world into a new advance, far away from the medieval past, and far away from the supernatural.

Realizing their dreams and their ambitions; to rid the world of that which was old, and entangled deep in the gut of superstitions.

And where ignorance can be replaced by the spread of knowledge.

So that mankind can live together, in peace forever, instead of in broken pieces scattered all over exposing danger.

But that was never going to be completely the case, since some of the past could not be erased. So into the future some traveled with time, leaving the rest to weather behind.

To be forgotten as dead and gone, because into the future they didn't belong.

And this was true, into the future some things went, such as superstitions and their beloved mother religion.

Still influencing people from generation to generation, regardless of the progress made by mankind. Yes indeed, religion had great influence, it always did and always will.

Especially upon those who ask no questions, easily they were led to the gates of hell.

Only to realize when they got there, they thought they were heading elsewhere.

And yes, it was also true for languages, and the creation of nations divided.

And the uninterrupted spread of knowledge, from the institutions of schools, universities and colleges. And not for a moment forgetting the survival system, 'capitalism' with its many financial institutions.

Infested with a range of calamitous problems, with money it's only faithful friend.

And of course too, the many sins of yesterday, all traveled together from the past, first class, to be a part of the world today.

Contributing in one way or the other, making things worse or making them better, making them whatever.

That's how it was as human beings were developing, and the world progressing, with knowledge the key to everything; even opinions were now geared from superstitions to rational thinking, humans were now using their senses, which were awakened from years of hibernating.

And as the old with the new blended in together, in a progressive world that was getting better.

The world was seemingly forming into shape, with things eventually falling into place.

But no one knew exactly how things would turn out to be, the future was too far away for anyone to see.

But as far as anyone was able to see, there was a glimmer of hope for success and prosperity.

With the many changes that were occurring, more and more opportunities were appearing.

And that created a sense of security, with the feeling and belief that sometime eventually, things will be as good as they should be.

Yes, that was the feeling which was developing in the hearts and minds of human beings as things were changing and changing again, fate and hope was accelerating.

But it never always turned out as was expected to be, disappointment was often the unforeseen reality.

With new things replacing the old ones one after the other, most things did, but some did not make life much better.

Even in clothing, lifestyles were changing, from naked exposure to the gracefulness of clothing, men were not sure if they did the right thing.

And with words put together in the art of communicating, distance was no longer a problem whenever speaking.

And onwards to wheels that rolled in transportation, with same day deliveries regardless of the distance.

And to fly in the sky just like a bird, humans were doing so many things they never thought they could.

And they did transplants of organs saving many lives, and countless developments, some foolish, some wise.

Indeed, electricity was king, it was involved in so many things.

It was involved in death and destruction as much as it was in saving lives, and in progressive development, it was there all the time.

And yes indeed, humans built pyramids, and that of bridges, joining distant lands together.

From across rivers, the seas, and in the skies, bridges were stretched for miles.

And yes it is true, humans also built deep under the ground, removing the minerals they had found.

Building some breath-taking tunnels, and with the conveniences for humans to live.

Not to mention upon the land, they planted buildings stretching upwards to heaven.

Buildings standing deep in the ground, and stretching upwards towards the clouds just beneath the sun.

Scraping the skies to look into heaven, and taming the wind long before it hits the ground.

Yes indeed, human beings built deep inside mountains and upon hills, and also upon the oceans.

With their knowledge obtained, like Nimrod the king, they were always searching for a passage leading into heaven.

So they ventured out into the peacefulness of the beauty of space, just to observe how the stars live. And with their arms outstretched, the wonders of the universe mankind embraced.

Astonished by the wonders of nature's distant perimeters, there was to be no end to humans' ambitions.

Searching maybe for the horrors of hell, or perhaps for heaven's splendors.

Searching yes, for something or the other, always going further and further, cannot find whatever they were searching for, further they ventured into forbidden corridors.

So with determination and a very strong will, humans continued to travel even further still. Reaching out to Mars, distant stars, and even to the furnace of the Sun.

And as they reached the Moon, they landed there upon; then unto Jupiter they circled around.

Humans were curiously exploring the universe, with the intention to find out just how things work. And of course to find out if there was anybody else, and where exactly they all dwell.

Whilst down on earth humans forged ahead, sometimes even going backwards instead.

And with desperate efforts to progress, the advances they made were not always the best.

In some cases, they succeeded as well as failed, then they started all over again turning a new page. But the page they turned was not always the best, so they sometimes ended up disappointed with little progress.

Still not yet defeated, humans continued towards the future with whatever progress they made, be it good or bad, right or wrong, all bundled together they passed them on.

Always creating something new with the knowledge they acquired, changing from old to new was always desired.

They changed things today, and changed them tomorrow, that was the norm wherever you'd go. And it did at times create unparalleled hope that things would be better, that's how it did look.

But then eventually it became very clear that the ambitions of humans were focusing elsewhere.

Exploring the lands, the seas and the skies; reckless and aggressive in a pursuit unwise.

And that they did with no regrets, and obviously without care, not even with a little remorse; that was never there.

Humans ravaged the forest like a beast that was savage, causing many lives lost, plants as well as animal lives, lives of every sort.

And yet still for them that was not enough, so they contaminated the seas with plastics and dross.

Affecting lives even deep down on the seabed, coral reefs, fish and plants all ending up dead. But that did not even stop there, it was as though humans hated fresh air.

So they polluted the skies, ignoring the advice that what they were doing wasn't wise.

And that they did, they created climate change causing effects that were devastating.

Effects that were most profound with heat that's more fit for the Cerberus hound.

And with even more consequences yet to come, that may push sea levels above higher grounds.

Causing destruction that was never seen before; not even during the perils of the Second World War.

And despite the threats from a complex and angry nature, yet still humans continued to ravish their only planet, just as they were doing years before.

They had a world to develop and couldn't just stop, so they continued with the destruction as if they must.

And they did so as if they had no other choice, but the splendors of nature they must destroy.

Believing it was right for the development of humans, they grabbed and destroyed whatever they could, regardless of the consequences, bad or good.

And that's how the world was developing, time and time again, during yesterday, today, and even tomorrow.

Passing it on with their sins, and with every joy and every sorrow, passing from today onwards to tomorrow.

Yes, passing on both destruction and progress, not sure of the outcome, success or a mess.

Humans were always passing from the present to the future, the things they created, and the sins of their fathers.

It was what was passed on to them, so they passed it on again and again, although they did so with a bit of change, it was still a world heading into ruins.

So what was really humans' intention? What were they doing? What exactly was their aim? What kind of a world was mankind developing?

Progressive yes, and even doing their best, and still the world was always in a mess.

Indeed the evidence is here with us today, it was not by chance the world developed this way.

Everywhere in the world human beings have been ruthless, they have been superstitious, they have been very sinful and yet religious.

Yes, they have been progressive, and yet still destructive.

Indeed, they have been very selfish, obsessed with their own interest; and that's why the world is as bad as it is; no unity, no equity, and everybody is always sorry.

And that is how humans have been right through the ages, right through their development stages.

From century to century that's how it had been, despite humans' efforts to come clean.

So yes indeed, the worse had taken the better of them, as if it was something they could not prevent.

And yet it is not that they were hit by a meteorite, and their attitudes changed overnight.

That's how they developed during their journey which was very long and weary, during a perilous existence in years counted in centuries too many.

So how much wiser now are humans? How much have they learned from so many years of experience, and from the centuries they left forgotten behind?

The answer that was given to those two questions, in three words rolling off every slippery tongue, was; "just look around!" That was the verbal explanation voiced with a tint of sarcasm.

But then the answer was already there in humans' creations as well as in their destructions.

It was there in their ambitions, their dishonesty and corruption, their avarice and selfishness, as much as it was in their injustice.

They were visible in the way mankind was developing the world, which, although progressive it was very sinful.

Doing most things over and over again, whether they were right or wrong.

And it mattered not of the consequences, things got done as they had to be done.

And they were done with zeal and with confidence, conscious that they were a part of development.

Conscious also, that they were progressing, so humans tried to do their best with everything.

Yes, it was to do their best they always tried, but their decisions were not always wise.

Still their failures were not always discouraging, in fact, they made them even more determined.

Pursuing both rights and wrongs; whatever was in their interest, regardless of the consequences, they were gambles humans were prepared to take, and so in many cases it was what they did.

Building the world with labour from slaves, with their sweat, blood and pain; and with their sorrow and grief again and again, it was indeed a disgusting shame.

Yes indeed, exploiting and cheating, labour was cheaper than anything.

Producing many luxurious things, the world was indeed progressively advancing.

But towards what it was advancing, which future was it romancing?

What the hell was it that human beings were doing? When at the same time they were developing, they were also repeatedly destroying nature's domain, hence creating the circumstances for climate change, creating the circumstances for destruction in ruins, and yes even creating the circumstances for death in pain.

Yes, that's just how it was, developing and destroying were both a progressive necessity, but they could have been done without the destruction of nature's boundaries, without the destruction of natural entities, without the destruction of life on the land, and in the sea, indeed, without the destruction of anything that was not necessary.

Yes indeed it was a necessity that was very frustrating, slowing the rate at which progress was dilating.

And yet not for a single moment did humans ever stop to think of the seriousness of the consequences of their boldness; their intransigent ravage of nature's domain.

With or without knowledge they carried on, it was for a better future so they felt, so whatever they were doing had to be done.

And it was in the future they were determined to reach, to enjoy the life they desperately seek.

Believing in the future things would be better, that kept them going in all sorts of weather, doing whatever was necessary or unnecessary, it didn't really matter.

They did whatever they felt had to be done, whether or not it was right or wrong.

So grasping at the opportunities for a better tomorrow, despite the tremors that brought woe and sorrow, and despite the many centuries already gone, it was still in the same direction humans were heading, and with all their problems, their pros and cons, it was what they were doing ever since they were born, each generation that came followed on, ignoring the consequences that may come.

Yes, it was always towards the future where they were heading, always in the same direction, and taking whatever they could carry with them, often it was more problems.

Taking their troubles and everything, so that they may not have to start all over again.

Yes taking their fears, their superstitions, inventions, and new ideas, in fact most things from the present they took with them.

Their toys, and domestic conveniences, they took whatever they felt had some uses.

Yes they took the past and the present, and towards the future was where they went.

And as humans continued their move in the direction of progress, more and more they realized that having knowledge was the key to their success.

They were consciously awake, make no mistake, they were now progressing at a rapid rate.

Opening up doors to a flood of opportunities, to every occupation knowledge was the key.

And that was so especially with the knowledge of science and technology.

Technology that would take humans far beyond the universal boundaries, and despite the difficulties, they could return back to earth in one piece.

And yes, that mankind accomplished quite easily, despite the confrontations with uncertainties.

Their journey so far towards the future, they have been succeeding, nay more than this: exceeding.

But unfortunately still, despite humans' developments, and their progressive accomplishments.

The world was always in a state of underdevelopment, regardless of humans' new-found knowledge and outstanding skills, regardless of their expertise and their experiences, the world remained an insecure place, darkened with humans' sinfulness.

And not very sure of their forward direction, nor when into the future they may arrive.

To this unpredictability they had no conception, not even if they would arrive into the future alive.

They were with doubt sometimes, with confusion in their minds, maybe they should have stayed behind, their troubled heads had lost direction.

Indeed, too often humans appeared to be in a state of confusion, behaving as if they were not certain what was right, wrong, or delusion.

And that was what led to their knowledge being badly put to use, giving rise to corruption and abuse. And the same went on from generation to generation, with a package of spoils as their inheritance.

Yes, the good and the bad were together in one package, that's what new generations always inherited, exactly what they never wanted.

And so it was the same with science and technology, and of course the inventions that were so many.

The skills and the arts from the medieval past, in fact most of everything.

The good and the bad, the rights and wrongs, everything bundled together were to be taken to the future in a package as humans' treasure.

And even superstitions too, although some were left behind to be forgotten, some slipped right through the security of hell's gates to mingle with the present as an intake.

Not forgetting the frequent battles, whenever there were disputes to settle.

Slaughtered in death was the price paid, that's how things were settled in those dark days. Killing each other was the norm, it was in a battle that different opinions were settled.

Yes, that's how it was and still is today, in many cases it's humans' only way.

Their only way of settling disgruntled disputes, because they were never able to find a peaceful route.

A route towards a peaceful settlement, with the understanding of an honourable agreement.

Humans always feared treachery and dishonesty, breaking agreements was a liability.

And when they were broken the consequences were dare, the price paid was never fair.

And that's one of the reasons humans always feared who to trust, which was a matter of concern very much.

Because they were left entangled with doubt, and with fear that they may regret that they had opened their mouths.

But it mattered not, whatever the problems were, throughout the ages they were repeated yesterday, today, and even tomorrow.

The same problems arrived again, right upon your doorsteps came the mail, and were settled in the same way, with many people dead, some badly wounded, some captured and enslaved.

Problems that were created from the divisions of mankind, often they were too complex to understand.

Pointing fingers at others to blame, with either suspicions, accusations, discrimination, exploitation, hate, bigotry and even despair.

Oh yes indeed, the fingers of blame were always pointing at someone, guilty or innocent it made no difference.

Making decisions whether they were fair or unfair, that was the norm everywhere.

But unfair or not, no one really cared, that's how it was, that's what humans did, the things God forbids.

Yes, that was how things were done, regardless of whether they were right or wrong.

That's how they were done in the past, and for most of the time, that's how they were done in the present.

That's how things were done as the world was moving on, with the same mistakes made again. Solving them still in ways aggressive; come another day, and they are repeated.

So yes regretfully, that's how it was unfortunately, a resounding adversity.

Building a world from its foundations to the top, with whatever was sinful and corrupt.

Indeed, the world as it is today, one can only imagine what it was like yesterday.

A world where knowledge was still hidden in darkness, and terror roared everywhere on the surface.

Yet still with their courage, humans found knowledge, progressed and advanced, and many of nature's secrets humans now understand.

But the secret of a united world, in peace and harmony as it should be.

The secret of fraternity, in the way that things ought to be, everybody together happy.

The secret of peace instead of war, fighting each other not knowing what for.

The secret of compassion with some patience, and without anxiety and aggression.

The secret of love instead of hate, the secret of never making mistakes.

The secret of justice instead of injustice; in fact, the secret of life itself, always to be wise and never foolish.

How much longer will it take for human beings to know those secrets, and use them for their benefit? That is something that is still very troubling, and with no progress in the making.

So the world remains yet a wretched place for century after century despite the many changes, and with everyone stumbling, still racing along in a dubious rat-race.

Racing with the crowd going where, it could be only one place and no other.

It was towards the future everyone was going, and in no other race but the rat race, the only one that was heading towards that place.

And carrying with them both their problems and whatever they had achieved, taking with them what they believed that in the future they may need.

Developing and making mistakes, always with intentions to make the world a better place.

So why is it that the world is as it is today? When it was never intended to be this way.

From the beginning of humans' creation, to this present-day development.

After numerous years counted in centuries. What could be said about humans' progress?

Why is the world in such a mess? What kind of a world have humans developed?

Indeed, after so many years of progressive development, and the success of outstanding achievements, the world still appears to be in a mess; human's dignity is not yet at its best.

Progression yes, benevolence no, and it is the same wherever you go.

And yes, it is true, although perhaps it is not as bad as it was in the past.

The measure of poverty and human destitution remain a problem that is expanding.

Unfortunately, the numbers are not showing any signs of deductions, in fact they are growing all the time, upwards they climb.

From the many centuries of the past to today's progressive age, the world as it is, that's all the progress humans have made.

With millions of people living in a state of destitution, and sadly to say that includes children.

But it matters not, human beings have landed on the moon, so perhaps those minor earthly problems, they may deal with them one day soon.

Yes indeed, human beings have made considerable progress from their naked existence in the rainforest to this present day of outstanding success.

They have searched for, and acquired knowledge which led them to their present-day progressiveness.

And it could indeed be rightly said without grudge or favour, that humans have taken a very long time to reach this stage of their development.

Indeed, it is true that their progress was very slow, too many things which they could have done yesterday, were left for tomorrow.

And that is why today there is so much that is so badly wrong, and this is so from top to bottom.

And yet still despite the wrongs, the harrying pros and cons, with the unrelenting ups and downs, the struggles and the difficulties, the injustice, the sweat, the tortures, the intimidation and the unnecessary deaths, the hate and the unfairness, whatever it is.

Despite all of that, a bundle of problems together tightly wrapped, with the superstitions and fears that were a constant daily threat.

And yes indeed, the long years of torment from gods and demons, and the many other problems and difficulties that came and went.

And despite that bundle of relentless troubles wrapped into a very heavy load, as their inheritance they carried with them wherever they went.

Human beings still managed to achieve for their needs the knowledge to progress, and they have done so at their very best, they have done so deserving some merit.

With threats often hanging over one's head, every other day was a lucky day just to be able to get out of bed, instead of being a corpse still in bed, lying cold-blooded dead.

But indeed, to say the least, mankind's journey was both a grueling challenge and a burden of a struggle to succeed, never in one single year were things that easy without problems and difficulties.

It has always been a struggle, with problems developing today and tomorrow, often it did look as though human beings may be left far behind, lost in the wilderness among forgotten time.

Indeed it was never easy, and always compounded with difficulties even to acquire the little that humans had achieved.

And the time it took, century after century, progress indeed was a bit lazy.

Yes it is true, no need to argue, humans were always trying to do their best without regrets for a better today, and even so for a better tomorrow.

There was always a need for better, whatever it was it didn't matter.

But in doing so, progress was not always without headaches, nor was it without sorrow.

It was never without challenges, and with it came many mistakes.

So yes, those were years that roared and trembled with fear and trouble, pushing things beyond man's bubble, it was indeed a relentless struggle, survival was always formidable.

And as humans hoped for a better tomorrow, without knowing if they would ever succeed.

The world still continued developing, it was always short of so many things.

And it did so although, no one was certain what kind of a world they were developing.

With many of the wrongs and the rights of yesterday, into the present they found their way, to be a part of the world as it is today.

Wrongs and rights which shaped the world whether or not they were useful.

And that's the direction in which humans were traveling since the beginning of their time, with everything heading in one direction, towards the future was their only destination.

With much of the old brought in from the cold, to build the present as it is today.

So whatever it is that human beings have got now, is what they have achieved in the past, and more of the old will disappear in time, as new inventions arrive.

Yes, as long as the world continues changing, few things will always remain the same, and others, only for a while they will last.

New things will come and they will go, always replacing yesterday with tomorrow.

And what will come tomorrow will not always be known, but whatever comes, some things will be better, and some will be worse.

So it remains for human beings to decide their ambitions and their aims.

In which direction they should thread along, when they all look just the same.

Hoping that all will not be cloudy and dark, like the destructive deluge before the ark.

But with knowledge the future will be much clearer and bright, aiding us sapiens to do much more of what is right.

Conscious of the fact that there is still a fair distance to go, and a lot could be done for a better tomorrow.

And the world as it is, if it is still corrupt, every effort should be made to clean it up.

And that is something humans should be certain that they are doing, using their efforts for the purpose to prevent the world from being corrupt.

Indeed, the wrongs of yesterday are the sins that aren't in pattern reconstituted.

And not to be taken into the future, or else, the future would never be better.

And that is a fact, not fiction; Indeed, many people believe that it is one of Nostradamus' predictions.

And yes, it has been said yet another time again that over the years mankind has made tremendous progress, no one can deny that, it is so compelling, transparent, and conspicuous, indeed it is very obvious.

And often equal in numbers were humans' failures, with irresistible forces pushing them backwards.

Indeed, humans have explored the skies; the seas and the lands, and they have polluted them as much as they can.

Whilst at the same time acquiring knowledge, boosting their confidence and courage.

To the point of prolonging human life, for the many who would have died otherwise, and sent to an early grave without a smile.

And yes, no one could forget that within those progressive miles, humans have explored far and deep into the vastness of space, reaching to the edge of the universal skies.

And despite this, they are planning to go much further still, with a space detector to do a search.

Yes indeed, humans have created and developed an abundance of things, during the centuries of their reign, and yet still many more they are investigating on every inch of sea, land, and space.

And it has already taken a very long time, this they have confessed, so yes, they could have done a great deal more to clean up their untidy mess.

If human beings expect a better future, indeed they need to do a lot better.

The present is not good enough, they need to make much greater efforts.

They need to try much harder, working together; instead of always enraged in anger confronting one another.

Yes indeed, they need to be trustworthy instead of being aggressive and crazy; to be a pillar of integrity, to each other be friendly, and as wise as they could be.

And now taking a look back in time, in a final search for what humans have done during the many centuries of their progressive development.

The time they took cannot be overlooked, it has been indeed far too long.

Not measured in miles but in millennia, and many it took to arrive just here, within the gates of the twenty-first century, indeed, the length of time it took, not much has been achieved.

So yes, the time it has taken to achieve so little progressive development, mankind had more than enough time to design and create an earthly heaven.

There is no doubt that humans had sufficient time, in fact, much more than enough.

And during that time, they could have developed a world more progressive, and indeed with less problems, more justice and less crimes, indeed a world without destitution, only smiles, music, love, and rhymes.

Yes, they could have developed a world without destitute poverty, and with all human beings living in dignity.

Indeed, they could have developed a world that is just and fair with happiness everywhere.

So what went wrong? What tilted the world in this doomsday direction?

With the world as it is today, its progressive development is far from okay.

With human beings refusing to be emancipated, their perennial problems they take for granted.

So the same questions popped up again, but there was never anyone who could explain.

Why was it that in every age the world was so corrupted?

To survive, crimes were committed, some so brutal, no one could forgive.

Why was it so very unjust and very sinful too? With crimes spreading everywhere, and yet no one knew what to do, no one ever seems to have a clue, so the crimes just continue, when indeed they didn't have too.

So why was it in that direction humans went when they could have been prevented?

Was it because no one never tried, or just as things were, they were satisfied?

Or was it because it was too much of a bother? How things were didn't matter.

And as it remains a world divided, no one could be trusted, and that was one of the main causes of the many problems assembled.

And yes of course it is particularly because of the many fools, one after the other for centuries they ruled, implementing ill-judged rules.

Some of them were so foolish they even claimed to be gods, others were just mortal Dictators.

But whatever they were, they all abused their powers, the wrongs they did made men cower.

And without accountability, they led the world into the dangers of the sea.

And as a god, or a Dictator, a king, a Pharaoh, or an Emperor, whoever were the rulers; today's world is the result of their successes and their failures.

Because as rulers of the world, they had the powers of control; so on the whole they could have developed a much better world.

So sadly to say, as it is today, it may still get worse before it is okay.

But however it is, human beings will have to live, and perhaps with each generation living a little better than how their ancestors did, and with their own wrongs, rights, and mistakes, and acquiring their own experiences.

So what in the world went so badly wrong? What steered it into this dismal direction?

What dragged it along? What trampled it in the mud into the ground? What turned it on its head upside-down? Why is the world as it is today so divided in so many ways?

With humans embracing so many negative attitudes, often confused, and don't know which one to use.

Treating each other like dogs, pigs, or mules; equality it seems is against the rules.

What is it that is so very wrong, that after centuries in existence, yet still with each other humans muster resistance? can't get it right, too often wrong.

Is it that they really never tried? Perhaps that is the reason why.

Or was it that at some point in time they all took the wrong direction?

Not knowing exactly where it would lead, they just kept on going with the belief that it may lead them somewhere into heaven.

But that indeed was a dream, a dream full of expectations, a dream wet with sweat and overwhelmed with temptations.

A dream that was without reality, just full of myths, taboos and superstitions.

A dream indeed without meaning, without the reality of anything.

A dream that had no interpretation, forgotten in the darkness of the night, forgotten the moment daylight strikes.

Until there was nothing left for mankind to expect apart from doing his very best.

So, what was it that humans did with the time they spent during the many centuries of their existence?

So many years one after the other which came and went, never together.

Did they spend most of their years partying or warring, making love or making hate?

With so many years and little progress; instead of a utopia, the world is in a mess.

With people living in fear of something or the other troubling them all the time, something they worry about, can't pay the bills, no job, can't find peace wherever they look, just don't know where to search.

And that leaves them with their minds in pieces, scattered in confusion beyond reaches.

Yes indeed scattered everywhere, and when they look, peace is not there.

And as the years went by like a thief in the night disappearing into the dark.

Some left in history what they had to offer, some left nothing whatsoever, nothing to remember.

Some left blood and death, and some horrendous other things one cannot forget.

Yes, the years came and for a while they stayed, and when they left, they had no regret, they never came back again.

Some years were wasted, and for sure there were many of them, some were productive, some for many they were years of penury.

Some brought death to millions of humans slaughtered in wars, and many other deaths by some other cause.

Years that were drenched heavily in blood both on land and the oceans; blood from men, women, and children killed during wars and for no justified cause.

Some were put to lie one on top of the other in shallow graves with their heads separated.

Some were lying in their graves still with their heads, but the rest of their body had no arms nor legs.

Some were put in their grave before they were dead; whatever was the culture, in mother earth they were buried.

Yes, those were years very wet with blood and tears, some years came and went, without any difference.

Indeed the years went by, and many things people tried, some were very foolish, some were wise; some were useful, some useless, whatever they were, humans tried their best, but not always with success.

Indeed, only the truth in history can reveal the dark and hostile reality of the years that witnessed unimaginable cruelty among human beings.

Those years of BC and even AD. Years that were full of blood and tears, years that were for many a living hell.

Years that were angry, years without mercy, years that were familiar only with brutality.

Yes indeed, years that brutalized mankind, years that were very unkind, years that were never easy for human beings to survive, much less to stay alive.

The things humans did, no one was surprised, those were very difficult and unusual times.

Many were years of insanity, some things people did during the years they lived; they were even beyond the extremes of madness.

There was and there is, yet no word created in any language that could describe accurately the beastly savagery of inhumanity.

Searching for knowledge with human sacrifices, including children taken away from their parents, only to be used as guinea pigs in the horrors of experiments.

Yes indeed, it was very real, humans were searching for knowledge on healthy men, women, and children, with very cruel instruments used in their experiments, death came too late for many of them left to die in excruciating pain.

Knowledge that was gained from excruciating pain, when it could have been found in other humane ways.

Nothing was too gruesome; nothing was too vile, humans just did whatever they had to do, whatever it was they just continued.

And that could have been anything, and as horrible as anyone could imagine.

And so it did, as everyone expected, the years passed away each day, creeping from darkness into light.

And with the air heavily contaminated with fear, no one was able to breathe clean air.

And as the sun rises and sets each and every day, almost every home was visited by fear of the unknown the moment the sun went away.

Fearing the darkness of the night, and every sound that was hidden out of sight, humans were always anxious for the return of daylight, the hours of darkness were a threat to themselves.

But no one knew what each day would bring; whether it would be joy, sorrow, death, or sickness with pain, or whether it would be sunshine or rain.

And despite the countless criminal activities, and the ruthlessness of the authorities; the spread of knowledge and human courage were daily on the increase.

Yes indeed things were getting better, from century to century progress was moving faster, into the reality from age to age.

And now into the twenty-first century, the age of science, technology, new skills and expertise; humans are releasing an abundance of new discoveries.

Discoveries that were often beyond belief, and to the credit of knowledge in the field of new technology.

Nothing was so challenging in the years before, and yet still to come are even more.

Bringing with it rapid changes which are very sophisticated and inspiring.

And in some ways irresistibly addictive, resulting in certain disadvantages.

Which may show itself one day in the future, that technology, whenever it is not used properly, quite destructive it could be.

Not forgetting one of today's biggest problems already spreading like a virus and settling like dust on the platforms of communication; one of the disadvantages of development which often brings new problems.

Indeed, human beings are still communicating physically with one another, but not as much as they did before.

The numbers are reducing worldwide, as technology knocks upon every door and enters inside.

Yes, humans are communicating and that is for sure, communication has no end, it is of fundamental importance.

But they are communicating through material things, and not face to face any more.

Disregarding their family and friends, with nothing to say directly to them, as face to face communication enters its retirement.

'Things were getting better,' that's what people were saying to one another, progress was moving faster, it was the reality of a technical age; no need to communicate face to face.

Speaking through recordings or some sort of robot, face to face contact may soon be replaced with back to back.

No more face-to-face communication, smiling with each other in jubilation.

No more eye-to-eye contact, that was something of the past many years back.

Instead, it is what they called 'Artificial Intelligence' humans have embraced as their new friend and companion.

Yes, that is already happening today, with robots getting smarter day after day.

So who can tell what the future may be? Perhaps with nobody communicating directly.

Communicating yes, and even more than before, but not face to face, not anymore, that may even be against the law.

Because stupid laws are often made, and when made they are executed until they are changed, and that could be for a few decades or even for centuries.

So face to face communication, it may come the time when it is completely forgotten, indeed, that's my prediction.

So yes indeed, it is already a new world order, a new age that is very different from the ones before.

Creating material things which are not living, and yet daily, smarter they are getting.

It is what humans called "Artificial Intelligence," and they are now concerned about how it may end, whether it may have damaging effects, arousing concerns for regrets.

As it has already invited suspicions with accusations among nations, leading to threats of economical aggression, and perhaps still yet to come, are even more severe world problems. Indeed, it cannot be avoided, progress in science is often with both advantages and disadvantages. Both are a product of science associated with new inventions.

So yes indeed, Artificial Intelligence has already created a tsunami of problems, and with waves gushing higher in all directions, and doing so all the time.

Bringing with them problems that may pose a global threat, and likely with disastrous effects.

Problems which are nothing less than a new wave of crimes which are already in the systems.

Using artificial intelligence, humans were committing new crimes all the time, and they could even be miles away from the scene; indeed, it's a nightmare, it's a bad dream, it is a calamity never heard of nor seen, it is a real problem for the police.

Sitting on their arses behind closed doors, the crimes humans commit could even start wars.

And with threats, abuses, and blackmail, online crimes are the source of nervousness, sleeplessness, and headaches.

So with the same question, ask again once more, and this time be very sure.

What kind of a world are human beings developing? What are their intentions and their aims?

What to expect the future would bring if anything?

Is it more science with more new crimes, and getting worse all the time?

Could Artificial Intelligence be the answer to bring criminals to justice?

Or is there more technology still yet to come that could leave criminals with their legs broken, unable to run?

Criminals caught with no legs to stand on, because the scientific evidence is far too strong.

Delivering justice upon the culprits, who otherwise may have escaped.

But isn't that happening already with DNA technology?

Yes indeed, but it has to be further developed so that criminals would never be able to stand up. Too many are still escaping already, despite DNA technology.

So when they have no legs to stand on, because the scientific evidence against them is far too strong, then they will never be able to walk free, nor run, and justice will be seen to have been done.

But science perhaps still has to look for more avenues to catch criminals, apart from DNA, fingerprints, and artificial intelligence.

Indeed, from science there could still be something better to come that could even catch criminals on the run, wherever they are gone.

Yes indeed, this is a technical age, and perhaps the final stage of humans' development.

So in this age, the final stage, humans must do the very best they can, or the world may submerge into oblivion, or perhaps into an abyss of darkness of humans' own making.

Yes it is true, very true that humans still have a very long way to go, and a lot to do to eradicate yesterday's problems before they could create today's heaven.

And without any doubt, they have the ambition and the will, and they will always continue trying still despite how hard it is to make the world a better place.

But indeed I repeat, humans have left it far too long, with problems upon problems piling on. And now the pile weighs much more than a ton; there is indeed a lot to be done.

So now unfortunately no one could predict, no one could guess how much longer it will take to clean up the mess that yesterday has left.

To clean up the crimes brought into the system, and by no other but artificial intelligence, and its parents technology and science.

Causing a lot of grief, leaving people in need, with disappearing bank accounts stolen by the ghost of artificial intelligence.

Still despite this new problem, straight ahead mankind kept on going, achieving more things, creating more robots smarter still.

Robots that may get not only into your bank accounts, but into your pockets, deep down.

Taking with them whatever they could get, leaving you sorry and to regret, as they head towards the future with no looking back.

Yes indeed, that's today's scientific age, and tomorrow it could be better or even worse still.

Because the present often enters the future, passing through from year to year. Passing through causing problems, with new crimes entering the system.

And passing from generation to generation, with things from the past taken to the present, things that were old and new, things that were right and things that were wrong, things that were real and superstitious too; the future was where they were all taken too.

Knowing quite well that the pathway was dangerous, very slippery and corrupt.

A pathway that was full of sin, where humans did almost anything; and all to do with making a living.

And that was what humans did, determined to take to the future everything they were carrying, and they carried them all, including their sins.

In fact, they carried whatever they were able to carry, both old and new, whatever they felt they could use, especially of course, their newfound friend; wherever humans went, "Artificial Intelligence" they took with them.

So towards the future mankind kept on going with their newfound knowledge that was becoming very troubling.

Yes indeed very troubling, and very convenient too, artificial intelligence was doing so many things, more and more jobs were disappearing.

But was it making things worse, or making them better? Was it indeed creating a utopia or a sewer?

Was it able to put the pieces together, creating peace in the world, instead of broken up pieces scattered all-over? Was it really changing human beings' lives for the better?

Could this computerized go-getter ever be able to change the world from its destiny of disaster to something much better? Could science really make that changeover?

Could it ever create a world with justice, kindness, and love for one another, without wars, unjust laws, and the ravages of nature, exposing mankind to nature's wrath to suffer?

Indeed, could Artificial Intelligence ever be that miracle in need, with humans' problems to heal.

Is it humans' final solution in their attempts for the creation of a better world?

Or is it just maybe, it is the master key that can open the doors to opportunities leading directly to prosperity without criminal activities?

Or, is there something still much better to come, that would be able to prevent everything that is wrong? Creating a world with justice in particular, and the elimination of poverty everywhere.

Indeed, a world without crimes, that's what everybody wants, hence a better world for the whole of mankind.

A world without wars and draconian laws; a world full of compassion and love.

Yes indeed, a world in peace with itself, without fear, pain and misery, a world that is much better than it ever had been.

Oh yes indeed, to which one of these, is Artificial Intelligence the master key?

Is it to paradise or to hell, or is it the master key to both of them as well?

Or is it just like any other invention, things could be better, things could be worse?

Already it is seen to be a discovery that is very solicitously worrying; and reaching boundaries where it could be devastating.

Causing less sleep and a lot of grief to those already affected by Artificial intelligence.

With many new crimes especially online, affecting institutions, families, and friends - yours and mine. With scammers, hackers and fraudsters hidden here and there, scattered far away over miles everywhere, committing their crimes with their conscience clear, and of course without any fear.

149

Yes indeed regretfully, there are hackers who get into bank accounts, cleaning out every single pound, wiping from your face every smile, just to create a pathway for the tears to run down from your eyes.

Hackers who unlock state secrets, who sit on their arses doing mischief.

No one can sleep because they worry, where next the hackers would strike to steal secrets, or their money.

With modern day things created without proper safety, hackers enter without a key.

So the question still is asked once more. How do you keep your bank account safe under a locked door?

How safe it is, and are you very sure, could hackers steal my money from under the mattress or the floor?

For how much longer, and how much more time does mankind need, to make the world a better place than what it is?

Each day just seems to be getting worse, a hacker just emptied another person's purse, just after one was reported five seconds ago, and the police still don't know what to do.

So how much further to reach the future humans have to go, without creating still more problems with technology and science?

And indeed the many more crimes associated with artificial intelligence.

Where on earth should humans go from here? In what direction should they steer?

Is it for humans to disappear and robots take over everywhere?

Leaving the world in a hell of a mess, and yet still calling it progress.

With real progress always moving very slowly, hindered by mistakes, bad policies, and the side effects of technology.

And yet all together they are executed, technology, bad policies and mistakes, all were the cause of a lot of damages, and that has been so throughout the ages, and it is still so even today, there seems to be no escape from the wrongs of yesterday.

So then where on earth shall mankind find peace, without first being engaged in a very clean sweep?

Where on earth must humans look to find justice? hidden somewhere it is instead of being in service.

And where? if there is really somewhere humans could disappear from the problems they create year after year.

Yes it is true, mankind has been developing and progressing too, and although it has been very slow; humans' efforts have been very rewarding; although not perfect, the world today is a much better place, indeed much better than it was yesterday.

And this is what everyone already knows that mankind still has a very long way to go, and indeed it is very unfortunate that the new generations always have to clean up the mess their ancestors have left.

Yes, cleaning up the world to make it look good, if they are not already doing what they should.

Instead of repeating the wrongs of yesterday, with Artificial Intelligence things could be done in a much better way.

And so hopefully in this scientific age, human beings have a good measure of knowledge, so they should be able to make wise choices and less mistakes, doing things in better ways.

And that is because it is the right choice they will have to make, if it is a better world they want to create.

But yes indeed, and this is no secret, I may have already mentioned it.

It took mankind many centuries to succeed, and to create a better world than that of yesterday, the world as it is today.

151

And it was not for a moment easy, with or without technology, there were always difficulties.

Yes it was little by little, and millennia after millennia one after the other, that's how much time it took to make the world better.

Making mistakes and trying again, hoping that it is not all in vain.

But then again, for most of the years humans were without knowledge; and blinded with superstitions they could not see their way, so they were not as progressive as they are today.

Nothing came about over-night, mankind always had to fight to execute changes from wrong to right.

And the reason for that, the world has been very corrupt, but today perhaps not as much, yet still there is a great deal of mess to clean up.

But that was only because of deep rooted superstitions, corrupted leaders and their bad policies, creating wars, implementing draconian laws, and ignoring problems, while at the same time creating more of them.

Yes indeed it was very real, it was never a dream; one after the other corrupted leaders came and went ignoring problems, leaving their mess behind, creating a larger pile.

And that was why it took so very long for humans to move on with their progressive developments.

But the time it took from yesterday to today, it cannot again take that long, too much wasted time had already gone.

These are times humans can move fast, much faster than they did in the past, with Artificial Intelligence, there is no limit to the heights humans could climb, among the stars their light will shine; creating yet still a better world until it is as perfect as it should.

Until it is serving everybody equally with justice, and peace; until it satisfies everybody's needs.

So yes, it has already been seen that humans have traveled a very long way, and as exhausted as they are, holding on tight to their umbrella, they are still traveling together, heading directly towards the future.

And that is because they haven't reached the future yet, but in this technological age, they can now travel by jet.

But tomorrow no one knows how much further humans will reach, that is an answer not for human beings, but for science and technology.

But one thing is certain, humans may be forever traveling, heading towards the future wherever that is, somewhere beyond the edge of the universe maybe, somewhere beyond our galaxy.

And always still developing they will be, still progressing, still executing a lot of wrong things, and still making mistakes and changes.

So it looks like a journey without an end, with determination to reach the future, but no one knows when.

And that is because they haven't reached the future yet, and they still have a very long way to go. But as things are today with progress, humans can now use a jet, instead of traveling so slow, bare feet, and getting their toes and their ankles muddy and wet that sometimes they often slip back.

So yes, with artificial intelligence humans can safely travel, and as far as they would like to go. And if they want to go even much further beyond, seats are available with Artificial Intelligence, leaving at any moment traveling directly to heaven.

Yes indeed, human beings have created some wonderful things during their years developing and progressing, and moving on from age to age, this I have repeated again and again.

Especially during the last three centuries, humans have acquired a great deal of knowledge, and they have made numerous discoveries, and sophisticated inventions such as objects with intelligence.

Constantly making new things all the time, leaving the old to perish behind.

And still today making them better yet again, for the benefit of the generations to come.

Although they were uncertain when they would get there, since they still did not know how much further the future was.

Indeed, humans have been moving through the perils of hell during the medieval ages, most of their time in darkness, and with little knowledge.

Traveling with time from millennia to millennia, developing and destroying year after year, progress was always what they sought after, creating things to make life better.

So yes, the world has always been theirs for humans to build, and whatever they sowed was what they reaped, whether the seeds were fertile or not, most of the time they got a good crop.

So today into the twenty-first century, it is as far as mankind has reached, carrying a bundle of problems, some from as far back in BC times, and yet still it is not the end of the journey, nor is the road ahead as smooth as it should be.

With obstacles and deep potholes, the remaining journey unfortunately, many lives could be lost in tragedies.

So yes indeed, and with good reason, humans always wanted to know how much further they had to go, that was understandable, and they were always worried about their safety too.

Indeed, they are not entirely creatures without concern, although that's how it often appears with most things they have shown.

Yes, they always wanted to know what it would be like in the future, they were very much concerned about their life when they got there, joking sometimes about what they would do, but the reality was, they didn't have a clue.

And yes, they were also worried about their security, how safe and secure was the rest of the journey, that's what they were not certain about, and that's what troubled them with doubt.

But in this new age of Artificial Intelligence, technology and science, both good friends, although not reliable ones.

It has given humans a great deal of confidence, ready and determined to crack any problem.

Yes indeed, with science and technology, a new world order humans may yet accidentally create, and it may come sooner rather than later, bringing with it what is not expected, and even perhaps what is not wanted.

And it could very well be, with or without sunshine, with temperatures on the rise, and sea levels just beneath the sky.

And it could be with a lot of water and fire, each keeping their distance from each other, each destroying whatever is in their path; making it very difficult for humans to make a new start.

But as mankind keeps on going, still developing and progressing with changes to make life in the future much better. This mankind should know and always remember.

Life is not just to survive, but to gather knowledge and be wise, doing the things that are right, not for oneself but for the benefit of each other, indeed, for the benefit of whoever.

To gather knowledge from nature, unlocking its secrets for humans to benefit.

Only then human beings would have reached the future, the type of future in which they belong, where life could be lived without doing wrongs.

Where everyone can live peacefully together, regardless of the difference of their opinions, and the difference of their race, culture and religion, or whatever may make them different.

Otherwise then, what is the purpose? A great deal of progress and no peace nor justice, a great deal of progress and the world in a mess.

So, as the people continue to develop and progress, let it be in the right direction, let it be for the best, let it be a world without sinfulness.

That should be human beings' ambition and aim, and not to colonize the moon.

Indeed, humans have no business there, no need to interfere, the moon has its purpose that's why it is there.

Yes, humans have been developing and progressing ever since from their origin, and tomorrow they will continue to do the same.

And this is because progress has no end, with new ideas there are always better things.

So humans must be wise and do things right, or a cataclysm coupled with armageddon may visit mankind with devastating forces of annihilation.

And this is already seen to be happening, there is an urgent need for change.

So listen to the voices of wisdom regardless wherever they come from, listen to their advice, listen to what they have to say, and respond in deeds which are wise, least the consequences which could be, a very devastating catastrophe.

Yes indeed it could be a devastating end, but this is something which humans could and should prevent, it is what science will recommend.

BELIEFS

Indeed, human beings have today reached into a new age of wisdom, knowledge and understanding, after relentless centuries of traveling, developing and progressing.

After an uncompromising journey that was full of dangers and difficulties, humans have now reached the age of science and technology.

Yes indeed, with patience and endurance mankind has traveled through the gates of hell to reach at this age of technology and science.

An age that poses numerous challenges, an age of less superstitions and more knowledge, with intellect now commanding.

An age indeed that continues to pose many difficulties, but perhaps not as much as they were during the years of BC.

And during the travels of humans to reach this age, passing through several development stages, they have been destroying, developing and progressing; doing them all together in different ways.

And this included developing their senses, acquiring abilities, knowledge and skills.

And one of those is the ability to believe, which mankind uses all the time, both constructive and destructive.

Yes indeed, human beings very often believe, and that they did about anything.

The less was their education, the more was their superstitions, which led them to believe in some very weird things.

So what are they? What are beliefs? Who can unravel this ability of mankind?

Why is belief so deeply rooted? Why is it so tightly held? Why does belief imprison thoughts and ideas kept locked inside one's mind, and no escape it could ever find?

Why is it so important what one believes? When it is possible, when you don't know you could be deceived.

And why is it that sometimes no one lets go of what they believe, treating it as something they know?

Yes, treating it as truth without any doubt, when it is not really so.

Holding on tight to whatever they believe, that's what humans did yesterday, today, and may continue to do so even tomorrow.

Holding on tight right through one's life to whatever they believe in, and that was regardless of whether it was wrong or right, or however weird or irrational.

Yes, whether it made any sense or not, beliefs were often taken for granted as credible knowledge, something positive, something to rely on.

Believing, and then doing whatever one believes in, and doing it again and again, despite the wrongs that are committed.

Indeed it is an insuperable influence upon the imagination that even delusions appear to be real, and in them people believe.

But whatever it is, it is just a function of the senses, unique only to one creature among all those living; human beings.

And with this function unique to humans, it has given rise to a mountain of superstitions, and suspicions, inspired by delusions, and indeed by dreams and misguided imaginations.

Superstitions and suspicions which were the cause of numerous problems, many which were the result of a death sentence in human sacrifices, in battles, and indeed as punishments.

So in this chapter, I shall expose the influences of beliefs upon humans' emotions, beliefs that were held during the many centuries of humans' existence.

Beliefs humans held and executed, and which differed from culture to culture in accordance with their customary traditional behaviour, and of course their experiences which could be the reasons for what they believed in.

Beliefs which are all irrational, ridiculous, weird; and yet cultural.

And were held by human beings everywhere, some beliefs to them were held very dear.

Close to their heart, hidden in their bosom, mankind held beliefs for no other reason but, from their ancestors they were passed on, within communities everyone conforms.

And without even an explanation to understand their purpose, they were passed on again to the next generations who just did the same as their ancestors.

Indeed, this is the truth that everyone already knows, that humans came into being thousands of years ago; but exactly when, no one knows, that is left to whatever you believe.

And during those years human beings developed several abilities, to aid them with their struggles and difficulties.

And that they did on their journey as they acquired experience, heading steadily in one direction, always towards the future.

And despite the difficulties they encountered, each year with step following step, towards the future they got a bit closer unimpaired with their hopes that things would be better.

Traveling and developing year after year, aided by their knowledge, or what they believed in.

And yes it was either one or the other, that kept them in the direction wherever it was they were heading.

Either knowing or believing it was the right direction, they kept on going closely attached to their problems.

So yes indeed, during the many years of failures and success, humans have developed some outstanding abilities that were useful for their purpose to succeed and progress.

And that included their abilities to reason, to think, doubt and to believe.

They either believe or doubt, or without an opinion they remain indifferent.

And that was quite often to their disadvantage, not benefiting anything.

And that may be because they never bothered to pause, and to take a little time to think and work things out.

They just believed or doubted whatever was said during the time they listened to someone else. And that may be why they were so easily misled, and too often led directly into hell.

They could never find just a little time for themselves to either think or to reason as well.

They were always too quick, never hesitated, they believed or doubted whatever was said.

They just believed or doubted whatever was the story, especially everyday gossip and hearsay.

And that they did, being persuaded by the degree of the scandal of the story.

If they like it, they believe it, no reason to question reality.

They believe what is not true and even argue to convince themselves with their view.

Take for an example the well-known phrase, "Seeing is believing."

That saying is spoken as truth in most languages, in every culture it is repeated.

Indeed it is well established, and repeated time and time again, perhaps it is the most common phrase.

It is repeated all the time, and by everyone, from people in the streets to those high up in institutions.

Everyone takes it for granted, the illiterate as well as the educated, they say, 'Seeing is believing.' And they say it with strength and purpose, and without hesitating, and without any doubt that seeing is believing.

And yet, how many people just for one moment have ever doubted its correctness?

Hearing it all the time, and yet not even for a little single moment at least to question its meaning?

Or even to think for a little while and try to understand the meaning of the 'saying'.

Whether it made any sense at all, believing what you are seeing.

The true fact is, seeing is knowing; that is a big difference, it is reliable, you know what you see, there is no reason to doubt nor to believe.

You know that Johnny is climbing up the tree, because that is exactly what you see, it is not what you believe.

And that is how it has always been, at no time it has ever changed, neither in the past or the present, and so in the future it will remain.

Whatever you see, you know what you see, that is how it was, and it will always be.

So to say, 'seeing is believing' indeed that is misleading, because when you see, that's when you know, and when you know there is no doubt whatsoever, it is always easier to remember.

So indeed seeing is knowing, it is real with truth inflowing, what you see you cannot doubt, it is reality, it has credibility, and it is a certainty.

And that is how it was with ancient humans, few things they were able to understand because they had little knowledge at hand, so they believed in almost anything.

161

Whatever story they heard, whatever they were told, believing made them feel good; brave and bold.

Whether it was possible or impossible, they just couldn't be bothered to think a little.

They believed whatever they were told, especially when it was about the spirit world, humans believed them, the young as well as the old.

Although no one was able to prove anything, they still believe it just the same as they did with many other things.

As it was the case with mother earth, for centuries humans believed that the earth was flat, they had absolutely no doubt about that.

But that belief eventually got lost in the wilderness of time when the truth was discovered by science.

And yes, that had shown just how little was known, hence the peril of the lack of humans' understanding of things at the time.

Yet still it was very comforting without knowledge, to believe with trust and faith.

So it became an area that influenced humans' behaviour, and often with consequences that were gravely severe.

Doing wrong things that were disgusting, and only because they were what human beings believed in.

And to no one's surprise, that had given rise to the successful spread of superstitions.

Superstitions of all sorts, especially about demons, goddesses, and gods.

And that eventually led to wild orgies, sacrificial feastings, rituals, and ceremonies.

All that was based on nothing more, than things unknown and unsure, inviting fear where knowledge was poor.

And that is how it was without knowledge, a vacuum of truth by all races, an emptiness which beliefs were free to fill, and that indeed was what beliefs did.

And in as much that there was nothing known, about the fertility of the seeds that were sown. There was nothing certain about what the people should reap, so without knowing nor even understanding, they just believed in whatever the sharman preached.

They listened yes, attentively and impressed, and believed in whatever was said.

And that had been so, with everything humans did not know, and that was how believing instead of knowing became more common with human beings.

Believing still more and more, in anything of which they were not quite sure; especially if it was for an illness or a curse, that they could not ignore.

Getting the feeling that what they believed in, it was just as good as knowing.

They had no doubt that whatever it was about, believing was the same as acquiring knowledge.

And as long as the feeling was not a threat, there was nothing for them to regret.

So they believed and did whatever it was, right or wrong there was no remorse.

But then it became very intimidating, with awe and danger conflating.

When beliefs were no longer just something one imagined, nor just a ridiculous idea.

And they were transformed from inner thoughts into outward deeds, as the norm in horrors of rituals and ceremonies.

And into whatever was heinous and unjust, the execution of deeds generated from beliefs, some were terrifying, some disgusting, some direct from hell was where they came.

And yet still they were what humans did, and for no other reason but what they believed in.

And that gave them purpose and meaning to their wretched lives, in their consciousness they were gratified.

They did what they believed in, and they believed in what they did.

And despite the savagery of their deeds, justified only from what they believed.

It was customary for many centuries, horrific deeds were repeated in rituals at anniversaries.

And that was always very compelling, traditionally exciting and entertaining.

The more brutal and terrifying was the horror, the more the excitement, greater the thrills, and so too was the pleasure generated from the manner in which humans were killed in sacrificial offerings.

Indeed, human beings always did love to see death, not just as a threat, or a solemn peaceful death, but the horrors of its reality, its savagery, it was exciting to see.

And it was customary, humans gathered in large numbers to watch the suffering of others.

That was excitement, that was pleasure, and for many people there was nothing better.

And that justified beliefs solid and strong, that nothing done during a ceremony, regardless of the measure of the barbarity, was considered inappropriate or wrong.

In fact, nothing was too savage nor too inhumane, that mankind couldn't entertain.

Believing of course that whatever was done, was what the gods wanted, so it couldn't be wrong.

And with the traditional drunkenness in feasting, in rituals, ceremonies and sacrifices offered to the gods and goddesses.

Whatever was done was done with reverence, and with the belief that it was fatalist, so it could not be avoided, that in itself would have been a sacrilege.

And so most horrors associated with beliefs, they were celebrated in rituals in yearly anniversaries.

The taking of a life as a sacrifice, in an offering to a god for its advice.

And that was believed to be an honourable privilege, a life to the gods to give.

And that was how it was in accordance with ancient cultures, human sacrifices were special offerings which were offered to the gods occasionally for favors or as thanksgivings.

And on very special occasions, the king's son or daughter would have been the victim of an immolator.

Sacrificing the son or daughter of a king, that would have been to a god of the highest ranks, and which indeed would have been the most divine offering, solidifying the bond between god and king.

Honouring a god with the life of a son of a king, that was indeed the most divine offering, and that would have been done in thanksgiving to the gods for only very special favours.

And that was done without regret or fear, because it was believed that the reward was fair.

And as beliefs were transformed from the imaginary into the reality of deeds, from just thoughts into actions.

Be it sacrificial slaughters in satanic orgies, or paganism rituals to gods and goddesses, or whatever they may be.

From the drinking of blood to the devouring of raw flesh, after decapitation and the removal of the breast; and the removal of hearts, livers, and penises too, even eyes were dug out as the beating of drums, the drunkenness, and the exotic feasting continued.

Yes, every act had a purpose and a meaning, different rituals for different things.

Different cultures had different ways, to their gods they offered their sacrifices.

And as everyone pranced and danced as if they were in a trance or hypnotised by demons.

Whatever it had been, regardless of the scenery, whatever humans did, it was what they believed in, and it was evil, to be rid.

Nothing was done that was not sacrificial and they believed in, especially on revered occasions.

Whether it was a sacrificial slaughter of a demonic nature, or however exotic was the charm of human behaviour.

They were deeds that had to be done, for the gods to be pleased and relied upon whenever mankind needed their assistance, and that to them was very important, it was the heart of cultural traditions.

The gods had the powers, so they were revered, feared, and depended upon by humans.

So yes indeed, humans did whatever they believed had to be done, there was no question about what was right or wrong whenever making offerings to the gods, and whenever needed be, heads were chopped off indiscriminately, or buried alive was somebody, or in oil a human was boiled; whatever was the custom on the occasion that's how things were done.

And that which was done was done in sacrifices to the gods and goddesses; in well-established cultures.

From North to South, and East to West, beliefs were very weird and devotedly held, as much as they were different.

But how did savagery originate to become established in cultures?

How indeed such cruelty became so commonplace and popular in every culture everywhere?

With man brutalising man without mercy or compassion.

What was its origin? What was its creed? Was it just something in which humans believed?

'What was the logic in such beliefs that were so weird and bizarre, beliefs with deeds of horror, and without any sense whatsoever? And yet no one seemed to know the answer.

No one knew, they just continued, it was what their ancestors believed and did, and remain in cultures deeply rooted, and well established, beliefs in deeds however cruel were put into practice in honour of the gods and goddesses.

So every generation believed it too, and did the same, conformity was to blame, no one questioned anything.

What was done by the elders must be done by the young, that for centuries has been the norm.

And whatever it was it gave them a feeling of belonging, and indeed, it gave them security within the community, bonded together with the same beliefs.

But unfortunately, there was no alternative, those were times of very little knowledge.

And as the beliefs passed from generation to generation, without anyone asking a single question.

They became the norm in traditions, deeply rooted, firmly established, and repeated on anniversaries in celebrations with rituals, songs, and dances.

Yes indeed, anniversaries were big occasions, with the sacrifice of a beast or even a human.

Just doing the same things year after year, and for no other reason but just because they were what they believed in.

And without any question, nor a logical explanation, they just did what they believed in, having fun celebrating.

Yes indeed, and very true to say that it was nothing more than human beings' lack of knowledge, their fears, their ignorance, and their stupidity, and indeed perhaps just traditional conformity.

Still, it was very important to them as a part of tradition, conformity in the community was necessary.

Believing and doing the same things kept everybody in the community together as one family.

And so beliefs with their horrors and pleasures, were passed unto new generations as spiritual treasures for guidance, protection, and for success instead of failures.

So from one generation to another beliefs were passed on with all their charms, their fears, and horrors to which they were accustomed.

Whatever was the vision in their imagination, became something they believed and took roots in their traditions.

Capturing the thoughts and the imaginations of mankind, trapped as prisoners of superstitions.

Yes, trapped in fear of the present and the future, especially of the forces of mother nature.

Yes indeed, trapped in fear of the unknown, fear was the seeds that were sown.

And from the day that they were born, right through their life until they were dead and gone.

Yes, it was only death that was an outlet, from superstitions and all the horrors that were a threat. But even in death there was still a threat, from the fiery flames of hell.

It was where you went, if the years you spent, you die without repent.

Indeed that's what people believed, that's what to them religion preached.

And that was how it was for many centuries in almost every country.

From north to south, east to west, without knowledge mankind was imprisoned.

Indeed there was no place, nowhere to hide, wherever humans had settled to live, there was always plenty to fear from a great deal of causes.

And yet no one ever quite understood why that was so. Why was there so much fear of the unknown, the invisible spirit world?

Yes indeed. fear was very real, especially off demons, or whatever was invisible; the ghosts of every kind of trouble.

Humans believed that their troubles came from them, or from their ancestors, or from the gods and goddesses above, and even from the stars, especially Mars.

It was either from the gods, the stars, or from their ancestors, or from evil spirits or demons.

That's what they believed during those years, and that's what fuelled their fears.

Their troubles always came, especially sickness, from demons or gods, so they did what they could to protect themselves from the terror from beneath and from above, the terror from the darkness of the supernatural world, so yes people wore charms and washed with oils and herbs to protect themselves from the spirit world.

So yes indeed, it just had to be, immolating and romantic feasting were part of the orgies of ancient living, rooted deep in cultures unforgiving.

It became a part of human culture, making offerings to the gods for favours.

To keep them safe and secure without problems knocking at their door.

And so it was in tradition to venerate gods for favours.

And that indeed was very important as part of their beliefs, which were passed on to new generations and celebrated yearly on anniversaries.

And not until humans had acquired knowledge, and superstitions completely rejected.

The celebrations continued as revered tradition, among the tribes in the darkness of the forest, and even among those in affluent civilisations.

Indeed, wherever humans had settled down to live, wherever the wind was blowing, in something superstitious humans always believe in regardless how weird it is.

And to a certain extent, it was influenced by their environment, and the natural forces of nature. And together they were an intimidating influence on the complex nature of their cultures.

Which they developed, and became the norm as something they did because it had to be done. For whenever there was something they did not know, this was what they did.

They either believed, or they let it go, or not convinced so they doubted.

And that choice to believe that one of the two; it caused a lot of grief when things were not true. But then again, believing can bring both a lot of joy and sorrow too, it has no borders, no boundaries or limits, beliefs can cause grief, as well as happiness.

It is a function of human beings, a part of their characteristics.

A part of their nature to believe whatever, and among what they believe there is a good mix.

And yet beliefs are just what they are beliefs, and nothing less, nothing more.

It is when they become operational, that's when beliefs can be ruthless or jovial.

They could be tamed, lamed, and as harmless as a dame, and they could be comforting and consoling as much as they could be threatening, intimidating, and as cruel and horrid as anything.

Yes, they could change your feelings about most things, just because of what you believe in.

And if you believe you are exposed to danger, even that can cause you unnecessary bother.

And it matters not whether they are false or true, the power of beliefs is absolute.

So yes, many things humans did, they did them for no other reason but just because they believe in them, even those beliefs inherited from previous generations.

And whatever was the purpose, or the reason, some were so foolish that madness deepened.

That's beliefs when they are transformed into deeds, they are either comforting or devastating.

Either bringing joy into someone's life, from the good news that was a surprise.

Or just as well it could be devastating, believing the story someone was telling.

Yes indeed, what humans believe can incite love, hate, or fill them with rage.

It can incite all sorts of problems, even vexation with family and best friends.

And when this rage is acted upon, it is taken for granted that it is right instead of wrong.

And that's when many sins are committed, sins of all sorts, some ruthlessly cruel, and all inspired by what was believed in.

Not knowing whether it was true or false, whenever you believe you are left in doubt.

And whatever you did cannot be undone, whether it was right or wrong.

That is the danger of believing, and then acting upon what you believe in.

Yes, to believe is what people do when they don't know, and to act upon it is taking a gamble; and indeed, it could lead to either joy or sorrow, joviality or misery.

And it could even lead to death, intimidation and threats.

Yes indeed, it is without certainty where it will lead.

And so in cultures everywhere, during mankind's existence from year to year.

Some beliefs became a traditional norm celebrated in rituals with sacrifices on anniversaries. Some were just a jovial feast celebrating a revered deed.

But whatever it was, and for whatever purpose, it was only because of what humans believed.

And that has led to some horrendous crimes committed during the years of disquieting times.

Times of fear of superstitions, times of evil of all kinds, times when punishments outweighed the crimes, death was the sentence instead of fines.

Yes, mankind believed in what they did, and did what they believed in without hesitating.

Beliefs that were nothing less than horrid and barbaric, and yet frantic in celebrations that were exciting and quixotic.

Which were occasions of lavish preparations with tribal songs, dances and bloody sacrifices. And with intoxications and demonic illusions, a moment of exotic self-indulgence.

Yes indeed, those were occasions celebrating beliefs, moments to rejoice and forget the grief.

Enjoying the occasions of what was believed in, gave their life purpose and meaning.

And so they did, whole villages would celebrate in a very jovial spirit, the occasion of a superstition.

And despite the bloody rituals, regardless of how savage, hideous or brutal.

They were always performed with gratification and jubilance, and with honour, pride and reverence.

And with a strong feeling held sincerely, that the deeds of their beliefs must be holy.

And of course, with the highest praiseworthiness that could have been offered to the gods, and goddesses.

And that became traditional in cultures everywhere, beliefs brought joy and jubilance in celebrations in a moment to be free from anxiety and fear.

Indeed, a moment to be jubilant, thinking of nothing, but praising the gods in jubilance.

So yes indeed beliefs were very important, especially those with an occasion to have fun.

They were the reason for some of the most celebrated occasions, bringing joy to hearts buried in illusions, it was now time for resurrection, lifting distraught spirits to heights beyond.

Lifting them to the skies, taking them into heaven, with beliefs you can reach to any destination.

Yes indeed, as Jesus had said when he was alive and well, you can move a mountain if that's what you believe in.

So yes, believing was the light inspiring what was right, with nothing else to guide humans through the darkness of the night.

So boldly and bravely they stepped right ahead, although sometimes they stepped backwards instead, and into a confrontation with the living or the dead, both were dreadfully feared.

Doing whatever they had to do, with nothing else but with beliefs to guide them through.

Mankind forged ahead day after day, and in the same direction all the way.

Keeping on track wherever they were led, but always towards the future straight ahead.

Taking with them whatever they believed in, because without whatever they believed in, it made them feel naked as if they had no clothing.

So yes, their beliefs were very important to them, it made them feel like they had some learning, it made them feel responsible, and that may be the reason why they never let go.

And as they continued on their journey towards the future, our ancestral kins did some ghastly things which they repeated again and again in cele-brations year after year.

And all without knowledge or a good reason, but just because they were what they believed in.

So what were these things that became so culturally influential, causing humans to repeat them on anniversaries considered consequential?

What were they that were so important? And celebrated every year instead of being forgotten.

Yes indeed they were something very important, the ceremonial offerings to their gods and ancestors, to whom they were devoted with both fear and love.

Offerings that were thanksgivings for the favours received from the gods and goddesses above.

And to whom they offered lives as sacrifices, both humans and animals.

In the belief that the gods would remove curses, grant them good health and prevent illnesses, and protect them from the wrath of demons.

In fact, to grant anything that the people wanted, the gods or ancestors were contacted.

And that was done often through a sorcerer, a voodoo priest, or an oracle; they were the professionals who corresponded with the gods for you.

And that was what humans did to win battles, the gods were contacted through oracles.

And to have a good harvest at the end of a season, the gods were invoked, not logic nor reason.

Fearing drought from the lack of rain, and the loss of a crop yet again, the spirits were contacted to prevent it from happening, hence sending a shower of rain.

And even for someone to have a child, who may have been cursed by an evil eye, and made childless in miscarriages.

Or it could be for the sex of a child to be granted, a boy or a girl as requested.

The gods would deliver whatever was wanted, as long as mankind continued with the sacrifices.

And even to make right decisions, there was no reasoning, no discussions.

It was the gods that were contacted for advice and guidance; indeed, it was the gods that were contacted in matters of importance.

And the ideas they got came from the gods, that's what they believed, so that's what they did whatever it was.

Yes indeed, the rulers of the world contacted the gods, especially whenever lightning struck and the heavens roared.

Fearing the wrath of the gods, they contacted them to learn what caused their anger in such a rage for them to roar.

Nothing was to them as terrifying as thunder and lightning, as the heavens roared in a rage.

Nothing to them was so frightening, fearing the gods may invade.

It meant to them that the gods were angry, different cultures did different things to guarantee their safety. And that meant anything, even human sacrifices.

Someone could be taken from captivity, and in a ritual boiled in oil as a sacrifice to the gods.

Yes indeed, the threat of the dangers of thunder and lightning was never taken lightly.

It was always seen as a warning, and the response was swift and obligating.

With live sacrifices to appease the gods, and hence prevent the wrath of the heavens.

Yes it was a moment of anxiety and fear, confusion was everywhere whenever thunder and lightning appeared.

And at that moment especially, they contacted the gods urgently with requests of all sorts.

No favours were left forgotten, no promises to be broken, the gods were well assured.

And they were asked for cures for sickness, and for advice in all sorts of matters and business, and for protection, in fact for whatever did come to their minds.

Yes they were asked for protection from evil spirits, and from the blight of curses.

And for all those regarded as enemies, let them be struck down on their knees.

And let them be forever cursed, that each day for them things get worse.

Yes it was true, all of those things the gods were able to do, and a lot more they'll do for you.

That's what ancient humans honestly believed, from tribe to tribe in every community, and they held their beliefs for many centuries.

Humans' faith, hope and trust were in the gods, and they depended upon them for special favours.

Doing whatever they believed in, regardless of whether they caused death or suffering.

And that had given rise to a reign of terror, in communities everywhere.

Especially beliefs associated with religious superstitions, from the horrors of the pagans to the terror of the Christians.

And since the Christians believed in one God only, and a devil that was his enemy.

It was indeed a period that was very brutal, and in some cases horridly fatal, for those accused as witches, wizards, heretics, or devil worshippers; all the enemies of God, a natural death they never had, they were at the mercy of the Christians, often burnt alive., or hanged.

Yes, it was the Christians, from victims of persecution they were converted to masters of retribution, hypocrisy indeed was their religious creed.

In the name of their God, they did some horrid things, and they did them because they were what they believed in.

And they did them with their conscience clear, no guilt whatsoever, the horrors of their murders left nothing to compare; whatever they did, they believed it was their God's will.

They were serving their god with ruthlessness, and that they believed was justice.

So yes it was certainly true as it was regularly seen, Christians' retribution was painfully slow and without a measure of mercy.

Words cannot yet describe the cruelty, or get close to it, not in any language; the pain and the agony suffered by those accused falsely, who were often women especially.

Yes indeed, they were arrested and hanged, or burnt alive, after confessing under the pressure of torture to whatever wrong they were accused to have done.

Yes, they confessed to anything, to stop the torture with unbearable pain.

But that only ended their lives, as their confessions made their death sentences justified.

Indeed, the roots of religion were buried in sin, its brutality was inhumane, and yet they believed it was their God's will.

And that went on for centuries, humans did the wicked things they believed.

And it was their beliefs that kept them blinded, affecting the function of their senses.

178

Don't know what was wrong or right, without knowledge there was no light.

So to prevent that from ever happening, humans believed whatever religion preached to them. And that they did without ever questioning any of the things they believed in, lest they be seen, and be judged as heretics with fire or a hanging to end their days.

So whatever they believed was always right, that's how they accepted it, and as their guide to a righteous life.

That's how much their beliefs had meant to them, it had given them strength, direction, and provided guidance.

So yes, it was true that whatever humans believed was very important to them, despite the fact they never asked any questions, it did not matter to them if they were right or wrong, believing meant to them that they belong, and safe from persecution.

But it was even much more than that, everyone believed and felt that they were on the right track. They were on the track to a spiritual paradise, where people went after their demise.

So whatever they believed in, they felt quite certain that there was no need to question anything, religion was infallible in its teachings, sins had to be paid for with suffering.

And that kept them on a solid path, with no reason to ever look back.

Their beliefs meant everything to them, there was nothing to doubt whether or not whatever they believed in made sense or not.

And it was just that which kept humans subdued, easily deluded and confused.

Believing most things and knowing nothing, it slowed the rate at which mankind was progressing.

And as beliefs were influential in decision making, it was paramount when deciding.

From the building of places of worship, to the severity of the penalty of death sentences.

What should it be, a hanging or a burning, or the purification of water by drowning?

A sentence must be severe enough as the sin, that's what human beings believed in, and the more severe was the punishment, the more compelling was the warning.

And from the horrors of live sacrifices, offered to ancestors, gods, or goddesses.

To the beliefs that sent many to an early grave, whether or not they were guilty of whatever was the crime committed.

And only because, what they were accused of, it was believed that it was what they did.

Others were kept in torment with chains in slavery, in the belief that it was good for the economy, and that was their purpose in life, to be a slave in bondage, and to be used as sacrifice.

Yes indeed, beliefs were cruel and very much so within the embrace of religion which, among their divisions, hostility was very common.

Keeping human beings separated, one is better than the other, so they can't be integrated, not ever.

'That belief was used to impede miscegenation,' that's what they said; to cure is more difficult than to prevent, it was a natural rule of purification.

And of course, not forgetting the mass murders of millions of Jews, and the thousands of women and children who in experiments were abused.

And all because of beliefs, indeed, and most regretfully, the brutality of humans was stretched far beyond the realms of insanity, in fact there were no limits, no boundaries inhumanity could not reach, and yet generated only by the forces of beliefs, no facts from logic or the reality of reason.

And yes indeed, it continued, with beliefs in eugenics to create a master race, to keep different groups in their place.

Sterilizing women to deny them their God given right to have children.

And that was done in the belief that their children will be inferior.

And the purity of the master race could be exposed to a whole mix of contaminated dangers.

Creating mongrels, albinos, Jews, blacks, deforms, homosexuals, lesbians and gypsies.

So to prevent this danger of an inferior racial mixture, it was believed that sterilization was the best answer.

And so it was done on a massive scale, believing it was right, so that's what humans did.

To prevent contamination of the master race, from those inferior and had no right to live.

Yes indeed, that was what people believed, and it was what they did without any guilt, their conscience was uplifted in what they did, and they smiled with pride feeling great.

But that was not all in the horrors of eugenics that were executed from beliefs.

In Germany baby factories were also created for the security and development of a selective creation of an elite master race population.

It was the ambition and the pride of their leader Adolf Hitler, a staunch believer and pioneer of the master race idea.

And they were used by those who believed in selective procreation, to guarantee the purification of the master race population.

So, in the baby factories of the state, selected couples were chosen and sent there to mate.

And their children were raised in state orphanages as children of the state, with the best of care and privileges.

Yes, they were to be the leaders of the world, that was what everyone was told.

And as such they were treated with the highest courtesy, conscious of the fact that they were different from everybody; they were to be leaders of leaders with a sense of superiority.

They were to be above Kings and Emperors, mould with the consciousness of having divine powers.

So yes indeed, it was very important that they were guaranteed a one hundred percent blood purity, that was the purpose of the baby factories.

Providing leaders for the brave new world, in the baby factories they were mould.

However, unfortunately, as the war came tumbling down towards its miserable end, and the orphanage children did not know their parents, the consequences were devastating for them, they became society's pariahs, society's despised victims.

Yes, they were abandoned and neglected by the state, they became children no one wanted to take.

They were a reminder of the horrors, which beliefs in eugenics was the cause.

And other cruelties by the Nazis, imposed upon Jews and minorities.

So yes indeed, they had a very difficult time: they were hated and were not trusted, their identity they had to hide, responses to them were not very kind.

And to make their way however they could; leaving the master race dream to perish and die, as history said it should, as it was an idea that was no good.

A belief which was useless instead of useful.

Yes indeed like most beliefs, they were executed without remorse and without any guilt, and without any feeling that they were wrong, despite the cruelty that was done.

And with determination and a deluded sense of dedication, indeed, they were executed with thrills and excitement deep into the core of fanaticism.

Yes, wrongs after wrongs humans committed, regardless of whether they were extremely brutal and wicked.

They were done time and time again, and for the same purpose, and the same thing, only because they were what humans believed in.

And even wrongs committed by governments and religion, believing what they were doing was for the benefit of the nation.

So whatever wrongs they had done, believing they were right, they just moved on and did the same things another time again.

And with their conscience as clear as water, human beings did some things as hideous as ever. And they did them without any other reason, but just that they were something in which they believed in.

Things that were passed on to them from earlier generations, things that were believed in by their great grandparents.

So maybe from hell is where they came from to be able to commit so many hideous wrongs, or perhaps it would have been better still if they were never born, then their horrid wrongs may have never been done.

But humans were born and that's what they did, horrendous wrong things most of the time. Influenced by their beliefs, they did as they pleased, whatever was the deed, it was what they believed.

And yet they claimed to be wise and civilised, doing so many wrong things they should despise.

And those were the very things they continued to believe in, and passed them again from the present onto the next generation.

Following in a path that was slippery and dark, right from the very start, following in a path with no questions asked, and especially when committing murders.

Following a direction led by religion, believing whatever was told to them; the existence of a God, the devil hell's denizen, and the pathway in which to follow to enter into hell or in heaven.

So yes indeed, human beings lived their entire lives without ever knowing many things, to believe was good enough for them, so that's what they did, and with success quite often.

But there were disappointments too, whenever what they believed was not true.

But true or false, whenever someone believes they harbour doubts, and it is the same when you believe in God.

And yet the evidence exposed in nature is there in places everywhere.

Right before the eyes of mankind is the true knowledge of God's existence, knowledge so simple for everyone to understand, and yet they never exploited it, not for one healthy moment.

So yes, it is within nature that the evidence is there, and likewise nature it is everywhere; humans have only to recognize it.

And with the evidence they would be wiser, because then they would know that God is everywhere.

And that's what makes all the difference, not in believing, but in knowing that God exists.

Because when humans know that's when they will be certain, and that's when they will have confidence, that's when they will do the right things.

Because when they are certain, there is no room for doubt; nor is there any need to believe that there is a God.

Because when human beings know, and that's how it should be, when asked the question, 'Is there a God?' then they can answer without any doubt. 'Yes, certainly there is a God.'

Unfortunately for the many, the people had chosen the easy way.

To be led hastily and blindly on the edges of darkness day after day.

Only to believe where they were heading, without ever finding out.

But they never really cared to know, because in what they believed they had no doubt, so there was nothing more to find out.

And as human beings weaken with anxiety, they are always too quick to believe, rather than to know.

They seem to think that what they believe in, things are really so, there is no need to know.

And they all act upon what they believe in, doing things that are wrong.

Although it meant sending someone innocent to the grave, to them it made no difference, they couldn't admit to themselves that they were wrong, because it made them feel weak instead of strong.

So in the same direction, and with the same intentions, eagerly they continued to go.

Grasping tight to their beliefs in a God or the gods, there was nothing more for them to know.

So with the feeling they were doing the right thing, they felt safe and secure on their journey wherever it was they were heading.

Doing whatever they had to do, right or wrong, humans did whatever they believed in, and today they are still doing the same.

So unfortunately, into the open sea of uncertainty, there was where mankind was led by religion in an old disrepair boat.

Left exposed to sink or float, they were at the mercy of an unpredictable sea.

Crowded together tightly close to each other, they started their journey, exposed to the hostility of the coldness of the wind, and the turbulent sea, and of course too, to its peacefulness, whenever the wind and the sea were in calmness.

And for century after century, in jubilation or in misery, unto their religion and their superstitions, mankind held on tightly for safety and guidance, and indeed for their peace of mind. Their religious path was always right, there was no darkness, only light.

So grasping at their beliefs, religion dragged them along.

Keeping them dazed with joviality in rituals, ceremonies, prayers and songs.

Just to make them a bit secure, comfortable and happy, with the feeling they belong safe and sound, under the protective shelter of their religion.

So that they go to their church regularly, then off to commit whatever was wrong, another sin for their conscience.

An assault maybe on someone they hate, or perhaps commit a rape, or a church to burn down, that was plenty fun watching the worshippers they hate on the run, or some cash to take from an old lady, a vulnerable victim to rob.

But that was okay, because they went to church today, where children were abused every day, and by those who preached right from wrong.

Indeed, and sadly to say, boys and girls were abused by pedophiles who joined the priesthood as a safe place to hide.

Where they find protection and cover for the evil of their sexual behaviour.

Hundreds of children were sexually molested within the holy premises of worship, and by those highly respected and trusted, their double life was hidden, covered with a cloth made of smiles, and lies, while reflecting the image of a respectable person.

Indeed, they had found a safe haven, no need for them to be on the run.

They were free, relaxed, and at ease, committing their sinful deeds.

Using their charm and fear as a weapon, they influenced and sexually abused children.

Living a double life of piousness and sin, fooling everybody with their honest faces.

And that of course was a part of the problem that gave support to atheism.

Priests committing their crimes of abominable shame, and within the premises of holy churches.

So yes, that created the non-believer, the atheists who began to think things over, searching for truth, searching for answers, with many questions asked within themselves.

Realizing the hypocrisy, which made them feel a bit uneasy, they questioned what was preached, and believing they were deceived by priests, in God they no longer believe.

But then again, the atheist also does not know whether there is a God or not.

God is nowhere to be found wherever they go, sin is in every slot.

Yes unfortunately it is quite true that they are left with their minds confused, don't know what to believe, what is false and what is real.

But then if such abusive sins are committed by Priests, they must be deceiving people with what they preach.

So the atheist remains quite convinced, and attached to their belief that there is no God at all.

Too many wrong doings, and even from the church within, too much pain in the world, that's the reason why they doubt.

But that is indeed a very feeble explanation, and yet still it is what they believe in.

If there was a God, there would be no suffering at all, no one doing wicked things; that's what they believe in, and seemed convinced, that's what a God would be doing.

He'd be preventing sin and all wicked things, preventing mankind from ever suffering.

But then again that's very wishful thinking, it is human beings who are the cause of their own pain, they choose to commit sin.

Indeed, they are given the ability to think, and that's what they should be doing before their engagement in wrong things.

So yes, mankind's suffering comes not from God in heaven above, or from the devil deep down below, but from humans themselves, always doing wrong things, inviting suffering, their urge for committing sin they hardly try to restrain.

So now let us go deep into the minds of human beings and do some serious thinking.

Let us be wise and try to understand the origin of creation, this morphology that has for centuries baffled humans beings, leaving them in a state of doubt, not knowing what to believe, what is true and what is false, confused with their thoughts, human beings are always in doubt, hence always searching for answers.

So with these questions ask yourself, and for the answers, look even in the darkness, look in the muddy waters, and in the unexpected places.

Who created the universe? How did it emerge? How did it come about?

To answer those questions perhaps one has to be wise, prudence is the voice.

So now we can all get involved in this subject for discussion, together we can search for answers in what to believe, what we must know, and what to doubt.

Those are questions that are still very puzzling from the beginning of humans' creation, with most people in belief, others in doubt, and some still searching for the answers.

And after so many centuries of humans' existence, they are still searching for the answers to those questions.

And with nature so perplexed as well as complex, and governed by rules of law.

What learned men in science have come-up with, some believed some doubted, and some still not quite sure.

'It was from a very big bang', that was what was said by the voice of science, 'it was very noisy and loud, that's how the universe came about, there was never any God at all.'

Yes, it was from a big bang that everything came about, even the unwritten natural laws.

It was all a matter of chance, that's how things really happened, by chance they all came into existence.

With self-creation and development after the big bang, everything happened purely by chance.

No designer, no creator, no one with infinite power; that's how things just came about without a doubt, the atheist is convinced that's how it was.

But what caused the big bang? That's another question causing frustration, it is never at rest in one's mind.

There must have been something already existing to release such tremendous power, and then thereafter the formation of whatever, into a universe with order.

So what is the explanation? What is the answer? Did it all happen by chance, no God whatsoever?

Whatever it was, that's the belief of the atheist, no God exists, and with that idea he is convinced, to nothing else he is listening.

There was no God to create anything, whether or not it was living, purely by chance they all came into being, every plant, every animal, every situation universal.

And it all happened billions of years ago, after an explosion in space.

Although they said that nothing existed, the big bang they said they could trace.

And from then onwards things developed very slowly, millions of years they took.

With no God to determine their form, their size, nor their shape; and not even how they may look, nor how much time to develop they took.

Although each species develops perfectly, everyone has the abilities to function in accordance with their environment and their needs.

And yet it has been said that it was purely by chance everything developed to be as they are, including the design and the perfection of life of every creature.

Their size, their shape, their complex life forms; were they all something which were created by a designer, or just by chance they developed as they are?

Yes indeed, it has been discovered that it is written in their genes how they should be, how big, how small, how short, how tall. Was it by chance those instructions in the genes came about?

And what gives them all continuity, is it by chance it just happens to be?

And if it was in their genes where instructions were written, exactly how each and every creature should be.

Then who was the designer? Who was the author? Who decided on such a complex matter?

Did chance decide the size of the pig, the size of the giraffe, and that of human beings, the rhinoceros, the bat, and the cat?

Did chance decide where the eyes should be, and indeed how many?

Yes indeed, those things were decided, and that's why they are as they are, they could not by chance just appear as they are, chance is not a designer.

So yes Mr. Atheist, just for one moment be silent and get deep inside your brain, and have a good serious thought, on the subject please do think.

How did everything get their size and shape, and with different abilities they function perfectly in accordance with their environment and their needs?

Did it all happen by chance, from the rotating wheels of evolution?

Not forgetting the many things that function orderly in the universe; black holes, the sun, gravity, dark matter, the earth, the moon, mars, and the stars, all of which of course have their different functions.

And even the laws of nature too, they have their job to do.

Yes, it is with nature's laws there is universal order, hence preventing from ever happening, a cataclysm of the most terrifying disaster.

Are they all events of chance, no creator, no God whatsoever? No supreme universal being?

Was everything just left to chance to function however they can?

And doing so in harmony together and with the right measure.

Just think about it carefully should everything be left to chance.

Then how could things be so orderly, when they are left purely to the forces of chance?

With not a measure more, not a measure less, everything is accurate, or else the universe could have been in a mess.

Indeed, it is somewhat difficult to believe that if left to chance, there could still be harmony within universal order, hence everything working smoothly together.

And by chance, so was evolution which brought into existence the complex formation of all life forms.

Are you not missing something here Mr. Atheist, perhaps you need some special set of glasses to see clearly the complexities of the wonders of living bodies, and so too the wonders of the universe.

Indeed, it is within good reason that if chance can create things so perfect, then surely no God is needed, God doesn't exist, and Mr. Atheist truth is yours, God is a fraud.

But who really believes that chance can do it, creating things so perfect, with every little thing in its proper place, and without any mistakes?

That's not how chance operates, chance always defies logic, it knows no other way, whatever it creates is imperfect.

So yes, indeed there must be a God, the one and only, one who knows what he was doing to create so many amazing things.

All life forms as complex as they are, left to chance to develop, they would all be a disaster.

With so many things left to chance, it could have only been a pool of confusion.

Yet still, despite reality and logic, despite good reason, intelligence, and common sense; so says the clever atheist "God does not exist!"

And so, still convinced and determined he explained. "It was by chance," he says, "purely by chance that everything happened, there was never any need for a God at all, chance engineered everything from the existence of nothing, into development towards perfection, it all happened by chance."

Yet still he could not explain with good reasoning the complexity of sizes and shapes, and the intricate forms of internal organs functioning to the beats of the rhythm of life, and without compromise, every organ with its purpose in life, functioning without sacrifice.

Not to even mention the mystery of growth, from the invisible sperm to its expansion in birth.

And to continue doing so thereafter, until it reaches a size determined not by chance, but by a creator.

And of course, the very laws of nature, sustaining the universe in order.

How was that possible without a creator? Is chance some sort of miracle worker?

'It was nothing more than an accident, sprang into action purely by chance, and driven by the forces of evolution, there was no other creator, only the unpredictable occurrence of chance, indeed, chance is the creator of nature, by chance everything all came together, and indeed in such splendour.' That was the atheist answer with doubtful words put together.

So yes, it was by chance, in the form of evolution, that brought into existence the complex formation of the rose as it is, and so too the tulips and orchids.

Not forgetting of course all life forms that exist, chance was the creator, so says the atheist.

But if that was so, and it was really by chance, then I have no criticisms, perhaps the Big Bang too was really by chance.

And indeed, everything as we know them, everything in the universe, black holes, gravity, and all the planets so perfectly orbiting in their orbits.

193

Everything and anything, they appeared and developed purely by chance, if of course that makes any sense.

But then again, I would have to be without a brain, unable to think, or at least to be a complete fool to think that it was all by chance the Universe appeared with all its forces so well engineered.

Chance has no stamina for the creation of order, and the making of things that are so complex; chance could never start to put them together, much less to finish them with order.

Left it to chance, and the Universe would have been in a hell of a mess; with no one knowing what will happen next.

And that is because of the way chance operates, nothing is put in its proper place.

Every fool knows that whenever anything is left to chance, it is a gamble that has no accurate prediction, nothing could be relied upon, anything can happen.

So yes, it was not purely by chance that everything came about; and that included the living no doubt; there must be indeed and without a measure of doubt, that there is a creator, there is a God; there is more evidence of certainty, and none of doubt.

Not forgetting of course, even a tiny component as the atom, within it there is order in its tiny construction.

So who can say that happened by chance? Perhaps it is something too complex to understand.

Yet still that's the belief of the atheist, who still does not know that God does not exist.

If he is so convinced then he should try and know, unfortunately, there is no evidence he can follow.

Switching from believing to doubting, and yet still without any sense of good reasoning.

But that is what the atheist believes, and until he knows, with what he believes he will be deceived.

Knowing that all things natural could have only been done by an intelligent designer, and not by chance, not ever.

Not in this universe or any other, not anywhere where there is order.

But then, who with good reasoning can make such a poignant claim, without being unwise, very foolish or insane?

The complexities of living bodies, with immune systems, brains, cells and organs, all in such fine operation, designed and tuned to a specific function.

Doing only their specific job, just what they were created to do by the omnipotent above.

Indeed, the power to develop and function, and within some form of order.

It must be generated from someone, from a source with unimaginable power.

Things that are so very complex, could never be left to chance to flower.

Or else nothing would have ever been made, chance for sure would have still been struggling with so many things to be created.

So, it is indeed hardly likely that something like chance, can ever be depended upon to deliver a universe with order.

And if that reasoning is not an adequate enough explanation that there is a God existing, a God who designed and created everything.

Then mankind must be cursed, or perhaps it could be something even much worse, that prevents him from acquiring the knowledge in knowing just how things came about in the universe; hence the knowledge of knowing instead of just believing that God exists.

But then just for a moment, try a little to think for a while and glimpse a bit at reality.

Is it very wise or just foolish to admit that the laws of nature simply appeared from nowhere, to govern the universal forces of nature?

Is it wise to admit or foolish a bit, to even consider such an idea?

Then how did the laws of nature all come about? Purely by chance no doubt.

Or what other explanations has the atheist? Perhaps the next thing he may say is that the laws of nature don't really exist.

And yet just a little bit of common sense is all it takes, no need to reason with anyone.

It is a matter that is so simple, it doesn't require any explanation.

My family just like anybody else, we want to be together in a picture, a family portrait.

So, we got someone, an artist was she, to paint the eight of us together as a family.

Sitting on a bench one next to the other, close together, she must use her skills with her brush to create a family portrait.

And with every stroke of her brush to be precisely accurate, a positive identity she must create.

Producing every little detail, the colour of eyes, hats and ties, and even the dent in every smile.

And with eyes gazing upon the skies, or in focus on the ground.

Everything must be right, even the dark patches and the sunlight, not a bit of it must be wrong.

Yes, every expression upon every face must be right, whether it is a frown or a smile.

And with everyone together just as they are, sitting relaxed under the skies.

And when she was done, the portrait was perfect when looked upon, recognising everyone sitting together under the sun.

Knowing that it could only be done, by the skillful art of someone.

And never by chance in any instance, with chance, there was no chance.

But now let the same painting be created by chance, indeed, let mankind give chance a fair chance, as did the Universe.

Let chance be given the chance for the atheist to see exactly how chance works if he really doesn't know.

First to consider is, "How long would it take without any mistakes?" giving the commission to a blind man representing chance, the only fair representation.

Yes, it is a challenge for chance, as it is for a blind man, a portrait for him to accurately create.

Giving him all the time in the world, and with the opportunities to do the best he could.

Any fool can know what the result would be; he would never ever be able to complete the portrait accurately, there is nothing he could see.

With the expressions in every smile, the colour of eyes, and the hair style of every adult and each child.

Yes, with every spot on their face, and whose nose is straight, every brush stroke must be perfect creating an identical image.

Identifying each person individually, just as they are sitting together as a family.

Indeed, that is not something a blind person can do, neither was the universe created by chance too.

But then again that is what is expected from the unpredictable forces of chance.

It is never with a purpose, so it has no aim to create anything, it is random and unreliable; totally independent, whatever happens, happens.

You cannot depend upon chance for anything, with chance it is never certain.

When, where, and how it will appear, chance is a function that just doesn't care.

It may, or it may not happen, that is how chance operates; it is never reliable, always a gamble, it could be on time or very late.

And that's what happens when someone places a bet; he takes a chance to either smile or to regret.

And although it may be a very good friend, one thing is certain, you cannot depend upon chance.

So it is very clear that the universe did not appear, from the unreliable forces of chance; be it from a small or a very big bang, or from any bang at all.

Chance could never create any part of it, it is not a designer, nor a creator, and perfection is not in its nature, indeed, it hates order.

It is too complex a universe, to be left to chance for development and growth.

And like a blind person, chance can never be a creator of things so full of complexities.

And with each functioning exactly as they should be, this is what you should know, chance would never take on that responsibility, chance is too lazy.

So now please sir, Mr. Atheist, wherever you are I have a question for you to consider.

Will you commission a blind man, upon your brain to perform an operation?

He cannot see and doesn't know what he is doing, so he depends upon chance to do everything.

So Mr. Atheist, would you depend upon him to operate on your brain?

If not, why not? You believe in chance very much. Perhaps indeed, chance would need a lot of time. But will it ever be able to complete the operation?

For this is what happens when it happens by chance, it is so simple and easy to understand. Chance doesn't like responsibility, so it does whatever it does haphazardly.

There is no continuity in manner orderly, nor is there completion with perfection, nothing will ever work left to chance, and the more complex, the more confusion.

There is no aim nor certainty, and not even the right place where things should be.

One eye may develop on the knee, and the other perhaps sitting on the belly.

This is how chance operates, it has no directive, no orderly perspective; it is not an instrument for perfect development, indeed, it cares nothing about beauty or perfection, whether or not it happens.

Yes indeed, it may create beauty, but that will be random, not a plan.

Because chance appears from anywhere, it just doesn't care, and you can only guess if it will be fair. So it is always better to wait and see, whenever depending on chance.

There is no prediction with certainty, nor is there a prophecy, whenever one is taking a chance, you can only wait to see, whatever will be will be.

Yet still despite all of this evidence of the unreliability of chance.

There are those who still believe that there is no God, whether it made sense or no sense at all. It is as if they are blinded and cannot see, or perhaps they have no sense of reason.

Holding on tight to their opinion, to change their mind, to an atheist it would be like getting blind.

But all of that which I have written is no proof of anything, but just an elucidation in wise reasoning, in the credibility of knowing that a God exists.

And if anybody can do the same; with a wise reason he can explain just how everything came into being, without a creator, without a God, and with chance the master of it all.

Then for him so be it, to be that wise it is an invaluable gift.

But for the majority it is not that easy for them to know that God exists.

They are content to believe he does, and do wrong things in his name, proclaiming God is love.

They just believe whatever they are told; religion is their spoken word, and yet their lives are still sinful.

Believing and doing whatever was the norm, regardless of whether it was right or wrong.

The only thing to them that mattered was to conform.

And that's what everyone did, they believe in God because everyone else did, especially within their family, and within communities, common beliefs create unity.

Their belief was one, a solid bond creating family and community unity, and that was so in religious beliefs especially, which was passed on to children very early.

Indoctrinating them to religious superstitions without any rational explanation.

And only because they had to believe in what their parents do, which has always been a cultural tradition, with their ancestors too.

And since beliefs had no boundaries, and neither were they measured.

Human beings believed whatever they wished, and some of their beliefs they even cherished.

Even beliefs in the supernatural, especially in the new life after burial.

And that had been so right through the ages, passing through every development stage, going right back to the origin of mankind.

When humans were without knowledge, they looked for guidance from the supernatural.

And that they did, regardless of what it was; without a good reason or an explanation.

And that became known as superstitions, with physical effects and spiritual attrition.

Effects that were felt in the execution of deeds, ghastly as they were, they were what humans believed, and executed in their deeds.

Indeed, it was without any doubt that mankind's medieval years were years of little knowledge, years of taboos, myths and superstitions, years with fears of gods and demons. Yes, it could be rightly said that early humans were very superstitious, and were troubled all the time by the invisible world of demons.

Yes indeed, humans existed most of the time without knowledge, their vision was in darkness, so they were always in fear of the invisible, and sounds which were heard and left no shadow.

The order of living was determined by superstitious values and disciplines.

The forces of nature to mankind were very threatening, and hence quite frightening.

Believing that they were forces from the gods or from demons.

And both forces were feared more terrifying than the venom in a serpent's head.

And even the darkness of the night gave them a fright, especially when noises were heard and no one was in sight.

Their first imagination was drawn upon, there may be a demon lurking around.

So their fear intensified with every sound, and their hearts beat in rhythm racing along.

Loud and very clear, beating with fear, and racing to hide somewhere.

And yet this is still happening today in cultures here and there.

In cultures in places around the world, superstitions are still very much revered.

Some beliefs are held so devotedly tight, right or wrong, rational or weird, no one cares.

And as medieval they may be, they are still taken seriously, fixed into cultures as a way of life, following in the footsteps of their ancestors, whom they considered were wise.

Repeating traditions that lack common sense, only because they were the norms of previous generations.

And that is true in many cultures, with different beliefs executed.

Some parents mutilate, and some even murder their daughters, in 'honour killings' inherited.

In their barbarity and vexed with rage, they set their daughters ablaze.

And only because they rejected their parent's choice, preferring to choose their own husbands, which by their parents' values was not allowed, it was not a choice for daughters.

And that was established as a norm in their culture, with consequences of disrespect and dishonour, deserving death in cold-blooded murder.

Yes daughters were murdered for making their own choice, and the reason, it was not allowed.

Not by the law, but within the family, so they were murdered secretly.

And only because of a cultural tradition established during the medieval years.

In belief which steals the life of daughters, without remorse, without tears.

So what was it in the belief rooted so deep to sway such a brutal rage?

Despising love to embrace hate to the extent of such a horrid act of inhumane disgrace.

What was so wrong for one's daughter to choose her husband, without the embarrassment of family dishonour, so depraved to commit murder?'

Why was it that daughters were not allowed to fall in love, and to marry someone of their own choice? Instead of giving them away like objects on display, that's what makes their parents feel proud.

Yes that was the hidden reason which was so important that in breach death was the sentence.

But there could be some other reasons too, conformity has always been a strict family value.

For whatever it was and it still is maybe, then the belief must be indeed super strong passing on from generation to generation for centuries on.

Yes, passing through the passages of time, and today it is still very common.

To murder one's daughter could only be madness, to invite such measure of sadness, whatever is the belief it must be wrong, insanity is its crown.

Especially in such a personal matter, the choice should always be that of the daughter, because she is the one to live with her partner, and perhaps for many years thereafter the parents are both dead and gone.

So what could be said of such parents to live with such horror on their conscience?

Indeed, the sin they have committed deserves no forgiveness, it would have been better that they were never born, than to commit such an abominable wrong.

But that's what they believed had to be done, and what they did, they committed no wrong; indeed, that's what they believe.

But believing does not make a wrong right, nor in condolence it makes the weight light.

Indeed, there is no scale down for wrongs, their measure cannot be reduced in any form.

But this has been and always will be a very disdainful part of human existence.

To murder one's daughter, and only because she fell in love and made her own choice who to marry, hence, that dishonoured her family, so the execution was death as the penalty, and perhaps as a warning to other daughters in the family; honour killing is its name, and even today it is still the same, in many cases culture reigns, from century to century without change.

That is how it is in some cultures around the world, daughters must obey, they must do as they are told.

Yes indeed, those were family values, the unwritten family rules, and whenever a daughter breaks them, the consequence could be house imprisonment, or even a death sentence.

Sadly, this barbarity established in cultures like several others, were more often to the disadvantage of daughters.

Yes, daughters were treated very badly indeed, in cultures where they were groomed only to get married, and to husbands chosen by their parents.

But that was just one of many beliefs both rights and wrongs which humans daily executed against women.

Especially during the days of little knowledge, beliefs claimed many lives in human sacrifices, in false accusations, and of course, the many other lives that were lost in deeds executed from superstitions, myths, taboos and accusations.

So yes it is true, and transparent too, around the world it has been happening throughout the ages every day in areas that were both primitive and civilized.

Many beliefs were taken very seriously as family values, and were executed as a code of practice restricting lives.

And particularly the lives of daughters, their lives were restricted with family values that became home rules and taken for granted.

And by those very rules, with no excuse, daughters were oppressed and disadvantaged.

And that had been so for many centuries ago, passing on from generation to generation continuing the cycle of female disadvantages, with oppression and abuses.

Yes indeed, values that were only beliefs and had no merit, no reality, not even just a little bit of credit, and yet in cultures they were well established to daughters' prejudice.

Executing inhumane deeds within families, with daughters especially as the victims, in silence was their suffering.

And as family values became the norm in cultural life, in communities both primitive and civilized. Those same values, whether foolish or wise, effectively they affected lives.

And they kept on repeating, time and time again, and for no other reason, but just because they were what humans believed in.

And because it was something that was traditionally believed in, by parents, grandparents, and great grandparents; going right back perhaps into BC times.

It was customary and very important to pass beliefs on to every newborn, and so they were passed to each generation, in conformity with tradition.

So yes indeed, it was very real, family values had oppressed, enslaved, and abused daughters especially, denying them independence, even respect and an education, and that went on for generations; with myths and taboos as family values, with which daughters were abused preparing them for nothing more than to be a slave to men.

Values that made them less important, only useful to have children, and of course to be a servant.

And yes indeed, preparing them to be compliant wives, obedient and tolerant for the rest of their lives.

And to be dependent too, because that's what parents believed their daughters should do.

And because they believed it, they must be right, so they enslaved their daughters throughout their lives. To be subdued to the unwritten rules of the restrictive family values.

And although beliefs may, or they may not be the worse of human characteristics, and whether they were, or they were not.

Many deeds that were executed from beliefs during the dark ages, were indeed very ghastly and barbaric; and yet still they were traditionally executed in jovial ceremonies on yearly anniversaries.

Providing occasions for celebrations, a time to get drunk and disorderly.

Releasing the tension and vexation that gave them an appearance always angry. Indeed, people believed in all sorts of things, many which gave them a fright; and with deeds often ruthless and barbaric, yet still they were what they liked.

They were exactly what they believed whether they made sense or not, and when they were what their ancestors believed, they were not just for them to forget.

Their superstitions were the knowledge of the times, and were with consequences very unkind. And all because no one had any doubts, that what they did was right.

But it mattered not if they were wrong, the feeling was, whatever they were doing had to be done.

That was their beliefs which were very strong, beliefs that were inherited from previous generations, stretching back to many forebears, beliefs that became the cultural norm, and for many centuries without hesitation the same deeds were done.

But that was how human beings felt when they believed, whatever they did they felt it was right, and what was right could not be wrong, so that justified the deeds that were done.

Everyday humans did many things, and that included what they believed in.

And it mattered not how weird and ridiculous it was, they did what they believed in because they felt it was the right thing; and that was their justification for whatever they had done.

And the greater the measure of the barbarity, the more inflated was the good feeling that circulated deep within the nerve-racking frame of their bodies.

Indeed, there was a feeling of joviality in barbarity, the sensations were really good.

It was a feeling of ascendancy direct from the spiritual world.

So yes, people felt good doing what they should not do, excitement was in every tissue.

207

Releasing the tension and irritation which were in their bodies hidden.

Celebrating what they believe in, was an occasion to suppress the daily hustle.

So without feeling any guilt, whatever they had to do they did, and that was not going to change anything, not until maybe after several decades.

And that was because just how it was, that was how it had always been, and with the feeling that they were doing the right thing, with no doubt whatsoever, they felt better.

So yes, this has been so throughout history, and it has been so with everybody, and it is still so even today, it may never ever go away.

When beliefs are transformed into deeds, quite often a very heavy price is paid.

As it happened only recently, one of many incidents of the twenty-first century which with today's technology, was exposed for the world to see.

And by no other but by the biggest democracy, exposing its whim for hypocrisy, in a display of stupidity.

Believing an election was not won, but instead it was stolen, stolen by the opposition.

And many people were enraged, both the illiterate and the educated, very disorderly they behaved, protesting their objection to the theft of the election.

So with a bang was their emotional explosion, creating chaos and mayhem, as the world watched, deeply shaken by the confusion and the idiocy of a literate nation.

And as the heart of democracy kept on a vigorous beat, with no effects despite the heat, with hate and rage synchronized in rhythm.

It was not surprising that the cause of it was just what they believed in, and without evidence, that the result of the election was stolen.

And that they did, they demonstrated how the deeds of beliefs could be destructive.

And the price paid for their confounded belief, a more divided nation in pain, hate and grief.

But that was not just a bad smell from a few rotten eggs.

Everywhere in the world beliefs in deeds are executed, regardless of whatever it is for.

Some are for pleasure, some cold-blooded murder, some for no reason whatsoever.

But that's exactly how it is, too often the general public is easily led.

And that is something politicians do all the time, they confuse the public, bent to their satisfaction.

They confuse, and they convince, and then mislead the public into believing anything.

And as the misguided public is convinced, without even good reasoning, they transform their beliefs into deeds which are rarely constructive, more destructive, a heavy price is the consequences.

Causing chaos and riots, and with disorder very serious, and for no other purpose but what they believe.

And whether or not it made any sense at all, beliefs were often the cause of broken laws. Leading directly to tragedies affecting individuals, businesses, families, and even communities.

Yes indeed, lives are often ruined by deeds committed, and only because of what people believe in.

But beliefs were not all darker than darkness, nor were they all stories of madness, many were consoling and reassuring with brightness, many delivered hope where there was only hopelessness.

Indeed, beliefs are like dreams, they can lead to very positive ends, some are real, some are misleading; reality's amends.

Giving you an inspiring feeling, making you feel as if you really know what's happening.

They can be uplifting as they bring you joy in the news you were expecting, whatever it was about.

Yes indeed, believing could be very elevating, it is a feeling worth experiencing, it is a feeling of joviality, that's the reality.

What you believe in could put a smile on your face, but that always depends upon what the message is.

Just as much as it could cause you suffering, and embarrassment with disgrace.

But then again the sad thing is, whenever you believe anything it cannot be always taken for granted, and that is because you don't know whether or not it was false or true, you took the risk, you took a gamble, and when you did, it was either one or the other, into heaven or hell you stumble.

Doing many very foolish things, and for no other purpose, but just because they are what you believe in.

Going into danger or whatever it may be, whenever you believe you are trapped in uncertainty, which could bring joy as well as sorrow, which will appear when you know.

And that is how things are when you do not know, and that is the difference between the two.

So yes indeed it is very true as it is real that humans have accomplished some wonderful things inspired by their beliefs, many things they have achieved.

They put their efforts into them, with or without determination, and they achieved what they believed.

And as beliefs are of anything, and are of all sorts; some are indeed extremely weird, some bizarre, some ridiculous.

And despite this known fact, humans still believe whatever is the story, and commit to their pleasure some terrible deeds.

Whether it was a life slaughtered in a sacrifice in offering to the gods, or someone as a punishment was burnt alive or hanged, although the person was innocent, no one cared a damn.

Whatever humans did which was something they believed in, regardless how horrid, they often did it without feeling any guilt, embracing the feeling they did the right thing, and upon that conviction, another time they did the same thing again.

That's how human beings were, and that's how they are, they do both good and bad things together.

Feeling no guilt, feeling no blame, especially if it was something that they strongly believed in.

Take for an example life after death, this has always been an area full of superstitions, fear, and threats; an area no one knows about, not yet.

An area which influences humans' behaviour, right through their development, it has always been a subject of interest, and yet still no one has discovered the truth about it.

A subject fascinating, compelling, and at the same time incomprehensible.

Indeed, it has always been an area of darkness as well as light, divided into hell and a paradise.

And it is something humans always believed in, and they prepared for it without hesitating.

It was never a dream or wishful thinking, the afterlife to mankind was always something real, something certain, something they felt deep within themselves; something they embraced as well as feared, preferring much longer to live than to be dead.

211

Yes indeed, humans believe in the afterlife with a feeling they embrace deep inside, feeling that they really know that it exists, so with weird ideas they prepare for it.

And that has always been at the heart of religious teaching, prepare for the afterlife without committing sin, to enter heaven the soul must be clean, or in hell is where it will be seen.

Yes, indeed, different cultures prepared for the afterlife in different ways, but along the same one and only passage, a one-way ticket through a grave.

And for some reason which no one ever knew why, most people were never in a hurry to go to the paradise of the afterlife.

They were never in any hurry to die, regardless of the problems in their life.

Yes, they believed that the afterlife existed, not like this, but they couldn't explain it.

So they felt it was better the devil they knew, and to hold on to their life for as long as they were able to continue.

And it mattered not how desperate they were, to paradise in the afterlife, they were never in a hurry to go.

So no one really knew what happened after death, because no one has come back yet; to tell the world what is the real threat that awaits mankind for his sinfulness.

So, all that mankind can do is to believe one of the many stories that are told about life after death, whatever is the reward or the threat, whether it is in heaven or in hell, or wherever it is for humans to dwell.

What are the criteria needed to get there, and how should one prepare?

So believing whatever mankind wishes to believe, whatever is the story, with its doubts and certainties.

Some people prepared for the afterlife very seriously, as if there was no doubt whatsoever of its reality. They made extravagant preparations, to take

212

their earthly treasures to the afterlife with them, which they securely buried underground, and left protected with curses from demons.

Yes indeed, many treasures were found in tombs under the ground waiting to be carried away to the afterlife somewhere behind the sun.

Treasures that were never delivered to the afterlife, the delivery was never organised, or perhaps maybe they were all on strike.

And that was done especially by world leaders who had treasures in plenty, and yet foolishly they never organized the afterlife delivery.

Yes, they were Kings, Pharaohs and Emperors, and anyone who had valuable treasures.

Fearing that their treasure may be looted, they had it protected with demonic curses.

Leaving signs of warning so that no thief would dare, with their belongings to interfere.

And although not knowing exactly where in the afterlife they were going, they still wanted to be certain that when they got there, they would at least have their treasure, and would not in the afterlife be a pauper.

So they had their valuables buried with them when they were dead.

To be transported either to heaven or to hell, or to wherever they were going to dwell.

So when they got there their treasure should arrive after a safe journey mile after mile, to give them a good start in the afterlife.

But their treasure never got there, that was never organized, there was no delivery service neither by humans nor by spirits.

And as their bodies remained in their grave until rotted, so was their treasure until it was looted by those who had no fear of curses.

Yet still that belief got stretched a bit further, and by no other but by an Emperor, who was obsessed with his sempiternal desire, to rob the angel of death, and live forever.

But he was not the only one with such a deluded ambition, but he hoped to be the first to be overwhelmed with the experience, to be glorified for his achievement.

Indeed, he had such a very good life, with many concubines and a beautiful wife, he believed he should never die, he believed he had the right to eternal life.

Yes indeed, one could see why he never wanted to die, with so many concubines at his side.

And he believed that there was a possibility, regardless how unlikely it seemed to be.

And if eternal life was for no other, perhaps may be, it was for rulers, for Kings, Pharaohs, and Emperors, believing they were special.

Indeed, that was something he strongly believed in, and was prepared to do anything to continue living, death he believed was not for him.

So, with good intentions, despite being troubled by his conscience in a muddle of confusion, he summoned his physician, and dispatched him on a fool's mission.

It was to find the secrets of this revelation, so that with it he can proceed immediately towards his aim of acquiring immortality.

Yes he strongly believed, in fact it was much more than that, he felt convinced that it was possible to live forever, getting the right treatment was all that mattered, and his continuity in life wouldn't sever, that thought had possessed him, it was like a tumour in his brain, so he was willing to try anything.

And his idea came a bit close within his reach eventually, now he was able to sleep peacefully, giving him a little glimmer of hope of the possibility, when the Emperor, after months of waiting not knowing anything, he saw his physician returned, and with news which were comforting with a feeling which was better than anything, indeed there was hope.

Yes it was from miles away in the wild forest in some foreign land, where danger was constantly lurking around, the Emperor's physician returned safe and sound, and very confident with what he had in his hand.

It was pure mercury, the only treatment for immortality, the only treatment he found after his exhaustive search in the exposed dangers of the forests of several foreign lands.

Nothing else was found but mercury, believed to be an elixir of human's immortality.

Unfortunately, there was some danger, with it there was doubt, since no one who used it lived forever; so there was no one with experience, no one to advise about the treatment.

And because there was no one to advise on the immortal experience, that trivial hindrance did not deter the Emperor from his immortality ambition, it was something at the time that his mind was set upon, he really felt it could be done, as Emperor he could not be wrong.

But he knew that changing from mortal to immortal physically was not going to be easy, he expected it to be painful, but despite that he was hopeful.

Yes indeed he was ready and somewhat in a hurry to make his journey towards immortality, he just couldn't wait to take the mercury.

So the mercury the physician brought back to the Emperor, he was very excited and thrilled, anxious to take it so that forever he can live.

Believing now he had immortality in his hands; he gazed at the mercury very curiously, trying to understand the nature of its powers which were now in his command.

Yet still he was troubled with fear, anxiety, and pessimism, all together they stirred confusion; his body and mind were already showing a state of decline, fearing death may be close behind.

Still he was determined, his belief was solid, with no doubt whatsoever that he could live forever.

Yet still he was a bit confused, trapped in the middle between doubt and certainty.

Trapped without consciously knowing whether it was real or just a dream.

Trapped with his stupidity between cowardice and bravery, he decided that for the benefits of immortality, he couldn't ignore the opportunity.

So because it was what he believed, and not something he knew, he was a bit cautious, and particularly so because mercury was the only medicine, conscious of the fact that it was a deadly poison.

So yes he was troubled like all humans, he wanted to live not to die, he wanted to live forever, and to go down in history as the first one to try and succeed, opening the door to other human beings.

So with his trust in the wisdom of his physician, the Emperor was delighted that he had returned with news of a treatment, regardless whatever it was, mercury or not, he started the treatment drop by drop.

Yes indeed it was a challenge, and it made him feel good, with fate he re-covered, showing signs of jubilance in his belief held tight and deep, that soon he could be, nay, he will be immortal.

Indeed he was overwhelmed with confidence which was obvious in his eyes and smile, and captured with optimism believing it would work, anx-iously he took his first dose, his immortality already seemed close; 'death shall be conquered' were his unspoken words which got stuck in his throat as he took the first dose.

Yes, his eyes were swollen with delight, and his smiles exposed just how he was feeling deep inside, with his confidence brimming he felt he was doing the right thing, no need for panicking.

So yes, his immortality was now well within his sight, anxious to prove that he could never die, anxious to prove that all along he was right.

So he did exactly as he was advised, taking two small doses daily, day and night.

Poisoning himself very slowly, with the delusion that he was acquiring immortality.

Enduring severe pains and discomfort, believing that his body was changing for the purpose.

And as he became weaker and more deranged, still possessed by his imaginary delusions, and still believing in his preposterous imaginations.

Reality stepped in for the final solution, to take his soul where it belonged.

It was the arrival of the angel of death, and with the Emperor she was very vexed, so she took away the Emperors' last breath, leaving his body not in the companion of a threat, but in the reality of death; so with immortality he never met.

But that was not the only act of fatuity impelled by the Emperor's beliefs.

And because he believed in achieving immortality, that was never a certainty, nor a guarantee that it would ever be, it was purely imaginary, a delusive fantasy, no reality, only what he believed.

That was something no one knew, or with any treatment what to do.

So as a human, troubled with doubt, as he tried to figure it out, questioning his own misguided thoughts, while still, his daily doses he kept on taking, enduring the pain, believing that it was just some internal change his body was undergoing.

Yes, he was indeed a bit confused, his belief was becoming overshadowed with doubts.

So if not on earth he could live forever, he decided to the afterlife he would take his treasure, which was his most forgoing decision, scrambled from his imagination.

So he prepared for his death as well, as he was advised by his close relatives, and of course by a few good friends who advised him that death was a more likely event.

And so he did, still deranged with weird imaginations, troubled and confused with marauding superstitions.

And acting as if he was possessed, with ideas which were weird, he created the amazing Terracotta army, to guard and protect his dead body, on its final journey to the afterlife.

And to ensure that his travel would be safe on his journey from his grave to his perpetual sovereign state.

Safe from attempted assassination by revengeful spirits and demons.

Safe too from the dead and their restless spirits, which hated him while they lived, and may try to capture him.

Safe from the wind that may be blowing, with consequences devastating.

And safe too from the rain that may shower him, and leave him exposed to the roars of thunder, and the swift speed of lightning fire.

Yes indeed, safe from everything he imagined may try to harm him, safe from whatever it was he believed in.

Safe from the devil and his angels, that may attempt to kidnap him and drag him into hell.

Safe from the threats of his own imaginations, and from the many things that could go wrong.

So his safety on his journey to the afterlife, was the duty of his Terracotta army to guard him through to paradise.

And that was what the Emperor believed, and his beliefs to him were very real.

His fear of the unknown had everyone deeply concerned, he was almost at the edge of madness with his imaginations perverse and delusive.

Yes indeed, an elaborate preparation was what the Emperor made, no risk was to be taken for him to be spiritually assassinated.

Unfortunately, he never traveled, nor did his army; like everyone human, he rotted in his grave, and his army remained frozen in captivity; as an act of stupidity for nations to see.

Yes indeed, during the mediaeval times, many beliefs humans held were ridiculously weird, elaborate, bizarre and idiotic, without logic, and especially without good reason or reality; superstitions were the knowledge of the day, and humans' behaviour swayed.

And yet humans believed in them with such an obsession, there was never anything to be said that was able to influence their change of mind.

Humans appeared to be hell bent, holding on tight to their superstitions.

And although superstitions as they were, ridiculously weird and bizarre, there was no rational explanation given, and yet still humans believed and did what they did.

Whether it was an individual, a commoner, or a king, or be it a family, or even an entire community.

Beliefs were executed with or without logic, and even though they were idiotic.

As it was done by a Buddhist Monk, not yesterday, but just recently in the twenty-first century. Yes indeed, another example of someone with beliefs in which they were troubled.

Believing that his personal sacrifice would bring him better luck in his next life.

So he took his life swiftly and quickly, with a guillotine he separated his head from his body.

And that he did on his sixty-eighth birthday, he decided it was time for him to get away, in this life he no longer wanted to stay.

Inspired only by what he believed in, the sacrifice of his life was his praise in reverence to Buddha, so that Buddha would grant him his most beseeched desire.

To be reincarnated as a much higher human being, that was his only dream.

He felt his present life was worthless, often depressed, and sometimes in a mess; better for him to go now and come back as a Prince or a Princess, that's what he believed; and that was what led to his suicidal death, believing that Buddha would grant him his request.

So yes indeed, all sorts of beliefs by anyone and everyone, convincingly and sacredly they held on tight to what they believed, and put it in practice when in need.

Especially beliefs concerning the dead, and that was so yesterday, today, and maybe tomorrow as well.

Preparations were made for the afterlife by every culture, and in whatever ways they believed were right was how they made their preparations for the afterlife.

Some were elaborate, some were simple, some were indeed very humble.

Some took a concentrated lengthy preparation, as it was done in mummification.

It was indeed a very gruesome preparation of the dead body, for its first-class journey to the afterlife.

A preparation that was bizarre, as was the whole afterlife idea, which was somewhere beyond the stars, no one knew exactly where, whether it was on Jupiter, Uranus, or Mars, but wherever, it didn't really matter.

And as that was what humans believed, so too it was what was done, the art of mummification, a preparation that was very common among human beings from different lands with different cultures, and religions, mainly pagans.

And yes, it did involve the removal of blood, internal tissues, and the same was done with the organs, including the brain, no soft tissues in the body were to remain.

And after the gruesome internal preparation, with the removal of blood, all tissues and organs; the body was washed, dried and stuffed with bodily preservers.

Then it was stitched up ready for its final external preparation with holy oils and incense.

Which were gently massaged upon the body, to ward off any evil during its journey.

Then finally as the body was tightly wrapped, it was sealed during rituals and prayers, and then gently put in a place to rest, until it was time to travel, whoever was next.

Yes indeed, those were some beliefs that were very absurd, and yet they were only just a few of a great many very weird beliefs executed in different cultures all over the world.

Many which human beings staunchly held on to, and for centuries the practices continued, executing deeds year after year in rituals and ceremonies, accompanied with exotic feasting to bring to life what they believed in.

And as demented as it was, this whole idea, that the dead with their earthly treasure could appear somewhere, into the existence of an afterlife either among or beyond the stars.

Yet still it was what humans believed in, to the afterlife they were emigrating, so they had to do whatever they believed in, because they believed it was the right thing.

Believing that it was not only right, but that it was also very wise.

And if for some reason it was not done, nothing could be worse than spiritual damnation.

To be left perhaps where they don't belong, surrounded by demons.

Indeed, beliefs and fear too often together are always there.

They are always there where they are not wanted, and usually to one's disadvantage.

But that never changed anything, people still believed and did whatever they believed in.

And they did them with confidence, never with a drop of hesitation.

As were nations' elites, Kings, Pharaohs, and Emperors, who made lavish and fanciful preparations for their journey to the afterlife.

But that was only one of the many weird things human beings believed in.

And from culture to culture in places everywhere, irrational beliefs, some with very cruel deeds were venerated, as well as executed on anniversaries in rituals and ceremonies.

Yes, they continued year after year, in celebrations with colourful exotic dances, songs and prayers, and with rituals in ceremonies that became the norm, from generation to generation they carried on in colourful gatherings humans sing hymns, in honour of the dead instead of the living.

So yes indeed, every culture has the things they believed in, things which passed from generation to generation regardless how weird and ridiculous.

And it is when those things are actually put into practice, the horrors exposed are beyond madness.

And yet it happened all the time, time and time again; right through the ages of humans' existence. For many years humans did the same things, and always with dedicated preparation.

From the past to the present, and from the present to further beyond, year after year those senseless things were done.

Believing and doing ridiculous things which they passed on to their children from generation to generation.

And doing them just because they believed in them, which was their main reason; they never had a better explanation, can't find one, not whenever concerning superstitions.

Doing them at anniversaries in celebrations year after year, and probably for centuries they did the same things for good luck, or for whatever, even to ward off their fear, and of course for better prospects another year.

Yes indeed, even going on a spirit hunt, in some cultures that was done, saying that it was to clean up the cities and the towns, so with traps they travelled up and down through the cities and the towns catching ghosts, spirits, and demons.

And since they couldn't see what they were catching, believing they had caught enough, fire was set to their impending traps.

And after the superstitious evils were burnt, they were all confident that it was safe to go home.

No longer fearing the darkness of the night, nor the whispers heard, and no one in sight.

Yes indeed that was real, an Asian cultural belief celebrated on anniversaries, believing that there were too many demons on the streets, the spirit hunt was a yearly feast.

A day to go out and clean up the streets, to catch and burn evil spirits, it was indeed a day to celebrate.

Releasing excitement, thrills and delight, with the hopes of a good sleep during the night.

And yes, so too were thanksgivings to the gods and goddesses, for whatever the people believed they did.

The giving of a good day to go fishing, and a good harvest to reap yet again.

Indeed, the kindness of the gods and goddesses were never mistakenly taken for granted.

Human beings everywhere, regardless of their different cultures, always showed their gratitude, offering sacrifices in a festive mood.

Something superstitious to celebrate, an event people believed was immaculate.

A day of superstitious jubilance was always a day with excitement and fun.

A day to forget your troubles, with everyone mixing together in a friendly manner with whoever.

Indeed, that's when it was rooted deep, celebrating what they believe in, a moment of crazy dancing and rejoicing, yes indeed, forgetting everything.

So yes indeed, as it has always been, many things human beings believed in were often very ridiculous, especially those with links to the superstitious.

And as will be expected, there were very many of them, celebrated for centuries on anniversaries, there were the occasions of community celebrations, the getting together in exotic dance.

Doing so time and time again just because it was something they believed in.

And even though whatever people believed lacked common sense and reality, it was never that easy, always with difficulty, to get them to listen to reason.

And indeed, that was so in kingdoms here and there, some monarchs were obsessed with a very silly idea, believing that they were gods, and communicating with their ancestors high up above, often asking for advice and favours, especially in the event of battles.

Yes, they often communicated with the gods for advice, so that they may make decisions that were wise.

And because they believed that they themselves were gods who came down from above.

To keep the godly bloodline without contamination pure in the family, in some kingdoms incest was common to preserve blood purity, mating was within the family.

Godly blood was not to be mixed with that of earthly commoners.

That indeed, would have been a sacrificial sin, and perhaps with their privileges confiscated.

So brothers and sisters, uncles and nieces among themselves got married to keep the god bloodline within the family, hence preventing contamination which then would have been possible with consequences unimaginable.

And that belief was without a measure of doubt, especially when supported by priests and sorcerers, and it was held very tight indeed, and with absolute powers firmly sealed.

Powers they claimed were theirs given from heaven, and which by no one could be taken.

And yes that belief was the same, for kings and Emperors who claimed, not that they were gods, but that they were sent down directly from heaven, with the commission to govern, and that they had the same rights as gods, because they came down from above.

Yes, that's what they claimed, and that their authority was absolute, they were the only ones to rule; and by earthly humans they could not be removed.

To rule over mankind gathered as a nation, that they believed was their God given mission, and so it was the only reason why from heaven they were sent down, in the bodily form as a human.

That was the only purpose of their birth, so their ordainment to rule could never be revoked.

And with that belief they lived their lives, ruthlessly corrupted, almost demonised.

And with the abuse of absolute power, the rule of law was always to their favour.

They did what they did right or wrong, and with no concern for anyone.

Believing that they came down from a heavenly kingdom, so whatever they did they couldn't be wrong.

Indeed, some of the things mankind believed in over the years were very fatuous and unimaginably weird.

They were unbelievable some of the things people believed in, they were ridiculous to say the least, and that was among every race, every culture, and every creed, in fact that was so with whoever was a human being, a King, an Emperor, a slave and his master, they all believed in some very weird things, things which made no sense whatsoever, things which were not only ridiculous, but the absurdity was a bit too much.

And despite that, they held onto their beliefs very tight, afraid to let go, believing they were right. So inspired by their beliefs, mankind did all sorts of bizarre things, whatever they could imagine.

And they did them because they were what they believed in, some in experiments to find out things.

And they believed in them whether or not they made any sense, some from their own ideas, and others passed on to them through previous generations.

Beliefs that were the subject of all sorts of stories, especially sex and pregnancies.

Stories that youngsters did love to hear and grew up with ideas demoralising their character.

It was an area with disgusting behaviour, full of myths and taboos.

What one should, and should not do, especially during a full moon.

Doing whatever they believed were the right things to do to prevent unwanted pregnancies.

Things they believed in, and not what they know, and regardless of enduring pain, they did them still because they believed in what they were doing.

And one that became very common, it was to soak sponges in vinegar, then up it was pushed into their vagina, believing it was a miracle worker.

But the one that was the most popular, the sponge would be sprinkled with a little salt and pepper, and that women believed did guarantee a quick and successful end to their unwanted pregnancy.

And that belief was with roots deep and strong, nothing was known to ever go wrong.

Indeed, with beliefs and deeds there was a bond, and that's why beliefs lasted so long.

And not until beliefs were seen to be wrong, throughout the ages they were passed on.

Passing on, and then on again, each generation believing in the very same things.

No questions asked, no criticisms, what was good for the old, was good for the young, so they were passed on again to new generations.

And so it was the same about getting pregnant, all sorts of weird stories were told by the young and the old in different cultures all over the world.

From north to south, east to west, all sorts of stories were heard, each claiming to be the best.

Especially stories about the sun, the moon, mars, and the stars, they all had something to do with women getting pregnant.

Yes, you heard this, and you heard that, whatever was the magic it was superstitious.

Indeed, it was an area full of myths and taboos, and with one not much different from the other, they were all stuff fit for a sewer.

And with absurdities, from culture to culture they varied, the same things were done differently, different cultures held different beliefs with different remedies.

So yes indeed, there were so many eerie stories, so many of them, from place to place everywhere one went.

Women especially were victims of all sorts of beliefs, many which lasted for centuries.

And failing to get pregnant, that especially was labelled with taboos and myths which were so many in story after story.

Yes it was believed, whatever was heard in gossip, every word of it, accusing women in tongues of different languages wagging derogatory words of mischief.

Women were seen as less than a woman in every culture wherever she went just because she couldn't get pregnant.

And although it could have been the fault of her husband, blame always fell upon the woman.

No one could ever imagine that just maybe, this lack of a baby, the man's fault it could be.

And that was because every man was always ready to grasp at the opportunity to impregnate any woman with a baby.

And so it still is today in some places, the taboo is still on the surface.

Failing to get pregnant is an embarrassment that is often associated with superstitions.

And not until a woman was able to prove herself, blame always fell upon her head as the only place for it to dwell.

And so it was everywhere, different weird things were done in different cultures.

And as it was known to be customary in India, women did anything to get pregnant, to avoid the gossip even from friends, with everyone pointing their fingers.

So on special celebratory events, in the honour of the deity Adi Shaki, women were treated to procure pregnancy with one of the most idiotic efficaciousness that anyone could witness.

Yes, hundreds of women who couldn't get pregnant, believing that they needed the treatment.

From all over India they travelled long and short distances in their colourful sarees and dresses, to this one place where they gathered together for their treatment to assist nature.

And orderly together with their arms outstretched stranger to stranger, relaxed and calm, and with their curiosity entangled with anxiety, they lie belly down on the ground in rows of nine or ten, awaiting treatment; not individually, not privately, but altogether openly, and wondering perhaps what the treatment will be.

And as they laid face down pinned to the ground in the open hot air under the sun, with their arms stretched out flat on the ground; it was a moment of dead silence, brimming with suspense and expectations.

And as their discomfort took a grip, so too was their restlessness.

Hoping to be cured from whatever it was, deep in their consciousness for a moment they controlled themselves burying their thoughts, while curious and anxious they waited for the treatment, not knowing what it was, when it would begin, how long it would last, and how it would end, whether they will be cured; and at that moment, it was the only thought that troubled them all.

Oh yes indeed they were deep in thought, whether or not they will be cured.

Until suddenly it began taking everyone by surprise as holy men arrived dressed in white, and as if they just landed, came down from heaven to cast out the demons.

Walking upon the women row after row, with their bare feet they walked very slow.

Chanting in prayers and showering flowers upon the barren victims in reverence to the gods, to remove the barriers that were their barren cause.

And at the same time, one of the holy men walking upon the women, one by one he hits them upon their head with a bunch of sage, as he mumbles in prayer to whichever god was listening from somewhere observing.

And as drums beat out in rhythm of approval, blessings were showered upon the women from the shouts of the curious gathering observers. And that ended the unorthodox treatment to make the women pregnant, releasing them from their discomfort, from a treatment which appeared to be nothing but a fraud.

Indeed it was, just another ridiculous belief in the world of superstitions where reality is never transparent, always absent.

Still, that's what the people believed, and what they did, like everyone else wherever they live. Doing the things they believe in, and they may continue to do so for a long time still, until their hibernating sense of reason awakens.

So yes indeed, it's all about beliefs, women tried all sorts of things, whenever getting pregnant was their aim.

And that was so wherever you went, women did different things, but whatever they did were all what they believed may do the trick, regardless of the magic.

And yet on many occasions it was their husbands, they were the barren ones, the infertile culprits.

Yes, conscious or unconscious of the fact, blaming their wives, they were satisfied with that.

Until it came to light when a woman got married again, after many years of guilt and abuse taking the blame.

Taking the blame and trying all sorts of things, but nothing worked because the treatments they were taking were all in vain, nothing was wrong with them from the beginning, it was their husbands to blame.

And as life went on still with superstitions, anxious to have a baby and the choice of its sex, spirits were sometimes contacted with the request.

Many decisions were made for clients by voodoo priests, sharmans, and sorcerers, claiming that their decision came directly from the heavens above.

From the stars, Venus, Jupiter or Mars, or from the horoscope of the woman giving birth.

So whatever was the advice given, it was taken very seriously, in the belief that it came from signs within the skies, especially from Mercury, or Mars.

So for most women wanting the choice of a boy or a girl, a sorcerer's advice was always very useful.

Indeed, even today, horoscopes are studied before some decisions are made, and even by the educated.

Human beings all over the world, before they make some decisions, they take a good look at their horoscope; it's in the supernatural where they look for advice, and answers, especially from the writings in books written by astronomers.

Looking for what? Perhaps they themselves don't even know, but with an urge to be certain, they feel they should consult the spirits behind the sky's curtain.

And yes they feel better, more confident, when their horoscope approves their decisions.

And if it didn't, then they would change their minds, or make their decisions at some other time.

And as beliefs penetrated the barriers of privacy, for centuries women's menstruation was clouded with superstitions, taboos, myths, and secrecy.

In some cultures women were treated very badly; especially by their own family.

Each time they underwent what was to be, they were humiliated, and treated as something dirty.

And it differed in degree among different beliefs, the taboos in menstruation brought women a lot of grief.

But men were also caught on the fisherman's hook too, in many cultures they were victims of sexual taboo.

And that was so especially when they were unable to father a child, especially a baby boy; in cultures where male children were taken for granted, that was the sex of a child most parents wanted.

So yes, men were ridiculed and seen often as victims of voodoo, when a male child they could not produce.

Indeed, all sorts of stories were concocted as the reason why such a person could not father a child who was masculine.

It was such a degrading stigma, that even friends wanted answers.

The general opinion which was held in the community was in the belief that it might have been curses from evil spirits, or a punishment from a god or goddess, or a demon from hell was another such fable, indeed, whatever it was, it was not natural, it was from the spiritual world, that they believed and without any doubt, that the spirit world was the cause.

And as they had no doubt that whatever was the cause it was not natural; believing it came from the spirit world, so treatment had to be very careful.

Yes indeed infertility was always seen as an unnatural condition that came from the spiritual world as a punishment.

A punishment that came upon the victim, directly from God in heaven, or from a demon from hell, so then the treatments were always different, and different still for men or women.

Prayers were said to retrieve the punishment from heaven, while a mix of herbs with animal blood and bones were used to dispel demons and their curse.

But how did they know which treatment would work, which was, and which was not a curse?

They didn't, it was just an act of mumbo jumbo, a voodoo gamble, treating the patient with both prayers and herbs, and animal parts too.

Each culture did whatever it took, especially if it worked.

Doing whatever it was that they believed in, to have a son, men would have tried anything.

And as beliefs unfolded into the reality of deeds, deeds of every nature, deeds of every kind. It became common in every part of the world, beliefs and culture were tightly welded together, and for as long as ever.

And that partnership gave rise not only to intimidation, but to all sorts of accusations.

Accusations that often led to physical and mental abuse for whatever some-one was accused.

Yes, people were harassed and tormented, just because of what others be-lieved in.

As it happened to women and different races, subjected to beliefs to keep them in their places, and in different economical divisions, separated into different classes with those at the bottom in degrading conditions.

And that had led to the shrinking of heads of those from different villages, inferior races captured in warring skirmishes.

Yes indeed it was real, heads were chopped off before or after the person was dead, then shrunk and preserved through a gruesome process and put on display to ward off spirits.

Its purpose was to ward off the dead person's spirit from within the village where it was not wanted.

Hence, to prevent the haunting by a demon, the evil spirit of someone just died and passed on.

And that was to guarantee safety in the community, without intimidation by the spirit of the deceased, now a demon that hell has released.

Yes surprisingly, and without logic or a good sense of reason, people were feared much more after they were dead, because then, they had powers from hell; that's what communities believed.

Powers which the living could not easily control, as the demons from hell grabbed hold of their body and soul.

And this belief is still commonplace today, that religion has become much more engaged.

Performing rituals of exorcism to cast out the offending demons from the people accused of being possessed, those with conditions in liking to madness.

To cure them religion does whatever they believe in, especially with prayers, because they know of nothing else.

Doing whatever it is that they believe in to get rid of the demons from within the living.

A common practice among priests and religious deities, they do whatever in what they believe.

So yes, beliefs are about anything, and they are always about what one does not know. "Is there really such a thing as a spirit or a ghost?"

Some would say yes, some would say no, and those who are still not yet convinced, they will say, 'I really don't know.'

And yet it is said that all humans have got a soul. Where do they come from, does anyone know?

Their presence is never felt so no one knows, maybe they came from the spiritual world.

And yet as ghosts they have been quite often seen, by many who would tell you just that.

Not as something that they believed in, but as something that is real, something they know as a fact. Because they have witnessed the things spirits can do, right in their presence in their home. Things that would scare the hell out of you before the spirits leave you alone.

Things that are no mumbo jumbo, neither they do not believe, but they know.

Because they saw the things spirits can do, and they know that they are real and true.

So the question now put to the atheist; 'Do spirits exist, and from what did they evolve?'

If you don't believe that they do exist, don't be content just to doubt.

But get yourself into a haunted house, it is there you will find out.

Yes indeed, science has not yet revealed the evolution of spirits, and that may be because science doesn't believe that spirits exist.

They have no theory, it is still a mystery, in fact they don't know how they evolved or whether or not they exist at all.

And they may never find an answer, because into the world of spirits, they may never be able to enter.

Indeed, no mathematical calculations, no earthly predictions may ever unlock the mysteries of the world of spirits' evolution.

So until then, science will have to be content with whatever they believe in.

And the same could be said about Aliens, in that too some people believe in.

From wherever they were, they came and went, bringing knowledge to mankind, planted in their footprints, the artefacts, and other objects they left behind.

Oh yes indeed, that's what some people believe, and even in UFOs and Extraterrestrial life.

The appearance of strange objects they swear they saw up in the skies, not with borrowed, or artificial eyes, but with their own natural eyes.

Yes, Extraterrestrials came and went from among the stars, bringing knowledge to mankind.

Now you see them, and now you don't, appearing and disappearing like ghosts.

Strange objects doing tricks with technology humans have not yet accomplished, leaving some behind for humans to find.

But that view is nothing new, in medieval times Extraterrestrials did arrive, so said mankind; the proof is there in their artefacts, and the many other things they left behind, things that were centuries old, things mediaeval humans could not have done, so they must have been left by a well advanced civilization.

And even in skeletons found, many which were thousands of years old, intact with evidence of the life of Extraterrestrials roaming the earth.

Skeletons that were neither animal nor human, but indeed Extraterrestrial aliens, so said the convincing voice of science, and those who believe that they were the skeletons of extraterrestrial aliens.

So yes it is true, there are people today who believe that Extraterrestrials are their ancestors, and they say that they have no doubt about that whatsoever.

They believe that they are progenies from Extraterrestrial life.

Indeed, the evidence is there in the many strange artefacts found, and in the technology brought to earth by Extraterrestrial aliens, all defying conventional explanation.

Yes, from distances far beyond, in objects that came and went, and even today their objects still appear, and those who see them curiously stare, wondering within themselves, how the hell did that get there, and within seconds they disappear.

Yes that is what humans claim they have seen, and many believe, and from the pages of the book of Enoch and other ancient writings, and archaeological findings, there is where humans may find the evidence of Extraterrestrials existence.

Indeed, ancient writings are on the pages of yesterday's history, in several books including the Bible, stories which todays' generations could read, doubt, or believe.

And with wise reasoning humans can understand and know the truths in history.

Because they were written as they happened, so that knowledge could reach the people.

And because they were written they may never be forgotten, whatever they are, Extraterrestrial alien life or whatever.

Whether or not they are within the reach of humans' understanding, or they require a great deal of explaining.

Yes indeed, there are some things which human beings for a very long time may still never know, hence only believe.

As it is with life after death, and many other stories of the superstitious, which for centuries humans believe, and still today what is the truth, they still don't know, so they still believe.

But whatever it was they did or did not see, it was what they knew, or what they believed they saw in this modern age, and right beneath the clouds in the skies, right before their eyes, playing hide and seek was the appearance of some sort of swift alien object.

Nothing to do with imagination, drunkenness, hallucinations or illusions, but the reality of objects disappearing and appearing again and again, sometimes as swift as lightning.

Yes disappearing, don't know where they went, as swift as lightning their appearance came to an end.

So yes indeed it is very true, I said it once and I say it again, human beings believe in all sorts of things, and that they will continue to do without knowing whether they are false or true. So indeed, humans will continue to believe all sorts of stories, whenever they do not know, and that is something which will continue.

Just as they did yesterday, believing in all sorts of things, from the history books and ancient writings, and from daily gossip, while still searching for the truth so that they can know, instead of believing.

So yes it is true that humans are still digging into the past beneath the earth searching for the evidence of truth.

There is where the truth lies in hiding, and without digging there is where the truth may always remain, peacefully at sleep, silent, and disengaged with humans.

So yes it is believed that many truths are today still held in the bosom of mother earth, secrets that one day may be unearthed and disclosed; because humans believe that they do exist, and in their search they may just be fortunate.

So yes indeed, in the meantime humans will still continue to believe, and even in the impossible, and with or without reason, as their ancestors did centuries ago.

Believing in all sorts of things, and for the truths, digging and searching so that they can know instead of believing, wisely so, that is what they prefer; to know.

So yes humans have, and they will always have the urge to know because knowing is certain, knowing is reliable knowledge, it is without doubt, it is positive.

So they may search for the truth whenever possible in whatever they believe, regardless how bizarre, from fake medicines, to good luck charms, rituals, sky burials, and self flagellation, to human sacrifices, and demonic curses, eating the dead in endocannibalism, and of course in ritual cannibalism too, which was common among pagans, and indeed many more beliefs, their truths may never be found, as they lie silent beneath the ground, so there they may remain peaceful and undisturbed, until comes the day with a dig they are disclosed, and brought as knowledge into the world.

Yes indeed, there was always a reason for ancient human cannibalism, that too was something the people believed in.

It was not done just for fun, or that they were hungry, but something superstitious was the reason, it had to be, in those days of sorcery.

Indeed, it must have been something very demanding, to influence humans into cannibalism.

Something they believed they had to possess, something needed for their success, and the only means of their achievement was to devour their enemy's flesh; and that they did, and hoped for the best; with the powers of the dead to manifest within themselves.

Giving them super strength, and being able to move as swiftly as lightning, that's what they believed happened to them when they ate the flesh of their enemy, indeed, that was what some cultures believed, and without hesitation, that was what they did, they ate the flesh of their enemies to fortify their strength and courage.

239

And yes, there were hundreds of fake medicines too, medicines humans believed in, when desperate they will try anything.

All sorts of concoction from animals and plants, for different causes were taken by humans.

Treatments were always in demand, especially from people in distress conditions.

And this was true in many cases among human beings anxious for a cure, they were willing to try anything whether or not they were sure.

And that's when they were deceived, they were never sure what to believe, humans always took advantage of those who are in need, an unfortunate reality.

That's one of the problems when people believe, especially if they are in need.

And that is true when deciding what best to take, don't know what is real or what is fake.

In fact it is true for most things, too often human beings are left disappointed in what they believe in, and whenever they are at a disadvantage, most of the time that's when they are cheated.

Not forgetting the butchery of carcasses, chopped up with roots, herbs and mixed with spices.

Then scattered upon roofs, and around houses, to ward off demons, evil spirits and witches; yes indeed, it was a common practice in several cultures among the tribes in villages.

Safety from evil was of the utmost importance, especially for their children.

And of course, the herbs hung upon the front door, although they did not know what they were for. But people believed that they must hang them up, regardless of whatever was the purpose, because that's what their ancestors did, and that's what they inherited, so they continue to do it still to guarantee safety in the village.

And of course, the festive celebrations in marriages too, that was something people believed that they had to do.

It was a tradition as weird as it was, and as like many others, it was the norm in some cultures, it was one of those bizarre things that they believed in and what they did like most other things.

Yes the celebrations were weird, like most superstitions, idiotic and sense-less.

They were for marriages between animals, something that was done in some cultures.

Marrying frogs, snakes, cattle, pigs, dogs or whatever, in festive offerings to the gods for a favour. For rain, or to heal the sick from whatever was the illness, or for protection from evil spirits, or tomorrow's battle to win, what-ever was the favour it didn't really matter.

That's what they believed in and that's what they did, celebrating events of animals' weddings as offerings to gods and goddesses.

And of course too, the belief in powers radiating from crystals, especially from the 'skull of doom.' That was a fascinating story wherever it was heard around the world.

And especially among Kings and Emperors, bamboozled with the belief that the skull of doom had powers.

It was a belief in several cultures that a particular crystal skull had magical powers.

The knowledge of it passed from generation to generation and bamboozled many people for centuries, indeed it had bamboozled the world wherever the story was told.

Many people journeyed in search of it, despite the dangers especially in darkness, convinced by stories heard from gossip, going wherever they be-lieved they could find it, risking their lives to find the mysterious object, in the belief that there was power to be gained from it.

Yes indeed, many lives were lost searching for the skull, believing it contained mystical powers, it was indeed something worth having, with the power of the skull, people believed that they were able to achieve anything, especially every battle to win.

But no one knew if they had really seen it, because of the many who claimed they had the skull, no one knew who really had it, or if it really existed at all.

But regarding crystals in general, in many cultures it was believed they had some sort of mystical powers, hence the psychic's crystal ball; still in circulation bamboozling us all.

It was just a matter of knowing how to use the powers from the crystals, and that was if they really had any magical powers at all.

So yes indeed, there were many other objects people believed had magical powers, not only crystals, but objects they believed were from the gods, and even too from Extraterrestrials.

And to get those objects people fought for them, putting their lives at risk for what they believed in.

And yet all they were, perhaps just rumours, but since no one was sure, it was better to take the benefit of the doubt than to be left without.

Indeed, they were all just beliefs, and that's for sure, that's what they were and nothing more, and yet when put into practice there was trouble.

In some areas they were devastating, as in areas of health and sex, superstitions were blamed for most things that happened both bad and good.

And whether they were right or wrong, bad or good; they all came from the spirit world, that was the common belief, there was no other reason told.

So illnesses were indeed full of taboos, believing that they were the effects of voodoo.

Or from the gods or goddesses, inflicted upon humans as a punishment.

So into the skies sorcerers glued their eyes for signs of advice, how best to deal with the pestering disquiet of the sickness blight.

So animal parts and plants were the regular remedies used, indeed some were effective, some abortive with absolutely no usefulness.

Using the parts with the intention, to cast out the affecting demon.

Or as in extreme cases, an animal's life would be sacrificed.

Offered to either a god or goddess in order to save someone's life, or to promote a successful business, or for whatever was requested.

So the cure which was nothing more than something superstitious, was indeed a very slow process with everyone hoping for it to be beneficious.

And the best was often nothing less, but an unnecessary death, because what the people believed was a cure, was nothing more than something superstitious, hence it was useless.

But then again, as it was with everything, it was either superstitions or nothing, medicines were not yet found, no one knew where illnesses came from, believing that it may be either from above or under the ground, inflicted upon them by demons.

Yes unfortunately, those were days with little knowledge and skills, so for many centuries, superstitions claimed lives from those who were ill.

Indeed, the angel of death was very busy, claiming many young lives, some very early.

With all sorts of cures supposed to be from the gods, whether they work or not, there was no other choice.

So yes indeed regretfully those were the days of very little knowledge, humans lived with superstitions, they lived by superstitions, superstitions indeed were the everyday norms.

And so it was the same everywhere, health care was very primitive, humans gazed upon the stars in search of signs to cure illnesses.

Medicines were often that of superstitions, no knowledge was yet known of the medicines of science.

So medicines were in all forms of mumbo jumbo, including prayers and sacrifices also.

And that was why death came so very quick, superstitions did not always cure anyone who was sick.

And because that was their only treatment, like a thief in the night death came crawling, and it did so to victims of any age, regardless of the triviality of their illness.

So yes indeed, life expectancy was no more than thirty or forty years, and that was reserved for those who were in good health; and those who were not, well, their fate, hope, and trust were all left to the superstitious.

Yet still without knowledge superstitions continue in different ways around the world, from nation to nation, from religion to religion, and from tribe to tribe in every direction.

And although time was moving on often with progressive development, superstitions were still the healing force to repel illnesses at any cost.

It was more like an exorcism disabling the offending demons, and returning the sick back to healthiness, after cleansing their body from evil spirits.

Yes it was a struggle to cure the sick with some voodoo trick, most of the time it failed again.

And with each culture doing things differently in accordance with their beliefs, either in rituals or in ceremonies, dancing and feasting were part of the orgies.

Yes, inviting the heavens, the sun, the moon, the stars, and the gods, believing that they all had magical healing powers, so the exotic drumming was a means to summon the powers of the skies, bringing to earth all those that were wise.

And whenever someone was cured, rest assured, there was more exotic feasting in thanksgivings to the gods.

And that humans did in gratitude and reverence, it was always important to them to show the gods their appreciation.

The evil demon was cast out and the patient healed, once again the devil has been defeated. So yes, that was a jovial occasion which was real, that's how humans felt and what they believed.

And so it was in times of need, those were just a few things humans believed in, despite not knowing or understanding why, they were never that curious deep down inside.

Beliefs that were superstitious, of a nature curious, and even suspicious, yet still they were all just beliefs executed in deeds, they were what people believed.

Things unknown, things uncertain, things which caused a great deal of fuss, things which were useful, useless, and dangerous; indeed they were all beliefs, some false, some real.

So yes beliefs are not only about grief, sometimes they give humans some hope in life, especially when they felt they had lost everything, believing has the power of joy and suffering, in both cases the sad thing is, not really knowing.

And so it did cause Johnny to divorce his wife, when all the time he was guessing.

Causing himself unnecessary worry and anxiety, believing his wife was unfaithful in adultery, just because she started coming home late regularly, and he didn't believe her story.

And now as a fool he has lost his wife because of the malicious gossip he's now mired in strife.

So believing instead of knowing, has been proved again, its powers could be devastating.

Causing problems that are unnecessary, falsely accusing, and just because of what you believe in. So then it is wise to always be certain, which can only be achieved by knowing, and not by believing.

And that's the power of beliefs; a power of irresistible influence, acting upon humans' emotions which could either be misleading and dangerous, or leave you feeling cheerful and magnanimous.

And that's when you believe that he loves you, when the fact is that's not true.

And yet you continue to believe the lies he tells you, because he tells you the things you love to hear, and that makes you believe that he really cares; it gives you a wonderful feeling; oh yes indeed, a feeling that makes you believe in whatever he says, until you found out that you were not both on the same page.

So it is always better to know than to believe, because that can prevent a lot of grief.

And it can prevent disappointments, and even the desire for revenge.

But then again to know may not always be possible, so it is better to believe only after being convinced, and that you are very certain you are doing the right thing.

But then again, everyone knows that is not always possible. So what are you left with?

Leave it alone, or take the gamble.

So yes, as it has been written upon the pages of history, in stories from medieval centuries. A lot of beliefs were really weird, and a great deal of them were focused on the dead.

But that is how human beings have developed to be, in the spiritual world they vent their curiosity during their life existence over many centuries.

The world of spirits was always fascinating, fearsome and intimidating with unknowns curiously challenging.

Regretfully in those days humans had little knowledge, so they believed many weird things about the dead and the afterlife, the gods and goddesses in the skies, they were bamboozled by superstitions all their lives, finding it frightening, exciting, and indeed enchanting.

And when humans' beliefs were about the living, they captured a terrain of all sorts of things.

Believing in this and believing in that, to get rid of the back pain, you must swallow a rat.

But that was not meant to be a joke, human beings believed and did some very strange things which were even much worse than swallowing a rat, things which were many times worse than that.

Whatever humans could imagine, was something they would believe in, and even putting into practice as their fate.

So yes indeed, it was often from something they imagined which human beings believed in, as it is the case in this fact.

There are many people who believe as a faith, that when they die, they will come back to life in some other life form, a bird, a snake, a horse, a bat or a cat, or even another human being; their new life form depended upon the merits of their previous one.

And there were others in accordance with their culture, they ate the dead bodies of their enemies they killed, and that was inspired by what they believed in.

Yes they believed that in devouring their flesh, they were extracting the strength of their enemies, their courage and their will, making them ferocious, invincible, and difficult, but still not impossible to be killed, it just improved their chances of survival.

So with a roasted human body they had their fill, hoping that in battle they would never be killed, as they were now prepared with a stronger will, fearsome, and with greater courage.

247

Yet still, there were many more horrid things people did, and they did them yet again and again, and for no other reason but just because they were what they believed in.

Until it came that time when they realised that many things they believed, they had in fact been deceived.

Believing in things worthy of nothing, and executing deeds that were inhumane, creating death, grief and pain, because it was something which they believe in.

And although some beliefs were inspiring, just as some were horrid and disappointing.

That is what happens when people do not know, hence, they are never quite certain which way to go.

Be it forwards or backwards, or should they go at all, or should they just wait a minute until nature calls.

To make the right decision is never easy, especially whenever the truth is hidden.

So what is it that mankind should believe? With doubts and confusion their heavy chests heave.

They are bombarded with reasons as they listen to a story, and whatever they are told, they swallow each word, until they are poorer mentally.

And when they believe, grasping at the feeling deceiving themselves that they were quite sure.

Surprise and vexation arrived, heavily printed on their faces the moment they realised that the key which was taken couldn't open the door.

And that is how it had been throughout the reign of humans' existence.

For century after century, blinded to reality, superstitions found a comfortable home on the quiescent consciousness of humans.

So beliefs were passed on from generation to generation, carried from one to the other with a bundle of problems all stacked close together.

And as they were passed from one to the other, there was never ever any filter.

Everything got passed into the future; good and bad, terror and pleasure, all got passed squeezed together.

Beliefs that were executed with blood and horror, and without any guilt whatsoever.

Believing that no wrong was committed, not even the murders in human sacrifices.

Believing that the right things were done, just because for centuries the same things were done by earlier generations.

And that of course was their justification for whatever wrongs they may have done.

And that was so in every culture, most wrongs committed involved cold-blooded murder, human sacrifices were a common engender.

And yes, not forgetting the cruel fate of deformed babies, an abominable atrocity, an insanity that was the norm in some societies, innocent lives were condemned as victims of superstitious beliefs.

In some cultures around the world many centuries ago, deformity was re-garded as a demonic curse, in need of relief instead of a long life tormented with misery.

So such babies were killed, believing it was necessary to save them from a life of perpetual suffering, and worse still, their murder was savage; it was indeed very cruel.

And with no concern of right and wrong, deformed babies lost their lives the moment they were born.

There was no caring for a deformed baby, it was a superstitious stigma in the community.

A stigma of evil, a stigma of shame, a stigma which haunted the parents as the ones to blame.

It was a life of ridicule and shame upon the family of a woman who gave birth to a deformed baby.

A stigma cursed with superstitions that made life difficult for a child deformed, and so too for their parents who were unjustly ridiculed and scorned; they had to be cleansed with the healing powers of superstitions.

And that's how it had been unfortunately, in some cultures the fate of a deformed baby was a cruel one, buried dead or alive, in the belief that they were cursed, and that it was better for them not to survive, because they will be tormented throughout their life.

So in accordance with tradition engaged with a witch-doctor's blessing, deformed babies' lives were brought to a hasty end by a family member or their parents.

And that was to guarantee that the child's spirit would rest in peace instead of becoming a restless beast, better known in the spirit world, as a demon.

But that was not the only belief that claimed the life of many babies.

In cultures both primitive and civilized many babies lost their lives because of the taboos and myths people believed in, hence inviting dishonour and shame.

Some lost their lives because they were black, some because they were white, some because they were girls, some because they were bastards, and some for other social reasons pressured by beliefs from within communities.

And all those lives taken from babies, they were only because of beliefs in certain human values.

Values that were nothing more than disgraceful and sinful, values developed perhaps during the mediaeval period when dishonour was a deplorable stigma with a weight too heavy to bear. So because of those cultural values, values which destroyed lives, values which were unwise.

Babies' lives were cowardly taken just to hide from dishonour, shame, and disgrace.

To hide from the displeasure from the things society rejected.

Yes lives were taken to obliterate dishonour, and with an easy escape from the consequences of murder.

And yes, it was never a secret, in many cultures during medieval times the spirit world was taken very seriously, as well as honour within communities.

And that was so because community life was in unity, conformity, and fraternity; they all felt what they believed was real, it had significance, it had importance, and especially beliefs in the spirits of ancestors, and demons.

And yes indeed it was what they believed without a spot of doubt, that spirits were able to possess anybody, causing them ill health, death, or injury, causing them whatever the spirits wanted it to be, a life of success or misery.

And they were able to do so either before or after birth, and that's why demons were always a threat. Indeed, they were able to make one's life as though they were in hell, so much so that it was better to be dead.

And that was why they believed that a newborn deformed baby was indeed better off dead, rather than to prolong its life in torment in the darkness of hell.

And they were also able to make life unbearable for an entire community, getting rid of demons was never easy, the fact that they were invisible, and were never seen.

Indeed, it was sad, humans did things as if they were mad, without knowledge humans were really imprisoned, living their lives in captivity, always in fear of the silence of darkness, and without the consciousness that they were imprisoned in bondage.

And yes, locked up in darkness with their consciousness terrified of superstitious forces, feeling threatened by the unknown, which never left them alone, with fear residing in every heart as it's home.

And as humans advanced during troubled times, some beliefs they kept, others were left behind as mankind moved on with time.

Civilisations came and went with some cultural beliefs disappearing, indeed humans were moving on from old to new civilisations, and yet still people kept in their heads many beliefs that were bizarre and weird.

But those were times still with little knowledge about anything, so people kept on believing without ever knowing.

Their beliefs to them were their light and their guide, to wherever they were heading.

It gave them inspiration, fate, hope, and courage, it was indeed their knowledge.

And it was those same beliefs that kept them going, they were what made their life worth living.

Because whatever they believed and what they did, they always felt that they were right, it was the light which kept their pathway bright.

And because it was right and it kept their pathway bright, whatever they believed, it was an important part of their life which could not be changed overnight.

And as the world was still with little knowledge, and indeed with little progress, and with cultures still very much primitive.

A world which was still engulfed in superstitions, with voodoo and sorcery embedded deep in traditions.

And where beliefs generated fear that was as threatening as a wild hungry bear.

During those times it was not a crime to execute beliefs of any kind.

And that humans did, despite however cruel, at traditional anniversaries the same crimes were repeated.

The taking of lives as a sacrifice, either humans or animals slaughtered with an axe, boiled in oil, or burnt alive, or whatever cruelty justified their imaginations running wild.

And all those crimes were frequently witnessed, for no other reason horrors were committed as fulfillment to weird beliefs.

So yes indeed, they were committed in the belief that they were suited either as punishments or sacrifices.

And both were very cruel, even barbaric, the punishments were displayed as a deterrent, believing that no one will dare to be disobedient.

Some sacrifices were committed in rituals on the occasions of marriages, in offerings to the gods to grant happiness.

Some after death to secure a safe passage to the afterlife, to guard and protect the deceased on their journey to paradise.

Some were to repel demons and their curses, some for the excitement and the thrills in celebrations to gods and goddesses.

Indeed sacrifices were made for all sorts of reasons, and they were occasions taken very seriously, whatever was done was done devotedly.

And yes indeed they were very cruel in cultures everywhere in the world; barbarity in beliefs was customary, especially on festive occasions; the more bloody were the sacrifices the more exotic was the madness, and the more humans got excited and jubilantly overwhelmed, believing that the gods had possessed them, and rewarding them with a heavenly experience.

Yes indeed that's what they believed, that they were rewarded for their deeds, with their sacrifices the gods were pleased.

And with that satisfaction between gods and humans, the barbarity in sacrificial communications were always meant to be jovial occasions.

But not necessarily for the victims, as was the belief in the horror of suttee, a belief that claimed women's lives without mercy.

And despite the screams of horror, from human sacrifice in smoke and fire, this barbarity claimed the lives of many faithful wives who were burnt alive, as it could be described, as nothing more than a monstrous human sacrifice.

And it was what humans consciously did among other wicked things, and maybe it was a religious custom, belonging to Hinduism, and likewise all religious barbarity, during mediaeval times, they were more often likely to be women as the victims.

And the explanation for this horror, which for women was considered an honour, and yet despite the honour, no one ever freely volunteered for the honour of being burnt alive with their husband already dead.

It was forced upon women, never a choice given to them, whatever was the reason.

Yes, they were shoved, dragged and pushed, like a criminal led to the gallows, upon the pyre where they were secured to be burnt to death in flames of terror.

Indeed it was very cruel, not deeply expressive enough to use the word savage, and yet it was a cultural norm, an abominable injustice against women, but it made no difference, it was what men believed in, and without compassion it was what they did to women.

And when asked for an explanation, without any remorse the answer was given.

'It was tradition, in the honour of the god of creation, it was a privilege for women.'

And that had justified the ghastly sacrifice of many women forcefully burnt alive.

With no logic, no reality, no good reason for the monstrosity.

But perhaps, this was what they believed, if not, it's what they did; deceased husbands going to the afterlife should be accompanied by their wife.

And so it did, and for many years, suttee had forcefully claimed the lives of many beautiful young wives, burnt alive on a cremation pyre, with their dead husbands silent at their sides.

A religious tradition maybe, developed from mediaeval times when barbarity was not a crime.

Both were burnt together, the dead and the living, and only because of what people believed in; their cold-blooded murder was no sin.

Indeed, those were the days, days of horror, days of savagery in murder, days of darkness with no consciousness, days that terrified the living as well as the dead.

Days with every hour which were feared.

Days which were nothing less than a living hell, for many, that's where they dwell.

Yes indeed, whatever it was that humans believed, it was the reason why so many women died in such a ghastly human sacrifice.

It was a question without an answer, no one can explain with good reason, the logic for doing such a horrible thing.

It was like most superstitions, it had no logical answer, no reasonable explanation that made sense.

And yet it passed through the gates of the ages for many decades, as an honourable ritual that was very sacred.

Claiming lives one after the other, with the living and the dead reduced to ashes together.

Man and woman, husband and wife, burn together, one dead one alive.

And that was so with only wives, husbands were never burnt alive, because that was considered to be foolish and unwise.

Indeed it was always women, from the grip of torment there was no escape for them, even religion always persecuted them.

They were always disadvantaged in some way or the other, and in every culture, as easy victims to injustice, abuses and even murder, and that has been shamefully happening in every culture of human existence, and passing on from generation to generation.

So yes, for many decades suttee claimed the lives of old, young, and beautiful wives.

Burnt alive on cremation pyres, in the belief in human sacrifice.

Women who had no right to live after their husbands were dead.

Condemned to death in the horror of flames, and for no other reason but what others believed in. Yes, it was nothing more than belief put into practice, and freely continued for many years without an opposition to it.

So it became a cultural norm well established with the pros and cons in a fiery ritual.

Which were executed like others during ceremonial feast and sacrificial rituals.

Fortunately, suttee was abandoned eventually, by the foreign power that governed India.

Putting an end to the barbarity which was nothing more than superstitions only, and which brought terrifying horror to grieving families one after the other.

Putting an end to the intimidating terror that brought fear to wives, condemned to flames to end their lives with their dead husband at their side, so that they could travel together to the afterlife.

What a taboo, what a myth, for so many years this barbarity existed; and from a religious perspective.

Committing cold-blooded murders year after year in a spectacle of horror considered to be honour.

Humans indeed had appeared to be nothing more than savages, that's how they could be described for the horrible things they did.

Indeed, everywhere in the world superstitions had a grip, and it was not with politeness.

Yet still it was what humans believed in, there was no rational explanation for the barbarity of their sins.

And that was everywhere, in every culture, barbarity was common in something or the other. Either in sacrifices to the gods, or maybe just for fun, or for punishments, it made no difference.

Cruelty was everywhere, it was in the air, blowing here and there.

It was what was shaping humans' mentality, and that's how they were developing to be.

With no consciousness, no compassion, barbaric deeds were committed without consideration.

They were committed time and time again, and more often with women as the victims.

Yes that's how the world was developing, that's how it was progressing, it was indeed a world consumed in sin.

But then whenever beliefs were rooted so deep, regardless of the purpose or the reason. It did not matter whether they were right or wrong, especially when they have been going on for far too long, they became the norm rooted and flourished as tradition.

And as tradition, right or wrong, beliefs became very difficult to be broken, passing instead to each generation as established and acceptable cultural norms.

In fact, whatever was the reason and it was superstitious, then it could only be right regardless of whatever was its purpose, there was nothing to discuss.

So everyone gets infected, and that's why beliefs, regardless of the horrors of the deeds, for so very long they lasted.

And that had given credibility to the insensitive barbarity in burning, raping, doing anything, chaos was often the result from the deeds of the things humans believed in, as it was recently transparent in evidence, in the belief that an election was stolen.

And that was so wherever humans went, regardless of their culture or tradition, or even their literacy or their ignorance.

Human beings did the things they believed in whether or not they were ignorant or educated, and they did them without remorse or guilt, and yes they did them even for entertainment.

And they did them most of the time with or without consideration, often causing chaos and mayhem.

And whenever they did them for their pleasure, the more destructive they were, they felt better.

Realizing indeed that it really could, when they did what they believed, it made them feel good. And it mattered not how cruel it may be, that even life becomes secondary.

Quite often what people believe in were considered when making decisions.

Making decisions based on what they believe, often drifting away from reality.

Yes indeed taking a gamble, but that has always been the case in their daily struggle.

Humans took gambles all the time, it became the norm in their struggle to survive.

Unfortunately, that's how things were throughout human beings' development, that's how they have been, and they are still the same today, but perhaps not as barbaric as the dark days of yesterday.

But yes, people's beliefs to them were always important, especially that of religion, that even to save a life it made no difference if it was outside the creed of their religion.

As it is in the giving of blood, that's when a belief is tested for its weaknesses.

Allowing even one's own child to die when a transfusion of blood could have saved its life.

But that is what is their religious creed, that's what they believe; whatever it is, and not until they let go, they will believe it still; and to save a life, not a drop of blood they will ever give.

And that is because their belief is deeply rooted, very solid, and that's when it is unshaken, nay unbroken; indeed, some beliefs are firmly planted, and are not that easy to be uprooted.

So yes, beliefs will always continue to be inspiring, whether they are right or wrong.

Inspiring mankind to do things they should and should not do, but still with the choice to choose.

Things that are either right or wrong, in rituals, in revenge, or even just for the excitement.

And whether or not they are an offense, yet still people always did whatever they believe in, believing it gives them strength, and with the feeling it was the right thing.

But believing likewise knowing, they are both just functions of humans' nature.

Embedded in the development of mankind, to become a habit firm and solid in humans' behaviour.

And during their lifetime there are numerous things humans encounter and believe in.

Yes, things they have read, things they have heard, and things that were passed on to them bad and good.

Some they abandon on their way to the future, as they acquire knowledge and become a bit wiser. Others with time they travel on, passing from the previous to the next generation.

From the past to the present and unto the future, beliefs were passed on from one to the other.

Passing from parents to daughters and sons, especially beliefs rooted in religion, creating a strong family bond.

Intact with dogma and cultural norms, especially among those with little education.

And so beliefs once held by ancient humans, many today are still very common, still with roots deep in the past, buried deep down in the soil of tradition.

The feasting in ceremonies to honour the reaching of age, from boyhood to manhood, as well as from a girl to a woman.

That was something taken very seriously and traditionally celebrated, especially among cultures which held the belief that with the spirits of their ancestors they could engage.

So from generation to generation the culture was passed on, in an elaborate celebration to honour the occasion, crossing over the age barrier from minor to senior; from a boy to a man, and from a girl to a woman, and for the young achieving that status it was very important, it meant a great deal to them, it brought into their life a big difference.

And it was celebrated with superstitions too, that gave it credibility, importance, and a reason to continue as a necessary means of thanksgiving to the gods, for taking the young ones safely across.

Yes, for guiding them along their journey, and to continue to guide them safely.

But why was that seen to be so necessary, and by everyone within the community?

Perhaps it was just another occasion, an excuse for a celebration, just like any other situation.

Something to celebrate was always appreciated as an opportunity to communicate with the spirits.

Or perhaps maybe, there were some superstitions attached to the idea of social transformation, from dependence to independence.

But whatever was the idea, for the young ones crossing over, to them it made a lot of difference, their status was enhanced, more responsibilities they were given, treated like men and women, now they could be married and have children.

And so it was too with male circumcision, and of course with female mutilation, to the elders it was very important, a tradition never to be broken.

And although both were given at a youthful age, claims were made that they were for hygiene purposes, and yet in superstitions they had their roots deep down.

Yes indeed and for good reason, superstitions were always the cause whenever logic was lost, that as a fact has been endorsed.

261

But that did not really matter, no one cared to know, superstitions or not, what was important was their culture to follow.

And many celebrations that became the norm, from the womb of superstitions was how they were born.

Celebrating remembrances year after year, with all sorts of aberrant beliefs deeply rooted in events nations held dear.

Granting holidays to celebrate ancient beliefs they commemorate, beliefs which belong to the dark ages and have no present day usefulness.

And yet still humans celebrate them year after year, the superstitious celebrations were a very good idea.

A holiday to rejoice, without the superstitions it would have never come about.

And that kept superstitions alive, without the feasting they could have been demised.

And so it had been perhaps for centuries, the celebrations went on whatever was the belief. And regardless of the horrors in ritual formalities, year after year the celebrations continued in joviality, and especially among pliant families.

Embracing the past for a bit longer to last, with the belief that whatever was the cause for the celebrating purpose; it was good enough for the present generation, just as it was for their ancestors.

And that was what was hereditably passed on from one to the next generation.

Beliefs that should have been discarded, and scattered like dust in the wilderness.

Beliefs that should have been left buried in the sand or washed away in the oceans.

Beliefs that should not have lasted so long, but left forgotten in the past as mankind moved on.

Yes indeed, beliefs that belong to mediaeval humans, and should have gone to the grave with them.

But that was not always the case, and as it was but no disgrace, beliefs were passed on from generation to generation, moving with the pace in the rat-race, and sometimes on the capitalist's bandwagon.

Moving with the times instead of being left behind, whether they were ta-boos, myths, or superstitions.

And passing on again and again without any change, from parents to chil-dren it was always the same.

So beliefs continued for a long time to last, from one to the next each time it was passed.

With humans doing whatever they believe in, right or wrong, virtue or sin, that's the way humans were living.

Yes, it could be argued whether or not it is true, that it started in the homes beginning within the family, and outwardly within the community.

Where beliefs were passed on indiscreetly to each and everybody.

And with the fear of a parental watchful eye in sly focus upon every child.

Religious beliefs especially were passed on to each child in the family, as an essential moral gravity. Whatever religion was the parents, so too were the children, the salutary fruit with all its juice was passed on to them from their parents.

And with it was love and hate, depending upon the other person's race, some you love, some you hate, and that was believed and executed by many families, and it became a self-fulfilling fate with their god it's executive.

And so it was also with family rules, which everybody in the family fol-lowed, believing in the same things was an unwritten family value.

And executing deeds in accordance with beliefs that were a part of family life.

And those beliefs were values to follow, family values from yesterday, and for tomorrow.

Passing from one to the other, values that made no sense whatsoever.

And yet those values influenced lives, especially daughters including wives.

Yes indeed I will repeat, women have always been disadvantaged victims of beliefs, and in every country, and in every society, and often by every male in the family.

Something that developed during mediaeval times, and passed on from generation to generation, with roots deep down in the soil of religion; perhaps there is where it began, religion never encouraged equality for women, it was never a part of their sermon.

They all have unjustly treated women, which was mirrored as a precedent.

And their bad example took hold in homes, and went out into the world where for women it hardly ever did look good as things unfurled.

Beliefs in values that became a part of the family code of life, yet no one questioned whether they were wrong or right, or even if they were foolish or wise, or why they were to the disadvantage of daughters.

Treating women not as equals, but as dullards, or a bunch of flowers, always giving them a doll, and giving their brother a football.

Yes, treating their daughters always as someone beautiful and delicate, but mentally and physically ill, who must always depend either upon a husband, a father, a brother, or whoever was without a soul or interior.

And this belief developed with a mix of taboos, influencing women's lives to keep them under control, to the point of what they should and should not do, restricting their lives with bogus family values.

Creating an atmosphere of idiocy, heavily contaminated with ridiculous beliefs that were discriminatory in matters concerning women's role in society.

Beliefs that denied them their fundamental human rights, and oppressed and abused them right through their lives.

Their right to drive, to vote, to own property, to be accepted and treated equally; and to choose their own husband, even that fundamental freedom was taken away from them by their parents.

And also too, to be educated and employed in any capacity, beliefs had also denied them those opportunities, and sadly so it went on for centuries, as were many other beliefs which were within cultures and rooted deeply.

Believing that women must be always under a man's control, as their natural birth right place in the world.

And that disparity was made perfectly clear by a far right Polish Politician, a one-time member of the European Parliament, a leader of a nation, say no more, those are the kind always in leadership wherever you go.

Yes indeed, he believed that he was speaking for the majority when he stood up and declared with a voice of solidarity that women did not deserve equality, especially in salaries.

And that was because as he said; "women were weaker and less educated."

And that was something that men really believed in, affecting women throughout the world.

Affecting them in numerous ways, including their livelihood, which for no apparent reason was always better for boys than for girls.

And yes it may be true that women were less educated, but that was only because of how they were treated, not given the privilege to be educated, not given the same opportunities.

As it is still sadly happening today, women in many places are still not receiving equal pay, neither are they receiving their right of an education, there are those who still believe in some of the old traditions, and those who believe that it is against their religion.

According to their parents, guided by beliefs held for generations, finding a suitable husband in marriage was their priority; so to give their daughters an education was just a waste of time and money; it benefited nobody.

Indeed and most regretfully, reality was lost completely, hence, it was as if humans were crowned with stupidity, and most sadly, it was among parents especially.

And so it was believed and very strongly too, that what all daughters were supposed to know was only how to raise a family, be a good wife and keep their husbands happy.

That was tradition, it was the custom, it was a cultural belief executed by their great grand-parents, and even by those before them.

Yes indeed, it has been well established in several cultures as the norm, and for centuries so it was done, a tradition men said should not be broken.

So yes it was both in the home and in the workplace too, in fact everywhere the injustice to women continued day after day, and from year to year in cultures everywhere.

With deeds executed only from beliefs, and yet they kept women disadvantaged for centuries.

Even today, women are still exploited and paid less than men, yet they are expected to work as hard as they could, and to shoulder responsibilities more than they should.

A culture developed from the past, and yet it seems forever it may last.

But then again that has been rooted as a part of the system of capitalism, to enslave and to take advantage in whatever ways.

That's how capitalism has developed over the years, it is not a system that is fair.

Indeed, the system has been used to take advantage of workers; men, women and even children were normally treated as slaves, no more than objects exploited.

And it happened especially to women and children, they were exploited again and again, for centuries it has been happening, and it is still happening today, the end still appears to be far away.

And yet again, it was just about the same, the opinion from another politician, a US Congressman expressing his disparaging opinion about women.

In his wisdom, or maybe in the face of his stupidity, he credited rape and incest as acceptable normal contributions, to prevent a decline in the human population, that was the message from his misguided tongue flapping up and down.

That is what he believed, that is what he revealed, and perhaps that is how he would like it to be. But then again, believing is not a sin, human beings can believe anything, and that is exactly what they have been doing during their years existing.

And with believing anything and executing the deeds of their beliefs, which were in many cases deeds of savagery.

The world has developed not as it should be, but brimming with injustice and cruelty.

Yes brimming with beliefs with all sorts of persuasions, some good, some bad, some right, some wrong.

And when they are done, they cannot be undone, and history claims both the rights and wrongs.

So yes indeed that is so, it is what humans have been doing, during the many years they have been existing, during the many centuries without knowledge, during the years of superstitions and ignorance, humans believed whatever was in their imagination, and what they heard, and what they read, they believe things that don't even make sense.

Believing and doing some disgusting things, and doing them from year to year over and over again. And by both the illiterate and the educated, both believe in idiotic things.

And they executed deeds from what they believed, without credibility, nor a good reason.

But that mattered not, they have fulfilled their purpose, believing and doing is like thunder and lighting.

Indeed as I have written all along, humans believed in what they did, and they also did what they believed in, some with good, and some with bad intentions, and many were just what were passed on from previous generations, most made no sense at all, especially beliefs in the supernatural.

But whether or not they made any sense, the effects were still felt from the deeds executed.

Which could be something very good, indeed something useful, as well as something which is so very horrid, that there is no word to describe it in any language.

But whatever it was it didn't matter one way or the other, it made no difference whatsoever.

So yes indeed whatever humans believed, regardless of the nature of the deeds, to them their beliefs were as important as the air they breathe.

So yes indeed, beliefs made their lives worthwhile, something to live for and even to die.

And yes still humans carry on executing deeds of whatever they believe, and especially on anniversaries; it was the big time for excitement, time for exotic feasting, time for an embrace and a good cuddling, time to get on romancing.

Time for favours as well as revenge, whatever it was it made no difference.

Yes indeed, it was the time to communicate with ancestors, especially when in need of favours.

Time for dancing and prancing, and for getting drunk, and with the gods and goddesses to communicate, someone on your list to be punished with the effects of demonic curses.

Passing from generation to generation, beliefs with jovial celebrations, beliefs that were held for a very long time, some were held for centuries, especially those which brightened occasions with the madness of colourful and hectic celebrations; noisy crowds in very large numbers, all celebrating whatever it was that they believed in, without really knowing its purpose or meaning, but it mattered not, it changed nothing.

And as beliefs were and continued to be, to the disadvantage of women, as they emanate from male institutions.

Beliefs have always enslaved them, to an intolerable measure of injustice, physical abuses, exploitation, sexism, and prostitution; all those were situations radiated from a pool of beliefs held in societies for centuries, which opened up a reservoir of male consciousness, that women were objects to take advantage.

Taking advantage only because the victim was a woman, always accusing her of most things wrong.

And that's how it was, and how it still is today in several places, even in the first world advanced nations. Many beliefs are still very common, exposing women to disadvantages which make it harder in the world for them to live.

And easy targets for all sorts of taboos, and myths, women today still receive sexual abuses and harassment, and from place to place wherever they went.

And that behaviour inherited by new generations, from attitudes developed by mediaeval men.

Keeping women in their place simply meant, nothing more than to exploit and enslave them.

Persecuting women throughout their lives, with injustices, exploitation, and abuses, and of course no human rights.

And even today around the world in so many places, they are still denied equality in the workplace, and justice for them especially in cases of rape, is as alien as a two headed snake.

The law enforcement system means nothing to them, instead of listening to them as a victim with a complaint, too often the law represented by men harasses women with abusive questioning, making them the offending culprits.

Yes, making them feel not as the victim, but as a delinquent, the one to blame.

Yes indeed, the law institutions from top to bottom, for centuries they ignored the rights of women.

So yes indeed it was never easy growing up as a woman, that history has witnessed and recorded on every page during the existence of every generation.

And yes it is very true, and without an excuse, beliefs blighted women's entire life, from at home, male institutions, and wherever they went a code of beliefs enslaved them.

Just for a moment, take a minute and focus on a bit of history of the past; consider the fate of Joan of Arc just a few centuries ago.

She was betrayed and burnt alive at the stake after the French handed her over to the English. Yes indeed history has revealed that the English had accused her of being a witch; her predicament was very transparent, it was only because she was a woman.

Indeed, she did the impossible: she led a French army and defeated the English in battle, so she had to be a witch; otherwise she could not have done it, that's what they did believe, there was no other way that the French could have defeated the English.

'The French could have never defeated the English under normal circumstances.'

That's what the English said, and to that they all agreed with revenge in their heads.

So she was betrayed by the French, and the English took their revenge, they brought her life to a painful end, she was burnt at the stake, condemned as a witch.

And that would have never happened to a man, so are the disadvantages of women.

Oh yes indeed it is real, it has been happening all the time, women have been treated very unkindly.

From childhood to adult women were restricted and persecuted in and out of their homes, the evidence is in the history books.

Yes, in many cultures they were treated with little or no respect, women were harassed, raped, or beaten to death.

And that was because of what men believed and took for granted, a woman could not walk on the streets alone feeling safe, especially during the hours of darkness.

For centuries men committed wrongs against women and went unpunished, nourishing the idea that there were no consequences.

And that attitude was what developed, so the wrongs continued, they never stopped.

And that had made it easier for the abuses, and all the other offences to go without nemesis.

Yes indeed, and for many centuries it has been a conscientious belief that women were very easy targets, and as such they were disadvantaged.

Consciously or not, the attitude developed over the centuries as a cultural belief.

And women were treated as objects for male aggression, like rain to be showered upon them, and conscious of the fact they will get away with it, so men took unlimited advantages.

And although that happened frequently all the time, for centuries justice for women was continuously denied. It was always one too many, injustice to women was with impunity.

And that was why it was only women who were burnt alive on cremation pyres.

And as though that was not terrible enough, many were accused as witches and were burnt to death.

And for having sex with Satan the devil; how indeed was that ever possible?

And yet many were accused of the act, with no one doubting that.

And those who were accused, well, there was no excuse that could have saved them from the torment that was to be their punishment.

Women were always victims of many accusations, and especially those of fornication.

Someone only had to believe whatever was said, and the woman accused was arrested.

Indeed, all she had to do was to reject a man's advances, and for that she could be accused of being a witch, arrested and tortured for a confession, then burnt alive for her rejection.

Yes indeed, that's how bad things were for women, things may have changed, but they have not yet been brought to an end; women are still disadvantaged in this modern day and age.

Indeed they are still forced into prostitution, and as sex slaves, paid low wages, exploited, frequently raped, and ignored by the police.

And with no end in sight to the unjustified disadvantages of women, the injustices just keep on brimming, and woe to the woman caught in the wrong place, if she is not harassed, she may be raped.

Indeed, although on most occasions the accusations that were brought against women were that of beliefs and without evidence.

Still it made no difference, they were arrested and tortured into making forced confessions.

Giving credibility to the belief that the devil was capable, and often did have sex with women for favours especially for their children.

What an absurdity that was believed, that the devil as a spirit, or in flesh as a human, came to earth to have sex with women. Is there no sex in hell? No pretty women?

But really, is the devil in need of sex? Stupidity indeed has no limits.

But perhaps it could be said that having sex with the devil was just an excuse, something which could be used against a woman to accuse.

Indeed, and without being biased, some beliefs were just laughable and ridiculous, as much as they were impossible, and yet the response in deeds executed were inhumanely terrible.

So yes it may be true that perhaps the belief in having sex with the devil was just an excuse to justify the means to execute.

Something which could never be proved, so the accused had no excuse, guilty was the only truth.

So yes indeed, it is never hard to believe that in those days ignorance was what humans breathed, it was so deadly, longevity was no guarantee, the average life expectancy was no more in years than thirty or forty.

And as this cowardly aggression continued against women, from culture to culture everywhere.

They were the ones who were stoned to death, because their fornication was a threat.

They were the ones forced into loveless marriages, and abused at home by their husbands and relatives.

They were the ones who secretly suffered into submission to genital mutilation, and by no other, but by their parents, a family member, or a friend.

Who believed not that they were doing something disgusting and inhumanely wrong, something which was offensive to women.

But something that was beneficial to their daughter as she advanced towards the future, with the intention to secure a husband; indeed, the holy grail of ignorance.

And that was what made it so much more painfully wrong, everyone actually believed they were right, so it had to be done; giving rise to an endless flow of genital mutilation which found its way even today among the new generations, still doing the horrors of their great grandparents, believing with the past they must conform.

And as painful as it is, just because it was a long held tradition, just because it was what was done by their great grandparents who indeed had no education, they felt that they had no route of escape from this inveterate popularization, so again, and still deep in silence, daughters are victims to this painful mutilation.

Yes unfortunately, women have been unfairly persecuted throughout history by generations that came and went, and the roots of this evil kept on spreading and getting more entangled with taboos, myths and superstitions.

Indeed, the disadvantages were so deeply rooted that even parents were just as bad with and without excuses, under their protection their daughters were still disadvantaged, and even suffered family abuses.

Yes it is true no need to argue, women were disadvantaged by their own parents, and family members, by institutions, and even religion, and not forgetting the law, that in particular made them feel insecure.

So yes indeed, that's how they did feel, too often their complaints were disregarded, not getting the protection they needed, just wasting police time, that's what the police believed.

Sending the wrong message to the public, that they could abuse women and get away with it. And that was exactly what was believed, and it was the cause of many wrongful deeds.

And that was because too often when women complained, they were either ignored, or simply rejected.

And that attitude was taken for granted, as the right way a woman should be treated.

And as they lived their lives as victims of taboos, myths, and omnifarious beliefs.

They were the ones right through their lives denied their basic human rights, equal privileges and opportunities.

And yet many of those beliefs are still executed today, although there have been some changes. After so many centuries with progressives changes, women are still not equally treated around the world in many places.

They are still very much disadvantaged, and suffer undeserving conse-quences.

And all to do with beliefs of some sort or another, deeply rooted and firmly established in the norms of cultural behaviour.

Firmly established centuries ago, wrongs that became common practice with women as obvious targets.

And that was taken for granted right through the ages, myths and taboos were to women's disadvantage, and that was the package from the past which the present inherited, a package full of disadvantages.

So yes indeed, traditional beliefs throughout the ages created divisions with disadvantages, and women always got the worst of it.

Some were the cause of hearts broken, or deep in sorrow they were left swollen.

Believing a woman must not be equally treated, that's how the world has developed to be, and in many places today it is still the same, places submerged in sin.

And after so many centuries this wound still hasn't fully healed, women are still suffering the aches and pains from a contagious sexist disease.

A disease created by men, and although it may not have been intentionally done, yet still they all reap the benefits of their wrongs.

And with no desire for a cure whatsoever, it seems very clear that men don't really care.

Things are in their favour. So why bother? Do men really want things for women to be better?

If that was the case, it could have been done very much sooner, indeed, women can't wait any longer, they could no more endure the pressure, for far too long, injustice they suffered.

And that may be because of long held cultural beliefs that were the seeds sowed for centuries, seeds that each generation reaped, from directly beneath their feet.

And which became part of cultural life, taken for granted whether wrong or right.

And that was so even among the influential and the educated, disparaging women was what men did, both in high and low places.

As was a Catholic Arse-bishop residing in Spain, he voiced his bigoted opinion to his spiritual gathering which was listening attentively to him.

In a speech he was making, or perhaps a sermon he was preaching from his sacred pulpit within the holy church.

He said to the gathering, that 'wives should obey or face a beating,' that was the kind of sermon he was preaching, and to the many who stared at him, in belief with what he was saying.

Yes, those were the words of an Ass-bishop, from within the church, and right from the top.

Expressing clearly his pejorative belief, in the subordination of women and how they should be treated.

Not as equals, but perhaps as domestic slaves, not to be respected, but to be beaten and humiliated.

But this is sadly already the case in many cultures worldwide, cultures with their roots in religion stretching for miles.

A culture from the past arrived into the present, with all the colours of enslavement, and to this day it has survived.

So yes indeed, domestic abuse is a worldwide problem, a problem that appears to have no end.

And ignored by both state and religion, that's why indeed it has lasted so long.

Both have shut their eyes, both have refused to criminalise the injustices women suffered throughout their lives.

Yes indeed, women were whipped, both private and in public, and even as victims of rape, for having sex, not within a marriage but outside it.

She was accused, she was blamed, everyone believed she was the one who committed the sin, and the whipping was done in Allah's name.

So yes indeed, it cannot be doubted that unfairness and injustice have been a woman's endless predicament, and it has often been so even from the most caring of men, from institutions, and even religion.

With excuses taken from the Koran, men claimed a mandate to discriminate, and abuse women.

Indeed, women have always been victims of unjust persecution, for centuries they suffered in silence.

And even today, after thousands of years of our species' existence, in a world that has been progressing and changing all the time.

Women are still victims of superstitions, victims of taboos and myths, and it appears for them there is no escape.

Yes victims of beliefs that drag them tangled in chains, beliefs that curse them as a good for nothing, beliefs that condemned them to abuses and beatings, and to forcefully marry their rapist, indeed, that too has been the norm in some places.

Yes indeed, and most regretfully, many wrongs especially to women were justified as rights, so they were committed all the time, no redress, no crime.

As it happened in Nicaragua, a young woman was stripped naked and thrown into a fire, by a mob of catholic fanatics.

Who for some reason, and again it was nothing more than their beliefs, they believed the young woman was possessed by the devil.

And that they said, 'it was better she was dead, than to be possessed by the devil from hell.'

So they did what they did, and without any consequences, no one did anything about it.

And that is the problem with the world's justice systems, with their eyes shut they are indifferent to women's problems, in short, they couldn't care a damn.

And yet despite all this wickedness to women, they are the ones who men are so desperately dependent upon, for their services and as companions.

And yet still they treat women no more than slaves who must obey and serve.

And their services are always taken for granted as some sort of duty expected within the community serving everybody.

Yes they serve and never get what they deserve, they are the ones doing the dirty work.

And that's how it has been throughout history, time can tell, although perhaps some things may have changed, but several things which many people believe in most of them remain the same.

Indeed, in this progressive day and age, in several places women are still very badly treated. They are still at a disadvantage to beliefs which are very strong, so the wrongs continue against them with everyone showing indifference.

And as women continue to be badly treated, no one seems to know the reason.

And no one can explain the root cause of this impediment, this endless injustice to women.

But maybe it is just what has developed over centuries, as it happens each day again and again.

Spreading its roots ever so widely, everywhere it was the same.

Today it was this, and tomorrow it was that, both were taken for granted.

Humans moved on with no looking back, and in that situation women got trapped.

Yes this situation has been going on for far too long, passed on from generation to generation. Passing as rights instead of wrongs, and that may be why nothing was done.

Yes, it is very true no need to argue, women have suffered and continue to suffer physical abuses, prejudices, injustice, degradation, discrimination, and from each day to the next, and in both first and third world communities, equality is not yet a level playing field.

There are still too many bumps, too many ups and downs, there is still a lot to be done.

And that has been so because the roots of this evil which had entered and spread within the soil of medieval cultures, got entangled with a web of beliefs that were taken for granted for centuries.

And for no apparent reason, so they were never forgotten, hence the wrongs of yesterday like a bad apple, made today and tomorrow rotten.

And that has been so in many places where you go, and it is still happening today, and maybe tomorrow.

And into the future it may still continue, executing deeds from irrational beliefs in superstitions, myths, and taboos.

And as long as nothing is done to right those wrongs, and they are left to continue to be so, then women would still be unjustly treated in the world wherever they go.

There would be no end to it, as there will be no forgiveness, not until the beliefs are fully discarded, and women receive their deserving justice.

But in this world of corrupt practices, it was not only women who were targeted as victims of beliefs enduring disadvantages.

Minorities too were often targeted, they were accused and abused, for reasons supported only from beliefs; evidence was never a required need.

Believing they were the cause for whatever wrong it was, wherever there was trouble, there were the foreigners.

And if they were not causing trouble they were pinching jobs, or cheating the systems, or creating slums lowering standards.

Yes, there was always something people believed in, something to degrade minorities.

Something to their disadvantage, to impede their courage, and even to get them enraged.

So yes, Jews in particular, they were accused for whatever, and they paid with their lives, even for someone else's crime.

And the same was the fate of black minorities, they were often scapegoats for atrocities.

Yes indeed, they only had to be in the wrong place at the right time, and that got them arrested and blamed for the crime.

Only to be persecuted in some way or the other, thousands were condemned to slave labour.

And that was because of the beliefs held against blacks and Jews, beliefs that condemned them as victims for abuse.

Beliefs that were passed from one generation to the next as contributions supporting injustice.

Injustice to Jews, minorities, women and children, injustice no one would prevent, or even make an attempt to stop it from happening.

So yes indeed, injustice has been a side effect of beliefs, in fact it still very much is.

And very often it was very cruel that even murders were committed without consequences.

And yes of course, during the difficult period of world wars, Jews were even accused of creating capitalism, and using it to exploit women and children.

And that was because Jews were affluent, they knew how to make good use of the system.

And that had intensified the hate and bigotry, especially because wherever Jews were, they were seen to be an affluent minority which ignited the flames of jealousy.

A minority that had no right to be affluent, so what they had was stolen from them.

And that was believed to be justified, in policies that made it right.

Policies that were rigidly enforced, to annihilate the Jews at any cost.

Yes indeed, it was very sad, painful, and regretful, beliefs did a great deal of damage especially when they were taken for granted.

Destroying lives, destroying families, and even sometimes whole communities; with deeds wrongfully executed, inspired only from what was believed in.

So yes indeed, unfortunately, lives were often claimed because of what people believed in, many were victims buried in graves.

Indeed it had been so in the past and in the present, it had been so throughout humans' development.

And that was in evidence, the many who were killed including millions of Jews denied the right to survive, and even the right to be alive.

It was an ideology, a premise of importance, with beliefs that were very strong.

And although without logic, it mattered not, most beliefs are just like that.

And that was done more often in the name of politics and religion, supported with policies that created divisions.

And where there were divisions, there were always suspicions, generating beliefs tainted with fear, and all sorts of antisocial problems with disturbances year after year.

Yes indeed, even problems that were the cause of wars, problems of which superstitions were the cause, problems that made no sense at all, problems that politics and religion couldn't be bothered to solve, problems they ignored and left to take their course.

And after the damages were already done, that's the time when they realised that they had problems.

And because human beings believe in whatever it is, whenever they were executing deeds, they hardly hesitated.

They just get on with it, especially beliefs with something to celebrate, for such occasions they couldn't wait.

And the reason for that was the feeling they got, feeling they were doing what was right. Feeling good inside, no need to lie or to hide, no cause for regrets or remorse, humans did what they believed in, no need for rational thinking, it never changes anything, good or bad, right or wrong, whatever it was had to be done.

So yes humans destroyed lives by the millions in wars, and in slavery, in serfdom, imprisonment, and even as guinea pigs in experiments.

Yes some lives were even threatened with accusations that were lies, and when lies were believed, consequences could be vile.

Consequences that were not always just a threat, but sometimes delivered with death, which was commonly executed as a means of redress.

Committing murder in revenge, although the accused was innocent, but that was not what anyone believed, so no guilt was felt, no sleep lost, no troubled conscience, no remorse.

Yes indeed, it is as true as it is, beliefs were often threatening, even when they were false, they were what people believed in, and they couldn't care a damn if they were wrong. They just did what had to be done, especially whenever they were persuaded by someone, they got agitated and committed wrongs.

They believed he stole it, or perhaps she did; they believe he is having an affair, or perhaps she is, pointing their fingers at blame, although they are not certain, and yet with a readiness to commit sin, to inflict severe pain.

Yes indeed, it has always been the same, beliefs could be convincing and persuasive, with false accusations often made, and the consequences very grave.

Indeed, whatever humans believe is what they don't know, and that's the big problem, they are never sure, and yet still it is what they ignore, punishing the innocent as they did before.

Again and again they did the same, it never stopped them from taking revenge, and they assaulted the wrong person once again, and only because of what they believed in, whether or not it was convincing.

Unfortunately and sad to say, that's how the world has developed as it is today, human beings often believe anything, and most of the time without even thinking.

Right through the ages, despite the progress human beings were making, always in the same direction they were heading.

And with beliefs that became cultural norms, with deeds executed that had no legs to stand on, except of course the wobbly legs of suspicions and superstitions.

Superstitions that were irrational and barbaric, and yet they were what humans believed was what the gods wanted.

So they did what they did in offerings to the gods, or for whatever was the purpose.

And it was that which kept them on their evil path, afraid to let go, afraid to make a new start.

And so it has been, whatever human beings believed in, it was always to them the right thing.

So having a desire to do what was right, it was wrong they did, and when they realised what they did, it was much too late.

But that made no difference, they did what they believed in, and whether or not it was right or wrong, they felt no guilt for what they had done.

So with their conscience clear they did the same things again, just because it's what they believe in.

But not all beliefs, although they were many, were superstitiously tainted with blood in sacrifices. Not all were horrid deeds executed in rituals, inflicting death in cold blooded murders.

And not all beliefs were disadvantageous to women, some indeed were very good to them.

And some again were very rewarding, you hit the Lotto Jackpot with the numbers you believe in.

Yes indeed, you believed the numbers you dreamt would win, so you put your bet in, and towards the bank you were heading, smiling.

And as believing is something people will always be doing right through their life.

Since it is impossible for people to know everything, some things they doubted, some they believed in.

And what they believed, sometimes they were very useful, and led to success even though the odds had appeared to be very doubtful.

And in their pursuits, they accomplished things which they did not know, but they believed in.

Making good use of what they believed, they succeeded as much as they achieved.

Indeed, the measure of their success was often very impressive, and yet inspired only by what they believed in.

So yes, indeed it could definitely lead to success in what you believe, even though you didn't know.

But then again, it is always a chance you are taking, whenever you believe in anything.

And as a chance it is a gamble that can lead to success, failure, or trouble.

Because when you believe, whatever it is, you still don't know, and that is the gamble, because you are never quite certain how things will go.

So you can lose as well as win, whenever you believe in anything, because it is a gamble you are taking.

And as a gamble you are never certain, so you cannot guarantee what it will be.

And as mankind continued to develop the world, year by year and century after century, progressing and advancing steadily.

Creeping slowly from one age to the next, with the things they created making progress.

And with their beliefs all taken to the future, passed from one generation to the other.

Beliefs that were absolutely ridiculous, and yet to some people advantageous, but whatever they were, from the old unto new generations they were contagiously passed on.

Some dating back from the superstitious darkness of woeful times, and passed on again and again many times.

Traveling with the times from the past to the present, the journey of superstitions has not yet reached its final end.

Indeed, humans still embrace superstitions today, they seem to need it for some reason.

And as they differ from culture to culture, with differences in some way or the other.

Each culture with their own beliefs held dearly, and celebrated on anniversaries.

Giving reverence to gods and goddesses, and even to the spirits of friends, and relatives.

Yes, in anniversaries that came and went, bringing with them only excitement and no enlightenment.

So in that same direction still, humans kept on developing, always drifting from the past into the present with new ideas and inventions.

And towards the future still heading, with their package of beliefs tightly held neatly in storage in their heads.

With each nation racing along, as if with each other they are in a competition.

Still doing some of the things that were done in the past, those that seem forever they may last.

Doing whatever humans knew or believed in, and with the same confidence they did both things.

And since knowledge was still not yet easily available, to believe was the next choice reasonable, and that was accepted at every stage in life as the only choice that could have been made that was wise.

So yes, if you listen carefully again, 'I believe' was what you heard many times every day, and from every person on their way.

From the man on the street, to the man in the pulpit from where he preached, 'I believe' is what he keeps on repeating, each time it is something different he says he believes in.

I believe in this, I believe in that, always something else they believe in, their brain becomes a storage full of crap, no need to think about that.

So yes, to know something, that's when you are certain, and that's the moment when you are educated, indeed, you have got knowledge.

But when you believe, you are stuck in the middle, drifting between certainty and doubt.

Stirring in your head a mix of confusion, don't know the cause of the altercation.

And that is because whenever you believe, you are always with doubt, and yes indeed troubled with uncertainty, troubled with not knowing what it could be.

Can't rest, can't sleep, not knowing what is false or true, not knowing the cause nor what to do, each turn in bed troubles you.

But to know, that is something else, it is a function positively unique and reliable.

There is no room for doubt whenever you know, it is solid and undeniable.

Yes it may bring you joy or it may bring you sorrow, but it is the truth, that you know.

Just like seeing, which is knowing, and that's when you remember, that's when you feel bad or better, there is no doubt whatsoever, and because you know, many things you can avoid, no need to take a gamble to find out.

So yes indeed, you cannot be fooled whenever you know, because whenever you know whatever it is, you are very certain that it is so.

So yes indeed doubt is lost, and from uncertainty you are divorced.

But it is when you do not know that's when you believe, there is no reliability, and you are left to guess what it will be.

You are left with doubt and uncertainty, disappointed that you may have lost an opportunity, but the fact still is, you don't know, so you are left in a state of limbo.

Yes, you are left depressed, you are left in a mess, you just don't know what to do for the best.

And that has always been a precarious predicament, when humans don't know they often make bad judgements.

Yes indeed, when humans are not sure, that's when they are cautious and hesitant, and that's when they make bad decisions, something which they do most of the time during their progressive development.

And regardless of whatever it may be, be it creeds, dogmas, ideologies, a lie, a joke, or just bedside stories.

When you don't know that's when you believe, and that's when you are often left deceived.

And that is very common in daily life, human beings are more foolish than wise.

They are deceived a lot of the time, believing in things they should decline.

And even sometimes getting themselves into trouble, believing that they were capable in their belief-bubble.

When the true fact was that they were not, and the problem they caused, cost them a lot.

But human beings whenever they are in a desperate need to achieve, regardless of whether they are right or wrong.

They very often assumed to be right in whatever they believed, and would trample good reasoning to the ground; don't want to know that they are wrong.

They would not listen to good reasoning, regardless of whether it made good sense.

They stubbornly just don't want to know, whatever they believe they would not let go, right or wrong they are holding on, and sometimes not even after they were convinced with proof that they were wrong, hell bent, they are stubborn.

So yes, their stubbornness often led to side effects, claiming lives in innocent deaths, inviting injustice, intimidation and threats, what they believe is what gets them in a mess.

And it was still in that direction the world was moving on, heading towards the future with whatever were the pros and cons.

But then human beings had nowhere else to go, that was the only direction in which to follow.

And that led to no other, but straight down the line; the winding line of time where terror and pleasure await their visitor.

So humans never strayed away on their journey, regardless for whatever reason, neither were they in any doubt that when they got to the future things would work out.

Yes, they always believe in that, but never know it as a fact.

Still it was towards the future humans were always heading, right through their lives to get to the future was their aim, any other direction led only to a grave which someone was already digging with a spade.

Yes, and taking with them whatever they knew, and what they believed in, many which were superstitions, and passed on from the old to the young generations, indoctrinating them to the mystical world of the supernatural where all things were invisible and spiritual.

And with so many wrongs believed to be right, and sustained as traditional norms in daily life.

Wrongs that were taken for granted and coupled with superstitions, with family values and of course with religion.

Wrongs coupled with capitalism, racism, sexism, discrimination, and divisions, or whatever were the wrongs that had caused the altercations.

In fact, wrongs that were coupled with wrongs, few things were right when many were wrong.

And that's how the word was developing, each year the same, doing the same wrongs over and over again, until whenever they were corrected, it mattered not how long they lasted.

Whether or not it was believed to be the right thing, humans did them still, unerring.

But that was the nature of human beings, wherever they were it was the same, they held onto their beliefs and wouldn't let go, whether they were wrong or right, they didn't want to know, to get them to change their minds, impossible.

They would trade reasoning just to believe in something; they couldn't be bothered to reason; it wouldn't change anything.

And given the choice humans would not reason at all, considering it to be a waste of time, as there was nothing that could be said to change their minds, yes they would listen to opinions, and yet still they will not change their minds, nothing would change what they already believed in, what they believed sunk right in, stuck in their brain.

Because what they believed in made good sense to them, and according to their judgement, there was nothing beyond the Commandments, ten.

So for this folly mankind paid a heavy price, they lost their way to paradise.

And that was because they refused to know, refused to be convinced, standing firm in what they believed in.

Because what is the truth if they did know, what they believed in they would have to let go.

And that may bring not joy but sorrow, so they prefer not to know, believing that the truth was impossible, so to reason they wouldn't listen.

And although they were told time and time again, yet still hardly ever they were listening, nor did for a moment their weary ears strain.

And that was because they didn't want to know about anything that may influence a change in what they already believed in, that to them was most compelling.

And when they acted upon their beliefs, that's when they committed many wrong deeds.

But to them it didn't matter at all, right or wrong, in one way or the other things had to be done.

And with that attitude humans were easily deceived, since they didn't want to know, nor to reject what they believed.

They kept it in them for as long as they could, although it was something they hardly understood.

But they believed it nonetheless, and they felt much better when what they believed was believed by at least someone else.

Yes indeed, beliefs shared had the effect of a shared piece of bread.

It bonded people together, people with common beliefs always get on better.

But beliefs were not only about the colour of history, associated with primitive and illiterate man.

Yes indeed, beliefs have taken humans to the bottom of the ocean, in search of treasure deep beneath the waves motion.

And only because they believed that treasure was there deep down below, although they did not really know, but the evidence was compelling, so they had to go.

And even into the peacefulness of outer space, in their search for Aliens, or another human race, which human beings believe exist.

But some say that they know that they do exist, like ghosts in the skies, they saw them with their own eyes, appearing, and for a time in the skies they remained, then they disappeared as swiftly as lightning.

And yes, into the dark corners of the world, in their search for black gold, because humans believed it was there under the earth, so they sent their drills deep down in search.

Oh yes indeed, there were many things humans felt very certain about, they believed in them without any doubt, and with success they found out.

So yes, they were successful in many of their pursuits, as well as failures and disappointments too.

Believing in things and pursuing them could be very rewarding in the end, because not all beliefs are misleading, you could be right or wrong like guessing.

So yes it is absolutely certain, belief is about all sorts of things, it is about all events and non-events, it is about the future, the past and the present.

It is about anything you are told, and even what you were not told, but just what you imagine.

And yes, it is about heaven and even hell, and so too it is about the living and the dead.

And about the afterlife somewhere to dwell, and about the weird stories daddy may tell.

And about the predictions of Nostradamus, recorded or not in history books.

And about gods, goddesses, ghosts, and evil spirits, demons, monsters, and mythical beasts, ancestors, witches, snakes, wizards, and vampires.

And yes it is about flying cockroaches, and the noisy parties on the beaches.

And the infamous vampires, a belief like many others which generated fear for years especially among the advanced cultures.

You may remember the infamous name Dracula, a living dead bloodsucker.

People did all sorts of things to protect themselves from being bitten and becoming vampires; that was indeed something they dread.

So they dug up graves of those buried and believed to be vampires, removed their bodies and chopped off their heads to be burnt to ashes to sprinkle around their houses.

And their hearts which were not spared, they were cut out and eaten raw, that was the cure to secure protection from the bloodsucking vampires' jaws.

Yes that's what history recorded that people did, that's what they believed would keep them safe and secure from the vampires' jaws; indeed, beliefs had no boundaries.

So yes, whatever it was and however weird, human beings everywhere, in every culture, did things to protect themselves from the evil forces of hell.

Yes indeed, from vampires, demons, evil spirits, witches, curses, or whatever it was that they were afraid of.

Indeed, there were all sorts of remedies, whatever people could imagine would protect them from evil forces; a mix of herbs, oils, animals' poo, blood and bones, their body parts, and even prayers.

Indeed nothing was too vile, nothing was disgusting, whatever it was, protection was king.

Yes, people did whatever they believed had powers of protection from the spirit world of demons.

There was no knowledge of anything, they were all what people believed in.

And it was very real, fear was no stranger, it was always there during those years of the supernatural with evil forces everywhere.

And without protection you could have been a victim of Satanic demons with your life turned upside down.

So yes people did the things they believed in, whatever made them feel secured and safe.

Indeed, they did all sorts of things, for their protection they would have tried anything, that's what humans do whenever they believe, not knowing whether it was false or true, not knowing what to believe or what to do, so they try to be safe, to be protected, to be out of the reach of evil forces.

As was the poisonous snake in your wardrobe that was not really there.

A joke that made you very scared and frozen stiff with fear.

So yes indeed what you did believe, your emotions change, scared for noth-ing, worried, or in joviality, whatever was your emotion you were deceived, and that was because you believed.

So the reality is that you did believe, and because you didn't know, you were scared, and that's because you believed it was there, a belief that trans-formed your emotions into fear.

So yes, beliefs are about truths as well as lies; and both have effects upon your emotions, delivering fear or jubilations.

As it is believed in the powers of the river Gangee, where people cramp together joyfully to wash their body.

Believing they are washing away their sins, and then off they went to get dirty with sins again.

And so too it is about the predictions hidden in their horoscope, where eve-ryone searches for answers in accordance with their birth.

And about what happened and did not happen, it is about everything and anything, it is about the end of the world and its beginning.

The dinosaurs, some with and some without claws, whatever humans be-lieved, they broke no laws, unless they committed wrong deeds whatever the cause.

So yes, beliefs are about the big bang too, and about universal development, evolution, and about fatalism, pancosmism, monogenesis, monotheism and polytheism, and of course asceticism and perdition; and especially about religions, every one of them, the dogma they preach, false or true, and about their influence in moral and spiritual guidance, and about their corruption too, the many children they abused, not forgetting the many good things they may have done, inspired from the teachings of religion.

And whatever it was that humans believed in, it was always the same, it was only about what mankind did not know, and that will never change, it will always be so wherever you go.

So yes indeed, there was never any doubt that some beliefs were very troubling with deeds that were inhumane, some today people still believe in them, and some for the truth humans are still searching.

Indeed, they are still searching for humans' origin, whatever they found they were never certain, and that's how human beings remain, still in doubt, not quite sure how the universe came about.

Yes, that has baffled humans more than anything else, the creation of the universe, humans, and life in general.

Yes indeed, it has baffled especially the educated in their desperate search for knowledge.

Some believe that God created humans in his own image, some believe humans evolved from apes.

Some believe that humans developed from Extraterrestrial creatures who came to earth from above.

Indeed they believe in Alien cultures, a civilisation they said existed maybe before, or alongside the dinosaurs, or perhaps not that very long ago, but they did exist, that's what they believe, since they don't really know.

Yes indeed the evidence has been discovered in the structures Aliens have built, and still exist in several places.

Structures humans could not have built, not during those times, human beings who may have been existing had not the knowledge or the skills to build such structures which were purposely in alignment with the stars as a means to communicate with the gods.

And that was indeed very important because from the gods came everything; sunlight, thunder, lightning, and rain.

Yes, lost civilisations that existed thousands of years ago, civilisations that came from the stars in the form of Extraterrestrials, and other weird looking visitors.

Yes indeed, for some weird reason, there are people who really believe that their ancestors were Extraterrestrials.

And yet they are no different from other humans, perhaps we are all from Aliens.

Indeed, humans believe that the truth may be hidden in their theories, and in desperation they search for the truth, not ever knowing exactly where to look.

But with determination humans are still searching, don't know what to believe in, only hoping that with the bones, the artefacts and ancient writings and drawings carved upon stones of mediaeval buildings, the truth of humans' origin will eventually one day be found, and spread as common knowledge among humans.

Yes it is true that the past has kept its secrets hidden, as though from humans they were forbidden, and left us all always guessing.

But some have been found by humans digging, some are still hidden buried in the earth, some in an unknown language are carved upon stones, and as they lay in silence, humans dig in search.

But none that has been found has not yet revealed all the secrets of the knowledge of the origin of human beings.

So disappointed but not yet discouraged, human beings believe they must carry on searching.

Searching for truth to eradicate beliefs, indeed, it is better to know than to believe.

So yes, that's what happens when you believe, you are scared of being deceived.

You never know exactly what to expect, nor with what numbers to place your bet, or where exactly to look for the truth.

The numbers you believe will win, most of the time they never do, and the place where you looked for the truth, you were disappointed with that too.

But although you believe that you cannot win, yet you still continue to place a bet again, hoping to walk to the bank with a grin.

And 'why?' that you did because of what you knew, that believing you cannot win, that was something that was never certain, so you just kept on trying again until at last you really did win, and towards the bank you made haste with your grin, couldn't care less about anything.

And that is how it is with what is expected, whatever humans believe in.

They believe it to be so, and refuse to know, always afraid that what they believe in, they may have to let it go.

And this is because although they do not know, they still feel certain and confident with what they believe in.

And so it is true, it has been proved that beliefs can be reliable too, but sadly to say you still do not know.

And when you do not know you can never be certain, and that's when doubt steps in.

Yes, doubt is often on your mind, although absent sometimes, and that's the moment when, although you don't know, you still feel certain about whatever you believe in, it gives you a feeling somewhat nerve-racking, as you try to figure out what you believe in.

Feeling certain with no doubt at all, and yet still disappointment is sometimes the result.

You are never sure what is the best thing to do, and what is right, you don't have a clue.

Yet still despite this fact, beliefs are often given credit, and even in undeserving cases. Beliefs are often credited with more certainty than doubt, especially when, whatever it is, it is frequently talked about.

And that is often gossip, people believe it, the more something is talked about, there is little doubt.

Accusing someone for doing wrong just because many others believe he did, and the evidence is decisive.

Believing in whatever was the hearsay, as it drifts in the wind day after day.

And that for people was the sensible thing to do, since it was hearsay and the gossip every day, then it must be true, and fair to say that's okay.

So their knowledge remains in what they believe in, since there is nothing that they really know.

And that of course could be very confusing, making matters even worse.

And because they believe instead of knowing, then of course they are never certain of the reality showing.

And because they are not certain that is when they hesitate, and when it was done whatever it was, it was done a bit too late.

But this is a fact that the people should know, and never forget wherever they go.

Believing and knowing are two separate things, and so they will always remain.

It is like superstitions and knowledge, one you believe, and the other you know.

And that is something that would never change, regardless of wherever you go.

And those two are never partners but are always separated like the darkness and the light; or be it even black and white, it is always one or the other, just like wrong and right.

Therefore people should never think that they know everything whenever they believe anything, regardless how sure they may feel; this is the human psyche's Achilles' heel.

And that is because many human beings have grieved, when it was revealed that they have been deceived, what they believed was not real.

And because believing is a function that leaves people uncertain, not knowing whether it is true or false.

To believe in God or anything at all, there is where you are left uncertain, you are left confused and troubled with doubt, the certainty in truth you are left without.

So what kind of a world humans have today, after existing for thousands of years?

Two thousand years after Christ came, and several more before he did.

How much about themselves do humans know, and also about nature and the universe?

How much knowledge have they gathered from mother earth, during their desperate and relentless search?

And how much human beings do not know, but they believe, from the things they have heard and from what they read?

What is the measure of the reality of their knowledge, and that of their beliefs?

Which of the two they value the most, and which to them is most important?

It may be true, or it may be unfair to say that people know less than what they believe.

Indeed, there is still so much to know, and so little is known, and yet despite this lack of knowledge, it is having pleasure, and not acquiring knowledge, that humans are more concerned with.

But whether they know more, or they know less, if what they believe is correct, then they have no cause to regret.

Yet still too often many things happened, and are simply left unraveled.

And that was because no one knew what the cause was, and neither what they should believe.

There had been too many different opinions, all tangled up into confusion, making them difficult to understand.

So yes the questions remain, after many years they still are the same.

What kind of a world has today inherited from yesterday's nobles, scholars and peers?

What kind of a world have they created and developed, from their acquired knowledge, and what they believed in over the years?

And from whatever they believed in, right or wrong, believing what they did had to be done.

Wrongs which they have done and passed on from yesterday to today.

Wrongs that were not wanted, and yet a heavy price paid.

Yes indeed, wrongs that made the world a place no better, and it could have certainly done without such untidy litter.

Scattered all over the world here, and here, today, yesterday's litter is seen everywhere.

So indeed, after existing for so many centuries, the same questions are still without answers, and are still being asked once again, perhaps this time someone can explain.

How much more knowledgeable have humans become? How much wiser are they today?

What have they learned from their years of experience stretching right back from medieval times?

Passing litter through the ages despite the development stages, yes that's what they did.

Passing superstitions and knowledge, passing whatever they had to give, from the past it's what the present inherits, and that's what makes it as it is.

So what is the choice of humans today in this developed technical age?

What in their heads should they lay to dwell superstitions or knowledge?

That is the choice they would have to make as they progress with development.

Both appear at the moment to be at equilibrium, together they dwell in humans' minds.

Yes, there are still too many things humans believe in, can't find the answers in history books, they can't find them anywhere regardless wherever they look.

And despite the truths in knowledge which human beings have found from nature's secrets dug from out of the ground.

After such a very long time in existence acquiring knowledge and experience.

What is humans' intention, to know or to believe, reality or fiction? What is their preference?

Is mankind to remain a creature superstitious, still foolish, selfish and callous, as were his medieval ancestors?

Still wicked, sinful, and unjust, taking wrongs for granted, as well as superstitions, taboos and myths, and executing irrational deeds in sacrifices to gods and goddesses in the belief that's how things will be achieved.

Deeds that were medieval and fiendish, deeds associated with taboos and myths.

Deeds that were common practice during ancient times of little knowledge.

Deeds that became the norm, although they were very wrong, yet still they were done.

So is it still in that direction mankind should carry on?

After many centuries in darkness without knowledge, is mankind still to remain foolish?

Or, should humans grasp at knowledge and create a paradise that is theirs?

Knowing quite well what is wrong and what is right, and not to be guided by superstitions, threading in darkness instead of light.

Indeed, this has been customary throughout many centuries especially at anniversaries, human beings have executed some deplorable deeds inspired only from the superstitions they believed.

Yes indeed, for centuries superstitions were humans' basic knowledge, they knew of nothing else, and beneath that rock, their beliefs were solid.

And during those years of medieval times, human beings did some extremely cruel things in human sacrifices and punishments.

People were punished in some horrible ways, including human sacrifices.

Yes regretfully, humans did things that should never have been done, things that were too cruel and horribly wrong.

Things that were beyond madness, and even things which were savage.

Inflicting pain upon another in the horrors of human sacrifices, or in brutish nemesis.

And they did so for centuries, repeating the abomination of their deeds in celebrated occasions on anniversaries, or in public executions for all to see the measure of the brutal severity.

Indeed, fear was believed to be necessary as a guarantee that communities will be orderly, obeying the strict rules of conformity.

And although what they believed made no sense at all, yet still in whatever they believed they never had any doubt.

Nor had they any feeling of guilt, or any consciousness to question what they did.

They were occasions of punishments, or celebrations to venerate the spirits of their ancestors, and to the gods and goddesses; they were occasions to win favours from the gods in offerings and sacrifices.

In fact, most of the things mankind believed and did, whether they were horrid or not, they had their purpose.

Whether it was a sacrifice in reverence to the gods, or a punishment in revenge, whatever they did, I say it again, it had a purpose, and it was what they believed in.

So never for one moment they had any doubt, or were troubled by what they did, regardless of how horrible it was, never were they troubled by their conscience with a guilty feeling they did wrong.

'Whatever we did was the norm', 'it was our tradition', 'It was the beliefs of our ancestors, and those of our grandparents.' 'So it is also what we believe in, that which was done throughout the ages.'

Those were the simple words of their explanation, the words that slipped right off their wagging tongues to justify the executions of their beliefs in superstitions.

What was good for their ancestors was good enough for them, and without any questions or answers.

And that was just how they felt, deep inside them the feeling dwell, it was the attitude everywhere, they too must believe and do whatever had to be done, whatever was the norm in tradition, to conform was necessary as it was important, so from generation to generation traditions were passed on.

There was no escape, no hiding place, traditional conformity had to be respected.

And that was how it was in every culture, the norms might have been different, and perhaps too, the procedure.

But most beliefs were just the same, irrational and bizarre, just utterly ridiculous, and yet they were the traditional norms in many cultures.

So yes it is true that humans have survived a very perilous journey, with fear a constant threat that was in every breath, even when snoring fear was there, it hardly ever disappeared.

Wherever one went fear followed, it was there day and night, its place of abode was in everyone's heart, and its weight wasn't light.

Nonetheless, regardless of the fears with threats, mankind lived and did some very great things, despite the obstacles that were frequently engaging.

Indeed, human beings acquired knowledge and made very good use of it, despite the difficulties that were problematic.

Not forgetting the blight of superstitions that kept humans in ignorance, and to an extent in which they were bamboozled; indeed, with superstitions they were utterly confused, mentally they were abused, and always fearing that maleficence may fall upon them as punishments direct from heaven.

And that was so for many centuries, it was what people believed, in cultures everywhere.

Yes, that was so wherever there was a lack of knowledge, but despite the fears, it gave them courage.

Pursuing things not knowing exactly how they would turn out to be.

And yet they did them because they believed in them, and rightly so, although sometimes they failed, sometimes they succeeded in what they believed in; indeed, beliefs were often very rewarding.

So yes, and although often with regrets, the choice was always for humans to make, and it was always more difficult when they had no knowledge from which ideas to take.

And despite their intelligence and their good judgement, influenced by their sense of reason.

They may believe or doubt whatever was talked about, but they were never certain until they knew.

And whenever people doubted, they had nothing to hold on to, and then the truth was lost, and more often than not at a terrible cost.

That's when they were left in a terrible mess, not knowing what to do next.

Only to realize that it mattered not how hard they tried, it was never always that easy to know what to do next, what to do for the best.

So now left with the feeling not sure what to do when they believe in something, to make plans could be in vain, resulting in time and efforts wasted.

And as humans progress and continue to believe numerous things day in and day out, and not knowing whether they were true or false.

Most of which were without merit, just things they believed in, from their childhood to adult.

Things they grew up with as family values, things that were no more than inflated bubbles; and yet they were passed on from parents to children, such as religious dogma which they believed in, and never questioned nor even doubted; indeed, the culture of beliefs as family values was one of the most inveterate unwritten rules; conformity was a must, especially with things religious.

So unto the next generation they were passed on again, passing and passing with nothing gained, always with results the same.

Passing to the other what they did not know, so that more and more people would believe.

Creating a world very superstitious and suspicious, don't know who to trust, don't know what to believe without being deceived.

But believing is something people will always be doing, because it is a function of human development, it contributes to experience, and of course, no one can know everything.

And because humans cannot know everything, some things they doubt and some they believe in.

And that they will continue to do because there will always be things they do not know.

But only when they know they will be certain that it is true, while believing is uncertain it is like guessing, a chance taken; with the possibility of a nice smile on your face, or a frown in shame or in disgrace, depending upon what the news is.

So you could be right or you could be wrong, the problem is when you believe you don't know which one is right or wrong.

Yes indeed, it is customary with human beings, they believe truths as well as lies, and the same they doubt, because they don't know which one is right.

And what they believe is given credit, regardless of the uncertainty which is always open to a measure of invalidity; indeed, again I repeat, believing sometimes could be very rewarding, it is not always disappointing.

And yes, quite often too you didn't have to worry, because you get that feeling that you knew already.

But it is never a feeling one can rely upon, nor to be taken seriously.

And that is because the reality is, whatever you believe in, there is always the possibility it could be misleading even though it was very convincing, it is never ever certain, that will be knowing.

For whatever it was that you relied upon, when it was something you believed in, because you didn't know what would happen, you took a gamble, and that meant either one of the two, success or disappointment.

So it is always better to try and know rather than to believe in anything, this I have already explained.

And that is because believing could be misleading, and indeed very disappointing especially when you have already set your mind upon what you believed in, and prepared for the occasion, a hectic celebration now had to be cancelled because what you believed did not occur, it did not happen, no need for celebration.

Believing that you know just what to do, and when given the opportunity you are not capable.

So it is better to be flexible, don't believe and then think that you know.

It is always one or the other, it could never be both together, it is either that you believe or that you know.

And as the truth is believed or doubted when people do not know.

It is just the same for lies, that's how it is, and it will always be so.

Whatever humans believe in truth, or lies, they believe it because they don't know what is right.

So it is left for them to decide what they believe and what they know, and don't ever try to mix up the two, just because it is easy to do.

And if they did, they would be left bamboozled and confused, not knowing what is the right thing to do. And that's when, as it often happens, they are left with greater problems.

Still confused and bamboozled, not sure what to decide, can't make a decision that is wise, because they don't know what is the truth or what is a lie.

And as mankind's journey looks finished when it is not; after thousands of years on a slippery track, believing in this and that, with consequences both good and bad.

Heading in one direction, always towards the future, anxious to know when they will get there. Heading in the darkness and the light, with whatever they believed in wrong or right.

Today at this point in time in the twenty-first century, this is as far as human beings have reached on their journey with tired feet step after step still heading towards the future hoping things will be better.

Yes they have reached here after many centuries of weary traveling, with the knowledge and beliefs they have experienced, some they had discarded, some they kept with them although bizarre and very weird, some were successful, and some were still without answers so they remain doubtful.

Yes indeed, some were even from as far back as BC times, those beliefs then were very irrational, very eerie, and indeed very unkind most of the time.

So yes indeed this you could believe, in some cultures it was customary in accordance with traditions heads were chopped off, people were boiled in oil, some were buried alive or nailed to a cross, others got their pain from a hanging, or consumed in flames, some fought with wild beast to the death, which they did as entertainment, and all were entangled with what human beings believed in, and it was anything they were able to imagine, from the sane to the insane.

So yes indeed it was real, no fictional stories, humans believed and committed deeds which extended beyond the limits of savagery, inhumane barbarity was an everyday reality which was put on display for all to see, and people gathered in large numbers to watch the cruelty of others, in their search for satisfaction and pleasure.

And with a sense of the utmost curiosity, with no feelings of compassion or sympathy, they stared at those in agony.

And yes, in silence they watched, horrified with what they saw, struck with terror, they never felt like that before.

And it is also very true that those were days that were terrible, too brutal, too savage, too many slaughters as punishments and sacrifices, not forgetting those slaughtered in frequent battles, death to some was horrible, cut in half with an axe, that was one of the many vicious attacks.

So yes indeed, whatever the deeds were, whatever was the measure of the cruelty, in some way or the other they were associated with beliefs.

And that justified the horror, there was no compassion whatsoever.

So anything dehumanizing was very useful in the development of a sinful world.

And yes, human beings did so earnestly, as if they had no other choice; when the fact always was that they had very much to gain if they had made the world a much better place with more love and less pain.

But perhaps it was their lack of knowledge to blame, why the world in those days was so cruel.

Knowledge indeed is the essence of morality, and morality generates philanthropy.

So without knowledge there was a great deal lost, and that's why humans had embraced superstitions.

But with superstitions their lives were no better, fear and cruelty among them were always there.

Yes, they were among them every day, not for a short visit, but for a long time they stayed.

And although humans have moved on from such a ruthless past, with the reign of terror a diminished contrast.

Their ambition still was to go further and closer into the future, believing that things would be much better.

And with that thought they had no doubt whatsoever that things could not be worse than what they already were.

But this is something that human beings should know, and not just to believe.

It matters not wherever they go, the future is whatever they make it to be, that is the reality.

And to do so, this is a lesson mankind should learn.

Always think before believing, hesitate instead of doing the wrong things, and the superstitious horrors of the past should be crushed and buried far deep down below, not in the depth of the seabed, but deep in the earth's fiery crust within the volcanic flames of hell.

Never to return to the surface of the earth, not in thought, in deed, or in word.

Indeed, in this day and age, in the twenty-first century which it is, reality should be the norm, and not the uncertainty of superstitions.

No more barbarity in punishments, nor human sacrifices, and not even for entertainment.

So yes, with knowledge and understanding in this literate modern age, the world should be heading to be a much better place, without human beings still believing in weird things, and it should be getting better all the time as it changes, and not drifting forwards and backwards as it has been doing.

Replacing the old with ideas that are good, and each time, always creating a better world.

And although towards this, humans still have a very long way to go, with determination it could be accomplished before tomorrow.

So with bit by bit yes, as long as it was progress, avoid wars, superstitious barbarity, and the ruthless oppression of draconian laws.

So what is it that mankind should do to prevent a repeat of the wrongs of yesterday?

Especially the many barbaric deeds which were associated with beliefs, beliefs taken for granted, and frequently repeated.

Beliefs especially against women, and children, which were cultural norms executed to their disadvantage.

And deeds committed in sacrifices, offered to demons, gods, or goddesses.

Deeds of all sorts, whatever they may be, for pleasure, death, pain, cures or injury.

Indeed, all those beliefs should be buried, they have long outlived their 'use by date', there is no place for them in this present day and age.

So yes indeed, human beings should always pause for a moment to be wise, to be cautious in deciding what is right.

The world is theirs to develop and make it a perfect place, without yesterday's superstitions in rituals and gory sacrifices.

There is no need today for ancient traditions, humans have moved on, they have reached the pathway of technology and science.

Indeed human beings have had enough of a corrupt, superstitious, and wicked world.

For centuries they were guided by their beliefs, and as a result, they have imprisoned their souls.

And as new generations came, they endured the same, so now in this scientific age, it is time for real change.

So yes indeed it is time for better, wait no longer, and let the evil in beliefs be gone forever.

Regretfully, it is not that simple nor easy since it is a wicked world which has developed over the centuries when indeed it should never have been.

And so sins easily slipped through the ranks from generation to generation, believing what is wrong is right, and especially by those with power and might.

That is what has always been the cause of wars, nations against nations, neighbours against neighbours, and too often for nothing more but just for a trivial cause.

Nation confronting nation, showing off their strength instead of wisdom.

Causing more confusion, with hardening of tempers and determination, no one wants to back down, so the problem is solved with a gun.

Yes indeed, it is what humans believe, when confronted with problems and they don't know what to do, the gun is what they turn to.

And because they lack wisdom they grab hold of their guns, believing that it is only with guns they could solve problems.

And that's what they do whenever they have disputes, weapons of destruction are what they use. Believing that the gun is the only weapon which they could rely upon.

And after centuries with problems and gathering experience, still today humans don't have a clue how to fix disputes without the gun, and that the fools say is their right to have one in accordance with their constitution, which perhaps by some fool it was written.

But that may be because no one could be trusted, priority is always about self-interest, a lot of talk and still no agreements, only arguments which are normally with different opinions to which no one is listening.

So life continues just the same, with everybody expecting change, and when it did come it was usually late, and still had to change at some later date.

And as for the establishment of different religions, all believe in the same God.

That has been another predicament which has reaped the perils of divisions, and yet still they cannot find unity among themselves, and not even conformity with their prayers.

And they have not even contributed much to a better world; perhaps they never could.

Always fighting one with the other, each claiming their religion is better.

So what is it that human beings should believe?

Where is truth to be found among divided religions?

When religions cannot righteously lead with their belief in one God, one creed.

How should humans know who is right and who is wrong? Which one religion for the truth they can depend upon?

One believes in this, the other believes in that, worshipping the same God.

Creating divisions when they should not, divisions that are the cause of discord.

That is the mystery that troubles everybody, wrapped and concealed as religious treasure.

And perhaps only when the answer is found, beliefs then could be relied upon more as truths than false.

But at this moment with religious confusion, unfortunately that's what happens when humans believe, with different ideas many are deceived.

Whenever there are different opinions, it is not always easy to believe which is the right one, when only one is right, and all the others are wrong.

So yes indeed beliefs are beliefs, and believing is what all humans have been doing for centuries, they never stopped from the moment they wake up, something new is added in their brain, not what they know, but something they believe in.

Indeed, they believed so much, story after story one after the other, believing in this and in that.

Some false, some real, don't know what to believe, whether they make any sense or not.

Harbouring beliefs of all sorts and kinds; some superstitious, some just suspicious and malicious, some very weird, bizarre, idiotic, ridiculously foolish, revengeful and spiteful.

And some were also excellent news, they change one's mood, from feeling resentful to optimistic and hopeful.

News that was so good to hear, as they passed through the ears, depositing a feeling of hopefulness, yes, filling the ear with sounds of joyfulness.

Giving you a feeling inundated with jubilance, hoping that it will never end.

And yet those are but just a few of the characteristics of beliefs that can create feelings of gladness within a human being, as well as hate, sorrow, or grief; that's the magical powers of belief, it can cause death, as well as heal.

Oh yes indeed, it is real, it has happened time and time again, just believing could heal the pain, and you could feel it disappearing.

And as weird and bizarre some beliefs are, they still bind people tightly together in religion, cults, and secret societies, and even among friends as well as enemies, and certainly among families, and even within neighbour-hoods and communities.

And to be one of them you have to belong, to be a member, and do whatever it is that they believe in.

Whatever is the mumbo jumbo however weird, you do as they do, you lie on the same bed, your mind to their ideas is geared.

What they believe in is what keeps them together, and often it is for a life-time, it is forever.

Giving everyone the feeling that they belong to something, and that's what keeps them together, whatever they believe in.

And this is true with the Knight Templars, the Knights of God, and with the Klu Klux Klan, Munks, and Nuns, The Satanist and the Paganist, the Free-masons, or whatever cult or religion, to which one may belong, whatever secret society one may have found; indeed, whatever tribe, or language which may be their tongue.

Whatever was their transparent or secret ideology, or their philosophy, or creed; whatever was their mumbo jumbo, without being a member, no one could ever know.

Whatever it was, it was indeed what they believed in, and by a code of discipline, each member supporting the other like brothers and sisters united together is how they live.

Yes they live with values in which they believe and hold dearly, and when executed in deeds they could be intimidating as well as exulting.

And it matters not whether they are right or wrong, or whether they make any sense at all, or whether they are about demons or gods, or Extraterrestrials, or about the universe, or just the natural and spiritual worlds.

Whatever are the beliefs of whatever religion or cult, each member must believe without question or doubt.

And if ever they no longer believe, from within their fraternity they must leave.

And of all the things humans believed in during the many centuries of their lengthy and challenging existence.

The centuries of perils and jubilation that took mankind through hell as well as heaven.

The centuries of blood and tears in wars, love, hate, and prayers.

Centuries that witnessed some very weird beliefs executed in deeds most horrid.

And in deeds of jubilation, in festive celebrations, beliefs that were either one or the other, horrific or fantastic.

The one belief held everywhere in the world by every culture and every language.

The one that has been the most common, the most important, and the most revered.

The one from among thousands of beliefs, from the most inspiring to the most bizarre and weird.

The one that humans had engaged upon from the very beginning of their years, and at every moment during the pleasures and the perils of their existence.

Yes indeed, the one belief that has been a very strong bond, and held people together throughout their life, that's for how long.

The one that is steadfast in every culture, from place to place wherever.

The one in whose name people had claimed both good and bad things.

Doing wrong things in its name, believing they were doing the right things.

It was humans' belief in a God, goddesses, or gods, hidden somewhere in the skies high above the clouds.

A belief that held human beings in separated divisions together, whether they were foolish or wise it didn't really matter.

Yes, it was in the skies above where humans always gazed whenever they were engaged in their belief in God, or the gods, or goddesses.

Yes it was always above where they looked when communicating with their Gods.

So they must believe that they were somewhere up there, somewhere among the stars.

Or perhaps somewhere just above the clouds, somewhere not too far above, somewhere perhaps between earth and the stars.

And during the many centuries of human existence, as pleasant or as cruel the years were. People never stopped to think not for one single moment, "if there was a God, how could they know". They believed yes, that they would confess, and that is as far as it goes, no further no less.

317

They just believe whatever they were told, without any desire to know if God exists, to ask a question so bold as this.

Doing wrong things as if they were insane, believing that they were doing the right things, very foolish indeed, committing sins in God's name.

And that has been the path of religious teachings, with nothing to know, and everything to believe from their preaching.

Believe in God, love and fear God, without ever knowing if God exists.

And inviting absurdity, in their search for reality, they believe in man's image God must be.

Yes, the Omnipotent must be in man's likeness, with all his characteristics, that's what they believe how God exists, like a man, he is in his form and shape; he is in man's image.

Yes, God made man in his own image, and that has been the general belief for centuries.

I don't know where that originated from, but I would have no doubt it was from religion, and perhaps from the Christians.

Yes, humans always intend to associate God like himself, even doing inhumane things in his name.

And the ruthless things humans do to others, they seem to think that God will do the same. Believing as a man God is jealous, a God who loves and hates.

And although God forgives the sins humans commit, for some sins he puts you in hell from where you have no escape, he shuts the gates.

But even then, if humans use the full extent of their imagination; the reality is, they still may never comprehend the likeness of the divine Omnipotent, it could only be what they imagine.

But it may not be too late, the truth may be predicted, to those who want to know.

But it would not be that easy, humans must be wise to acquire the knowledge of God, and to know what life all is about, whether or not it is for some useful purpose, or just maybe it ends in the grave, dust to dust, and ashes to ashes.

So what is it that human beings should do? Should they just continue to believe, with doubt forever up their sleeve?

Or should they make an attempt to know, engaging with truth and not mumbo jumbo?

Yes, the same choice is for the atheist, he should try to know for sure, instead of just believing that God doesn't exist.

A commission perhaps that could only be impossible, since the evidence for that is absolutely zero.

Indeed, believing is not good enough, it does not satisfy the appetite for certainty and trust, it is very much exposed to ambivalence and doubts.

Indeed it has no certainty, no reliability, confusion is its reality.

And that is because believing nurses confusion, that is its reputation, and when confused, your senses you could lose. Can't think straight, not even twisted, your mind is in a state frustrated.

So in a matter that is so serious, humans should make it their duty to find out.

Don't leave it too late, that could be a mistake, believing is not an alternative.

So what could be said is the purpose of humans' existence?

What could be said about his intelligence? Why is it that humans from all other creatures are so different? What are the answers revealed from science?

For a very long time those have been unanswered questions, with different beliefs, different opinions, and still today there is no common ground upon which an agreement could be found.

Yes, indeed, humans are the only living creatures given the privilege to be creative, and with far reaching abilities to acquire knowledge, to create and invent, and even to reach to the stars high up in heaven.

And yes unfortunately, it is a resounding reality, despite human beings profound privilege, the life they have already led would take them directly into hell, and that seems to be without question, it appears that humans are already heading in that direction.

So better that they should know that which is true, that the purpose of life is to gather knowledge and be wise.

It is not to be wicked and be corrupted, believing and doing things that are senseless, brutally wicked, worthless, and stupid.

And above all, mankind should know that God exists, and not to be content living with doubt and in darkness, can't find a way out; believing it doesn't matter at all.

But matter or not, it is only with prudence and wise reasoning, that mankind would ever know the truth.

And when they know instead of believing, that is when, without any doubt they would be certain. But then, how could humans ever know that there is a God? How can they know the truth? Where must they look?

The evidence is already there in nature everywhere, the evidence of God is not hidden, it is transparent throughout the universe, it is there as knowledge and as proof.

Yes it is there among the secrets of nature, wherever the wind gathers, and it is there where humans must look, among the things natural, and not within the realms where they do not yet belong, in the corridors of the supernatural.

Yes it may be sad, but to living humans that door is not yet open.

And it has been there from the beginning of time, but humans never look, humans never find. But focusing now with their eyes wide open, and with their attention unwavering.

Providing they have got wisdom, knowledge, and understanding, it is only then that mankind will know that God exists.

Yes indeed, it is very true that mother earth is full of secrets, and so too is the universe.

And to humans the secrets will be revealed to them when they know where to look.

Only then will they know that God exists because of the knowledge they have found.

No need any more to believe, because with knowledge they can't be wrong.

And that knowledge when it is acquired, there would be no need to believe, neither there would be no need to doubt.

Because with knowledge, the answer humans are searching for, they will be wise enough to work it out.

Indeed, they would be wise enough to know that God exists, because they have acquired the evidence of it, they have acquired the knowledge.

No need any more for beliefs in mumbo jumbo, no need to wonder what life is all about.

Because humans then will be very certain that they know that there is a God.

And they will always appreciate the difference in believing and knowing; because they know the most important thing.

They know in the universe there is a God, and because they know they will have no doubt.

And because they know that God exists, they will have the wisdom to know the right way to live.

LAW AND DISORDER

As I continue to examine the world regarding humans' progressive development over the many centuries they have existed.

And to come to an understanding why the world has developed to be as it is, an unjust and sinful place.

Now I am taking a look into law and disorder, so as to appreciate what humans did in their efforts to make the world better.

And to understand why it has always been as it is, sinful and corrupted.

Beginning from the moment of humans' origin to this day in time, which is measured in several millennia.

Through the passage of time humans have moved on, always with problems from the day they were born, and most were of their own design.

From their beliefs, their doubts, and their deeds, their suspicions and superstitions, and from their lack of trust from one to the other, creating hostility from brother to brother, all a part of the effects of law and disorder.

With problems that came about as they ventured through the passages of their development, problems that came and went.

Some stayed very long causing mayhem before they were gone, some came, a short while they stayed then disappeared only to return with the wrath of hell.

Problems humans encountered right from their origin, they were often their own making.

Creating problems time and time again, with the law and disorder often blamed.

So now I shall examine Law and Disorder, a necessity human beings created like any other. A necessity yes, but never together, law and disorder are always separated from each other.

So yes, I shall examine their purpose, their function, and humans' response.

What Law and disorder have done for humans during the many years of their development.

How they may have affected humans' lives as they struggled to survive.

It is indeed an unusual partnership, and yet still law and disorder do exist.

They are both around all the time, law and disorder are functions of human life.

And it is true that the only time you see them together, it is when they are angry opposing each other.

And yet both serve the people, and serve them well, each enables; one in chaos, the other stable.

But with law and order, that's a different matter, both are seldom separated from the other.

So it would be reasonable to concede that where there is law there is order, and where there is no law there is disorder.

Yes indeed, law and order appear to be closely related, with a bond that cannot be separated, indeed their bond is endurable knitted.

So yes, law and order will always be together supporting each other, and maybe forever, especially whenever disorder is threatening to take over.

And it doesn't really matter how difficult it may be; law and order would always be in each other's company, with one always supporting the other whenever necessary.

So yes, law and order are like twin brothers, always supporting each other and nothing else.

And when they are not, look no further, that's where you'll find disorder.

"So what could be said about disorder if anything at all?"

'Is it something to despise or something to like, something popular, something to ignore, or something to which you just couldn't be bothered?

'Has it got any merit towards humans' benefit?' 'Or is it better to prevent it, get rid of it?'

Yes indeed, the three are well known to one another, just like members of a family.

But with family problems unfortunately; law, order, and disorder, all three could never be together peacefully, and that is because disorder keeps bad company.

Hence casting aside disorder from the family, it is always on the stand-by with a watchful eye, waiting for opportunities.

Opportunities to cause chaos and confusion, and even destruction whenever it can.

Taking over from its orderly brother, in moments of protest; giving its support to protesters in uprisings, revolts, and unrests.

That's how disorder operates; although not always, but usually it is in response to injustice.

It becomes like a wild hungry beast upon its release, to fight the injustices in societies; no justice no peace, that's disorder's unwritten ideology.

So it could be said that disorder always supports protesters, fighting for justice is its prerogative.

Fighting with the oppressed, causing a mess, fighting with them for their rights, nothing more, nothing less.

So yes, causing chaos and mayhem, fighting with them, fighting for the rights which belong to them.

But make no mistake about it, disorder is not a friend of protesters, it simply hates injustice, it gets irritated by it.

So to victims it gives its services, and its services could be chaotic, it could be really destructive, indeed wherever there is injustice disorder is often engaged with rage.

So then indeed it could be said that disorder is not necessarily always a menace to societies.

It was more often alongside with the public to get things done; things ignored by the politicians.

And this was true particularly in cases of injustice, passed on from patrician to patrician.

Things which never got done, because changes never came when they were asked for peacefully, and orderly; that has often been the reality.

One had to be content with a very long wait, embracing patience sometimes for more than a decade before the application of any change.

And that was because politicians were never in any hurry to change unjust and oppressive policies.

So yes indeed, and regretfully, the injustice that is in the world today, must have been there for many centuries.

A long way back from the past to the present, that's how it was, without the presence of disorder change never came, injustice remains the same, day after day, again and again.

Passing injustice from generation to generation, injustice especially to women.

And although affecting lives, change was never swift, it never came overnight, it never came without protest or a fight, it never came without disorder in sight.

And the reason for that, without protesters and disorder operating together, change always came much later rather than sooner.

And that was because usually, that was how long it took when one was engaged in orderly protest for change.

It never came swift, it was always late, bringing with it little to celebrate.

So disorder always did seem to be a much better solution, change came about much quicker, instead of having to wait, for a much later date, for things to be better with change.

Take for an example the many years of peaceful protest by African Americans, led by Dr. Martin Luther King for justice with change which never came.

And the South African apartheid system; how long did that last after peacefully begging for change time and time again?

Oh yes indeed, as it is recorded in history, it was the same for slavery in many parts of the world, disorder often had to be engaged to put an end to that which was savage.

And the same could be said about the injustice to women, and many other disadvantaged groups in places wherever you went.

They only got what was rightly theirs, not with peaceful protest and prayers, but by joining forces with disorder; only then changes came about, and they came about sooner instead of later, that is the effect of disorder.

So now at this moment in time, it could be scrutinised just how the family of law, order, and disorder get along together in a world with problems one after the other.

How they served human beings with their problems, keeping the peace or the pieces in a nice straight line.

Yes, it has been often heard from the scientific world that which everyone knows, it is very common to hear the expression 'The laws of nature'.

But how many do understand the meaning of those words put together, and why does nature need laws?

327

Indeed, it is clearly exposed in its meaning that in the realm of nature there is law.

And that it could be said, but only from a wise head, that order is the purpose of nature's laws. Otherwise, why have them? Law has only one function; order, and no other.

To maintain order within the universal borders, preventing disasters from star wars.

And although there may be a lot of natural disorders, they too are influenced by laws.

Hence in mankind's world it is somewhat similar, as it is in nature.

The laws of mankind are for the same purpose, to maintain order for all of us.

So, the criterion for order is clearly the law, and without it, that is when disorder takes over.

So the purpose of law, and of this I am quite sure; it is for no other reason but to maintain order.

To maintain order in every aspect in man's world as it is in nature, its function is the same everywhere.

In every environment and in every culture, just as it is in the universe, where nature's laws are successful.

Maintaining the orderly function of everything, as they were created to function from the beginning.

So now the question is raised as one's mind is now fully engaged.

What is law? who can tell what it really is, and describe it in accurate details?

Perhaps it would be true in an oath to say that law is nothing more than rules to obey.

Rules that sustain the functioning of that which must function as it does.

Be it a game, an aeroplane, the forces of nature, or humans' behaviour.

Be it whatever it is, the reason is the same why laws were made.

And without the rules which are the laws, that's the moment when disorder crowds the floors.

And that is an illness in the world today, as it was yesterday.

An illness that is still without a cure, and appears to be getting worse, that's for sure.

In the world mankind progressively developed over many millennia, implementing laws for whatever cause, they were often very unjust, and the systems they served were very corrupt.

Systems that were bent and very twisted, with draconian laws ruthlessly implemented.

Laws that were different serving divisions, as they were for the rich and for the poor.

But why were they different?' no one was sure, only perhaps those who made the laws.

But the laws for whites and for blacks, neath bigotry did reside, different laws then applied in the name of segregation, and apartheid, injustice was part of it, one had privileges, the other subjugated.

Keeping races separated as masters and slaves, to be chained and whipped and kept in bondage.

Not forgetting for men and women too there were different laws, that is true, no need to argue.

Laws that denied women their basic rights, with no protection from abuses, and harassment right through their lives.

And yet despite the injustice and the rule of an iron fist, whatever was the law was the law, written or unwritten, it was the law that kept nations secured from the disasters of chaos and disorders.

And yet although disorder had been a disruptive force, it had appeared to be frequently necessary, and indeed, needed to acquire equity.

So yes indeed disorder was a force, supporting protesters fighting for justice, or opposing whatever was aggressive.

And the reason for that was to bring about change to the laws that were flawed, unjust and oppressive.

Indeed, laws were even made to justify wrongs, with the law makers knowing quite well what they were doing, so they made laws to oppress, to exploit, and to enslave, laws to deny justice and to segregate.

That's the type of laws humans made, and that's why the world has been as it is, with laws that were brutal, inhumanely unnatural, laws that needed change immediately, and yet remained in the systems for centuries.

Indeed, with the laws which were implemented in many places for centuries, little attempts were made to redress wrongs in societies, and little attempts were made to bring about change.

Passing them on from generation to generation in a package with injustice that became the norm.

And so they remained as a part of the systems, with legalized wrongs very common.

Yes indeed, they were common in every society, in every culture, in every country.

They were common everywhere, wrong was right, and right was wrong, those were the laws by which things were done.

And that was so throughout the ages in many places where despotism reigned.

Ruling with an iron fist, and the excruciating sting of a slaveholder's whip.

Indeed, the law was anything that was not perfect, so any form of retribution was executed.

And that's how it continued for many centuries with laws which were hostile, laws which were brutal, laws implementing injustice even claimed lives.

And to break them was a tragedy, retribution was often a painful reality, it was indeed with the utmost severity, in fact, it hated leniency.

So yes indeed, the law had clipped humans' wings keeping them under control.

Preventing them from doing wrong things which could create a chaotic world.

So yes indeed, it is the law, draconian or not; it is the law that keeps the peace even when it is unjust.

And yet of course, it is those very same laws which are often the cause of disorders.

And that is because they are seldom just, but brutal, and ruthless.

So yes indeed those were the days, the days of ruthless despotism, and the rule of law was nothing more than the legality of barbarism.

People feared, and so they should be, retribution was without mercy.

And so it had been as it was seen, there were laws that claimed heads just for stealing bread, others were hanged for stealing a horse or a gun.

Some were whipped in public for whatever wrong they did, and it mattered not what they had done, or how trivial was their wrong.

And yet they were condemned to several lashes, splitting their backs into bloody pieces.

Some again suffered pain, and to use the word excruciating cannot describe the flailing whip-hand, excoriating.

And that went on for quite a long time, until the masses got fed up with oppressive laws that were unjust, disorder was the only weapon they had got.

And that was exactly what they used, very confused, they had no other weapon to use.

And it was only after some sort of disorder, that changes came about sooner rather than later.

But yet still, and in many cases, regardless of the chaos disorder caused in the demands for change to the unjust laws, yet still the demands for change were often ignored, so for many centuries again injustice still remained the same, no change.

And the law as a force remained as it ought to be, altruistic and exemplary, differentiating right from wrong, what could and cannot be done.

So that the people would know which path to follow, without drifting into where they didn't belong. But instead, unfortunately, not always was the law as it should be.

Too often it was biased, giving rise to demonstrations and riots, the result of laws which were unjust was often unrest, with disorder and chaos joining the protest.

But laws are just rules to follow, aiding security just like a guard.

Guarding humans through their next tomorrow, without the need to worry or to be sad.

Rules that decide how to settle a matter whenever parties cannot agree with one another.

Rules that determine how it should be done, hence differentiating right from wrong.

Rules that endorse criminal activities, giving them credibility to exploit and enslave.

Taking advantage of the weak in society, with rules that kept them shackled in poverty.

And even rules for them to be treated severely, whenever there was a need to be.

Rules that are made in the home, they too are laws, keeping the family close together in and out of doors.

Rules that are made in the office; in the factories, jails and schools, and in the banks, hospitals, and churches; they all have their own set of rules.

Rules that save lives on the roads, without them it would be disorder and chaos.

Because that's when disorder steps right in, causing many more lives to be lost.

And within small and primitive societies, hidden in the darkness within the forest.

With their set of rules written or unwritten, in revenge a life was taken.

And that too perhaps it was their rule of law, in accordance with their culture.

What is right or wrong in different societies, is as problematic as the answer could be.

And as rules for whatever purpose, they are the laws that prevent chaos, so whether they are written or unwritten, the law decides what is permitted and what is forbidden.

And that is true in many environments, even in advanced societies too.

Where laws are frequently bent or broken, or they are with loopholes letting criminals slip through.

Different in beliefs, language and culture, and with different rules from one place to the other.

Rules that determine different punishments, from stoning to death to a suspended sentence.

Rules that also determine how to play the game, what is and is not allowed in order to win.

Rules that are necessary and even unnecessary too, some wise, some foolish, some just and unjust, whatever is the rule of law, it has its purpose.

Because the rules are what human beings live by, and they live by them all the time. Despite whether they are wrong or right, humans live by rules all their life; they can't be trusted to do otherwise.

And for whatever cause were the laws in society, regardless how crooked, bent, or twisted they may be, they were the laws to maintain propriety.

And for whatever was the purpose that the law was intended, be it for a good cause or to justify injustice.

Whatever was the rule of law, and regardless of what it was for, it had to be implemented and to be obeyed, and when it was not, there were consequences.

And that was how it had been for centuries right through the ages since the creation of laws, since laws were made that's how it was, and that's how it still is.

And they were made for all sorts of purposes, to guarantee liberty as well as to enslave.

Indeed it is true that in some places, order was maintained with laws that permitted the sting of a whip, and in many cases even with shoot to kill.

There was no escape from the sting of the whip to keep order in place, which had condemned the masses to nothing more than objects ruthlessly treated.

Yes, that's how human beings were treated in many places for the wrongs they did.

And those who were slaves were chained and locked up in cages, and that was within the law during the harsh reality of mankind's survival policies designed to control the poor.

Yes indeed, locked up in cages, raped and tortured, and no one cared a damn, not even when someone was sacrificed like a lamb, it was no cause for compassion.

Because that was the everyday norm, it was within the law, written or unwritten, to death you could be beaten, and no one was held responsible, indeed, no law was broken.

So yes indeed it was real, an everyday reality, those were years of brutality, numerous crimes were committed by those in authority, crimes the laws permitted right through the ages, throughout the dark years of BC and AD.

Coerced sterilisation, to prevent women from having children, that was within the law in some civilisations.

And one child per woman to keep the population down, that too was the law in another culture.

And of course, the many many more, thousands of men, women and children tortured as guinea pigs, in cruel experiments that ended with many killed, after enduring the torment of overbearing pain.

And the many more who were slaughtered as prisoners of wars, and as victims of unjust laws.

Yes indeed, it was no secret that many men, women, and children, together they died of exhaustion and starvation.

And that was if they were not shot, or simply worked to death, dying in privation.

And that would have been within the law written or unwritten, in wars all sorts of things do happen; no questions asked, no answers given, no one held accountable.

Because whatever was done nothing was wrong; in times of war, one must be strong.

Mass murders, rapes, beatings, and torture were often the faith of prisoners of war, and as slaves they laboured in hunger, and were not even given a drink of water.

Soldiers from different cultures tortured, raped, and murdered; men, and women, leaving them in the ground blue; and even the children captured, they were often murdered too.

So yes indeed, entire families, some killed, some wounded, some kept as slaves with their families separated, and it was all lawfully permitted.

Brothers, sisters, husbands, and wives, all separated and kept as slaves by different masters, that's how they survived, with their families divided; lost and forgotten, exploited, rape, and often beaten.

And all of this which was witnessed as a duty lawfully accomplished.

Human beings did what they did, they wounded and killed with the weapons they created.

Executing laws that were criminally brutal, and in some cases even savage, and very aggressive towards their captives; that even heads from bodies were often separated.

And all which was done was done within the law, some laws were written, some unwritten, some were no less than centuries old, and still a part of the statutory code.

Transforming the law into a bad-tempered ass, to oppress the poor and the working class.

With injustice they did not deserve, making their lives a great deal worse.

And the law as it was, good or bad in whatever way, was still executed every day.

Carrying its full weight as a guarantee, that order will be always maintained fully.

So as to prevent chaos and disorder from ever spilling over.

The law was often ruthless as much as it was unjust.

Its severity had always guaranteed a fearsome and peaceful community.

And that was how it functioned; the law was never wrong, as long as order was maintained.

And that's what was important, its only purpose, its only aim, and that function it had to sustain.

So, with fear was how the peace was kept, everyone was under threat, to utter a wrong word was an arrest, and in several cultures, it was even death.

That's the way the world was developing, that's the way the law was sustained, that's the way order was maintained, ruthlessly oppressive.

So the law for centuries implemented in many places had been draconian and a bully, restricting freedoms wherever necessary.

But then mankind should understand that being a human, by his very nature he is a creature who cannot be accorded absolute freedom.

And that is because he lacks self-control, and is always doing things with the wisdom of a new-born foal.

Just imagine how chaotic the world would be, should humans be left completely free.

There is no such a thing as free speech, it has never been, nor is there a free society; those are dreams that could never be, it is not a possibility.

Just imagine the chaos, mayhem and disaster, all wrapped together in a bundle of disorder.

Just look at some places how chaotic they are, it is as if there is no law and order.

Indeed, in such places any fool can see the reality of, without law and order, how chaotic it could be with disorder a lasting reality, and the ghost of crimes haunting everybody, roaming freely in senseless acts of cruelty committed repeatedly, no law, no order, everybody free to do whatever.

So yes indeed, it is a misleading interpretation to think that human beings have the right to absolute freedom.

Wherever there are laws there is always less freedom, and that is because of the restrictions.

And this of course meant some form of order, so the more laws the more restrictions, reflecting more order within institutions.

You cannot have law and at the same time be left uncircumscribed, that is simply not wise.

The law is what ties the hands of humans making them law abiding with restrictions curbing their movements, hence limiting their freedoms.

But this is too often taken a step too far, with hostile and oppressive laws.

Giving rise to formidable situations, infringing upon the liberties of mankind.

Restricting their freedoms yet more and more and causing resentment each time.

Putting liberty secured in chains, until the people can no longer endure the pains.

So they are forced into disorder yet again, in a vicious cycle to bring about change.

And yet despite that, whatever were the laws, just or unjust, oppressive or not, so they remained, and quite often for a very long time before they were changed.

Regardless of however unjust, biased, lenient or severe; without any change, unjust laws were enforced year after year.

Just as it was yesterday, today and tomorrow, and for every other day that follows.

Making little changes in the laws now and then, in places wherever you went.

And yet still despite the changes, many laws remain unjust, lenient or severe, in countries everywhere.

And although mankind was progressing continuously, and making rapid changes frequently.

Yet still unjust laws, for far too long, with their loopholes and flaws they remained in the systems.

Draconian or not as the laws may well be, they were often ruthlessly implemented, keeping a tight grip on communities.

And that was how it had been in the world as human beings were progressively developing and advancing, making new laws and creating new things.

So within the law the people were controlled, within the law they did what they did.

And that was how it was, and so it had always been with laws changing all the time, and yet still they were not always much better than the ones left behind.

And with the purpose to prevent disorder and chaos, it was those very same laws that were the cause of disorder, and even wars.

And that was because they were unjust laws, prompting rebellions to correct their flaws.

And that's how it was in every age, regardless of the progressive development stage.

Wherever there was a war, death and destruction came with chaos and disorder, there was a brotherly bond among those four.

So yes, and for sure, law was always required to prevent chaos and disorder, hence keeping the peace from tripping, and then stumbling over with disorder filling the floor.

Keeping the peace in one piece, instead of scattered broken up pieces.

And regardless of whatever was lawfully expected, at all stages the law had to be successfully implemented, whether or not it was just or unjust it had to be seen serving its purpose, maintaining order at any cost.

So with rules and laws for whatever cause, written and unwritten, unjust very often, and regardless of whatever happened.

It was always the law that kept the peace, although quite often it caused some grief.

But that was mainly on the occasions, when the law was bent or broken.

And the weight of the law came tumbling down, smashing those in its path squeezed to the ground.

So the law was often seen as a necessary evil, but evil or not, it was always necessary.

It was indeed like an unsavoury medicine, although useful, it was detestable.

So without it the world would be sick, and driven into a chaotic epidemic, and then looted into an existence of a very bad experience.

So yes indeed, the world would not have been as it is today, although not perfect, without law it would have been many times worse still, and perhaps indeed very chaotic.

And yes, despite this fact, laws were often badly written, endorsing laws to justify wrongs which were then committed by anyone.

Wrongs in the form of oppression, discrimination, inequality, and the inhumane conditions of exploitation, serfdom, and slavery.

Indeed, laws had sanctioned those wrongs and many others, making them lawful, and they had sustained those conditions with the freedom to operate, and because it was legal and lawful, there was no exit for the victims to escape.

Indeed it was seen, and by everyone, that those things were right, not wrongs, so it was written, and so it was done, within the law, wrongs were sanctioned.

Mankind made laws that vindicated wrongs, and even wrongs that were in many ways grossly inhumane.

Indeed, the law makers themselves must have been insane, creating laws which were inhumane.

Yes indeed so it had been, within the law written or unwritten, victims were tortured, and badly beaten.

To their death some bled-out in a public hell, others lived another day with their story to tell.

And yes, that went on again and again, and it went on despite the protesting.

It was the norm in a developing world, with injustice and brutality one and the same goal.

And most of it was particularly so to the disadvantage of women, minorities and the poor. Giving rise to a resentful consciousness, that there were different laws for the poor and the rich.

And that had created a quandary in even law-abiding communities, and especially where the laws were unjustly implemented, which was so in many cases.

Indeed, there were laws that were seen clearly to be made deliberately to keep women oppressed in poverty.

Denying them their basic right of ownership to property, and equal pay for equal responsibility.

And with no prospects of ever being independent, that was the final blow to cripple women.

Not forgetting their basic human rights, that too were kept away from their sights.

And of course, from abusive husbands, and public harassment, for many centuries the law had given women no protection, it simply turned a blind eye, and wet with tears, women cried.

And as wrongs against them became the norm, they got rooted and accepted as normal customs.

So yes this culture, just like a bush fire, drifted around the world everywhere.

It became socially established in every place, although it was very unfair.

Indeed it is true, religion too, unjustly discriminated against women.

And they were doing so centuries ago believing their injustice to women was God-given.

Yes that was in their fate, believing from the heavens it was established to be on earth as it is.

And that bad example caused a lot of trouble, whatever religion did, was taken for granted.

Creating a precedence to the disadvantage of women, religion indeed was a big part of the problem. It never protested nor objected, but turned a blind eye to the wrongs committed.

To disadvantage women, although it was unfair, religion had shown no concern, not even that it had a care.

In fact it was as if they had created the problem, throughout history they unfairly treated women.

And still those are the same problems today, they are what the present generations have inherited.

And with the conviction foolish as it is, it is the way women have always been treated.

And that has been so sad as it is, even in their homes, it has been the rule written and unwritten established as family values.

And in some way or the other by those same values women were abused, using the values as an excuse.

And that was very true in every country and in every society, in fact in every culture wherever you may have been.

That was how the world was developing, that was how it was progressing, with laws unjust, oppressive and corrupt, both written and unwritten.

And nothing mattered one way or the other, women were always victims of the law, that's how it was and that's how it is, even today they are still unfairly treated, disgraceful as it is.

So yes indeed, it is very much still the same today with problems inherited from yesterday, some have changed, but in many cases and in many places women are still unfairly disadvantaged.

Women are still victims of abuse and injustice, wrongs against them are still taken for granted, and often the culprits are not even punished, whether or not it was reported, the police are the least concerned in most cases, their indifference is a disgrace.

So the criminals get away with it, no one is arrested, no one is charged, and crimes against women shoot up on the rise.

And that is in a world that has been developing for thousands of years, with laws changing and the same crimes repeating with women always the victims.

Indeed, they are still not yet treated equally, in every aspect of life, and in every country.

They are still too often disadvantaged, especially in the workplace with low wages.

And the reason for that, it is the law; there is either none in place to prevent the disadvantages, and those that are made, from women's rights they are disengaged.

So yes indeed, make no mistake that the world is as it is today, because of the policies that were implemented yesterday.

Policies inherited from previous generations, policies that have not yet changed, disorder has still to be engaged.

Yes indeed, they are the past generations' failures and success, all together they led to this present day's mess, and yet they claimed that they did their very best.

But humans' very best isn't worth their efforts, if an unjust world is what they develop.

But that may be because of the laws humans made, and didn't make, that could be the reason why the world is so disparagingly engaged.

Because after thousands of years with many changes and new laws implemented, still mankind cannot yet get rid of injustice. Why is it?

Is it because it is so deeply rooted, stuck in the heart of cultures?

And the only way to deracinate injustice one may have to leave it to the vultures.

Or is it maybe because of some other reason? To deracinate injustice could be treason.

And that will indeed be a heavy price to pay, so it is better that injustice stays where it is.

"So then, what kind of a world were humans creating?" 'How successful were the laws they were making?'

Laws that were flawed, laws that were unjust, laws that were discriminatory, as much as they were biased.

Laws that were oppressive and very aggressive, ruthlessly implemented.

Creating a world without sexual equality, full of hate, vexation and hostility.

A world that seems always angry with itself, can't find a comfortable bed upon which to rest its head.

A world that cannot find peace, nor from the torments of hell, can't find release.

In fact, it is a world with so great a measure of hate, and a much greater measure still is injustice.

For justice and peace human beings have never stopped searching, and today, after thousands of years, for the same things they are still searching.

Maybe because they were always at war, regardless of whatever for, and that too perhaps it was the law to create war.

Or maybe because they never searched in the right places, and that's why they never found peace nor justice.

Or it could be that they never searched at all, knowing quite well that injustice is a part of the laws.

So the law remains just as it is, despite the frequent changes, it remains as good and as bad as it is. And regardless of being corrupt and unjust, order has always been its main purpose.

And despite its many legal wrongs frequently affecting individuals.

Life continued, humans moved on, stepping forwards in the same direction, towards the future their only destination.

And that was how life went on for century after century, and in every country.

Human beings moved on creeping along, developing continuously.

Creating a world very corrupt, reckless, progressive, confused, hostile, and unjust, and at the same time religious; the concoction was a very toxic broth.

With nations in dispute or fighting with each other, with suspicions, and accusations, they point their finger, which then ignites the fire.

And regardless of the world's conditions, regardless of the situations, whatever was the state of law and order, there was always hope that the future would be better.

And with laws for the very same cause, and yet from culture to culture they differ.

What was right or was wrong, was influenced in accordance with the norms of local traditions.

Yes indeed, doing things as was the norm, as per tradition, some things were done in the same way for centuries on, change was alien.

Things that were both right and wrong, they made no difference, together both were done.

So yes, it was only with the law, regardless how badly it was flawed, or how old it was; life was orderly and secured.

And for that it was given credit, with some security and order human beings were able to live peacefully with one another.

Feeling secure within the law regardless of its imperfections; feeling secure within the law, conscious of its protection.

So the more laws that were applied, the more freedoms were the price, and the more secured was everyone's life.

Indeed, freedom was the price for a secure life, so law was necessary even for survival.

And that was the direction the people had taken, trotting along day after day.

To the future was where they were heading with a portfolio of laws from yesterday.

Yes, with all sorts of laws, some faultless, some flawed, some made no sense at all.

And conscientious or not, one could not forget, to disregard the law was to disobey, and the consequences were, a heavy price to pay.

So yes, the law was a whip, and like the sting in a scorpion's tail, it fell upon those who disobeyed.

Yes, true to say that the rule of law was an indestructible pivot; and it is still the same today.

And right or wrong are just modes of conduct, and not necessarily the law.

Yes, that is something worth remembering, and not just to pass through both ears in vain.

Because one day you may slip on your way and might be left with a very heavy price to pay.

Hopelessly trapped with a heavy weight on your back, the weight of unjust laws.

For whatever were the laws, and for whatever they were for, right or wrong that's what had to be done.

And that is how it was, and that is how it is now, and that maybe is how it will be for always.

For the law is what it is, it doesn't only protect but it enslaves, and that is because whatever are the laws, they are not natural, but man-made, and with a mixture contaminated.

And whatever was the law there was a punishment for sure, be it lenient or severe, or however it was meant to be including the death penalty, which was in any forms of cruelty, even to be tortured was a possibility.

To be nailed to a cross, or trampled by a horse, or in a fire to be burnt, or your head from your body to be separated by an axe or a guillotine, or to be stoned to death or buried alive, or to be hung by a rope from the ground very high; or to be shot, or perhaps boiled in oil, whatever was the law that's how you died, inhumane barbarity had no shame, no reason to hide.

Yes indeed, when punishments were severe, they were often very severe, and so too when they were lenient, sometimes they were very lenient; punishments never fit the crimes.

So it was within that area, in places everywhere, that injustice was a frequent visitor.

And that was how it was regularly seen, with watering eyes in tearful grief; expecting retribution as a relief, what victims got was more agony.

Expecting a punishment to suit the crime, so that victims can move on feeling justice was done.

But instead, the punishment was so lenient, very surprising and a shocking disappointment.

The retribution given was beyond belief, it pierced the victims' heart with further grief.

348

Causing more pain, outrage and hate, the traumatized victims were left to suffocate.

Already in pain as victims of crimes, injustice struck another blow at their heads; this time from behind; too lenient was the punishment for the crime, it served no purpose, not even a little satisfaction.

So yes, retribution was measured from purgatory to hell, from too lenient to too severe.

The problem was to get it right, so that victims could sleep a little better at night.

Believing that the wrongs against them which were committed, the perpetrators would receive what they deserved as justice.

But instead, some perpetrators received just a pat on their backs, and the victims in shock were left to wonder, 'What the hell was that?'

And as was expected, justice became a laughingstock, and the judiciary system something to mock.

And that has been particularly so in the advanced world, where punishments for crimes were no longer centuries old.

They were changed from time to time, from barbarism to just a fine.

But as they still are in the third world, many punishments for crimes are without control.

In some places it is as if there are no regulations, so anything could be the punishment.

Creating a disadvantaged inhumane difference, with the execution of very severe punishments.

Regardless of the triviality of the crime, punishments were severely unreasonable most of the time.

And so they still are even today, in countries where their system of law runs away.

One can get the death sentence for a loving gay embrace, and a few months in jail for a brutal rape, which is the logic of their reasoning; idiocy is a possibility, like a crown it sits upon heads in applying justice when sentencing.

And in those places, no one is safe, people disappear without a trace.

Even journalists are arrested and persecuted, some are killed just for investigating and exposing wrong doings, and too often in those cases, no one is arrested and brought to justice, no need to hide, the murderers are safe, nothing will be properly investigated.

And in jail in most of those places, jails are hell, they are filthy places of torture, beatings, and murders as well.

And make no mistake, it is a shameful disgrace, homosexual rapes have also become commonplace, and by both wardens and bullying inmates.

And yet still the jails are filled, many overcrowded, and perhaps with more innocent suspects than those with guilt.

But the corrupted systems bother no one, case closed, they got someone paying for the crime, it troubles no one whether he or she is guilty or innocent.

Someone is paying, that's the main thing; no need to investigate the same thing again.

And the system continues in the same way they function, without disorder there is no change whatsoever, not for a long time which seems forever.

And now, I shall move on after this conscientious introduction.

Moving on directly into the system gathering information of just how today the systems work.

After centuries of development with trial and error, and with repairs, amendments, and acquiring experience from mistakes made, frequently smoothing out the rough edges.

I shall now take a look at how good the best systems work, how reliable they function serving justice instead of injustice with laws that are at least almost perfect.

Looking at the best, as it is claimed to be in the West, in mankind's developed and progressive first world.

Taking a journey through the system, to observe just how the law deals with unlawful situations.

How exactly is the law implemented, whether it is a deterrent, and how effective.

Whether it is beyond criticism, serving all the people in the best way it can.

Whether or not it serves justice, or it serves as a judicator in the favour of those who are privileged.

Or be it that it is just being used conveniently, sometimes severe and sometimes with leniency.

Or to a point of no regard for the law, that crimes are committed even more and more.

Giving rise to a crime spree society, where criminals survive committing crimes, and doing so successfully.

In fact, to scrutinize the wisdom of operation within the judiciary system of Western Civilization.

How good or bad is the system of law? And for how much longer it will continue to be, just as it is serving western societies.

Yes indeed, in the first world as it is. Will humans still be searching for justice?

Searching for it in every place, searching for it every day, and yet still can't find where it is.

Or have they found it? Or will they find it? Have they stopped, or are they still searching for it?

So now let us step forward together and enter into the system and assume that a crime was committed, and of course it was reported.

That may or it may not switch the system into action with some responses at a police station.

And if it did, there could be a staff shortage, and the police are few in numbers, or they may be already engaged in crimes of others.

Or it could be that they were corrupted and lacking in resources, or just that they were not interested, especially with trivial cases.

Or that they simply didn't want to know so nothing was done, they made no attempts to redress the wrong, exposing police integrity as nothing more but something to scorn.

So the criminal goes about his business laughing at the police, and thinking contemptuously;

'The lazy fools couldn't even be bothered to do their duty.'

Unfortunately, that is what happens because quite frequently the police don't always do their duty properly, this happens in most countries.

So another crime was just ignored, and the culprit was overjoyed, he got away with it again.

Feeling that he has beaten the system, he commits crimes most of the time.

And only because the police could not be bothered to do what was their job.

So criminals gain confidence at the expense of the police's unwarranted indifference, so criminals are free, and victims at their mercy.

And yet this is just one small example of the best system in service to the people in Western Civilisation; no need to consider Third World situations.

But there is also an alternative, things are not always as bad as they look, some operate to the book.

So yes, the reported crime was followed up with a cursory investigation right from the top.

And that led to someone arrested and charged with the crime committed, someone who fitted the accusations of the offence; someone who was in the wrong place at the right time.

So now at this stage, a suspect was locked up or released on bail, pending a hearing on some future date to entail.

But also, it could be that the police may be conscientious and dedicated, and yet incorrect, doing their best to serve the public.

They may or may not have enough resources, and yet still the crime was thoroughly investigated.

And only then was the offending suspect apprehended, as the police was satisfied that it was by the suspect the crime was committed, as it was supported by the evidence collected.

And yet the police could be wrong, or they could be right, but still the suspect was arrested, and released on bail, or thrown into jail, where he remained for many days.

And that is the machinery of the law so far, but there is more to come, things I shall expose which may trouble your conscience, things which are done as part of the system.

Yes indeed we have reached the stage at which an arrest was made.

But even to achieve that requires a great deal of police effort.

To make an arrest, police require a great deal of patience, courage, and integrity.

Quite often it takes a lot of time to get to the bottom of a crime protected with thick barriers of lies, and a suspicious silence supported with no comment.

And those two together they waste police time, prolonging the investigation.

Investigating with all sorts of obstacles and difficulties, no-measly; investigating a crime is not entirely that easy, attitudes are frequently hostile against the police, the public is not always cooperative to say the least.

And that involves the lack of public co-operation, and witnesses fearing criminal intimidation.

And as the police must operate within the perimeters of their limit, doing their best to secure an arrest. Whatever they did, whatever victory they scored, they must be quite sure that they operate within the law.

Yes indeed, there are rules to follow, or the police could be in big trouble.

So they do their job with their hands tied, their limits within the law are not very wide.

No one is obliged to answer police questions, 'no comment,' Habeas Corpus beckons.

And that makes it difficult for apprehensions, and wasting police time too.

And even when gathering information, the police must be cautious in their operations.

Or risk the evidence being declared inadmissible, and wastefully thrown out through a window.

And all because the evidence was not lawfully obtained, so the dedicated efforts of the police were all in vain.

Hence, to protect the public from unscrupulous police, the law had burdened the job with difficulties.

Making it more difficult to arrest criminals, with laws that disable police powers.

And yet that difficulty had become necessary because of police brutality.

Anxious to obtain confessions, perhaps to close the investigations, or even frustrated by their efforts, police often applied intimidation in methods of coercion.

But it was not only from the police that criminals were protected.

The law protects them in a number of ways, covering criminals with a designer coat of rights, hence leaving victims exposed in the cold day and night.

For their right to justice, victims must fight, no point in waiting, it never comes overnight.

And even when they fought there was no guarantee, to obtain justice was never easy.

Some victims felt they must commit a crime, by taking the law into their hands, or be prepared to wait a very long time; too often it is very late when justice arrives.

Yes indeed this folly, as in one example of how bad it is, was recently exposed in a murder case, forcing a solicitor to resign in disgrace.

And the crime he committed was to help catch a criminal, by passing on papers that were considered confidential.

Yes it appeared that confidentiality was king, even if it meant protecting a murderer from the consequences, indeed, another hindrance to justice.

And perhaps it is even more important than saving a life, as procedure and law go together like husband and wife.

That was the type of reasoning that one could be receiving in a world progressive and civilized.

And it was all lawfully binding, confidentiality indeed deserving of its preservation.

And preserving maybe at any cost, regardless of how many lives may be lost.

Indeed, criminals have more rights than what they deserve, that even unlawful protection is sometimes reserved.

Leaving them free to roam the streets, no wonder crimes are on the increase.

And this again is the best in the West, where the systems of law are clearly in a mess.

And in this area of confidentiality and disclosure, matters are often very sensitive and even highly explosive.

It is an area that is badly abused, and even with an illicit excuse.

To cover up crimes their best excuse is. "It is confidential, sorry, can't speak at will."

Concealing information in the name of confidentiality, often it was because it was too big a scandal and full of debauchery.

Covering up crimes which ought to be exposed and brought to attention.

And it was in that area where the troubled conscience of the whistleblower threatened those with criminal behaviour.

And yet they were the ones who were persecuted, when they should have been encouraged, protected, and perhaps even compensated.

But instead, they were the ones who were looked upon with hateful eyes, as if they were the lawbreakers to be despised.

When indeed, and with great courage, they were the brave ones who exposed wrong doings. And for doing just that they got the sack, and the message sent out to the public, 'better to keep quiet. 'Indeed already, cowards do just that.

So yes indeed it is no secret, everyone knows that whistleblowers are never appreciated, they often lose their jobs for whistleblowing, and more often than not, it is for exposing those at the top.

So they lost their livelihood and just for doing what everyone should, and to obtain redress, they were left out in the cold.

But that is just how the rotten system works, manmade as it is it often gets worse, and it may remain so beyond tomorrow. But for how much longer? Without protest with disorder no one knows the answer.

But then again, that is just one very small problem among the many which human beings are living with already.

And when tomorrow comes with whatever is on its way, there could be yet still many more problems, more than yesterday.

So what are the incentives of a whistleblower? What benefits does the law have to offer? 'Must he expose or ignore crimes?' hence to be troubled by his conscience all the time, leaving criminals free to offend yet another time.

'Which one of the two whistleblowers should do?' When to do what is right, their family lives could be jeopardised, and the law turns a blind eye.

Yes indeed, one could lose his job just for reporting a criminal who may be his boss.

There is no safety net for whistleblowers, anything can happen to them thereafter.

There is no guarantee they would be treated fairly, with the protection of the law as it should be.

And that does not give confidence to whistleblowers, when they are re-garded with a stigma affecting their reputation in an ugly manner.

Indeed, they are not criminals, but perhaps the ones who deserve a medal.

A medal for their bravery as well as their honesty, the courage of a whistle-blower doesn't come that easy. It is not for cowards, and there are many, in any one group it could be everybody.

So reporting those who have done wrong, could only be the right direction in which to move on.

A direction which should be encouraged, and with the respect of a good image which is deserving to those who are brave, indeed, proper laws are needed to be put in place, so that whistleblowers could feel safe, hence, more crimes could be reported.

Oh yes indeed they deserve it just as much as they earned it, because what they did took courage, and they don't have to be rewarded, but at least to be respected, and by the law, protected.

But instead, not much is done to encourage the reporting of crimes, neither by the law, the police, or the public.

That has been an area full of fear, to report a crime, there are many people who wouldn't dare.

And those who did are often left with intimidating experiences, abused and threatened with consequences.

Even at schools at a young age, bullies discourage children from reporting wrongs, and those who do so are intimidated, called by names, bullied, and even lose friends.

Indeed, they are often bullied and picked on, to snitch they are told is very wrong, they must keep their mouth shut, don't utter a sound, never report a wrong.

And that's how they grow up weak inside, instead of reporting crimes they keep their mouths shut or they tell lies.

And that is exactly what they should never do, it is what allows criminals to continue, and when witnesses behave cowardly, criminals feel secured, so they continue offending breaking laws.

And that is exactly what should be prevented, especially when the wrongs that are committed are at the top where they are least expected.

Yes indeed, feeling secured at the top, should not be with guarantee that to the ground they couldn't drop.

And that indeed could only be a very bad example, when from the top the law is broken.

That's when the law is not properly implemented, then all sorts of crimes are repeatedly committed.

Hence giving rise even to police brutality, which becomes the norm and then happens frequently.

To a point of being very troubling, as the abuse of power at all ranks is then taken for granted as a right to good policing.

And with that measure of police corruption, affecting law and order and the judiciary system.

Injustice becomes like a water pipe burst, spreading itself everywhere and getting worse.

Affecting the pillars of an orderly society, with things continuing, but not as they should be.

And with the judiciary paralyzed, crimes certainly escalate on the rise, daily affecting many lives, which could have been better otherwise.

Now at this moment in time before I get carried away any further.

Let me get back onto my fact-finding mission, observing the implementation of the laws in the system.

Observing some more how the system works, the system they claim to be the best in the world; to see how wisely they function, how bad or how good, how towards serving justice they are useful.

How it works to the benefit of the masses, redressing crimes committed, in both low and high places.

With laws daily taken for granted, laws that are bent, some broken, some twisted, and some perhaps perfect; but all are laws which are manmade, so anything could be expected.

So for this investigation I must keep an eye open, and perhaps ask a good few questions.

At this point in time an arrest was made, concerning a crime committed.

The suspect was charged and locked up in jail, because he could not afford the bail.

So in jail was where the suspect had stayed, before and during the period of his trial, whether progressing or delayed.

And during all that time, it was bars where the suspect was behind, for months and even for years, and sometimes he was still not even charged, indeed, that often happens.

And it was indeed very depressing as well as emotional what the suspect was enduring.

Within an enclosed environment, and subjected to discomforting regulations.

And yes, stripped off his possessions adding to his loss, from a respectable person he was now divorced.

Yes he lost his job, there was no doubt, and so too was his freedom and friends, his dignity, his privacy, and his respect as well.

And he had brought shame upon his family, whilst he was kept as a suspect in custody.

He lost everything, and even the will to continue living; suicide was constantly threatening him. And yet the law said he was guilty of nothing, until in a court of law he was proved guilty.

And this is something very important to remember, this is what is at the heart of the matter.

An innocent person as a suspect, in accordance with the law, in prison he was legally locked up. And that is no lie, it is what the lawmakers decide, whether it was foolish or wise.

They did it nonetheless, the innocent is incarcerated with a burden of misery weighing heavily upon his chest, that's the reality of his innocence.

Yes, whether the suspect was guilty or not, he was lawfully locked up by the same system that says he was innocent, enduring the torments of imprisonment.

And although the law was very clear in the light of its wisdom, or just maybe from the darkness of its fatuity.

The affirmative in law has been very clear indeed, honest and representative in serving everybody.

And so it was declared as a provision within the law, from times of yore, that suspects were innocent until they were proved to be guilty in a court of law.

And yet despite that wise or foolish declaration which ever one it is, into the jurisdiction of law it may have been written, and perhaps for a very long time; during which suspects suffer the torments of imprisonment awaiting trial whenever bail was denied, and that without doubt on many occasions, it was often for quite a long time.

And that has been happening for many decades, or perhaps for centuries, and still no one has ever yet challenged this inveterate predicament.

Yes indeed, within the law this absurdity is a reality, it is commonplace, it is what happens controversial as it is, and yet no one has ever challenged this unethical confusion.

The law states that suspects are innocent until by a court of law suspects are proved guilty, and yet those same innocent suspects are arrested and locked up in jail if they can't afford bail. Indeed, where is the common sense in such a controversial statement?

Is it that I am the foolish one, and can't see beyond? Or just that I can't understand the language of legal expedience.

Or indeed this is something with its meaning confusing and left unchallenged for centuries without investigating, although it is out of touch with the reality of what is happening.

If indeed the law is not an ass, then what is it? When it always has to be making changes; seldom is it appropriate in the first place, and yet still that's how it operates.

So if that is the case according to law, and so it is in progressive societies.

The big question remains as it was before. Could anyone be certain, could anyone be sure?

Could anyone who is an expert in law explain this riddle which ought to be forbidden?

"Why punish someone who is innocent?" 'What is the reason for the punishment?'

Lock up in jail when the law says that the suspect is innocent, it makes no sense.

So what is the message when a suspect is punished? When the law clearly says that the suspect is innocent. Does that to anyone make any sense?

Yes indeed, that is a flaw in the law, and like all flaws it makes no sense at all.

'So what is the message of the law?' What from it, it is trying to promulgate?

Punishing someone already who is not yet found guilty.

Did the police after making elaborate enquiries, just grab hold of an innocent person to be locked-up in prison? Doesn't this make a little more sense? Guilty until proven innocent?

Then of course it justifies the arrest, and to be locked-up, while awaiting trial.

Instead of being locked up in jail because the suspect couldn't afford the bail, that's what is done to someone who is innocent; that's what the law says a suspect is, and locks him up still.

Or is it some sort of bad joke? The law is not doing what it should, but punishing someone who is innocent.

Or perhaps maybe the law is truly an ass, that's how it has been often described, both in the present, and in the past, a name it appears has been very much deserving, with little wisdom the law has been operating.

Indeed, the law is man-made, so probably an ass is what it really is, stubborn and often incomprehensible, its jurisdictions are not always sensible.

Is it any more difficult to prove which one, guilty or innocent?

And surely whenever an arrest was made, it was by evidence of the suspect's guilt the police were persuaded.

They don't go out to arrest an innocent suspect. So why has the law created such a mess?

Unfortunately, and with a sense of propriety, sadly to say the law is not always about what is right or wrong, although that is exactly what it should be all along.

And because it is made by man, it is often quite confusing, its interpretations are often patched-up with different opinions, no clarity in explanation, and so it remains full of difficulties to reach a conclusion.

Yet still, despite whatever the law is, despite its flaws and imperfections, it must be obeyed until it is changed, that's how it is, that is its mandate, regardless how long it takes.

And that is so whether the law is just or unjust, necessary or unnecessary, and even contradictory.

As long as the law is in the system it commands obedience.

So the same question is asked once again. "Why does the law punish someone who is innocent?"

Is there any wisdom in any explanation to such a simple question referring to a penalized suspect lawfully innocent.

Yes indeed, the suspect is innocent until by a court of law he is proved to be guilty.

How much clearer could that be?

So is there a reason for this contradiction when in reality the suspect is treated as if guilty.

"Or is it just another flaw in the system of law that makes it obscure even more?"

Adding to the system more reasons for criticism, piling flaw upon flaw with reasons for disorders as before.

But then again that's just how it is, and perhaps it has been so for centuries, just like other decisions that are man-made.

Thay are often done in haste after arguments instead of apprehensible reasoning.

And the damage is done right or wrong, and as human beings, mankind will still do it again, the very same wrong thing is repeated again and again.

Because that is exactly what humans do, and for as long as they live, they will continue; until perhaps they have acquired the wisdom to make wise decisions.

So now back to the heart of the system is where my attention is about to drift, still scrutinizing the best in the world, those in the West, which so far appear to be hopelessly imperfect.

So now I shall see for myself just how the system functions, how fairly it operates from within. Where the intellectual battles are bitterly fought, as innocence is put at risk.

With two players, a referee, and twelve observing adjudicators selected randomly from among the public, to listen attentively and use the circumspection of their ability, and deliver a verdict wisely.

Yes indeed, all burdened with the same evidence to be presented in their duty, in deciding innocence or guilt, whichever it will be.

And yet it is not immutably binding, whatever decision that was made.

Decisions that are made are overturned quite freely, by the reasoning of a more esteemed judiciary.

And that has contributed to the system's very slow movement, yes indeed it has.

Waiting sometimes for months for a decision, waiting even for years for justice to be delivered.

So this now poised yet another question, another one that no one ever asks.

"Why is it that when decisions are taken, they are always the ones made last?"

Overturning decisions that were previously made, and yet based on the very same facts.

Then someone must be lacking in understanding or may have fallen off the tracks.

For it is neither wisdom nor a judgement on merit, and therefore it could only be a myth, that the best decisions were the ones made last.

And yet still those are the ones that are always taken, and that is how it always has been with human beings, both in the present and in the past.

So why is it so dire a folly, for centuries it had been, and continues to be?

And unless this folly is eradicated completely, right into the future it will continue.

Making the system very shaky, affecting its integrity as well as its reliability.

And the decisions that are made in lower courts, they will continue to be thrown out of hand. Reflecting badly on someone's integrity, and the lack of their ability to make decisions, as well as on their feet to firmly stand.

Making a mockery of the lower courts, undermining its authority.

If those in the office are not suitable to make decisions wisely, they should not be given the responsibility.

But that is what it is to be human, having the ability to reason and understand in matters of any sort.

And to be able to make wise decisions, knowing there will always be different opinions.

And the previous could be much wiser than the last.

So yes indeed, there is a need for a better system to decide the best decision, and not to be stuck with one, just because it was made last.

But then again and quite often decisions made in the lower courts represented something quite frightening, it was as if there was no sense of reasoning, the ability to reason was completely lost.

And the result of that sent criminals back into societies to re-offend.

After serving whatever was their sentence, which was nothing but extremely lenient; it was neither a punishment or a deterrent, nor was it an act of reformation.

So what was it? What was the sense of it? A sentence that served no purpose.

If there is no meaning in sentencing, then the efforts of the courts as well as the laws, may well be in need of re-examine.

Not acquiring anything, not achieving anything, not redressing anything. Where is the logic in sentencing?

Still this hopefulness of further appealing overturning the decisions of previous courts. That could be seen as a very good thing, to curb extremes in decision making, and especially extremes that allow criminals to walk.

Exposing flaws in a system that should be flawless.

A system, when examined, should be the pride of humans' progress.

Seen only as a pillar for unblemished justice, and with the power to be sure and secure, that no one should rise above the law: de jure.

But instead, it has become a house divided, where some are below and some above the law. And it may be because the system is corrupted, in need of change, in need of a cure.

And yet it is the house where decisions are made, to redress wrongs and serve justice.

That is its fundamental purpose, a servant to the public, in good faith: earnest.

And that is why it is always necessary, for it to be seen to be fair in its deliveries, impartial and serene. Delivering justice wherever it is needed, regardless of the circumstances it heeded.

And despite of course that it is not that simple, neither is it that easy.

But then again it has to remain, always impeccable in its integrity.

Doing what it must, fulfilling its purpose, and being transparent even in darkness.

Unfortunately it had been, and too often it was frequently seen, that too many people who have been offended were left without redress, hence they were left without justice.

Time and time again, the system failed them, too many offenders walked free, unpunished, gaining confidence, laughing at the system, still offending again and again.

And the wrongs they committed for which they were not even arrested, were thrown out of the system, not enough evidence, allowing criminals to beat each dictum.

That was the excuse often given as a reason why nothing was done.

So the system remains corrupted as it is, with everybody just moving on and carrying on with the same problems day in and day out, problems which appear that they can't do without.

And as crimes committed go unpunished, the rise in crimes becomes an epidemic.

That's how it was and it still is everywhere, even in the progressive Western world.

The rise in crimes is now so severe, almost pedaling out of control.

And that may be because whatever was the law, it was flawed in some way or another.

And seriously affecting the judiciary, drifting away from its responsibility.

That even sentencing becomes very vague, not equated to the crimes committed.

Instead, so it has been, that quite often it appeared as though sentencing was given for revenge, or an act of hate, bigotry, or even compassion.

And with no regards for the seriousness of the crime committed, the accused walked free with leniency; appreciating he got no punishment, to commit more crimes off he went, brimming with confidence.

And that appeared to be the regular norm, with punishments too severe or too lenient.

When mankind could not find equilibrium, he did the next best thing, to be unfair.

And that was how things were done, whatever was created by humans.

Whenever it was a function in society, from profanation it was never free.

It was always exposed out in the cold, shivering with the effects of debauchery.

Affecting the effectiveness of whatever is the system, making it weak and loathsome.

And that has been so, and today it is still very common around the world, pushing social justice many moons away affecting both young and old.

And after several millennia of progressive development, with laws changing all the time; yes the world may be much better than yesterday, but social justice is still very far away.

And this has been so for women especially, throughout the ages they have been treated disadvantageously.

And in some cases, in many places today injustice is extremely horrific, still medieval and barbaric.

As it was exposed in the horror of this case in Pakistan where it took place, in the belief that it was implementing justice, when indeed it was the opposite.

Yes, it was a village council in Pakistan, a council of elders the people depended upon to represent them the best it can.

All heads came together with their opinions in a matter of a serious offence, and yes indeed they all agreed upon a barbaric decision; to dishonour the innocence of a young woman.

And with its impudent authority, biased against women especially, they made a decision to which all had agreed; that the offending rapist in this case, his sixteen-year-old sister must be repeatedly raped, as the punishment for her brother's sexual offence upon a younger girl.

Indeed, the sin of a brother visited his sister in a very horrendous manner.

That was the punishment the council ordered in revenge upon a child who was innocent.

And that was the wisdom in judgement imposed upon one known to everyone, that she had nothing to do with her brother's crime; not in thoughts, words, or deeds, or anything that was human.

And the culprit, her brother, got away with it; but perhaps he would never do it again, because the severity was a weight too heavy which his innocent sister was forced to carry, and in a very dishonourable way.

So perhaps in reality he did not get away scot free, because the horror he brought upon his innocent sister will be remembered forever; with that burden of guilt on his conscience all the time, knowing that it was for his wrong, his innocent sister was the one who suffered, for his horrific crime she was sexually butchered.

And yet still around the world today in many places there are numerous cases.

For all sorts of offences medieval chastisements are still executed.

Yes indeed it is real, brutal punishments are the written or the unwritten law, which could be even death during or after torture.

As it still is in some places where offenders are locked up in jail with barbaric codes of practice.

And even death it is, in some places, for a loving same sex embrace.

Indeed, fools as law makers had often made some ridiculous laws which were full of flaws, and of course very unjust, biased, horrid and brutal.

And to the disadvantage of the vulnerable, they were the ones always in some sort of trouble.

And among them there were many fools, many who ended up in jail, and many again who were lucky enough, they got away without any fuss.

Indeed, many of them were not really criminals, but foolish enough to do what they did.

So advantage was taken because they were foolish, but by another fool smarter than them.

Leading them on to commit wrongs, 'no need to fear the consequences, there is none', very convincing was their persuasion, and they joined up together in gangs.

And that was because they were never caught and brought to the jaws of the law.

So realizing just how easy it is, they offend more and more.

And that made them feel very clever indeed, each time they got away with it.

With a smile on their faces, they brag their way, thinking of nothing else, with the same thoughts bustling in their heads, and wondering to themselves; How could the police be so damn stupid?

And that they felt was to their advantage, so more crimes again they committed.

Unfortunately, women and minorities were their easy targets, hence, shop owners too.

With their products regularly stolen, they just didn't know what they could do.

The law is ineffective, the police are not cooperative, shop owners become their easy targets, and for them a disquieting business.

And yet that is the norm, with police indifference and a rise in crimes, societies were in fear everywhere.

So yes, and sadly to say, around the world today crimes are endemic in low and high places.

Many which go unpunished; as it happened to a Turkish journalist, and the criminals got away with it.

Yes indeed he was murdered savagely in a Saudi Arabian Embassy where the murderers chopped up his body to dispose of it easily.

And with cowardly lies and accusative denials disgustingly ignored by world leaders; no one but the law was put on trial.

But then again that is just how it is, it happens frequently.

Journalists become easy targets, murdered or arrested and locked up in jail in many places.

Indeed, many people in high places commit crimes, especially to silence the voices of opposition.

And then everyone keeps their lips shut tight, just waiting for time to dissolve the crime, and left forgotten as if it never happened; no accountability, no justice for a journalist.

Yes indeed, sometimes the world shout very loud, but it is upon deaf ears where it falls, no one listens, no one hears, as it was the case with another journalist Shireen Abu Akleh murdered in Israel, shot in her head, and after more than a year, no one is still not yet arrested; in fact, the case has never been investigated.

So yes indeed, crimes are covered up by those at the top, too many leaders of the world are corrupt.

Yes, that is the corruption as it is, and so justice remains as it has been, just a political game for those benefiting.

Yes, a very sad world is what it is, led by corrupted leadership, and that's how it will be for another century if no one takes responsibility.

So yes indeed, regretfully, that is how it works in corrupted parts of the world.

In some places it is better, and in others it is worse; no common laws to prevent this curse.

And yes it is true, very true that today too many criminals walk free, and especially those able to hide, often paying bribes.

Often too it is the police to blame for doing nothing, but then again, they are often victims, weak links in a chain.

And this too is also true, both political and financial gains often override justice, in a corrupted world that's just how it is in many places with each pursuing their own interest.

And believe it or not, the world today is very corrupt, too many rogues are at the top, abusing their power for personal gains; and this has been happening right through the ages, and still nothing much has been done about it, and that's why the world is as it is.

And that is why jails are filled with innocent people, instead of those with guilt.

The systems are not infallible, in fact they are often contemptible.

They operate on the wheels of corruption spinning only in a financial direction.

Spinning sometimes out of control, and that's when anything goes.

But science fortunately has been rescuing many innocent people, and the guilty who may have walked free, are now paying the penalty.

Yet still a great deal more science is needed, especially in this day and age.

Too many crimes are committed over and over again, and in many cases the guilty offenders are not even arrested.

And this is because man protects man from the consequences of his wrongs, and this is so among everyone, both at the top and bottom.

And those at the top, in matters of the law they make quite sure, whatever it takes they must be safe and secure.

Covering up their crimes with whatever it takes, just like all cowards they can't face the consequences.

So they tell the world lies and make up denials, and they even accuse others in kangaroo trials.

And that's when the law takes second place, bent and twisted in disgrace, with justice so ashamed that it hides its face, whenever serving those in high places.

Unfortunately for many, and especially journalists working in corrupted places their lives are often at risk.

And for nothing more than exposing the truth, which sets into motion a chain of disputes.

With a journalist accused of the cause of it, he or she is either killed, or arrested and thrown into jail, and then with lies, the crimes are covered up in disguise.

And then, what is it that the world does? Nothing else but for a few days it shouts, no one is listening so it shuts its mouth.

So the culprits live to do it again, as world leaders failed to do anything.

So yes indeed, that's the way the world continues, from top to bottom with corrupted values.

And after centuries in existence, making and changing laws all the time, the world is still submerged in a mud of crimes.

Submerged so deep with nothing beneath, the chances are it may never recover.

And yes, that's the way it is today, with so many wrongs inherited from yesterday, wrongs which refuse to go away, as if they are here to stay.

And as criminals get away in high and low places, especially where it is corrupted with privileges.

In other parts of the world where the law is less corrupted, a fair price is paid although not always as was expected.

But at least justice was seen to be done, as it was in the UK system.

In one year alone, more than a hundred criminals, mainly rapists and killers, had their previous sentences increased in a court of appeal.

Overturning judgements which were too lenient, and serving no purpose, neither as a punishment nor a deterrent.

So yes Indeed, it had been a very unfortunate bad example of the lower courts, showing no regards for justice at all.

One may wonder what is its purpose, to be merciful and be a laughingstock, or to serve justice whatever the cost?

With criminals passing through the courts in and out, with a pat on their back instead of a good clout. No wonder criminals offend again, mocking the system which they themselves blame; it does nothing to help them change their bad ways, or even pay a good price for the wrongs they committed.

But then again, those were just a few and a very tiny drop of the impediments in the systems around the world, all covered in muck and need a good cleaning up.

Yes indeed, all sorts of criminal activities are covered up, and even by the very institutions responsible to prevent the rot.

Many criminals are allowed to walk, because the systems cannot be bothered to take them to court; "Not enough evidence" is the usual excuse given, and especially for crimes against women. And those who get to court, for them their sentence could be lenient or severe, that gamble was always there.

With countless numbers of sentences that do not even reflect a punishment, not for the crimes committed, hence victims are left not only disappointed, but with tempers raised they become aggressive.

Yes indeed, very aggressive and angry towards the system which always seems ready to let victims down, sometimes they are even treated as if they were the ones who committed the wrongs, especially women, they experience that kind of treatment all the time.

And as criminals continue to be treated with countenance, the full length of a given sentence by the courts, that too is ignored, and criminals are released early as a reward.

Yes, they are released sometimes years before serving their full time, they never empty the cup from which they drank.

Even murderers are released years before paying the full penalty for taking the life of somebody.

And when they get out, some even offend again, and then everyone blames the system, yet still nothing changes.

And still there could be even many more offenders serving sentences that heavily outweighed the crimes for which they were punished.

Punishments that were extremely excessive, and were very common during the medieval ages.

Punishments that are in one way or the other, still enforced today in many places here and there. Places where the rule of law is nothing more than rudimentary and insecure.

Places where prisoners suffer beatings and torture, and are dehumanized in some way or another, locked up in the filth of a squalid hole, and left forgotten by the rest of the world.

And sometimes locked up for years without ever being charged, for whatever was their crime that puts them inside.

Yes, a suspect can spend years behind bars without a trial, in places where corruption is traded with a smile, a common norm in daily life.

And yes indeed, this too you could believe, there are many such places scattered around the world. In Third World countries especially, justice is sold as a commodity, you can pay a price to be free; indeed, that is exactly how it is with bail, those who can't pay end up in jail.

And in some very corrupted places especially, within their jails is where you really suffer with physical and mental torture, there is where it has no limits, there is where institutional injustice like a productive vineyard flourishes.

Yes, you could even be beaten to death, everything cruel is a threat, even same sex rape is commonplace, for crimes in those places no matter what it is, a very heavy price is paid.

And that evil as it continues from yesterday to today, with no signs that it will ever change.

It goes right through the system from the past to the present, and even much further beyond. With injustice very oppressive, and that's how it is in the jails in many places.

And yes that is how it has always been, and it has been so for many centuries, as a part of the justice system, nay, the injustice system.

Mankind had always delivered judgements at the two extremes, failing to find equilibrium.

It was either very lenient or very severe, in both cases it was always unfair.

And that is how the system continues to be, ravished and blighted with inequity.

And of all the punishments the courts ditched out, both lenient and severe.

There is one in particular that really stands out, with its meaning not very clear.

And that is sentences for a hundred years and more when the criminals usually have already passed the age of twenty four.

A sentence that no one will ever live to serve, that is something that everyone knows, and yet still such lengthy sentences are imposed.

And although it may be just what the accused deserves, still it makes no sense at all.

And yet it remains a sentence that is frequently given, reflecting the shrewdness of the courts.

Just how wise or foolish it operates, how sensitive or insensitive it is, those are what are in need of thought.

But that's not a matter of any concern, because it is still the best in the world.

And yet as the best it still needs to change, because their justice system is still far from perfect, and not until there is a change, that's just how it will always remain.

So now, the punishment referred to in the above, just for a moment imagine that it was a garment that was extra-large.

Now, just imagine giving a person that garment, when his size is small or even medium.

Not only would that be foolish and ridiculous; but the garment would never be worn at all.

And yet something similar is in common practice in the courts of law.

378

Where sentences given are for a hundred years, and sometimes even for a great deal more.

And although it was clearly obvious that the sentence is ridiculous, because the accused would never live to serve out such a lengthy sentence.

The sentence will be still upheld, as if there was nothing wrong.

Not that something was wrong in committing an offence.

But wrong nonetheless, because the sentence didn't make any sense, written of course, with a fool's pen.

And because it lacks reasoning, it has no effective meaning, in the reality of sentencing.

And that is as foolish as could be expected, and from within a court of law.

Knowing quite well that the accused would never be able to serve the full term of his sentence, humans don't live that long.

Then, what is the purpose of its deliverance? Where is it hidden, the common sense?

To make such decisions invites confusion, better the accused was just given a life sentence, that indeed would make more sense.

And yet still there is another folly demonstrated repeatedly, when sentencing for life.

Giving a person a few life sentences, "What is expected after he dies?"

To be buried perhaps within the prison, to serve the rest of his sentence, dead or alive.

Luckily for everybody, there is no other institutional body that follows such ludicrous advice.

Any decision effective for life, it has the same meaning in every culture, and in every language. It has no other meaning but to terminate the moment one dies, and that's the only meaning that is taken for granted, and by everyone who is alive, whether they are foolish or wise.

And that is true everywhere in the world, and in every language, in every culture, 'for life' is well understood with the same meaning everywhere, and without disjuncture.

"So what is the wisdom in several life sentences?" When the meaning for life is so very clear, it means what it is; the meaning is understood very clearly everywhere, no explanation is needed, no need to be repeated.

And any other meaning contrary to that, it could only be confusing as it would be incorrect.

So to sentence someone to more than one life sentence, it does nothing to its meaning but to create confusion.

And when such decisions are made in a court of law, then it makes you wonder what the courts are for.

If it is a mass delusion, or a place that confuses confusion, with language that only a few understands.

And those decisions made are often in sentencing, some are so foolish they can't even be explained. Take this one out of many for an example.

A sex attacker who assaulted a woman on a train, the judge had considered his offence to be 'so serious', and for that seriousness he was sentenced to twenty months in jail, and banned from sitting near any passenger who was female.

Does any of it make any sense for what the judge called a 'so serious offence', and then gave just a twenty months sentence?

And who would police whether or not, by a female the accused must not sit whenever he is traveling from place to place? Could anyone see the sense of it?

And what if a woman or a girl sits next to him, is he always to get up and move on again?

And what must he do if the train is packed to the brim with women all around him?

Indeed, that is the kind of decision that serves justice, and believe me, there is a lot of it.

Many sentences are really ridiculous, they are not effective, nor serve any purpose.

And when they are, they are to the extreme, exhausting the endurance of human beings.

But that is exactly the type of logic that impedes justice in countries everywhere.

When from the courts as an institution of circumspection, decisions that were made seem to lack reason's care, or even simple common sense.

And this was true also even with governments, those who made the laws.

Injustice was always present, especially with laws justifying wrongs.

Yes, laws which they made after heated debates, laws to oppress the working classes.

And which remain in the system for years, until disorder appears and changes them, instead of logic or good common sense.

And that was because the institutions that made the laws, whether they were right or wrong, without some sort of protest and disorder, they never changed any law.

So they remain in the system, with blunders, loopholes and distortions.

Only to be changed at some time or the other, after the appearance of protesters and disorder.

Indeed, the law makers seldom seem to get it right the first time, so laws that were flawed enter the system.

And despite their imperfections, their weaknesses, and their ambiguous interpretations, despite the blunders and the injustices they cause.

They still remained in the system, as the laws everyone relied upon as their only means for justice to be done.

Yes indeed, despite its reputable need, justice was served with abortive laws; laws with loopholes, and laws that were flawed.

And that was why in many cases, there was never really any justice at all.

Indeed, it was always very clearly seen that with unjust laws justice could never ever be served.

So as such, laws were generally feared, with suspicions in troubled heads, the reality of their unfairness made people toss and turn in bed, some with thoughts wishing to be dead rather than to be a victim of the brutality of unjust laws.

Indeed during many years, and for centuries without doubt, the law has been very unfair in places everywhere, this is on history's records.

And it has been very oppressive, brutal and aggressive, and it has been even deadly, it hated the sight of leniency.

And yet its purpose has always been clear, regardless of the direction in which it steered.

And when the arms of the law were fully outstretched, everyone feared it could be a threat.

Yes, the laws were the cause of order as much as they were the cause of disorder, especially to be found in the form of street protests, revolts, as well as riots.

Protesting against unjust laws, or whatever justified the cause.

Such as stealing from the public both their rights and justice, yes indeed, the law was frequently seen as an adversary to the welfare of the common people.

And that's how it had been during the many centuries of humans' progressive development; in every age and at every stage, in every decade and century.

The law had aided and abetted exploitation and enslavement with heavy handed forces of chastisement.

Yes the laws shaped the past and the present, and then to the future they went.

Carried over from one generation to the other, were laws infested with impediments.

It was the way the judiciary was created, twisted, bent and corrupted, by past unreason's sediments.

Justice was often in the service of large sums of money, and those without it, well, they were at its mercy, thrown into a pit to be forgotten, or into the loneliness of a castle.

Injustice was theirs for months and even for years, locked up in a prison cell.

And where injustice was brutal and even sexual, and in most of those places whether it was legal or illegal; injustice was very cruel, it was hell, death was a means for justice's knell.

And that was the system of justice that was familiar to mankind in many places, and it is still the same for many today, despite the changes which were made.

Indeed, after centuries of humans' progress and development, with changes that came and went, yet still laws were always in need of amendments.

Indeed, there is no need to doubt that the laws may have been created with good intentions, but not with wisdom, and at some point in time some lost direction, and drifted into a path where they didn't belong.

Failing in their integrity, their trust and their obligations, failing in their deliverance, they became an unsocial nuisance.

And sometimes of course everything was lost, whether or not one was guilty or innocent. Claiming lives in torture for confessions, based on false accusations, and judicial transgressions.

Yes indeed, torture for confessions was very common, perhaps to justify the horrors of the punishments.

Under torture people were forced to confess more often for wrongs they did not commit, after which, they were punished, and even death they did not escaped.

Yes indeed, confessions were a very admissive proof of guilt taken very seriously, they were never doubted despite the methods used to obtain it, and were always unscrupulously accepted.

So it was necessary, it made the governors feel that they were punishing only the guilty.

It made them feel that their conscience was clear, whatever methods they used they had nothing to fear.

Lawful or not it didn't matter, there was no accountability whatsoever.

So believing that those accused were guilty, and it was left to them to get a confession, their methods used were without mercy, some victims even died in agony.

And that was accepted as an admission of guilt, it was the norm in the grue-some castigation.

To be accused in mediaeval days, from retribution there was no escape.

And it was never lenient, always severe; in many cases a sudden death was better.

Still, it was what most of those who were accused did, they surrendered themselves taking the blame when they could no longer endure the pain, and the warders felt justified, another confession without the lies.

But how much more cruel could it have been than that which was already inflicted upon victims?

Mankind had executed all forms of brutal torture which was the norm in different cultures to extract confessions of guilt, indeed, only that was accepted.

And that was whether you were guilty or not, only a confession would make them stop.

The moment you were accused, no one would hear your excuse; guilt was yours with pain to endure, and it came in all forms of torture.

And it mattered not, it made no difference whether or not you were innocent, torture guaranteed a confession, to guilt you must admit, or the torment continued until you did.

So yes it went on again and again, increasing the pain, until the suspect confessed as was expected from her or from him.

And yes that was what suspects did, with a broken will they confessed to anything taking the blame, just to stop the torture, to stop the pain they were suffering.

Indeed, admitting to guilt was never easy, especially when innocent.

You got the feeling what it will be, a definite death sentence.

But those words admitting to guilt, were the only words the torturers wanted to hear, to bring the torment to an end.

And no other word was dear to their ear, as the word of guilt which they wanted to hear.

And yet still victims were punished again, and even with death, after they had confessed, promises were never kept.

Yes, during the medieval years that's how it was from place to place, some places were better some were worse, every culture had their own laws, their own rules, their own methods of torture which they used.

Brutality was everywhere, and it was used to propagate fear.

But those were years of darkness, those were years of superstitions, those were the years it was often said that truth was nourishment especially in a confession.

Still, injustice was implemented in whatever way which was cruel, either from within or from outside the law, it mattered not one way or the other.

Those with the power that's what they did, knowing quite well there were no consequences, so upon their victims they took advantage.

Yes, that's how things were, that's how they were done, and they were justified to get a confession.

So the warders, anxious to get a confession, with their emotions brimming with confidence, they put the pressure on; increasing the heat, the torment, and the pain.

'You're guilty my son' those were the words loose on their tongues, persuading with pain, and determined to hear loud and clear in confession of a guilty admission.

Indeed, that's how it was, it was their duty which they took seriously extracting confessions from the guilty, and that was everybody accused of a felony, no one was innocent.

Yes indeed, a confession was important to the admission of guilt, and nothing was too cruel to obtain it.

Innocent or not, it didn't matter once you were brought to the torture, guilty in confession was the only required admission.

And not until it was admitted, the torment continued until you were broken.

And that was taken to be true, no one had any doubt in the confessions painfully forced out.

Indeed, it may be hard to believe, but they were all a part of the abuse and corruption of the justice system, the people, the methods, and their tools,

386

whatever, and however they were used, that's how it was wherever you went, written or unwritten it made no difference, it was the norm in the systems, confessions were important, and with torture they acquired them.

Yes indeed, there were no rules, whatever they had they used, and they did what they did with a clear conscience, to torture was their commission, believing they were doing a good public service, all in the cause of justice.

However, injustice as it was noticed, it was not always brutal and horrid; it was not always laced with death, torture, or even a threat.

Indeed it was in some places sometimes forgiving, and very lenient too, to say sorry, that will do.

Yes indeed with good intentions it was very lenient on some occasions, serving no purpose but to create a weak link in the system, and of cause to victims' disgust.

Thinking only should they take the law into their own hands, or was there someone who they could blame and sue to acquire justice, should they pursue.

And that was how it had been throughout the ages with laws man made, during human beings' social evolution at different stages of their progressive development.

Creating the world to be as it is today with what was right and what was wrong, both together were contributions.

Although human beings never knew what it would be like, because it was never within their sight. It was never within their imagination: humans simply did what had to be done.

They just did what they did, right or wrong, they got it done and then moved on.

Drifting from the past into the present, with a system of laws and retributions.

Which were hardly ever compatible, retribution for a crime was seldom suitable.

Some of the laws had no teeth and were not able to bite effectively deep.

Some had their teeth, and in the gum they were rooted deep, so that whenever they'd bite, they'd grip and hold on tight.

And as the law whatever it was for, it was a part of the judiciary system.

Which, as an institution, was affected by its many problems.

Making deals for confessions, such as pleads of guilt in exchange for a lighter sentence.

Intimidating the accused with threats and abuse, disregarding the fact that the accused may be innocent. So drawn towards malfeasance, entangled in corruption, and with fear of the consequences of the situation.

Innocent or not, and conscious of the fact there was not a choice, fearing the worst that could be imposed, fearing the threats of a long imprisonment, the accused would confess in exchange for a lighter sentence.

Indeed, that was common practice throughout the world wherever you went in countries everywhere, the systems of justice have always been unfair, hypocritical as much as they were brutal, some were really very unjust and ruthlessly merciless.

Yes for sure they were ruthless, in a hell of a mess, with fear a force that disengaged the masses from disorder and protest, indeed, it kept them under duress.

And that was because jails were filled with innocent suspects, admitting to guilt through the unbearable pains from torture.

To stop the torment they had to confess, that was the only way, there was no other.

That was the system of justice as it operated, and it is still the same today in many places where change seldom visits.

Places where there were very stringent restrictions, hence little basic freedoms.

Places with conditions as they were in the past, and the question never got asked; For how much longer will they last?

Indeed, innocence without science has always been hard to prove, and different cultures adapted different methods in the belief that they could find the truth.

Most were in torture to extract confessions, which were taken for granted as guilty admissions.

But some were more humane in acts to perform, to eliminate the guilt of doing wrong.

But there were also other methods too, in the search for proof to sustain the truth.

Most were nothing more than ridiculous, based on ideas superstitious, and still to the disadvantage of suspects.

And they often involved pain, with the suspect as the one suffering, who would then admit to anything, whatever was said was binding.

Yes indeed, many unusual methods were used in search of truth, or whatever was a good substitute.

The admission of guilt was all they wanted, and nothing else would suffice.

So they did what they did, no matter how horrid, as long as it extracted a confession of guilt.

Yes, with that they were satisfied, foolish or wise, they got someone who admitted to the crime, and that indeed was just fine.

So yes indeed, it is absolutely very true to say that the systems of justice provided by humans throughout the years of their progressive development have always been corrupt, that is how they were created bent and twisted, and often to the advantage of those at the top, laws were seldom made which were fair and just.

And despite the constant changes in some places, many wrongs committed were the direct result of unjust laws.

And that is the reason why the world is as it is today, infested with many wrongs from yesterday, wrongs the present inherited from the past, many that are today common crimes.

Yes, wrongs ratified by laws that were a common cause of injustice, and even the cause of wars.

And with countries with laws of injustice instead of justice, laws which even deny women basic human rights.

In fact, laws which deny them their rights even in the factories where they work.

Exploited and paid very low wages, from hand to mouth is their worth.

Yes, all those wrongs were permitted, and for centuries they lasted until disorder was invited.

Some laws disappeared and some remain, and with those laws things are still the same.

And after hundreds of years with new laws and changes, to keep up with the progress which human beings were making.

Yet still there was always the constant need for justice; despite the new laws that came with changes, and without any doubt, some things got better, and some got worse.

But they were never all okay, some laws were still flawed, some were with loopholes, and some made no sense at all.

But there were always a few composed of wisdom, with the enlightenment of King Solomon.

Yet still despite this, and all the changes over the years with both amended and new laws, there were always unjust laws which were frequently the cause of chaos and disorders.

And despite that, and the weaknesses that were in the system, measured in whatever way.

It has still remained a firmly established fact that the importance of the system of law and order, both together, were at the heart of every culture, protecting societies from the acrimony and the ravages of disorder.

And that was what had seemed to matter most, although it irked to witness how unjustly many systems worked.

Yet still, as everyone knew, without law and order sustaining good behaviour, nothing would be better, neither today nor the day after, progressive development would have been a failure.

And that was the idea that held things together, implementing laws of whatever sort, achieving order was paramount.

And for justice as sluggish as it is, moving like an ass blindfolded.

Taking many years sometimes to reach a decision, and yet still justice was seldom served at the conclusion.

Yes indeed, it has been an absolute disgrace the many years it sometimes took to serve justice.

Clearly, the awful length of time was not necessary, to the contrary, what was needed most was the ability to reason with the application of wisdom, without prolonging matters and making them worse. But then again, although things are not always the same.

Even the courts have rules to follow, guidelines they have framed.

Rules that made the systems crack and crumble, like a duck they are lame.

"So then, how can the world have a better tomorrow?" "How can justice ever be served?"

When the systems themselves are so corrupted, and to make right those which are wrong, no one is interested.

When so many criminals escape so easily with nothing more than leniency, and if they did not, then they escape through loopholes.

And the rule of law is broken once more, and by the same offenders repeatedly.

Whilst others perhaps were not so lucky, they suffer the fate of severity.

Condemned to a punishment so severe which outweighs the measure of their crime.

But then again perhaps it is a lesson they will learn, and never offend another time.

But who can ever tell what the right decision is, a decision to suit the crime.

Who can tell of that which is wise in efforts to serve justice without compromise.

Indeed, who can tell what is the best way to handle a criminal situation, should it be a heavy fine, a hanging, or a lengthy jail sentence?

Should it be a severe or a light sentence? Or whatever it takes to compensate, or something that is more likely to prevent the committing of yet another offence.

For justice it requires equilibrium, it requires a suitable punishment, it requires a justified payment, but what it does not require, is to reform.

Indeed, reform is very important in efforts to keep crimes down.

And as such, it is understood to be something good, it has nothing to do with serving justice, but a condition that serves the public's interest.

Yet, not very much attention is driven towards that situation, and criminals are no better after serving their sentence; indeed, it often has little or no effect, so they mock at justice, they laugh at it, they see justice as a clown serving no one.

And that escalates crimes, pushing them upwards on the rise, because the system is not operating wise.

And yet there is no aim to make it better, so things remain as they are.

With criminals evading the penalties of justice, serving very lenient sentences, and by them, crimes are repeatedly committed again.

Yes indeed, criminals become so used to the systems which in many cases cannot even be bothered to punish or to reform them.

So they take advantage of the weaknesses which keep the system disengaged.

Offending yes, again and again, and each time they escape, realising how easy it is, downwards goes the measure of their fear, driving up their courage to dare.

But justice for whatever it is, it is neither to be merciful nor to be merciless.

It should not be doing favours but redress, that is its purpose.

And it should never be expected to be anything more or anything less, even compromise is doomed to regrets.

So its only purpose then as it had always been, is for it to do its best, and so to be seen; to be very keen executing a balance in its duty.

Executing a punishment that suits the crime, giving victims some satisfaction, especially those who are seriously affected by criminal acts that left them badly wounded.

And what can be a better balance than whatever you took in the same measure you pay back. A tooth for a tooth, an eye for an eye, and the same would apply in a life for a life.

That it is said is written in the Holy Book, The Bible. So it should be followed as an example.

The big problem is that the law must be certain that it is not an innocent person it is hanging.

To be found guilty by a jury, it is very sad that they were not all able to wisely reason, so it does not necessarily mean that the accused is not innocent, whether or not he made a confession, which could be acquired through coercion, and in many places that is very common.

Unfortunately, that is a weakness of humans, their sense of reason is not always wise, and their emotions often run wild, affecting their ability to think properly, to reason and make good judgements.

So indeed, right decisions are often very difficult to reach, and that is the challenge human beings have to defeat.

Unfortunately all this time, human beings have not yet tried, and that perhaps is the reason why the decisions they make are not always wise, and that includes the laws they make, they don't all serve justice.

So yes it is very true, it is no secret, and it has been happening right through the ages. Everyone knows that many crimes committed are very brutal and savage, and some are even worse still, that no words in any language can accurately describe the measure of the horror and the brutality of some crimes.

Leaving victims who didn't lose their lives, to be in some way crippled or hospitalized.

Not forgetting entire families, permanently affected by criminal activities.

Therefore the punishment should be nothing more nor less than equal.

The measure of the weight, not measured with a tape, nor with the wisdom of an ape.

But with the wisdom of humans, achieving a balance that can compensate for the crime.

Yes indeed, criminals should feel the pain they inflicted upon their victims, and just maybe, there is a possibility, they will never offend again.

Experiencing for themselves the same measure of torment they caused, and that may just persuade them not to break the laws.

Indeed, justice is not about taking revenge, neither is it about compassion.

Its only purpose is to obtain a balance in the making of a fair decision.

And yes it is true to say that it is never that easy, nor is it that simple, and yet it could be done because humans are capable of using wisdom.

If humans can reach safely to the distant Moon and Stars, and even to Mars, then to execute justice they could be just as prudent, they could be just as wise and execute justice with or without compromise.

But first they must have a clean system of laws, justice cannot be executed with laws that are flawed, neither with laws twisted and bent, with such laws, injustice is difficult to prevent.

So unfortunately, justice seems to be still a very long time in coming, it appears to be many moons away; too many flaws, too many stumbling blocks, too many operators who are corrupt, sitting comfortably right at the top, and down below causing havoc.

So in the meantime injustice is what is at the service of mankind, and perhaps it may be there for a very long time.

It has always been there, well established, and without protest and disorder over the years, very little has been done about injustice by its peers.

And that is the problem with the justice system, to get it right without protest and disorder, no one seems to have the insight, no one seems to bother.

So the system remains unjust as it is, as long as there are no protesters, riots, and mayhem, the system never changes, just as it is, it remains.

Yes it is true no need to argue, human beings have travelled a very long distance in time, thousands of years starting from their point of origin.

They have crept out from the terror of the darkness of nature's forest, through the rugged passages of several ages, into the twenty-first century, today's age of science and technology, at this point in time is where they have reached.

A distance stretched far beyond their imagination, and yet they are still travelling alongside with time. And what they have achieved during the many centuries changing things all the time, they could not have been achieved without law and order; and even with disorder sometimes.

So yes indeed this is very true, during humans' travels they have put together a set of values for them to live by and to follow.

Values as laws are what they live by whether they are wrong or right.

And despite their efforts to get things right, many wrongs were done and became the norm in the services of injustice all along.

And yes they were acknowledged to be legally right and held consciously as ethical values.

Values that kept them in the darkness of a dungeon, values that kept them from the light of wisdom.

Values that kept them blighted with superstitions, to the extent that they were consumed with ignorance.

And with laws that were draconian most of the time, with injustice indeed very unkind.

That was the way humans lived their life, that was the direction they had chosen.

A direction which was darkened with the blight of injustice, and supported with laws that were oppressive. And yes, as each generation came and went one after another, what they all found was widespread injustice, it was transparent wherever they went, it was as if it was following them.

They found laws that were flawed inhibiting justice, laws which were very oppressive, all in a state of repair, all in need to disappear, indeed, all in need of change.

Laws which prompted the question from one to the other, "How could such laws sustain order?"

And yet that's what they did, with brutal and oppressive forces, that's how such laws were implemented, and true to say, human beings were often intimidated, everyone feared of being arrested, and left forgotten in a jail.

That's how it was in most cases and in most places during development throughout the ages.

And yet it could have been much worse instead of better, without the changes which came after disorder.

"So what then is really justice, who can wisely define it?"

Who can say what it is, and how it can be wisely executed?

"What about it that is so precious, so valuable to mankind?"

Is it, or is it not the measure of equilibrium, and the right of humans to be delivered without discrimination?

"Or is it just a punishment that suits the crime, or the satisfaction knowing that the culprit did not get away with it that time?"

"Or is it something else, something that everyone got to experience for themselves?"

Something you feel deep inside, the satisfaction it gives that is hard to describe.

For whatever it is, humans should know this, that in a world developed by humans, they may be searching for justice all the time.

And yes, even fighting for it too, throughout their lives that's what they may have to do.

Yes indeed, fighting and dying to obtain justice, that's how valuable it is.

And this appears to be very true and certain, because for justice humans never stopped searching nor fighting ever since law and order had been created, and still today they have not yet found it.

Indeed, the world has continuously witnessed injustice for many centuries, and humans have got used to it as part of the ruling autocrats' policies.

Every eye of mankind has seen it, inflicted upon the masses by the ruling classes, injustice was everywhere to be seen, ruthlessly transparent indeed.

And that's how it still appears to be, in this progressive age, so mandated.

Humans are still fighting for justice constantly, as they did right through the ages from BC into AD. Many new generations came and went, and still it made no difference.

The young and the old together they searched, but can't find justice no-where in the world.

Indeed for centuries they never stopped fighting nor searching, and still there is no reason to believe that tomorrow would not be the same.

And that is because regretfully, even today there is still nothing to date that allows one to contemplate that one day it will change, it will be different instead of being the same.

Even with having wisdom, humans still behave strange; they often behave very foolish as well as selfish, pursuing profits instead of justice, and of course, most things they did were in their self-interest, and to someone's disadvantage, which is the choice they often make, affecting the lives of the weak and vulnerable, and often even getting them into trouble.

So yes indeed, that's how it was yesterday and today, and still it may continue even into the tomorrow.

Still searching for justice for as long as it takes, and that could be every single day.

It is never easy to find, it is not among the rubble left behind, and it cannot be found anywhere in the present, so perhaps it is in the future that justice is hiding somewhere there.

"But are humans wise enough to really decide the substance of justice and what measure is right?" Not lenient nor severe, but the equilibrium must be fair.

"Is mankind without sin and fit to decide, the righteousness of justice without compromise?"

When everywhere today it is the reality that the systems of law are not all salutary.

And in several cases the laws are so inadequate, that changes have to be frequently made to update.

And even to do that, there is always a long wait, so the injustice continues beyond its use-by date. And those in its path know the pain, especially when it is aching.

And so today the world is still very much a troubled place, when it could have been much better than it is, time and time again efforts that were made have failed.

And despite the thousands of years of development and progress, one thing is always certain, and that is for justice today human beings are still searching, and tomorrow maybe they will continue still, and that's because there's still no sight of it.

Yes indeed, searching perhaps in the wrong places, no one knows where it is.

Searching perhaps in the right places, and yet still cannot find it.

Or perhaps no one is searching at all, to find justice is too difficult, so they just can't be bothered, and live with injustice as were their ancestors.

And that may be because it is not as bad as it was during the medieval years; years of torment, years in hell, injustice was the bed upon which they dwell.

Yes indeed, time has moved on with many laws changed; I said it before, and I am saying it again, and yet still they never all serve justice.

With some new laws enforcing human rights, and some still stuck in the darkness of the past, can't escape, no light.

With justice and injustice, both knocking on the opposite sides of the very same door.

Both want to enter, hoping that it will open, but from which side, neither was sure.

So, with laws bent and badly twisted, and with flaws mankind created, too many to be listed.

Flaws for which our genus has not yet found a cure, so injustice continues just as before as if it was mired in manure.

So, into tomorrow with a few changes injected here and there. the legal system gets patched up and amended, and continues to be useful yet ragged, a field poorly tended.

Indeed, this is very true, not an element of doubt to argue about.

The history of law and order everywhere in the world, was written in shame and disgrace legalizing injustice.

And from this there was no easy escape, so it just continued in every place.

So yes indeed, that's how order was maintained with oppressive laws that kept the peace with freedoms lost to hostility, the cost.

It was indeed a very bad experience, life was nothing more than an insecure existence.

And that's how history was written by each generation, all using the same words and the same pen, registering the cruel deeds of injustice as they happened.

It was indeed a reality of corruption, a system where justice was very much polluted; giving rise to disorders as the only force to change unjust laws.

And that was because those who made the laws, made them with too many flaws.

And indeed, as I have explained already, they even made laws to justify wrongs, wrongs which were too many, some trivial, some with a weight too heavy to carry.

Wrongs that kept humans in bondage, and as slaves; wrongs that whipped them when they tried to escape, and even shot or hanged in some cases.

"So then, what is the final solution?" What is required for a fair and just world with laws that are transparent and justice they serve?

When humans have already existed for such a very long time, and yet with nothing more than a dismal record in their international social achievements.

So what could humans do as they continue to develop? What are they not doing as they advance with progress?

Is it too late? No where on earth has mankind started with a plan to eradicate injustice from every land.

Why has injustice taken control, and in every part of the world?

And although it is everywhere, transparent even in darkness, causing resentment, anguish and hate, and yet there is no international plan for injustice to be obliterated to nothing less than its extinction, life just carries on, widespread injustice seems to bother no one.

Perhaps it is that humans have already started its obliteration, but are steering in the wrong direction, with nothing effective according to plan?

Yes for certain, the big question still remains. What are the leaders of the world doing?

It is indeed their commission, a momentous obligation.

Indeed, those are really some very explicit questions, and the answers still no one seems able to find, despite the many centuries of humans' existence, making and changing laws all the time, and yet they never seem to get things right, what they have already changed, often they still have to change them again.

But then, when those who rule make and break the laws as commonly as they do, then things are no better than they were before, and the laws remain just as they are, with loopholes to escape.

And when crimes are committed against the masses with unjust and oppressive laws.

That's when disorder is engaged with rage against the ruling classes, and fights with the masses for their just causes.

Yes, fighting on the side of protesters, fighting with them for their human rights, fighting with them for justice, which by the law has been rejected.

Indeed, for their just and deserving rights the masses always had to fight for whatever it was, nothing was given overnight.

So yes indeed, that's when disorder moves right in effectively creating chaos and mayhem; fighting with the oppressed for their rights which have been stolen, denied to them.

And that's when the arms of the law outstretched in motion shooting, and injustice then shows itself to be nothing else, but a bully heavy-handed.

But disorder really can only be defeated, not by shooting at demonstrators.

That is indeed very aggressive, and agitates the protesters.

So what is needed are laws that are just and are fairly implemented, preventing wrongs from being committed.

And whenever they are committed especially by those in high office, equally they should be prosecuted without favours nor special privileges, and certainly not to be sheltered in corruption's orifice.

For it should be indeed simple enough and easy to hold them accountable for their atrocities.

But when laws are flawed with impediments, and delivering injustice frequently.

With those in high office committing crimes and getting away with it scot free.

And ignoring protesters and criticisms, then it must enrage society.

And when society is enraged, disorder too is engaged, and often with regrettable consequences.

But surely that is something mankind should know already, and especially the law makers.

Shooting at demonstrators outrageously, is not the best way to stop disorders.

So to prevent this happening again and again unjust laws have to change, in fact, they should have never been made, especially as they were made by the educated, they should have known better, and make laws not to enslave, but to prevent wrongs with justified consequences.

Indeed, unjust laws cannot be implemented in a manner oppressive and expect to be tolerated by the masses day after day.

The law has to be just, doing what it must, serving everybody fairly, which ought to be not only its main purpose, but also its fundamental duty.

And yes indeed, it should be transparent, exposed for all to see that it is operating properly.

For it is very true that it is the purpose of the law, and it is something that everyone is quite sure, that the law is both to prevent and to cure; and not to despotism cow-tow.

So indeed, this question is asked again. What kind of a world do we have today, after centuries of progressive development making and changing laws all the time?

How just are the laws? How effective are they? Are they correctly interpreted all the way? Those questions were answered in the norms of yesterday, as well as every other day.

They were answered in the culture of every nation, the answer was in their deeds transparent or hidden, the answer was in the reality of what was happening, it was there on the streets with the people gathering.

Yes indeed after many centuries the world which human beings have created is still many miles away from perfect, and this is despite the progressive developments which have been going on.

Indeed, human beings are still heading towards even greater disasters, and this is because their laws are flawed, and often ignored, one or both are the cause.

Yes there are still too many unjust laws, too many indiscreet laws, and even laws that have no sting, not even a limb, nor a claw, so they are simply ignored, and in many cases they are bent, and even worse, they are broken.

And that's what gives rise to a world so heavily loaded with wagons full of difficulties and problems.

Indeed it is what gives rise to a troubled world with so many wrongs which were left for tomorrow, and when tomorrow came they were left forgotten.

So problems pile one on top of the other with the unavoided consequences of disaster.

And despite the many progressive developments, with changes that came and went.

That is the way the world has been developing, never was there a single day without problems.

Problems from the past that entered the present, then unto the future was where they went.

Piling one on top of the other, and yet no one noticed how the pile was getting bigger with difficulties, tragedies, and a wave of new problems all added together in weight more than a ton.

And even still creating many more problems with their progressive development, both seem to go hand in hand.

Indeed, problems and development are no strangers, they are always together shoulder to shoulder, and that was so every day of the year, from January to December.

Indeed it is no secret it happens frequently, humans are always creating their own problems, even those caused by nature were the result of humans' callous behaviour in some way or the other.

As capitalists they pursue their self-interest in whatever is good for their business, that has always been their priority, on top of the list of their duties.

So yes it is very true that they are responsible, humans are often reckless in what they do. Ravaging the delicate balance of nature, and that's what they did with or without laws they ruined nature for their purpose.

Yes they destroy lives of plants and animals on the land, in the sea, and even in the skies.

And that they did with broken laws which were the ones humans often used to get things done.

And so they did as everyone knows, with broken laws they made things worse.

And yet still it was those very same laws, despite the measure of their flaws, for justice everyone relied upon.

Yes justice was what everyone sought with broken, bent, and twisted laws, but injustice was what they often got, because the laws were not perfect enough.

So yes indeed, humans were trapped, wherever they turned they got stuck.

Trapped with laws that whipped their backs, until their skin and their flesh were badly cracked, injustice was the cause of that.

With a rope around necks just for stealing bread, or perhaps hands were cut off instead, and if it was a horse that someone stole, with a bullet he or she was dead, probably shot in the head.

Yes indeed, for fornication she was stoned to death, and for heresy he was burnt alive, and for treason, his body was separated from his head.

Not forgetting those who were strapped or nailed to a cross, whatever wrong they did, a slow and very painful death it cost.

Indeed, it was very real, punishments were very severe, humans were trapped with laws that were very unfair; brutality was the norm of the day, the only escape was to obey.

So yes indeed, punishments for whatever, most of the time they were very severe, more to the edge of the extreme; the pain was so intense, that even the deaf could hear victims scream, because every wall big or small the agonising acoustics travel through them all.

Yes indeed, believe it or not, but just don't ever forget, history will tell you that those were days of savagery, with laws that justified cruelty, laws that were no friend of mercy, in fact you may say that they were enemies.

And so the world had remained very much the same, day after day, century after century, and for as long as it could be.

Without some form of protest and disorder, the laws as they were, could remain forever.

Whatever were the laws, and for whatever cause, just or corrupt, perfect or not, to maintain order was their only purpose; yet still many used the laws to torture, to enslave, and even to murder. And that was so in many places where you go, including the infamous Guantanamo.

And yet still it was without any doubt, that without whatever was the law; chaos and disorder as partners together, they were always on the ready to take over.

To take over and demand changes with guarantees that draconian laws are never implemented again.

But that was never easy, disorder always had to wait for a good opportunity.

And that was something that the autocrats knew about, so they had no doubt that law was absolutely necessary to prevent disorder from taking over completely.

So they implemented laws of all sorts, with loopholes and flaws, and of course the many that were unjust, and all for the same purpose, to prevent disorder and chaos, so it mattered not if they were unjust, as long as the law had achieved order which was its main purpose.

So yes indeed, it was by those very same laws, and of course with intimidation, threats, and arrests; the peace was kept.

Keeping the peace at whatever cost, even with oppressive and corrupt laws, some to justice completely lost.

So yes indeed fortunately, and true to say honestly, that draconian laws were unnecessary, and yet they were common aspects in societies, generating fear everywhere as a guaranteed necessity to maintain order peacefully.

Indeed, there were some very oppressive laws which remained in the system for far too long; very intimidating and brutal, that was the strength of the laws.

And they were indeed very strong, with one arm of the law it could knock you down.

Yes some were changed from time to time, but only after protesters had voiced their opinion, embracing a firm stand with their demands, when they saw an opportunity for engagement.

But never did laws ever change overnight just because they were not right.

Human beings often had to protest just to get the right things done; and change only came if disorder was on their side, protesting with them for change from wrong to right.

Yes indeed, protesting for rights that were by the law denied, and the only way to achieve them was to revolt and fight, and usually with disorder on their side; that was their strength, that was their might, they had no other weapon with which to fight.

So what today is the solution, what must be done for a better world, when the systems have failed to achieve their goals?

When law and disorder have both failed, and the world remains unjust as it is.

This question has been asked so many times, it is now centuries old and still no answers, no predictions were told; Nostradamus has left the world shivering out in the cold, he left no prediction to unfold.

So the laws remain far from perfect as they should be, and still continue to be a part of the problems in societies.

Yes indeed, the laws are often the cause of injustice, everyone knows this, and yet still today no one appears to know how to fix it, or they just can't be bothered, it's not their business.

And after centuries of human progressive development; and still towards the future marching on; creating, changing, and amending laws all the time, many remained malevolent, oppressive, discriminative, twisted, bent, and corrupted, and most of the time still delivering injustice; uninterrupted.

And still passing from generation one to the other, within every nation, within every culture.

The same unjust laws which were the cause of unruly mobs, resentment, and disorder.

The same laws that are in need of change, gone past their use by date, yet still they continue to function just the same, fit and strong they continue to operate.

408

And as it gets worse from place to place, hopelessness is what embraces the human race, wherever they look they can't find justice, neither in the light nor in darkness.

There seems to be no solution, or perhaps just that no one cares a damn.

Instead of getting better, things are getting worse, the signs are there, new crimes are committed every day, and with more and more people worrying about their bills to pay.

Many are left with their purse empty as hackers and fraudsters get past security.

And this may be so for a very long time yet to come, because human beings are moving much too slow in the direction of redressing wrongs.

Giving rise to a dismal justice system and an escalation in crimes, crimes especially against women; they can't even walk the streets without harassment.

And yes it is regrettable as it is intolerable, and yet everywhere and everyday it continues.

And for how much longer? When this question was asked, no one knew the answer, so they passed.

But some said, 'it may last maybe for a day or two, or perhaps for a week or so'.

And with a smile and their sarcasm, they announced their unwavering prediction.

Carrying a ledger of inadequate laws, for whatever purpose they were full of flaws; indeed the world is drifting off its course, a better future could be lost, especially with the continuation of wars.

And that is because regretfully, even international laws are broken frequently.

Human beings don't seem able to be trusted, double standards step right in, and the law is broken once again by those in high places.

Yes indeed, it is their favourite, an inveterate malfeasance among those in high office, integrity is not taken seriously, so agreements are often broken; no one could be trusted, least of all those in high places.

And despite the progressive developments of mankind which were made over the years with flimsy inspiring attempts.

Attempts to create a world without injustice and crimes, that it appears would take an awfully long time.

And that is because human beings are not yet seen to be dedicated to the course.

They are not doing as much as they should, and not even when they said they would.

Too often problems are ignored, and promises neglected, they are left until they become too big a problem to solve.

So yes for sure, judging from the situation in which the world is in today, change for the better appears to be still many centuries away.

Much more than doubled the centuries already taken; and the reason for that, human beings are still very destructive and hostile, corrupt and unwise, lacking the ability to eradicate injustice and crimes, despite the fact that the two forces are steering the world into decline.

Yes indeed, human beings are lacking the ability to maintain order without disorder in the forefront, causing mayhem because an injustice has been done.

And also because humans haven't even started yet, neither have they any plans to reduce injustice and crimes.

So things are getting worse day after day wherever you go, with unnecessary random shootings, and terrorist bombings, youths stabbing youths, that's how they solve their disputes, and crimes indeed are escalating.

Yes indeed, during all those centuries humans existed, regretfully too many years went wasted.

Not doing the many things they should have done, creating just laws for the benefit of everyone.

Moving with progress from stage to stage, without wars and disorder on the rampage.

Yes, that's how mankind should have lived, instead of always being hostile to one another, a pain in their arses is what it is, can't find a doctor with a cure, can't find a simple pill to cure their ills, so the problems continue still.

And yet, despite this daily configuration with a concoction of confusion, it could be said truthfully that the world has moved on with law and order, indeed the world has moved on with both as friends still together, and doing the best they can whenever.

Keeping the peace from smashing into pieces and leaving everyone with broken dishes.

Yes indeed the world has moved on despite the laws with imperfections, the wars, disorders, and all the difficulties put together, difficulties which were often hard to overpower, difficulties indeed, which were never an easy turnover.

So yes it is correct that over the years humans have not done as much as they should; and without any doubt they had plenty of time, so they should have done the very best they could, which could have led to a much better world.

Yet still today, without any tears, and despite the drawbacks with difficulties, anyone can truthfully say that the world is a lot better than that of yesterday, a world that was very brutal of course, and very superstitious in its deeds, in its ambitions, thoughts, and dreams.

So still one day the world could be perfect, no need to doubt it, but moving at this rate, a very long time it may take, depending very much on the laws man makes, and of course the integrity of those in high office.

But no one could predict when that will be achieved, or even if such an ambition is possible to succeed. But yes indeed, that's what human beings should hope for and believe.

That it is likely that they can create a world with justice, and indeed, a world that is peaceful, a world without wars, and without altercations with friends and neighbours.

Yes it is true, very true that human beings have the ability to be wise, so not all things should be impossible whenever they try, wisdom should be their guide, and success their pride.

So definitely it is not all doom and gloom as could be seen in the mirror of tomorrow's world.

Let not oneself be intimidated with doubts that there are still better things to come.

And yes, without doubt there is a glimmer of hope, because mankind still has a very long way to go, and the world could be a much better place tomorrow, as long as humans did the good things they ought to do.

Indeed the time has gone, much of it, yet still it is not too late for mankind to clean up the mess from yesterday's mistakes, and move forwards with impartial laws in place.

And that I am sure that everyone knows, it will need a lot of courage and hard work to change the world from how it is into a much better place.

And that is because it is already in a very big mess, everybody is vex, doing their best and yet still with very little progress.

Still, I hope humans get there before next year, with just laws for whatever cause, creating peace instead of wars.

And it is just that what will restrain disorder, in fact there will be no need for disorder when fairness and justice work together, serving the public everywhere.

Just as it is already with law and order, fairness and justice should never be separated from each other.

Although one is as good as the other, when they are together, they are even much better.

And that's when injustice has no place, nowhere for it to appear exposing its deceitful face without care.

Whenever fairness and justice operate together, that's when injustice surrenders, and disorder crumbles.

So yes it is certain, there is no doubt within, only then the world could be a better place, with its laws operating in the service of justice, transparent even in darkness.

No more double standards by politicians, and the breaking of laws and agreements causing wars, and altercations.

No more lies covering up crimes, especially murders of journalists, whistleblowers and oppositions.

No more draconian or discriminatory laws because they don't serve justice at all.

No more nincompoops as world leaders, because they all should be of good character, not as those the world had before.

Indeed, no more crooked politicians taking bribes, because today in government there should be no place for them to hide.

Neither for the decisions of fools whose policies are not always useful.

And no more influence and the abuse of power to rise above the law, that should not be tolerated any more as it was done before.

Indeed, those are the things tolerated from human beings' weaknesses, which gave rise to the world as it is.

So now in this day and age it is time to slam the brakes, don't ever leave it too late, or the world will never be a better place.

And yes indeed, it should be clearly seen that within the law everyone should be treated equally regardless of their sex, race, religion, their disability, or their office; whoever did wrong should receive the consequences, without ever getting away with it.

And that should be an example as well as the message, that equally under the law everyone will be treated, and not just with words but with deeds.

And only when that is so, only when human beings have proved that they are capable, only when those in high office are suitable, only then there would be no need for disorder neither today, nor tomorrow; because human beings would be getting along peacefully with themselves, and indeed with everybody else.

With laws that are just, wisely made without loopholes and flaws, laws that would even prevent wars.

Yes indeed, laws that suit their purpose, effective and just, without any cause for riots.

And only when human beings have proved that they have achieved this, that's when they will find peace as well as justice.

Bringing to an end their very long and exhausting search for their lost two very good best friends, peace and justice.

THE ASSASSINATION OF REASON

I have now reached the final chapter of this awakening book, 'A Sinful World,' and I hope that I have unlocked some of your hidden thoughts which were buried in the back of your head, in your unconsciousness, lying undisturbed as if dead.

Now you can examine their usefulness; and do the same after you have read this chapter, the final dose to make you recover from the unconsciousness which for years in silence caused you to suffer.

Yes, the world today as it is, how it has come about to be this way, the world human beings have created and passed on from age to age, from generation to generation, making changes all the time, some no better than what was left behind.

And yet despite the many changes time and time again, the world has always been sinful, that has never been in any way doubtful, transparent as it had been, it was indeed very easy to be seen, not even light was necessary.

Oh yes indeed, it has always been corrupt, ruthlessly unjust, and very unkind right through the ages of humans' development.

Indeed, there have been many unpleasant situations which humans have experienced, situations they created themselves from the ideas which were awake in their heads.

Yes that's what humans have done and are still doing on their journey that has already taken several millennia, from their creation to this present day in time, and still travelling towards the future, and yes indeed, often with things a little better just as they have done in the past, with some things replaced, and some forever perhaps they may last.

Yes indeed, a journey that was uncertain about everything, dark and intimidating, every footstep was frightening, indeed a real nightmare was the uncertainties on human beings' journey towards the future.

And true to say it was dangerous, with supernatural encounters; ghosts and demons everywhere, not a moment was without fear.

Indeed it was a journey brimming with problems one after the other, and sometimes even all together, with no escape whatsoever.

Problems that shaped the world to be as it was at every stage during the progressive developments humans made.

And yet, there was never any doubt that humans could have created a much better world, one that was more equitable, and indeed less sinful, much more loving and peaceful.

Despite the unavoided numerous problems, created both by nature and humans.

Problems throughout mankind's development, many in which lives were lost in battles fought, and in many other unnecessary events.

Yes, problems which were caused by superstitions, when knowledge was lost in darkness hidden.

Problems that were the cause of problems, and without a clue of how to solve them.

So now onto the last topic which I have chosen, this unfortunate act of madness. 'The Assassination of Reason'.

After absorbing the sweet essence of this book, with its rhythms and rhymes which made you feel good, your mind should now be refreshed and younger you should look.

Because the wiser you will get, and you will not forget, that tomorrow could be better yet.

Having the knowledge that the cause of most of your problems were not your enemies nor your neighbours, but those who were in positions as world leaders, those who made the rules affecting your life, those who had the powers and delivered policies which were wrong instead of right.

Indeed in their policies that is exactly what they did, and that's why your life was affected, that is why the world is as it is.

So yes indeed, human beings are what we all are, and as a part of the universal creation, human beings have been created in a very privileged position, and yet there are those who don't even realize that to themselves they are sometimes a threat.

Yes, humans are the number one of the numerous life-forms; not the biggest, nor even the strongest, but indeed the wisest, and yet perhaps the worst, with ability to do bad and good.

But despite this, being the worst, human beings have been given the privilege to shape the world, to explore the universe, and to utilize nature's secrets for their benefits.

Indeed, they have been given the mandatory authority, they are in charge, they are the only ones who can take care of the others, even saving their lives.

Yes indeed, humans have the ability to acquire knowledge, and to be intelligent and wise, and to be as good as an angel, or in wickedness to live their life.

They have the ability to think and decide what is wrong and what is right, hence they can make a choice to take it or leave it, that's their prerogative, they are often left with a choice to make, a decision to take.

And yes indeed, they can choose even to reach far beyond the moon and the stars, and perhaps one day even to colonize Mars if that should be what they decide.

So yes, humans have the ability to make wise decisions, avoiding consequences, doing the things that are worth doing; doing them because they know they are right; indeed, they have the ability to decide.

Creating a world as it should be, with everyone living together in harmony, and not to be stuck in the darkness of the night searching for light.

Or they may just as well create hell, whatever is the choice they make, there is where on their beds they will dwell with the problems they create; that is their birthright, their privilege to decide, to make their choice wrong or right.

And to add to all of it, those excellent privileges humans were born with, they were also given the ability to know that God exists, no other creature can obtain that knowledge, human beings are the only ones enlightened to acquire wisdom.

Yes indeed, acquiring wisdom, knowledge and understanding, putting to use nature's secrets to their advantage.

And likewise all living creatures which existed and are existing, humans had a beginning and may one day have an end, the problem is that no one knows, no one could predict when.

So at this present moment in time, no one is bothered, no one seems to care.

As far ahead that humans are able to see, the end of their existence is not yet anywhere near.

So life goes on every other day, as it has been going on for centuries.

And the end, well, it could be still a very long distance away, no need to hurry, comes what may.

And that's the attitude human beings have developed over the years, with the desire to live as long as they can without ever being forsaken.

And yet it is what happens all the time, humans are often betrayed and forsaken by their own kind, and this carries on throughout their progressive development, it never stops, perhaps it has no end.

So yes it is true, human beings have already been here for several millennia, which is a well-known fact today.

But how long since they were here? The answer to this curiosity is not yet known with accuracy, but it is not very important, so humans are still carrying on, having already stepped close to armageddon.

And yes, that's how long it has taken them to reach today's point of development, with years of sluggish progress, and most of the time things in a mess.

With problems that cost a great deal of time, with one colliding with the other in a chain reaction.

Problems that cost innocent lives, because of foolish decisions, instead of ones which were wise. Creating wars, disorders, and mayhem; with valuable time lost, slowing the rate of development and progress with unnecessary problems, mainly engaged in battles fought.

Still humans made attempts and adapted with changing times, they were never with intention to stand still regardless of the formidable and intimidating obstacles which too often stood in their way.

They were always on the move making progress, although very slow, they were determined to keep on going, even though sometimes they felt that they really didn't know where they were heading.

And yes, that's what they did, and even today they are still developing and progressing in the same direction towards the future is where they are heading, and often accompanied with their sins.

So yes indeed human beings' journey was very lengthy, and like a relay race, passing from one generation to the next whatever the previous had accomplished.

But the race was never always pleasant, death was a constant threat, with fear in every breath which was heavily felt on one's chest.

But yes it is true that the journey was sometimes smooth, often exciting, rough and bumpy, and sometimes with good reason it was really scary.

Starting from the beginning and without anything, the world as it is, today is what human beings have created, during the many centuries they existed.

Building and destroying again and again, that's what they did with most things.

Yes, making them better as they got wiser, changing things all the time.

As inventor humans were no miser, old things they left to perish behind.

Developing in the present for the future, was how they lived together.

Heading towards the future towards somewhere, anywhere, hoping it could be a Utopia.

And as they survived, they kept on developing, always taking to the future whatever they needed.

Some things on their journey they left behind, as they progressed and moved on with time.

Other things they took forward with them, passing them on from generation to generation.

Improving on them year out and year in, getting better all the time.

And that continued for as long as humans lived, even today it continues still, and that is because the world is still developing, and indeed, there is still a lot of progress to be made.

Yes it has become a regular habit of change; creating and destroying as the new becomes old and no longer worth having.

And that went on for as long as human beings wanted new things, and it appears that it could be for always.

So they were always on the go; to progress was what they knew, and driven by their ambition, success came with determination.

But that of course depended upon one thing, that they had acquired the necessary knowledge.

So for knowledge they were always searching, sometimes even in danger-ous places, not sure where it was, they looked beneath the earth and above.

Knowledge was never easy to acquire, in some places it was even against the law; so progress was slow in one way or the other.

And that was how the world was developing, that was how it was progressing; the pace was slow but it was certain, mankind was always on the go destroying the old, and creating the new.

So now at this point in time, just shut your eyes and relax for a while, now try and imagine for a little while just how it was thousands of years ago.

Now strip yourself naked and enter into an unpopulated world with no knowledge of anything. Just what it was like, could you imagine?

Now take yourself into the bosom of the forest, deep into the darkness of a mix of terrifying noises.

Forget the luxuries of today's world, and for a moment take yourself far back deep into the darkness of BC times among your lost ancestors, behind the doors of medieval history and into the forgotten centuries.

Going right back into lost time as far as you can; crossing over from millennia to millennia where light came only from nature.

Going into the times with nature's darkness, the moon, stars, and sunlight, and with all the things that had given mankind a fright, the superstitions, and the noises in the darkness of the night.

Now, cast your thoughts deep down into the intimidating environments of those years, naked in the forest with only your prayers; and where darkness refuses to allow sunlight to enter, so it remained dark as if it was forever, hoping your eyes don't see, nor your ears hear anything to fear, not knowing who, or what was there.

And surrounded by uncertainty, not knowing what it could be when sounds are heard in the darkness, whatever is there you cannot see, so your troubled thoughts keep repeatedly asking curiously: Is it something creepy? And your heart is answering with more vigorous beats as you are captured with fear from your head to your feet.

Yes, living like an ignorant primitive man, who is without knowledge, but with imaginations brimming with superstitions, and with fear an intimidating companion.

421

Yes, the many things today that are all taken for granted, imagine yourself in a world without them, a world of hopelessness every day, not knowing if it will ever end.

Not knowing anything better, and can't even imagine a future.

A world where time was not yet even calculated, not ever knowing what time it is, and as humans, wandering in the darkness of the forest, and residing naked in caves.

Silence was golden, fear was in the wind everywhere, and in every sound, believing perhaps it may be a demon.

Indeed, fear was there night and day, it never went away.

Fear was in the heart and in the mind, it was with you all the time.

Fear which kept you awake at night, whenever you heard a sound and nothing in sight.

Fear which made you tremble wet with sweat, and sometimes dragged you close to death.

Fear from which there was no escape, whether or not there was an open gate.

Yes indeed, fear was there, and when it was not you felt better.

But unfortunately that was hardly ever the case, because fear made everyone's heart its dwelling place.

So yes indeed, in a world without knowledge, just imagine how it was, without inventions, and not even a spoken language to express one's imaginations.

A world where nothing was understood, and by the gods everything was in their control.

Every act of nature was either something good or bad; favours, and punishments all came from the gods looking down from above.

Whether it was rewarding or threatening, whatever in their imaginations was rattling, they just didn't know nor understood what was happening, no one was able to explain the many natural things that were happening; from where above the earth came the rain.

And the cause of that very bright light high up above, which appears, stays for a while and then disappears.

Some cultures believed that it was a god of gods, which they worshipped and revered.

And indeed, towards it they were very humble, the sun as it is known today, was something early humans dread, yes indeed, it was something they feared.

So now, stretch your imagination a little bit further beyond your reach, and into a world where knowledge was only what you believed, with demons or gods the cause for whatever it was, there was no other reason, no explanation.

Whether it was something that was natural; a shower of rain, thunder or lightning, or a nice good sunny day to go fishing, or that sickness struck someone again, whatever it was, joy or suffering, it was demons or gods that got the blame.

Whatever it was, it was always the gods, demons or ancestors, they were always the cause of whatever it was, they were the ones with the powers.

Especially whenever there was disaster, or during the darkness of the night lightning did strike, followed with a roar of the mighty thunder.

Indeed that had aroused fear, great fear, among tribes everywhere.

Believing that the gods were vexed, so they did whatever they could to show respect.

They did whatever they could to appease the gods, the roar of the heavens frightened them all.

So now just imagine without trembling, how intimidating it may have been during those early years of humans' development, years without light only when sun shines.

Yes, years of darkness with wild beasts in the forest, not one single moment was safe.

Indeed, how it had been for those who were living without knowledge of anything, and without light when there was no sunshine, tormented with fear all the time.

Indeed those were times humans needed to be brave, and that they needed with great courage as they stood unclothed in the darkness of the forest gazing at nature, fearing lightning and thunder, in fact, fearing any sound they could hear and could not see what was there.

So could anyone now imagine just what kind of a world it was at the beginning of human existence, those years without inventions, no knowledge, no education?

With so much fear of nature, and of the many things that were happening that humans did not understand.

During the many centuries without knowledge, how humans lived, and how they survived thousands of years ago in the darkness of the wild.

Did humans have dinosaurs for pets, or did dinosaurs have humans for breakfast?

Indeed not, that was too far back, humans were not existing yet, they were not the first to inhabit the planet.

So yes, imagine still, imagine a world without the many things today which are taken for granted and are profusely wasted.

Could anyone today imagine living in a world empty of those things, a world just as it was in the beginning of humans' existence?

Just for a moment, cast your imagination once again far beyond early modern, medieval, and ancient times.

Into a world without running water; no bath, no shower, and not even toilet paper, no hygiene paraphernalia whatsoever.

Yes indeed, are you viewing the picture? Are you getting the feeling of the times which were worse than ever? To be without all those little things in the world today, things taken for granted, things which make life much better than yesterday before they were invented.

Without them, humans settled on savannahs and beneath pines, making sacrifices to the gods for rain and sunshine; and for whatever was their heart's desire, the gods or goddesses were asked the favour, even though humans were not sure they would get an answer.

Indeed, human beings asked the gods for anything, that's what they did, especially protection from thunder and lightning, those were most feared more than anything else, there wasn't anyone in any village who wasn't scared of the natural forces.

Yes, as scary as it was, imagine a world with no conveniences at all; no toothbrush or toothpaste, not even a dentist or a pair of glasses, and nothing that looked or tasted like chocolates, and not even a gun with which to shoot the demons.

No music, no cigarettes, perhaps it was for the best, or perhaps they were not invented yet.

And whenever sickness did strike, it brought with it a great deal of fear because that's when you said goodbye, it was more often the end of a life, there was no guarantee of a cure with a sacrifice.

Neither did black magic or voodoo tricks always cured the sick, it was always a gamble very risky to take with animal parts and herbs in a mix.

Yes indeed, imagine a world without your needs, without fish and chips, no roast beef and yorkshire pudding, nor the fiery spices of a curry dish, and the succulent taste of a delicious dessert; indeed, no pizza, no ice cream, not even in your dream.

A world indeed that was unreal with no conveniences human beings needed, not even a comfortable bed with something soft to rest one's head.

No hats, no shoes, and worse still, not even some homemade booze.

Indeed, none of the material things that we have in the world today, were yet invented, not even a pin or a nail.

But fortunately, mankind never remained still, things changed and changed again and again century after century, as mankind developed and progressed from one stage to the next.

And as humans lived in family groups with social bonds well cemented, and without conveniences that were not yet invented.

Fear was humans' biggest problem, especially the darkness during the day, which came crawling gradually taking the light away from each day.

No one knew why part of each day was taken away by darkness, and left without light, so the dark part of the day they called it night, and that was because it brought along fear, you couldn't see, only hear what was there.

Everything became invisible, in the darkness they were hidden; gods, demons and evil spirits, and even raindrops on leaves in the bushes, they too were hidden in the darkness. and so too were the beasts in the forest.

No one was able to see anything, when the darkness came and claimed everything, it was indeed very frightening.

So yes it was real, with the darkness came a lot of fear, fearing what was and wasn't there, fearing the powers of demons and gods, and that of natural forces, and the wild beast that no one could see hidden in the darkness within the forest.

Yes, fearing every sound from creatures around, unable to see any of them.

Fearing everything, whatever humans were able to imagine, whatever mankind could and could not see; even the noises hidden in the darkness between the leaves among the trees.

Fearing whatever could or could not be, fearing the devil and sorcery.

Fearing hell and perhaps heaven too, but humans greatest fear was in what not, and what to do. Fearing the ploys of their imagination, they may get things wrong and slip right into the arms of a demon.

And yes, not knowing or understanding why the heaven roars with terrifying anger whenever lightning strikes from above, yes high up in the skies the sounds trembled with great might.

Fearing that someone had made the gods angry, that's why they roared in warning maybe.

And with so much fear what humans feared most, it was that they may do something that will make things worse.

And as they live their lives in fear all the time, whether or not it was justified, whether or not it was superstitious, fear was a force that pushed humans backwards, indeed it was a force to which most things were lost.

So who today can really tell whether life for early humans was some sort of hell?

With so much fear and little knowledge, surviving indeed, needed a great deal of courage.

Yes, it could only be true, humans started off from scratch with nothing on their patch.

They had to create every single thing, whatever they needed, whatever they wanted, they came into the world with nothing, not even with a piece of clothing.

And yes indeed, that they did progressively, year after year, century after century, humans created things continuously.

But it was never that easy; it was even much harder than it was expected to be.

And that was because it was a very unkind world; most of the time it was dark and fearful.

With death a real threat every single moment, approaching without warning and at any time.

Yes, coming sometimes like a thief in the night, not only without warning, but out of sight.

And with the forces of nature frequently raging, forces of which humans had no understanding.

It was always very scary during thunder and lightning, and at night especially, just the darkness only was very frightening, nothing you could see, and with every sound threatening, the velocity of heartbeats were rapidly increasing, and with fear in every beat, above and beneath, the ripples traveled downwards from heart to feet.

Believing that someone had offended the gods, and that was the reason why the heavens roared. So sacrifices were made to appease the gods who showed their mercy and sent rain as a reward.

And as humans were without knowledge, or the understanding of the natural things happening around them.

They believed in, and feared the powers of demons and the gods that were to them, very real and terrifying.

Gods to whom they offered prayers and all sorts of sacrifices, in exchange for their protection from evil forces.

And although there was never any reason to believe nor doubt that the gods existed above.

Our sapiens kin still believed, and they communicated with the gods through voodoo priests.

That's what the people believed, and that's what they did, during their difficult years with little knowledge.

And they did so in rituals with lavish feasting, sacrificing animals and human beings.

Ripping their guts wide open, or in a pot of oil to the death they were boiled, or in whatever way was the tradition to give a life as a sacrifice in exchange for favours from the gods.

Nothing was too cruel in sacrifices to the gods, to win their favours and to gain better odds.

And to win their protection from the dangers of superstitions, especially to be possessed by a demon. But not all gods were bloodthirsty spirits captivated with bloody sacrifices with no limits.

Some loved and enjoyed a bouquet of flowers, especially a bunch of orchids and roses.

And that was how it was in a world of little knowledge, humans believed in gods, in demons, in witches and in evil spirits, and still there are people who believe in those things today, and offer sacrifices for certain privileges.

But perhaps not as cruel as it was done in the past, and for human sacrifices, well, that have been abolished, lost forever in the wilderness.

So yes it is true, very horrid were the rituals in live sacrifices made to the gods for special favours.

To save a life from illness and death, or for a good shower of rain to prevent drought, or protection from demons, and evil spirits, in fact, protection from anything; yes, from the gods all sorts of favours were requested, a good seasonal harvest, and to win battles of course, and whatever was considered to be important, the gods were called upon, good reasoning was alien.

So yes indeed, people did believe in all sorts of things because they had no way of knowing, not even by sensible reasoning.

So, what they believed in, informed what they did, for a little life fulfillment and its riches.

And that was how they lived, without knowledge they did what they believed in, it gave their lives purpose, it gave their lives meaning.

So how did mankind reach this station of civilization after so many dark and troubled years? A very long passage filled with tribulations from which protection was only with superstitions and prayers.

And yes, with years of superstitions, years without education, years of fighting and many other problems, years that were full of fear, sorrow and tears, years in blood which history remembered.

And on a journey that stretched beyond its end, very rough and dangerous, and with fear all the time, fear of superstitions and invisible demons, and whatever wasn't or was a human.

A journey that was always death threatening, either by demons, by thunder and lightning, or by curses that struck again, bringing sickness full of pain.

And yet despite their fears, the journey was still bravely taken by each and every generation, towards the future they were always heading, everyone in the same direction.

Indeed it was never that easy, with problems arising daily, problems that were an intricate burden, they came without warning and were hardly single, in fact, most problems came in a bundle, and upon a shoulder was where they settled.

Yes, one after the other the years came bringing with them many problems, some the same and some different.

And for a while the years stayed, and then off they went, leaving behind either little or no progressive development.

And that was why it took humans such a very long time to develop and progress, costing not only a leg and an arm, but often too, their vertebrate spine.

And with many more problems that were frequent, there was always something or the other which human beings could not prevent, they had to deal with problems all the time; each day came, and brought another battle, some were difficult, some easy to handle.

But difficult or not the same price was paid, death claimed bodies filling graves.

Bodies scattered one on top the other, like a rubbish heap six feet under, with mother earth they were covered.

And that they did, whatever had to be done, both right and wrong, especially if it was tradition. Always cautious, fearing the unknown, fearing a ghost may visit their homes.

So for safety and protection different things were done in different lands.

Some hang bones with a mix of herbs on their doors and windows, others sprinkle the blood of a dead animal right around their yard, in jovial prayers, songs and dance.

Some sprinkled ashes in and out of their homes and displayed crosses with skeleton bones.

Indeed, all sorts of weird things were done, during the days of little knowledge and a consciousness brimming with superstitions.

Yes, humans did whatever they believed in to rid their fears of the supernatural, fears that troubled them day and night, fears that made their hearts tremble with fright, and beat louder than drums, beat after beat racing along.

And of all their fears what humans always feared the most, on their journey wherever they go?

There was nothing to them that could have been worse than hearing sounds in the darkness and not knowing what it is.

Yes, that troubled them, but they kept on going, they were not always easily intimidated.

So they carried on step by step, moving forwards sometimes with steps inept.

Going forwards both cautiously, and courageously, humans continued on their journey with their fear in their hearts beating vigorously.

Indeed, fear was always there overworking hearts, beating like drums, to scare the demons perhaps.

Humans were never quite certain if they would complete the rest, and do what they ought to do, make the journey right through.

Not really ever knowing where they were heading, and not really knowing what else to do.

So with their bundle held tight on their backs, believing they were on the right track.

With their heads outstretched and their feet flat on the ground, humans simply kept moving on, to the future bound.

So around the world was where humans went, and settled upon different lands.

And developed into separated different groups that came to be known as nations.

And yes they did so, because they really didn't know that there would be many serious problems.

Problems so grave that kept many in chains as slaves, and many more sent to an early grave. And all to do with human divisions, with each group classified as a nation, and which gave rise to numerous problems.

Yes, problems that were unavoidable, with frequent visits by death, grief, and sorrow.

Bringing more trouble into the world, as consequences of divisions began to unfurl.

Yes indeed, humans slaughtered humans to gain control in the savagery of wars, which always had a brutal end with the loss of families and friends.

Yes, man fought with man just because each had different opinions, and because one wants to steal the other's land, and today this is still happening, as it has been the case in Ukraine.

And that has been a reality in the world, the true stories written in history books.

Humans were creating a divided and dangerous sinful world, and that was what was always happening during the years they were developing and progressing.

And yet still onwards humans went in the same direction, straight ahead towards the future with whatever problems the past had to offer.

It was a dual carriageway heading one way, everyone racing along despite wherever they came from; in the rat-race they carried on, pushing and shoving to get to the front.

And yes, that's what new generations did as they came and went, towards the future they were always heading.

And with the same questions arousing suspicions, yet still no answer to the questions.

No one was ever able to guess, whether the future will be any better or in a mess.

Or whether it would be just the same, searching for an answer was very bewildering.

So without an answer human beings did their best developing and making progress.

They trotted along step by step, anxious to reach the future before their deaths.

There was where they wanted to die, and yet they could never explain why.

Only that it was very important to them, each step towards the future meant, another day gone wherever it went; they were still alive and that made the difference.

And as time took mankind nearer still, each year a bit closer to the future.

Centuries came one after the other, and as they left things were a little better.

Developing and progressing with language to reason together, understanding one another, things were definitely getting better, mankind had found a way to communicate with each other, after centuries scattered all over, and with no spoken language whatsoever.

So yes indeed language was created, it had to be done, without it too many things were going wrong, and it was almost impossible moving on.

So with language exchanging opinions in discussions together before making decisions, that was becoming customarily important, everywhere it was becoming the norm, reasoning together and understanding each other, that made everyone feel they belonged, with their opinion they had a contribution whether or not it was the final decision.

It was becoming a way of life, listening to different opinions helped to get things right.

But it was slow and sometimes frustrating, but the results were good and the world was progressing; language indeed was a very good thing.

And that's how it was for some time, people gathered and reasoned together making wise decisions, and so the world developed with progress, changing all the time with new inventions of material things providing domestic conveniences.

Changing yes, but not always for the best, bad decisions too were often made, especially by those seeking their own interest, and gaining the upper hand with their arguments.

Drifting apart was not very smart, over heated discussions were too often changing into altercations giving rise to uncontrollable tempers.

Humans were no longer reasoning together as they should, they were losing their trust in one another, and that wasn't doing any good.

Too often self-interest was taking over with bad discussions in heated arguments resulting with no agreements.

Indeed, self-interest was swift in becoming a very important part of arguments, everyone wanted to be heard, everyone with their own words.

Everyone speaking together loud and clear, no one listening whatsoever.

And the reason for this, as it was made public in widespread gossip, 'Reason was Assassinated.'

So no one was listening to reason anymore, reason existed no longer.

No more exchanging of opinions, no more reasoning to make good decisions.

Yes, reason was dead, no one was reasoning, it was a real mess the world was in, almost like the times before language.

And no one knew why, some rejoiced, some cried, some said, 'It was because everyone was always seeking their own interest, arguing instead of reasoning, which became very disgusting, something which everyone hated.'

The long arguments, disagreements with friends, and at the end they still made bad decisions.

So what was the point in reasoning when no one was really listening?

Everyone was just arguing in favour of their own interest, nothing was more selfish.

So humans took it upon themselves, now that reasoning was dead, no need to think, much less to reason exhausting their brain.

And although human beings' ability to reason was not yet fully developed during the medieval years of little knowledge, which led into the belief of things which were weird.

But as it was getting developed over the years, with things getting better as humans reason together, reason was assassinated, and that made it difficult for wise decisions to be made; humans were now acting as though inebriated.

Yes, and sadly so it was, reasoning was dead, so when exchanging opinions people argued instead with one another, and even with themselves if there was no one else.

And that had given rise to idiocy in the making and the execution of bad policies.

Taking control of the judiciary, in fact the complete law enforcement machinery, and of course capitalism and its institutions, and even governments and religions.

In fact, idiocy took control of control, it spread like water running down a road, no one was reasoning anywhere in the world, wherever one went you heard only arguments, reasoning was dead, and buried.

Indeed, the assassination of reason had left the world blindfolded, reasoning together had ended, with the result of devastating consequences.

It might be temporary for a decade or a century', that was the prediction of everybody; and with opinions only from guessing, nothing was said which made any sense.

Yet no one seemed to be bothered, it was nothing serious enough for them to be worried about, yes indeed, that's how people did feel.

The general attitude was they couldn't care less, not even if the world was in a mess.

Yes it was always with deep thinking and reasoning in debating, exchanging and listening to opinions, which had aided humans in the making of wise decisions.

It was reasoning in debating which led to successful developments and pro-gress; reasoning in debating is the key to wise decision making.

And it was often wise to compromise, from different opinions one makes better decisions.

So, without doing so humans were left with their eyes blindfolded, and with nothing to guide them safely through the slipperiness of life's passages, resulting in bad policies.

So then unavoidably, humans entered the wrong direction with just a little glimmer of light.

And in their desperation men fought with men, whether or not there was a reason, both sides stubbornly believing that they were right, so the battles continued day and night, and often with no end in sight.

Killing, wounding, destroying, capturing and enslaving; decisions were made unwavering.

Decisions that were often regrettable, and yet still for the same reason, and in the same pathway mankind continued to follow, season after season, and in battle after battle.

Causing unnecessary death and suffering, from bad policies implemented without a good reason.

Yes indeed it has been very often seen that leaders as rulers attack their own people subjugating them to oppression with bad policies, and they even attack other nations to enforce their interest in expansion.

Indeed, unity was never the reason for their colonialist enlargement.

It was always in self-interest to colonize, and in separation, indeed, some form of division was always important.

So the fighting never stops despite the many lives lost, they were always never enough.

So yes, those were just the sort of decisions that were made by rulers of nations.

By Kings, Pharaohs, Emperors, Dictators, and even Parliamentary Democracies, too often they sanction bad policies.

Yes indeed, policies of war and genocide, policies of murder in ethnic cleansing, slavery, segregation, injustice, and the denial of basic human rights.

All those policies were implemented, policies that created disadvantages, policies that made life as difficult as it is, policies that were the cause of disorders in riots, and chaos.

And yet despite how unwise the decisions may have been, the decisions were made and the policies implemented, no compromise, no reasoning.

And from those policies came the rise in crimes, with criminals getting away with it all the time.

Some commit their crimes for fun, some for something special they want, some for revenge, some just because their victims were different, some for no reason at all, it is as if crime is in their blood, and those are the dangerous ones, because for no reason they will attack anyone.

Yes indeed, policies were implemented with devastating effects, and yet the ruling elite showed no regrets.

Affecting many livelihoods in some way or another, as despots they abused their powers.

Despots in the East, North, South, and the West, wherever humans went if it was in a mess, there a despot had his nest.

Yes, many world leaders were ruthless and brutal despots, with an iron fist were the many wrongs they committed.

And they often did so without a just cause or reason, many people they murdered were wrongfully accused, or in opposition were the words they used.

Covering up their crimes, blaming others, indeed many world leaders were nothing more than insecure cowards, with no integrity, no honesty, and worse still were their policies.

And yes they were everywhere, in the Middle East, America, Asia, Europe, and Africa, everywhere their sins were scattered, warring with the intention to enslave and build Empires.

Empire building was just a form of colonizing for the benefit of the ruling classes.

And that they did with no good intentions towards those captured and colonized, usually they were treated as inferiors, enslaved and demoralized.

There was never ever any getting together, to find solutions for a united world Utopia.

Instead, world leaders did wrongs that were often inhumane, and yet they were never brought to justice or faced their shame; so they committed the same sins again.

Unfortunately, many of them remain in office for far too long, obsessed with power, they took it for granted as their right to abuse for their benefit.

And that they did, they abused their powers in many ways, inflicting misery upon the masses. So eventually it happened, Empires crumbled, and the divisions broadened.

There was nothing given in the building of empires that was in the interest of the indigenous masses.

They were exploited, and badly treated by their captives who considered and treated them as inferior races, worthy of nothing more than a life in bondage.

That's the history, that's the reality, so it was exactly.

So yes indeed that was the misery, it was reality and so it was the history, written or unwritten, that's how it was in the past, and that's what the past

439

bequeathed to the present; a world that was sinful, wounded and sick with policies framed from a recipe of madness.

Indeed, the world was governed as it was developing by corrupted forces within.

And although today maybe it is not so bad, the situation is still very sad.

With human beings trailing along still in an evil path, step after step in the dark.

Hoping maybe to find some brightness of light, so that they may see that wrong is not right.

Indeed, many centuries had already gone, and mankind was still moving on, each century with new generations and some of the old iterations.

Paving the way for an insidious world, in rhythm with autocratic rule.

By rulers with dictatorial powers corrupted and despotic.

With no regards to how the world was developing, no regards to their reck-lessness, indeed, no regards for anything, not even for nature's environ-ments.

So it could be very true to say that human beings have no enemies but themselves.

That's the way they have developed to be, to be self-destructive, and to themselves their own enemy.

And although they have been progressing all the time, from age to age and from generation to generation, the world they were developing was always unkind.

Unkind to women especially, that fact could be written on every page of history, how women were always treated unfairly, and in every culture, and in every community, and on every day of every century.

And that got worse ever since humans got lost, after reason was assassinated life became somewhat as though it had no other purpose, but to commit sins of all sorts.

It left mankind confused, not knowing what to do, they were always in search of an excuse rather than the truth.

Creating a world in which wrong was right, and what was right was decided by might.

And it was in that direction the world was sliding, making decisions without thinking.

Everyone felt there was no point in reasoning, and that led to policies without purpose or meaning.

Policies that were the cause of death and destruction, even nature was no exception.

Yes, nature too was ravaged by humans, ignoring the advice of science, and even ignoring the evidence of destruction although it was transparent.

And as human beings during those times were still indeed credulously superstitious, and with ignorance a blight on their conscience daily affecting their emotions.

They were always on edge, and persistently determined, just as much as they were optimistic about where they were heading.

They appeared to have no doubt that one way or the other things will be better the moment they get to the future.

So they were constantly destroying, developing and progressing, with new ideas all the time.

Passing them on to the next generation, until they became redundant and left with others forgotten behind.

Yes, passing them on from the past to the present, and to each generation.

So many of the things still in the world today are medieval in inspiration.

And with humans' problems constantly multiplying, with no end in sight.

They often got very frustrated, confused and agitated, that quite often they were not even very sure what was wrong or right.

And that led often to the decisions humans made, which were the cause of history's disastrous parade.

Disasters that claimed many youthful lives, and only because of decisions that were unwise.

Yes indeed, just think of the many bad decisions that claimed lives especially in wars, when with good reasoning lives could have been saved with wise decisions made.

But not all humans' efforts were doom and gloom, scattered in the wind, or laid covered in a tomb or a grave.

There is much evidence in the world today of what humans did yesterday, both bad and good, some things indeed were very useful.

Indeed, human beings often took from the present into the future the things they needed, rather than to start all over again, with all their progress seceded.

And what they took were the things they created for each and every generation.

Things they passed on to their newborns, things that were both bad and good; as long as in some way or the other they were useful.

Yes, such things as the creation of nations, language, culture, religion and divisions, and of course their experiences and skills, and the distribution of knowledge.

And all of those things they passed on from the present unto the future.

Hidden among them were a great deal of problems affecting mankind and even nature.

Yes, indeed, problems that accelerated the extinction of species caught in the middle of humans' ambitious developments, and their sense of arrogant distinction, and their recklessness with indifference.

And as humans entered into new environments, it was the same wherever they went.

They came and stayed, or they left, thereafter was a difference, the environments were never the same again.

For better or for worse, the conditions of the environments depended upon what purpose they served.

But humans also passed on many material things too, the many they had invented.

Each time making life a bit more comfortable and enjoyable, and even more dangerous too in the event of a battle.

Yes, they passed on many new weapons that killed and wounded people by the thousands.

But that was exactly what they wanted to do, each time there was another battle.

But whatever they were that mankind passed on from the past to the present, and then onwards to the future.

Good and bad, right and wrong, some made life worse, some made it better.

And of all the many things that were passed on from the past to the present, wisdom was one that was never passed on, and that may be perhaps humans had little, or they had none.

So the world continued just the same, with everyone doing the same wrong things again and again, and doing them as if they were insane, indeed the world was in pain.

Yes indeed it was in pain, and even in this modern age, soaked with blood running down drains, from corpses that were left brutally slain, as they were in Afghanistan, Syria, and Ukraine, and many other places which could be named where things were the same.

Oh yes indeed, death came slowly with pain to millions of people, in brutal slaughter their lives were taken, with a sword a spear, or an axe, they were brutally slashed as it was done in the past, or as it is done in this day and age, bombs are the weapons that fill the graves.

And as humans moved on over the years traveling from millennium to millennium with whatever they had despite the condition, good or bad.

Heading for, they weren't quite sure, maybe it was the future; they just kept on going in the same direction, hoping it would lead to anywhere that was better.

And as slow as it was that mankind was progressing, acquiring knowledge and getting new ideas. Creating and developing countless new things with the aim for a better tomorrow.

Yet still the world remained sinful, unjust, and corrupt, a world that was never without sorrow as it waited for a better tomorrow.

And that was partly because of the many divisions, each with their own opinions and missions.

With conflicting ideas from each and every one, arguments were common, agreements seldom.

So it began to look as if something was wrong with humans' thinking, their visions, and their mores: perhaps the assassination of reason was the cause, no one really knew what it was. And as humans continued with their progressive developments, still attempting to change the world as the purpose of their ambition.

Although by now many millennia came and went, humans were still very slow with their developments.

They held on still to superstitions, and to myths, taboos, and religions, they held on tight to the unknown with much concern, and still afraid to let go.

And they held on too, to the wrongs they considered to be right, wrongs that were taken for granted and were frequently committed.

Wrongs that were unjust right through the ages, beyond the light of history's pages.

Wrongs that affected women especially, always victims to hostility.

Wrongs that blighted their entire life, making them dependent whether a daughter or a wife.

And which got worse from place to place; everywhere in the world women were disadvantaged.

There was no escape from the injustice to women, injustice that men took for granted.

Injustice that came with beatings and abuses, and often just for very trivial causes.

And that was so in any home, whether it was a palace or a shack in the forest.

Women were disadvantaged in some way or the other, and often by their own father.

And that has been the progressive developing world, which is the same today, despite the many centuries of progressive change, despite humans' knowledge and experiences which they have gained, despite attitudes which may have changed.

Yes indeed, this you could believe, human beings have been making changes all the time, and yet still despite the changes which they have made, the world has always been a sinful place, and that has been the problem from age to age.

And so it continued year after year, how women were treated was very unfair.

They were denied their basic human rights, and even an education.

And although that was many years ago, in some places today it is very much still so, some things in cultures seem hard to let go, whether right or wrong they are solid norms with roots very deep in traditions.

So the wrongs in the past have not yet completely disengaged with the present, some are unchanged, they remain the same, they have been in the system for far too long, so without protest and disorder change may never come.

Indeed regretfully, that's how things are, and so they were for centuries, without protest, chaos and disorder, things never change, not ever.

And with everyone in rhythm with the status quo, things that don't bother them; they never want to know.

So the system remains with bad policies, until there is a cure, a remedy.

And yes, that could be for centuries, especially if no one is in a hurry to change bad policies.

And so it has developed, rooted and continued to thrive, the belief that a woman was useful only as a wife, and that was the purpose of her life.

That was the general male opinion without good reason, and it was held around the world within every nation, within every home, within every institution.

And it was that opinion from the past to the present, hinged tightly in cultures as the norm.

Denying women their basic human rights, and it made no difference whether it was wrong or right.

So yes indeed, the culture of contempt for women, disadvantageously treating them, this has been happening everywhere in the world and still no one

446

seemed to care, so it continued year after year, it continued for centuries, and today still causes grief.

Yes, it became a characteristic solidly welded in male behaviour, instinctively treating women as though they were inferior.

And it went on for century after century, in silence women suffered disparity.

So for their rights they had to organize and fight, nothing came easily overnight.

Nothing was given free, not even the end of slavery, mankind always had to fight for what was right, and even for rights by the laws denied.

And that was particularly so after reason was assassinated, no one was reasoning anymore; things just got worse, many decisions made were apathetic, and even constituting law.

Indeed that's how the world was developing alongside the progress it was making, century after century many things were the same, with too many bad policies implemented.

Developing and progressing at the same time together, with many wrong things destabilizing the prospects for a better future.

And it mattered not what age it was, although there were many changes which came about, and yet for far too long many wrong things remain the same, repeated again and again.

That even for their basic human rights, women had to fight, there were always those who opposed change, even slight.

And they were the ones with the weapons, brutalizing people to preserve injustice, yes indeed, that's what they did.

And that went on for many years too long, that today in many places it is still the norm.

Taking advantage of those who are weaker, as everyone raced into the future together.

Pushing and stumbling one upon the other, and for no good reason whatsoever.

And as life continued with gradual change, always changing and still changing again, moving with time from age to age; the future was looking bright and a bit promising.

And of all the many changes, there was but one that was so different from the rest, it was very conspicuous.

It had opened up several doors to heaven and hell which were tightly closed for many years.

Yes indeed it brought many more opportunities giving everyone a chance to live in luxury.

And that was the one which replaced bartering, like a good pill it had benefits and side effects, one of which was debt.

Indeed, debt was a threat, it was a devastating side effect, but like all side effects not everyone it did affect.

Yes indeed, it was rewarding too, but that was left up to you.

Yes, debt offered opportunities for vast rewards, but financial death was also in its claws; whichever one, the choice was yours.

And that was exactly what it did cause, financial death in large numbers, that even today people are still dying, no cure, no vaccine, debt seems immune to everything.

And it was the same from one place to the next, financial death was not just a threat, but something you could live to regret before your death.

But if you knew from debt how to rise up again, instead of, in financial death to remain.

Avoiding death financially, and of course debt socially, with only one way out, 'Money,' and that to acquire was never easy.

So yes money it was called, and money it was, money was its name.

And it had an alarming effect, as it was exchanged for anything, there was a price for everything, whether or not the currency was the same.

But it also had a perplexing effect during the time it took to settle in.

And as it was never a recluse loner, it brought with it several problems.

Problems of many kinds, problems associated with crimes; and even with death sometimes.

But when it first arrived it was a surprise, and it was treated like a stranger.

Until very much later as it got familiar, a scramble for it began.

And money became not a king but a god, very famous, worshiped and loved by everyone.

Because it was the one and the only thing, the more you had the more you were empowered.

And that had led to a new commitment, 'Borrowing' a commitment yes with a deadly sting.

So yes indeed, everybody was involved with somebody, and the common denominator was money.

You were either in debt to no one, or you owed a lot of money to either Tom, Dick, or Harry, and sometimes to all of them, and that's when the headaches began, and quite often spreading, that even your toes start aching.

And that's usually when you are threatened, yes, either threatened with eviction, or to be hurt by someone if you don't come up on time with the payments.

Paying back a great deal more than what you borrowed, sometimes even more than doubled, that is the disadvantage of every loan.

And it could be even more than that, indeed debt is a trap in which you could break your neck, and yes indeed, you may even break your back when in debt and can't pay it back.

And as money became so compelling, something everybody wanted.

And with the same ambition, to get as much as they can, because it was the only ticket to heaven.

It was the one and the only thing that could be traded for anything, no matter how small or how big. Or whether it was a wife, or someone's life; when you had money you could reach to the skies. And it was obtainable even without reason, yet still it was always very hard to get, and even when you placed a bet.

So whether or not it was good or bad, right or wrong, whoever had money was a king without a crown. And it mattered not whether you smiled or frowned, whether you were famous or just a boring clown, when you had plenty of money, whatever you did, although not always right; you were never wrong, and for friends, you were never short of them.

But of all the things money had changed, that was not a part of the norm before.

There was one so vile and yet it was needed to survive, always it was knocking upon a door.

And it became known with little concern, for creating a division between rich and poor.

A division that brought about many changes, changes that mankind had never seen before.

And the extent of it, although it was not deliberate, it kept on widening even more and more.

Yes, the name of the culprit money brought with it, was with name capitalism; a direct descendent and a loyal companion of money.

And they had adopted a very thrifty son within their avaricious family.

And those three together were very close, money, capitalism, and the capitalist.

And they each took good care of each other, protecting the interest of one another.

And as the world kept on moving on, still in the same direction.

Into the future was where those three together were heading, money, capitalism and the capitalist.

Keeping close to human beings, especially those who were in big business.

And despite the general feeling that it was a risk they were taking, yet still they kept on going as if they didn't care much about anything.

But with their arrival settling into the system, many more locked doors were opening up, with opportunities to get right to the top.

And that created an incentive for positive thinking, human beings were creating and inventing more and more new things.

Yes indeed, everyone wanted to get up there, most were unprepared, so it was with many more problems they were engaged.

With debt around their necks, tightening slowly, getting to the point where they can't breathe.

Even institutions tumbled and crumbled, and some governments had to have their debts canceled to save them from further financial troubles.

So yes indeed don't be deceived, debt often bleeds whoever was in need, and sometimes takes much more than that which was necessary.

It is a force that is very strong, it has no respect for anyone, and it is known to have brought large institutions tumbling down.

It also gives rise to a sea of sharks that are wild and very ferocious in their bites, biting off large trunks, not off the debt, but what they called interest.

Indeed debt destroys lives, those who are weak and don't know how to survive, but at least it could be avoided with good reasoning and intelligent planning.

Yes it could be avoided with the opportunities provided, indeed, the opportunities are always a gamble, sometimes risky and could be even illegal too.

But there was always money to be made from whatever you did, capitalism was the wagon to ride on.

Yes it was safe and secure, although not always very sure that there was a chance of arriving into heaven, especially with debt heavy on your chest, which was often the cause of an accidental death.

So yes indeed, money is the key to paradise, that's what it is, that's how it was established after it had arrived, there is no other key, so there is no need to try the others you have.

And yet still there are many people who say that money is not happiness, what foolishness, perhaps they don't know how to spend it other than on booze and chocolates.

Even to give to family, friends, and charities, you are rewarded with happiness from the smile you put on their faces, regardless how large or small it is.

But unfortunately, there is a big problem with money, a little bit of it is no good to anybody, that's when you remain in poverty.

So to say that money is not happiness, indeed that could be true, can't argue, but only when you have a very little bit of it, it gives you headaches, can't pay your bills, no happiness that's true.

But happiness or not, money is never that easy to get, not even in debt to acquire it.

One always had to have something to exchange, whether it was a service or an object.

And that of course brought a lot of sorrow and grief in cheating and exploiting.

Knowing quite well that there was no alternative, it was the only way to make a living.

And that as good and as bad as it had been, it was still passed on from the past to the present.

Money was becoming well established, and so too were capitalism and its forces.

Yes indeed, forces of ruthlessness, forces of selfishness, forces of dishonesty and avarice.

Those were the forces of the capitalist, used to exploit and to take advantage.

So yes, money was passed on and on again, it has always been on the move since circulating, and so it still is on the move today, although getting weaker every day.

Yes, each time it was passed on it lost its strength, affecting its health, so it lost some of its value as well.

And as it gets weaker it may retire, but exactly when, no one is certain.

Perhaps with technology it may quietly disappear, there are already signs of it everywhere.

It remains hidden in banks, too weak to travel around, and with a phone or a card it changes accounts.

And it mattered not how much one argued, to the point of being clever or confused, weaker and weaker money was getting, no one knows from what it is suffering, some said that it was something called inflation, but whatever it was there was yet no cure for the patient; and in the meantime always it was more one had to pay for the very same things every other day.

Causing poverty to expand with rising prices getting out of hand, currencies weakening, you pay more for everything, inviting a need for urgent change; everywhere there is an uprising because people can no longer afford the prices, and yes true to say, corruption is the culprit which everyone blames.

And yes it is said, despite the economical hell, there are those who are swollen fat with profits, they consume too much and yet more they will take, while others to the very bone they are skint, they have almost nothing.

Yes indeed, there are advantages and disadvantages, but only those who are skint, know just how bad it is.

Still despite the illness which weakens currencies, capitalism has been serving the people well, with opportunities to get out of hell.

But as it will be expected in the capitalist world prices are difficult to control, 'market forces are the real bosses,' that's what everyone says, and they listen to no one, whenever prices go up, they love it up there so much, they seldom ever come back down, they always keep on rising further and further, right through the roof they go whenever they reach up there, and that's when they never come back down; not in the market places, not in the stores nor the shops, in everyone of those places they charge too much.

Yet still despite this, despite the ill-health and the weakness of currencies, they manage to keep their usefulness and their influence, opening the doors to hell and heaven.

Yes money is still very useful to everybody, the only time anybody did not need money, it was because they were dead already.

So in a world intoxicated with corruption, money will always be circulating in the wrong direction.

In the direction infested with wrongs of all sorts, some with the most despicable nature, and yet someone would still commit for a price on offer.

That's how it was, that's how it is, and perhaps that's how it may be for always.

And that is how things may always remain, as long as money is a vital and an important thing.

And to this single dilemma, mankind may never find an answer nor recover, and yet perhaps an opportunity is there, hidden under cover somewhere.

So yes in the meantime, despite whatever was the problem, human beings carried on still moving on in the same direction, as if they knew they still had a very long way to go, and with that thought in their minds, they were often very troubled.

Reaching the future was always on their minds both at night and daylight, hoping all the time that things will be bright.

Trotting along in the same direction, everyone grasping their bundle they just followed on.

Very relaxed humans carried their sword and their axe, prepared for any attack as they kept their footsteps on track.

Indeed, the journey was often dangerous, especially during the hours of darkness, every sound was a threat, every threat was death, and that's when someone had their last breath.

But when will humans ever reach the future, and would things really be better?

Those were questions that troubled them the most, those were questions that kept them on their toes, those were questions with answers they wanted to know.

Those were questions still without answers, despite how much further they went.

And that had caused them a lot of bother, not knowing how much further; whether or not the future was any closer, after years of traveling together.

Indeed, it was really frustrating most of the time, no indication, not a sign, not knowing how much further they had to go, how high was the hill which they had to climb, as they were always traveling in an upwards direction, and very tiring was the incline.

But despite not knowing, and because there was no other choice, mankind kept on going and developing in a slow progressive cycle of change.

Which was more obvious and continuous mainly in the use of material things from nature rearranged.

While the social structures, as bad as they were, were hardly ever improving.

And whenever they did the pace was slow, it was so very slow, that it hardly ever looked as if anything was really changing.

But most things did change, not all things remained the same, change was slow, but things did change from old to new.

But that's how things did look with gradual change, changes that were no longer the same, and yet they were not always recognisable, the changes that came were so little.

And so it was, the years just pushed ahead, with all that were loved and all that were feared, including the sounds of terror that came from hell, all crossed over from BC into AD.

Yes indeed, for thousands of years humans lived in conditions that were very primitive.

Now they were crossing over unto another bridge into a new age, with hopes of acquiring more knowledge and making life better still, there were too many things still needed, life was still very primitive.

And at that point in time, the distance already traveled by mankind was very considerable.

It was indeed a good few millennia, and with so many changes things were getting better, and yet still no one was sure about the future. What would it be like when they get there?

No one had an idea, nothing was in their sight, it was a too far distance to see even in broad daylight.

And that was because humans did not keep up with time, so they were left very far behind, with many up hills they still had to climb on a journey that could be very unkind.

And with the burden of whatever they had achieved, and with all the things they believed they may need, they were determined to take them to the next decade, and that's what they did.

Whether or not they were good or bad, whether or not they made them happy or sad.

Things that became common and taken for granted, things people believed they could use them still.

And with injustice, corruption, oppression, exploitation, and brutality, all together in one package, humans took them over with them, crossing the line from BC into AD, yes, crossing the line with optimism for a better life.

True indeed, the past was always taken into the present, whether it was right or wrong it made no difference.

So the present was always loaded with things from the past, to be taken to the future if they could last.

And in that load was not only gold, but a bundle of trash which humans think may be useful.

So from the present they were carried to the future, where they may still be useful for some purpose or the other.

And so it had been, both good and bad things continued just the same, year after year with little change.

And that was mainly because in those days, those who ruled they governed like fools, with iron fists of injustice their tools.

They abused their powers implementing draconian laws, with most freedoms lost.

They created difficulties implementing bad policies that even affected nature in some way or the other.

And they also created not peace on earth, but an earth in pieces, scattered far beyond man's reaches. A world engaged in the pleasures of sin, which was the cause of almost everything that was wrong with our kin.

And it was also a world in which the people lived in fear, not just of the unknown, but also of one another, and especially of those who ruled abusing their powers, fear was always a part of humans' troubles.

So yes this is true, it was never a secret, the world had appeared to be very sick.

It was lame, disabled, too many things that were done were wrong, and that's the way human beings were carrying on; too much pleasure, too much corruption, too much self-satisfaction.

With oppression and brutality, people were locked with chains in slavery, many were slaughtered in wars, some imprisoned into serfdom, and even many more were condemned to a life sentence of destitute poverty, and although there were passages of escape, never was there an opportunity.

And that's how those who were unfortunate lived, a lifestyle that continued through the ages.

And it may be in the future too, and throughout humans' existence it may continue.

Because even today there seems to be no other way, humans are still engaged in the wrongs of yesterday, and added to that are the new wrongs of today.

Indeed, that has been the outlook, that has been the view; that was what mankind was able to see all the way through; that was the prediction from sorcery and voodoo, and from Nostradamus too.

That was the progress of a developing world, for tomorrow things were not always looking too good.

And that was because humans were seldom wise whenever making decisions to do what was right.

But perhaps they were not to blame, human beings were badly affected when reason was assassinated.

Nobody was reasoning any more, reasoning was dead and gone, everybody was arguing, self-interest they blamed; even those in high office, the blame game was their favourite.

Pointing fingers at one another, criticizing, accusing, blaming each other.

Whenever anyone tried to reason no one would listen, preferring instead to argue, the best they could do.

And because there was no one to reason with, exchanging opinions so that wise decisions could be made, the same wrongs got done again and again, until the time came that things did change, which was often several decades.

And as humans continued on their forward move, making the best of their achievements.

Heading towards, they still didn't know where, but they believed it was towards the future.

Yes indeed, everybody was always talking about the future, what they will do when they get there.

And that meant that they were not there yet, and as new generations came, they all raced along, anxious to get away from the present.

So gripping tight to whatever they had, they trampled upon whatever was on the ground, despite slowly moving on.

Yes, it was with a pace too slow, a bit too cautious as if they didn't really want to go towards the future, but that was not the case, it was the uncertainties which made them afraid.

Very cautious was each footstep, especially during the hours of darkness, with doubts troubling their minds, and confused sometimes, they were often tempted with the decision to stay behind.

Afraid of their footsteps, afraid of their shadows, afraid perhaps they were moving too slow, and may not get there until many tomorrows.

So yes indeed, confused sometimes, humans felt that there was no need to hurry, they could get to the future any time, finding it difficult to make up their minds with all sorts of ideas tumbling over in their heads, it was a bit of a problem for them to make a right decision.

But in the end, they felt that they had to go regardless how slow, they couldn't just remain in the present, that was not an option, so onwards to the future they travelled with their decision.

So relaxed and determined they continue on their journey, leaving the prints of their footsteps on the ground behind them, for history to record as an expedient event.

And as they traveled on in the same direction, still amassed with yesterday's bundle of problems.

There was one that was the worst with effects like a curse, it was the problems caused by human divisions.

There were so many of them, much more than ten, affecting men, women, and children.

So yes indeed with mankind divided, the problems it brought for humans to live with, the only thing that was worse, was to be possessed by a demon's curse.

And although it may be true to say that today things are not as bad as they were yesterday, there was always the danger that, instead of getting better, things were geared to be getting worse, that's how it often did look.

With divided mankind still always fighting one another, and for what reason, it didn't matter.

No one really cared, no one was afraid, with everyone doing a lot of talking, while the fighting kept on sending many people to an early grave.

Yes, men, women, and children, military and civilians, bombs don't know the difference, they are not yet that intelligent.

So yes indeed, right or wrong the fighting went on with everyone using their weapons of destruction as an instrument to reason.

And that had been the case since reason had been assassinated, mankind seldom ever verbally reasoned wisely together, and cooperating with one another.

And whenever they tried, it just hurt their pride, they couldn't even decide what was wrong or right. So it was with a gun, with threats and intimidation, brimming with ammunition, nation dared nation.

And that had always been the case when people were foolish, in the past, the present, and today, and as a result, bad decisions were made, and when too many were made, they were devastating, badly affecting several things that were in the first place, very difficult to gain.

Even affecting nature in some way or the other, decisions executed by humans were not very often wise ones.

And although it may be true that humans often knew what they should not do.

They still continue with what they pursue, and more often than not in a jolly good mood; they relish the wrongs they do.

That's when they admit it, and brag about it as if it was something useful.

Doing them only out of self-interest, regardless of the consequences which in several cases were devastating.

And when they did, they were hardly ever able to put the pieces back together, to put them in their places just as they should be, things were damaged so badly.

Indeed, what was left was nothing but a mess, nothing that was easy to redress.

And then when it was too late, that's when they effectuated, believing it was better than never.

And yet they said in so many ways, the same thing they said again and again, that prevention was better than a cure.

But they hardly ever prevent, instead they show off their strength, and even with provocations to start a war.

So, oh yes indeed, that's how it had been for many centuries, that's how mankind has developed to be, with a hostile mentality, especially after the assassination of reason, trust was lost, suspicions common, no one had confidence in anyone.

And that was because reasoning was dead and gone, and that's how it was with everyone, arguing became more common.

Disregarding the consequences, humans did whatever it was, right or wrong they did them still, especially when it was in their interest.

And it was in that frame of mind that human beings developed over time, influenced by the pressures within their environment; adapting the ways in which things were done regardless of whether they were right or wrong, most of the time they had no choice.

And that of course they never stopped doing, always developing and destroying, one was never done without the other deploying.

And that is what humans will always be doing, as long as the world is in need of change, there will always be room for better things to be arranged.

So the future to them was looking good, indeed there was some hope, that's what they believed, but without good reason, there was no certainty in their vision, in fact there were more obstructions.

And as human beings continued to move forwards from age to age, with efforts to progress as they turned a new page.

And still trying to make the world a better place, without injustice and suffering.

That they tried and tried, and failed again, because the world was too deeply submerged in sin.

Pursuing pleasures from injustice and wickedness, as corruption spreads in every place.

Indeed, humans were treated as property, bought and sold into slavery.

That's how the world had developed to be, that's how it was for centuries, no one knew for how much longer it would continue; the reign of terror was still everywhere.

Yes indeed, it was a world of masters and slaves for much of the period during both the BC and AD ages.

That was the choice human beings conscientiously made, they were developing the world with labour from slaves; developing a conscientiousness of ruthlessness, and where the air was no longer fresh but heavily polluted, contaminated with discontentment and hate.

So the years ahead were not really looking too good, but that was as far as humans were able to look, further than that, there was no certainty of what kind of a world it would turn out to be.

And yes indeed, everyone agreed, that humans were not doing the things which they should be doing, and for predictions, although uncertain, it was still going to be a world with better things, sinful yes, and perhaps in a mess, but it will be with a great deal of progress, so it was predicted by Nostradamus.

Yes indeed, Nostradamus had given the people hope which enabled them to cope.

And as the world developed even more and more, as centuries rolled over one after the other. So too were the problems created by divisions, for centuries they just came and went.

Problems associated with discrimination, advantages and disadvantages.

Sowing seeds of bigotry, suspicions and hate, adding to the problems of injustice.

Which had created opportunities that were seized, and were relentlessly exploited.

To degrade and dehumanize other races, by capturing, branding, selling and buying; and kept quite often locked up in chains, several world leaders indeed were insane, their policies were ruthlessly inhumane.

Indeed, many of their policies were oppressive and without mercy, and even beyond insanity.

And with so many lost opportunities, the world was indeed very angry.

And yes it was angry, and it had been so throughout history, and without any doubt it has been a very hostile place, that's how it was, that's how it is, that's how human beings have created it, and that's how it is to this day.

So with its anger it hasn't changed, passing hostility from age to age, because it was never disengaged, no one had the courage.

And although with many progressive changes, acquired with understanding and the use of knowledge, humans were still committing the same wrongs again and again, and with full consciousness of what they were doing.

Yes they did their wrongs for their pleasure and satisfaction, and to the disadvantage of someone.

Wrongs that became the norm, many committed still from beliefs in super-stitions, wrongs that were passed on, committed upon the weak by the strong, and especially against women.

Still it is true to say that despite the many wrongs of yesterday, AD times were much better than BC times, human beings were progressing with change, creating better things all the time, leaving the past behind.

Yes indeed, this you could believe, with time human beings were becoming more civilized, leaving many wrongs behind, and living within a code of rules, within a code of civilized values.

But they were achieving them slowly bit by bit, progressive development was never quick.

But civilized or not, and with values humans made up, they were hardly wise, too many wrongs they did were unjustified, even their so-called val-ues were discriminative and contaminated with inequitable rules.

But it was not that humans were not trying, but the forces of good were always failing.

Evil indeed had the monopoly, and it created many opportunities.

Opportunities of every sort, it was indeed like a broth.

Opportunities for humans to build the world in whatever way they felt they could.

Opportunities for them to create a heaven or a hell, whatever was their choice was where they dwell.

Indeed with so many opportunities, human beings were developing and progressing slowly but surely; they were putting the pieces together, unfor-tunately, not always as neat as they should be.

Shaping the world in whatever form, with the knowledge they had they carried on, hoping each day would be better than the day before, and hoping still that however better things were, they could be much better still tomor-row.

Passing their progress to the next generation, for them to add their own contributions.

And what the old generation did pass on, some were their problems they passed to the young.

Problems the young didn't really want, they were what the old had left after they were dead and gone.

And it was so the past entered the present, with a backpack filled with whatever.

Whether it was with love or with hate, it didn't really matter one way or the other; whether it was for the worse or for the better.

And so the world took its shape and form just as it is today, bumpy and rugged especially along the edges where danger silently waits.

Oh yes indeed, if you didn't already know you could believe; the world has developed to be an uneven playing field.

With bumps here and there, everywhere, it is so bumpy, that every step taken, lies danger beneath your feet.

And although it has been developing for centuries before and after Christ came.

The rugged surface of the world, although it has changed, there is so much still to be changed again.

And that is because most of the world leaders did so very little, or nothing at all to level up the playing field.

So that it could be said that Christ didn't die in vain, because humans indeed have achieved something.

But then again that depends on the world leaders, the politicians, whether or not they have got the ambition, it has always been their commission.

Yes indeed it depends upon them, they are the ones who make the decisions.

Unfortunately, just as the world is today with its uneven surface, and the many leaders who came this way, that's all the progress that humans have made during the many centuries they existed.

From the very beginning of humans' existence to this present day in time.

Building and destroying throughout the ages, there have been many changes at different stages.

And this is true as it has been recorded, the world was built with labour from slaves, labour that sent many to rest in an early grave, indeed, bad policies with exploitation to blame.

And with exhaustion, starvation, beatings, and diseases that were rife, they all claimed lives.

And driven by the forces of exploitation and injustice, the world has developed to be as it is, sinful and corrupted.

And yes of course you can be sure without any doubt, the world has not yet fully recovered from the sins committed by humans' ancestors.

Yes indeed, they have left their mark, they have left their footprints, they have left their history, and despite their irrational ventures, some cultures today, instead of rejecting the sins of their ancestors, are still committing the same.

And this is as far as humans have progressed during so many years doing their best.

A civilized world they say they have developed, and yet still it is in a hell of a mess.

A world where humans are still fighting with each other all the time, and with threats of weapons of annihilation, and still developing many more of them.

And yes, whenever they are not out fighting, crimes are what they are committing, even governments and law institutions are corrupted, from top to bottom, from the skies to the ground, nowhere is safe, the air is polluted.

And this has been more obvious since reason has been assassinated, more bad decisions have been made, and indeed, more crimes have been committed.

And yes indeed, certainly it was bad policies, the decisions that were made brought nations to the brink of catastrophes, affecting the health of their economies, hence the livelihood of families.

So yes indeed, it has been transparent and it was seen that the world has always been progressive as much as it has been destructive right through the ages, progress and destruction were always companions.

And that was because the leaders were not all inspiring, except of course in the engagement of wars, the ravishing of nature, and their profligate abuse of their powers.

They fought and conquered to build their empire, building it with slave labour.

But as battles raged and kingdoms tumbled and crumbled, governments were formed by the people.

Some took form as democracies, some took form as monarchs, and dictatorships, but whatever was the form of governments, progress was never easily accomplished.

Indeed, quite often it has been difficult to achieve progressive development, too often the problems were directly from the cup of corruption emptied, turned upside down spreading upon everyone.

And that might have been because the past was firmly seated.

Things that were done in the past, in the present they were repeated.

Yes, most things that were done in the past, seated in the present they still had influence.

And it mattered not if they were right or if they were wrong, these effects of time's confluence.

Just as they were in the past, in the present that's how some things were done, and whether they were right or wrong it made no difference.

In fact, what was either right or wrong, were not always matters for discussion.

And until they were, or that they were no longer needed and replaced by better ones.

Things from the past some lasted very long in communities where they became the norm.

And that was so with both rights and wrongs, to most people there was no difference.

Indeed, they were never concerned about whether things were right or wrong, tradition was always more important, and so too was to conform with whatever was the norm, had to be done.

So yes, life went on and things got done, still heading in the same direction, and still with the same problems.

Towards the future was where everyone was heading, passing from age to age, passing through different stages, passing through hell's or heaven's gates, passing for certain from one to another development stage.

Knowing quite well how bad things were, often shrouded in sorrow, and yet still humans never lost their fate and hope that there will be a better tomorrow, and with that thought lingering in their minds, that kept them going most of the time.

And although the expected better tomorrow usually came a bit too late, they never doubted that it would come, even with disappointment; but they never lost hope, they kept their confidence with them wherever they went.

Yes indeed things were bad, that's just how they were during those medieval years, but they were gradually getting better as humans moved onwards towards the future, things were changing all the time, some were taken forward, some were left behind, replaced by another kind.

And because of the frequent changes which always gave humans some hope that things will be better instead of worse.

That was something they knew already, as they continued on their journey, heading towards the future, their destiny, with so many changes made before, things couldn't be worse they had to be better, that was the feeling everyone embraced together, smiling with each other.

That was the feeling which kept them going, towards the future they were heading.

But it was always still a very corrupt world every moment in time, that's how it had developed to be; divided, vile, inhumane, very unjust and hostile.

Throughout humans' progressive development that's how the world was at every moment.

With draconian laws and brutality, riots and disorder became necessary.

In a world where sin was commonplace, especially among those who ruled, abusing their powers they tightened their grip with a pressure squeezing the masses.

A world where human species existed for a very long time, and despite all the changes mankind made, the world was still not yet a peaceful place despite the progressive development stages.

Even at the very best of times, it could have been suicidal to step out of line.

Daily mother earth opened up graves to claim lives that were lost in direct response to humans' altercations.

Yes indeed, the lives that were lost were unnecessary because the problems could have been solved peacefully.

But unfortunately, and regretfully, the lives that were lost were always one too many.

And often with or without compromise, whatever had a price, nothing was cheaper than a human life.

So yes indeed, in such a troubled world, about the future everyone was concerned.

Policies and decisions implemented too often were regretted.

So yes, it was really unfortunate that after reason was assassinated, humans seldom hesitated whenever making decisions, and that was why so many were wrong.

Instead of reasoning together as people did before: especially those who were educated; arguments became more commonplace, reasoning together was out of date.

So people did whatever they had to do, and this is no lie but the truth.

Many of the things that human beings did were unbelievably barbaric, it was as if humans were mentally ill, cerebrally acidic.

Or maybe they were possessed by a demonic ghost, or perhaps with something very much worse, whatever it was, it was a curse, things were getting worse and worse.

Indeed, humans did things that were so horrific, and the sad thing was, there was no need for it. Yes, going right back into history's primitive days, during or beyond the mediaeval ages.

Captured prisoners were often murdered as human sacrifices, some had their blood drained through their veins, some were killed by being chopped up into pieces, some were buried alive, some thrown into a pot of oil to be boiled, and some, with whatever worse could still be imagine, that would have been their suffering.

Indeed, nothing cruel that humans could imagine was not done, and none of it was considered wrong, barbarity in cruelty was the norm, it was even fun.

So yes, every culture around the world did in their own ways what had to be done, there was no question about right or wrong; not in matters of human sacrifices or punishments.

So yes, humans slaughtered humans just because they were different, it made no sense at all.

Not in the shape or the form in which they were born, but different in race or religion, and even in opinions.

So in battle with their sword was where they went, to slaughter those who were different.

And that they did with no remorse, regardless of how many lives were lost.

The more they slaughtered the more they rejoiced, the larger the number was their choice.

And that whatever it was they had done, it was something for which they would fight with anyone.

And that was true among those who rule, the decisions they made were often those of a fool. Decisions weighted with tragedies, affecting both friends and enemies.

Plots and counterplots were the fuel of flames, and fear was the oxygen that did the fire retain. And this still continues in the world today, not at any time soon it will be going away; despite humans' efforts and the progress they have made over time, wrongs committed were simply repeated again.

Clearly a better way is what is needed, or the world one day may crumble into bits receding.

With humans always sowing seeds for a world of sin in most things they did to their kin.

And making certain that if they did not reap today, at some later date they'll harvest bloody hay.

And with corruption at the top like a good crop thriving and flourishing, the fruit of evil was the most nourishing.

Delicious yes, so it was always tempting, the forbidden fruit was the most appetizing.

Making the world more of a reckless place, more insecure with more injustice.

Day after day, and year after year, things either got worse, remain the same, or they got a little better. With corrupted leaders abusing their powers, leaving behind tragedies and disasters.

And yes it is true that world leaders come and go, like the wind of yesterday and tomorrow, one after the other, and still things were not always better.

And that was so wherever you went, despite the fact that cultures were different.

Those who ruled sat on their mules galloping through opulent mews.

They never ever went where poverty was transparent, except of course only when there was an election.

Galloping along doing things wrong, believing that it didn't matter at all, whatever they did had to be done. Leading nations into destruction that would rise to the surface one day.

And when it comes it comes along, often with a very heavy price to pay.

And who pays the price? It's the working classes, and usually through their noses.

And so today it has come to pass the unwanted predictions, not knowing how long they would last, with yesterday's problems unwinding.

Unwinding so fast, causing disasters, but it was just the beginning of humans' blinding.

And with the forces of nature so devastating, with everything in its path left in ruins.

Those who rule are left scratching their heads, and don't know what to do next for the best.

They gazed at the problems with their eyes wide open, not knowing what to do, most of the time they didn't have a clue.

And yet, despite the obvious disasters, still they wouldn't even listen to the voice of science, preferring to gamble and take a chance with their bad decisions.

So they sit on their arses or confront the working classes, making speeches with promises that were broken like thin glasses.

But then again that is something very much congenial with the rulers of the world; politicians they are called.

From monarchy to parliamentary democracy, corruption was common among them all.

They created problems, although perhaps not with intent, still, often the problems were devastating, leaving many families with next to nothing.

And that was because they too were only human, and like everyone else they followed not common sense, they followed their emotions.

Yes indeed, they were made rulers to serve the people, but instead they served themselves, often ignoring problems.

And as they did so the problems grew, getting bigger all the time.

And that's when they failed the world, the problems became too difficult to make good.

But yes, as difficult as they became, yet still it had to be done, and in the process more things went wrong.

Indeed, politicians don't usually tackle problems in their infancy, they wait until the problems become a catastrophe. And yet still nothing is done, not until disorder comes along.

And that is exactly when they don't know what to do, most of the time they don't have a clue.

Arguing about how to solve whatever is the problem, often it is a mess they create in the end.

Failing yes, and failing again, and yet still they do the very same things.

And as for the laws they created for whatever purpose, if they were not flawed, they were often ridiculous and unjust.

And often to the disadvantage of women, the poor and minorities, indeed, to the disadvantage of the working classes to say the least.

They were always the ones most affected, as individuals, entire families, and even communities.

And yes indeed, not forgetting the repeated failures of the law against women, the discriminatory failures of the police against women, the failures of the judiciary against women, the failures of the systems against women, the failures of societies against women; shamefully, they are all failures of the politicians, failing in their duty towards women as equal citizens, and it is there transparent everywhere, in every country it could be found, politicians have unfairly failed women.

Yes, the numerous failures by politicians against women over the centuries, exposing them to an endless stream of injustice, and ignoring their complaints.

To give them a deserved compensation for all those years of injustice they have suffered, indeed, they will all be millionaires, and yet still perhaps not justly compensated for the numerous years of injustice they suffered, yes that's how bad it had been, and that's how bad it still is.

Unfortunately, women today are not yet entirely released from the imprisonment of iniquity.

For women the world has never been a secured place with equality and justice, and indeed compassionate.

They are still frequently raped, harassed, paid low rages, abused, and discriminated, and all without being compensated, in fact no justice. Is that a world in which to live?

And it is still very true that politicians one after the other have corrupted the world in some way or the other with policies that should have never been implemented, not ever.

And believe it or not, it was with their policies they created hell, opening-up doors they invited injustice to spread.

And yes this is also true, they built and destroyed too, in a cycle of developments that still continues.

And since reason had been assassinated, they seized more opportunities to enforce their will. Making decisions without prudence or good judgement, with devastating results at the end.

As was the terrible fate of hundreds of male babies, brought to their death and witnessed by many.

Yes indeed, it was with the blade of swords with smoothed and very sharp edges, everything they struck fell to pieces.

Oh yes indeed, that was a day to remember, all hell broke loose, and babies were taken from their mothers only to be slaughtered so as to guarantee the kingdom of Herod.

Indeed, how much more defenseless could the victims have been?

And how much more barbaric could have been the deed?

How much further could madness stretch beyond the extreme?

What crimes were committed by defenseless babies to be so brutally slain?

Yet they were slaughtered by the madness of authority, to prevent a newborn king his sovereignty.

And that was executed from the orders of a king, a king with the name Herod, very proud and sane.

But fearing that he may lose his kingdom and crown, to a Jewish King recently born, and tortured by his conscience in search of what should be done to hold on to his crown.

The answer he came up with was to kill all male newborn.

And death he ordered to every male baby within the entire community, all those who were born recently.

That was his orders in abuse of his powers, it was the orders of a king, kings were able to do anything.

Fearing that he may lose his kingdom to a Jewish newborn, it was male babies he ordered to be slaughtered.

Yes indeed, the henchmen of a king slaughtered babies because among them there was one who was a threat to him. So no one was spared to make certain that the threat was dead.

So to kill them all King Herod gave the orders, and that his henchmen did.

Obeying their orders from their King Herod they slaughtered all male babies who were, and under two years of age to make sure that their King's crown was safe.

Yes indeed, that was what he ordered and was done, to be absolutely certain that his crown could not be stolen by a Jewish newborn.

And because it was the orders of a king, no one dared to criticize him.

No one dared to oppose his order, fear was already mixing with the air, a six parts to one was the mixture.

Yes, fear was in the air spreading everywhere, screams were heard from pillar to pillar, and blood scattered everywhere from hundreds of babies slaughtered from house to house, nowhere to hide, the henchmen dug them out.

Some were sliced in half and thrown on the ground, some with their heads to their necks with a bit of flesh still hanging on, some with no legs nor even heads; wherever the swords struck, that's how they perished.

Indeed, the barbarity of this history could never be forgotten, least of all to be ever repeated.

It was, and still is too great an evil, to go to hell is too lenient a punishment for such a measure of wrong, in the name of God something worse has to be done, forgiveness is not an option.

And yet still that madness as it was perhaps insuperably contagious, it affected many world leaders right through the ages from yesterday to this present day.

Yes indeed, world leaders as humans, they have done some of the most horrific wrongs, abusing their powers they committed wrongs which could never be forgiven.

And that disease affected many of them, it inhibited their common sense, and woe to those awaiting their judgements.

Yes indeed, some very bad decisions were theirs, and the agony of their cruelty, no words could ever describe.

And so history once again witnessed the madness of another world leader, an Emperor abusing his power.

Yes, Nero was his name, with characteristics as though insane; in his insanity he set fire to a city, only to admire and enjoy the view, promising to rebuild it brand new.

But then, after the chaos, the confusion, and the many murders consumed by the spread of the flames, leaving families gutted, some burned to death, many left homeless, enraged, and distressed.

Realizing the weight of the measure of his madness, Nero acted swiftly to dodge responsibility, pointing his accusing finger directly upon blame, on a scapegoat he left his fingerprint.

Yes, he found an easy target to accuse and blame, one that was already a public enemy, and perfect it was to quell the outburst of the citizens' outrage; Nero knew that it was to his advantage.

Indeed he found the perfect scapegoat to shoulder the weight of the public's outrage, and like Herod the king, Nero knew that they were all innocent victims; men, women, and children, everyone who was a Christian, for most wrongs they were usually blamed, so for burning the city down, no one doubted that it was the Christians.

So without hesitation Nero shouted loud and clear for everyone to hear.

With the words "It was the Christians," at the top of his voice he shouted, as if choked with the words he took a little pause then shouted again.

"They burnt the city down, they are a real threat, we must stop them, they must all be dead, it is time for the lions to be fed."

Yes he shouted and shouted, possessed with madness, blaming the Christians for the wrong he did.

Those were the words he said as they appeared in his head, at the top of his voice he was shouting, doing his best to be convincing, then he disappeared, wrapped in his robes off he went swiftly to bed to hide himself from the revengeful noise of the roars from hell.

Oh yes indeed, when faced with the consequences, even world leaders are cowards.

And that is because they are humans like everyone else, yes they have the power, but that does not make them any better.

So yes indeed it was real, it was no sci-fi, the Christians were very easy victims, they were the ones everyone blamed for anything, there was no compromise, no reasoning; revenge was what everyone wanted, only revenge would cool their tempers, while their rage got overheated and blackened with the heat of the smoke and the inferno flames.

So Christians everywhere were rounded up and arrested, and for Nero's sin they were going to pay. But what was the price? It was kept secret.

And so it was eventually, as the gathered crowd waited anxiously for their moment of excitement on this special day of feasting in accordance with Roman custom.

So what was it going to be? Anxious in their waiting, they were very curious to see, and overwhelmed with anxiety.

Until the time had come and from the dungeons the arena was filled with Christians to be used as entertainment for public amusement, a spectacle it was to be, and for this thrill everyone was hungry.

And so it did the moment it began, it was hilarious, sensational, there was nothing that was in the arena that was better.

Christians were taken into the arena not knowing exactly what would happen to them, until it came that final moment.

The moment of fear which appeared as they were set upon by roaring hungry lions, as a means of fun for public amusement.

And as the horror got smeared with Christians' blood, and the roar of terror was heard everywhere amusing the ghoulish crowd.

It was a display never seen before, indeed very exceptional, and with an element of surprise, the crowd was delighted, never was fun so exciting.

Yes indeed it was a moment that thrilled everybody, very sensational, and they loved every moment with every drop of blood, believing, and without any doubt that the Christians deserved it for what they had done, burning down the city to the ground.

In fact, it was to everyone a master stroke of entertainment, every whim in their bodies had its fulfillment, they were consumed with what was to them, a moment of delightful excitement.

Oh yes indeed it was to them exceptionally brilliant, good fun and entertainment, the roars, the screams, the fear, the prayers and the singing, all mixed together in a package of horror for public entertainment and pleasure.

And as the Christians continued to pray and sing, to overcome their fear of what was happening, realizing for them there was no escape from the grip of the jaws of a hungry wild beast.

Nero was the one devastated, seeing the Christians with so much courage, it was not what he expected.

'Were they hypnotized?' he asked politely, looking bewildered and surprised, even the fear that was in his eyes he tried, but could not hide.

'Perhaps their god is protecting them,' he whispered, nervously looking around afraid of their superstitions, with anxiety to see what will happen next, he waited a little while, and then disappeared off to his bed.

And as the public expressed their overwhelming satisfaction with Nero's choice of entertainment, more lions were fed with more Christians, triggering an explosion of public jubilance. The crowd was delighted they got such an auspicious revenge, Nero was now like a god to them, able to think of such brilliant entertainment, which was no less than a majestic revenge.

Yes indeed the air was filled; polluted with horror, and with the smell of Christians' flesh and blood, and with the thrills and excitement of the crowd; the air was very heavy with the variety, it was heavy with impurity.

Indeed it was heavy, filled with a mix, with prayers, singing and screaming, fear, pain, and terror, blood and pleasure, the concoction couldn't be better, indeed it was more soothing than fresh air, they couldn't ask for anything better to arouse and excite their wailing tempers.

And that was it, just another case of a world leader, an Emperor abusing his power, in the delight of horror.

Committing mass murders of Christians as scapegoats for the Emperor's crime, in a spectacle of horror designed for public pleasure.

And if you are not horrified yet, there is still more horror to come, from within the madness of despotism.

Only this time the madness did not visit a king nor an Emperor, it visited a Dictator with the name Hitler.

So what was it that Hitler did to compare the horror of his abuse of power with other world leaders elsewhere?

Indeed, what he did, like many others, cannot be forgotten so in the history books they are written. What he did was beyond measure, evil had stretched a length too far, it was demonstrated in the gravity of his hate, everyone who knew, it made their consciousness ache.

It was as if he was possessed with the idea of Jewish annihilation, it was his commission, something he couldn't get rid from his mind, and achieving it would be to him his most auspicious achievement as a politician; that measure of aggression was his foremost ambition.

Indeed, and with one stroke, he wanted to wipe out an entire nation from the face of the earth, and that was no joke, neither was it an empty threat, nor were they just words meaningless.

That was his ambition, and his aim, so from Jews he stole everything.

Yes indeed, he stole their belongings, all their material things, and then he stole their pride, their respect and dignity, and he even tried to steal their love for their families, but in that he couldn't succeed.

So in condemning them, this was what he said, 'Jews were better off dead,' so all over Europe he chased after them with hate and guns as his weapons.

And in trains after trains, they were packed to the brim, and were transported to the place where they were going to be killed, to be murdered cold-blooded.

Yes, they were transported to a place to be embraced by the angel of death, after the Nazis had taken away their last breath.

Yes indeed, there were millions of Jewish men, women and children all arrested and taken to the gas chambers where they were told to undress naked, in the belief that they were going to have a shower, all stacked naked together.

Indeed, there were many Jews who were suspicious, but it mattered not, they didn't really know what to expect, some thought that they were going to be shot.

And naked together they waited anxiously until the poisonous air they began to breathe.

And still not realizing what was exactly happening to them, when they did it was too late, they had little consciousness.

And so it did happen as it was planned, they all together had their shower, a shower of poisonous gas released from the pipes above disguised as showers.

A shower from which they never recovered, as victims of evil, like lamb they were slaughtered.

And for what reason, what was their sin to deserve to be stripped naked then cold-bloodedly killed?

Only that they were Jews and had no right to live, that was the answer that everyone gave.

And that was enough to condemn them to their death, insanity indeed was never just a threat.

Too often it is real, and it makes no difference whatever is the horror of the deeds.

And what was common in the crime of those three world leaders as mass murders which is usually the case? Their victims were all innocent.

Yes, the decisions of world leaders may be insane, but when they are abusing their powers, the decisions they make are seldom in vain.

And if they become frustrated, that's when it becomes very dangerous, better to keep far away, because their decision could be anything, whatever they imagine.

As it had been during the years of the great terror, as it was known in Stalin's Russia.

Yes, years of terror ruthlessly executed by a Dictator during the purges of the communist era; thousands of families were sent to Siberia, condemned to life imprisonment, some of them, just for criticizing the system.

Many others were shot and thrown into graves, those who opposed the Dictator's ways, and even those who were considered to be a threat, although they did nothing wrong yet.

But then again who was to blame, that's what world leaders do again and again.

And likewise, those four fools with powers they abused.

There are many more world leaders who could fit in their shoes, indeed there were several world leaders who were mass murderers, the history books are filled, and so too are graves with the evidence of their horrid deeds.

Yes indeed, many mass graves have been found filled with humans' skeletons, and with marks of horror as evidence.

And still there may be many more buried under the ground, with the evidence of some horrific wrongs, just waiting to be found.

Indeed there were many world leaders who, with innocent blood from veins which they drained, could have had a bath or a shower, the murders they committed were numerous in number.

Yes, indeed, going right back into mediaeval times, many leaders have committed some barbaric crimes.

Leaders who, over many centuries, have committed some gruesome atrocities, and without a measure of accountability, that is the weakness of human beings.

So yes, leaders go unpunished, living in luxury, with their pockets filled and their hands bloody.

Indeed, this is very true, governments in the past and even today, be it democracies, monarchies or Dictators, were murderers.

And secretly some even plotted and removed other world leaders because their policies were not to their favour.

Abusing their powers is what they do, creating wars, committing crimes especially murders, and in several cases even genocide too.

So yes indeed, governments and some government institutions, both together plot and plan, murdering those in opposition, murdering those with different opinions, murdering those who don't toe their line, murdering those who expose their crimes, murdering those who are weaker than them, bullying is a part of the precarious political game.

So yes indeed, it is not difficult to see that in the arena of world politics, there is no place for weakness, strength is the only language spoken, one language, one tongue, which needs no interpretation.

And if you don't understand it, I am afraid it is to your disadvantage, there is no interpreter to translate.

Nor is there a place for wisdom or commonsense, decisions are made based on strength.

And yes, that is very common with threats of repercussions, threats against defiant oppositions, threats against those who don't toe the line, threats that are not only threats, but with consequences serious enough.

And with no accountability, governments commit crimes as a policy.

That's how it has been among world leaders, they commit crimes and create wars.

The strong are always invading the weak, that is a norm in world politics.

Living their lives as untouchables, committing wrongs without ever being held accountable.

Indeed it is true no need to argue, they themselves know that they are not above the law, but this is what they also know, and without any doubt whatsoever, they are confident and quite sure, that beneath them is the law.

So as despots, they abused their powers, someone to murder, or to start a war they gave the orders.

But not all leaders were despots and brutal, no leader is better than a good Dictator, without the ramblings of an opposition, he can pursue things and get them done.

But where on this earth could anyone search to find a good King, a good Emperor, or Dictator, a good President, or Prime Minister, or any leader with good character, honest and sincere.

Without ever telling lies, nothing to hide, and delivering the promises that they made to get elected.

Yes indeed, maybe there are many good leaders, but one by one they come, and very soon they are gone, either dead or they move on.

Good politicians don't last long; they are here today, and tomorrow they are gone.

But yes, all are not regrets, during the centuries of human beings' progressive development, both good and bad world leaders often tried their very best.

Both have done some wonderful things, splendid cities they have built.

And in wars they have destroyed them just as well, regrettable as it was.

They were the architects of the world, nothing could be done if they did not approve.

At one moment they created heaven, and at the next moment they created hell.

Creating whatever was to their pleasure, and a great deal with slave labour.

That was the corruption circulating at the top, and it was always there dripping downwards drop by drop.

Indeed, corruption has always been in the houses of power, where the leaders of the world gathered together, operating quietly and secretly behind closed doors, and with no transparency, not at all, not even accountability, and in the interest of their rapacity.

While the masses down below live in fear, fearing even their own shadow.

Fearing what they could and could not see, fearing the listening ear of everybody, fearing how their policies may affect the economy, affecting their lives financially, affecting the living standards of their family, fearing when tomorrow comes what it will be.

Indeed fear was always there, and among both the rulers and the common people, if it was not of superstitions, then you can bet it was of suspicion.

Yes indeed fear was always there, among human beings there was always something to fear.

Whether it was something natural or supernatural, fear has had a devastating effect on mankind, and so it did on several world leaders, except of course those who were not human.

So what did they want? Who was able to tell? No one was ever sure when dealing with corrupt world leaders.

No one was certain, nor were they able to predict what kind of a world the politicians were creating for the present and future generations.

But if it was heaven this was certain, they still had a lot of work to do, but if it was hell, very well, they were already halfway through.

And as leaders of the world they made the rules which they abused, and too often no one held them to account, although law was misused.

And not forgetting one of the worst things that they have done, that which could never be forgiven, they even made laws to justify wrongs which for centuries were the norm.

Laws that enslaved, exploited, discriminated, and justified injustice in numerous cases, including denying basic human rights to the masses.

Yes, those are things world leaders did, and that is why the world has always been as it is, sinful and corrupted.

Indeed, they even kept the people subdued and obedient to laws that were oppressive, discriminatory, and ruthless, laws that were hostile serving injustice, creating fear among the masses.

And there were even laws that made no sense at all, completely biased and systematically flawed.

And with all the laws world leaders endorsed, nothing was more tangible than the opportunities lost.

Not ever forgetting their double standards, a shameful disparity, corrupt as it could be, and yet a common practice among world leaders.

Indeed, in politics there is where it is, more hypocrisy than honesty, more corruption than progressive development, more double standards than the integrity that matters.

Yes, they play their game ever so cool, knowingly breaking or disengaging with the rules.

There are too many double standards in world politics, the rules are broken too often, and by those who made them.

They break the rules and agreements when it doesn't suit them, as if it was a privilege for politicians.

And seldom too they agree on anything, no reasoning only arguing, pointing their fingers at each other to blame, with accusations and no shame.

So yes indeed, it could be rightly said that in the world of politics, what is right or wrong often depends upon who is the benefactor of what is to be done.

Double standards are common practice, so it matters not who is right or wrong, in politics self-interest is what serves everyone.

Indeed, the economy is a priority, each government for their own country.

And yet still they often get it wrong, no foresight, no imagination.

That is how it is today after centuries of the implementation of world policies; as it was yesterday so it is today, everyone is geared towards self-interest at the expense of justice.

And that they say is politics, that's how it was created, and after many centuries that came and went, still today many things are no different, the weaknesses of humans are still the same, they will do wrong things for financial gains.

With idiocy and hypocrisy circulating at the top, and from there contributing to world problems from the bottom up.

And combined with corruption and bad policies, for the ills of the world there seems to be no cure, no remedy, not even from modern day science, or from medieval days' sorcery.

So the policies continue affecting human lives, making it more difficult to survive.

And as the world continues to develop and progress, with no one cleaning up the mess.

The mess piles up, up and up, only to tumble down one day into a cataclysm of chaos.

And that is certain it could happen, humans have already experienced some bad examples.

And what do they do? They still argue, on what to agree they don't have a clue.

And that's how it has been and how it is, a world overwhelmed with confusion and problems, that's how the world has developed to be, with a foreboding commodity.

Yes with sins from the past which today has inherited, and perhaps they are what humans in the future may have to live with.

A world progressive with material possessions, and stuck in a quicksand of divisions.

A quicksand with no safety net, and sinking deeper was a real threat.

And yes, with divisions that created cataclysms, and the only cause was being different.

With each division striving to be better than the other, always in competition with one another instead of working together in the interest of each other; for some reason, working together always seems to be more difficult than ever, no one can trust each other, self-interest was at the top of the agenda, it was always sought after, despite causing altercations with one another.

Yes indeed, it is an illness very true as it is, in a world full of opportunities and yet still for no proper reason women have always been denied equality, they were not given with men the same opportunities, and the reasons were often a mix of idiocy and bigotry which were far away from reality.

Indeed, the world has always been unjust with few rights and many wrongs, and despite this unpleasant fact, it was never short of politicians, politicians who came and went, politicians who did nothing, apart from expanding their bank accounts the only right thing they seem to have done.

Yes they came and went one after the other, some stayed as long as ever, those who loved the sweet taste of power.

Yes indeed, they were the ones with the building blocks, they built and destroyed subjugating their flocks.

Sometimes they advance forwards, sometimes backwards, and sometimes they do nothing at all. Doing nothing as if they did not know what to do, doing nothing as if they didn't have a clue.

Doing nothing as if they didn't care at all, so the situations remain the same as life went on.

And when they did something, it was often done in a haste, or too late, and that's when they made many mistakes with situations crumbling flat in their face.

And yes, despite the numerous problems, the arguments, and disagreements, the disengagements, and criticisms, it was still always the politicians as world leaders, the world depended upon to make wise and progressive decisions, that was their commission, in fact, it was their responsibility as politicians.

It has always been their duty to lead in a direction of progressive development without wars, chaos, and mayhem, which was always the result of unnecessary deaths, and the rollback of progress.

Indeed, and without reservations, every nation depended upon the politicians to keep the peace, every nation depended upon them for security, every nation depended upon them for development.

Every nation depended upon them for a better world to live in.

But instead, despite their duty for which they were paid, they created wars that could have been avoided, wars that took many young lives to an early grave, or were left permanently disabled.

And when it was not wars, they created insecurity with policies that affected families.

Indeed, they don't always even try hard enough to avoid wars, stubborn they remain arguing, no one wants to be seen as the one backing down;

believing it is a show of weakness that could be taken for granted, and then followed by all sorts of disadvantages.

But yes, perhaps it is very true to say that sometimes they try, and perhaps very hard, still, often in vain, someone is always complaining, trust is frequently missing with suspicion taking its place, and that may be why so often they fail.

That is the problem among nations, they trust no one, yet they smile and shake hands, pretending to be friends.

And that's what they call diplomacy, with their actions lying to themselves and to everybody.

And yes regretfully, with times too many, whatever it was politicians did in such circumstances, whether right or wrong, they were often attacked with criticisms.

So yes, it is true in everyone's view, politicians have a very difficult job to do.

The burden of leadership is not a light one, you get credit or blame for what is, and what is not done, and especially for what is wrong; indeed leaders ought to be strong, or better they resign and be gone.

And yes it is sad, they are not often given full support, their idiocies are news to report, and their privacy is often stolen, especially when they did something wrong.

Full support is seldom in their favour, wrong or right they are criticized, and that is not without arguments with one another.

So what can they do? If only they themselves knew, perhaps the world might have been a much better place, as good as new.

And as victims of political squabbles, burdened with problems and stuck in the middle.

It was always the poor, minorities, women and children, they were the ones who often bear the brunt.

Rejected, disadvantaged, discriminated against, and even by the law they were unjustly treated. With wrongs that were very much contemptuous, deliberate and presumptuous.

Wrongs that treated them as objects inferior, and with no respect whatsoever.

Wrongs that condemned them as second-class citizens, and left them exploited, harassed, and abused.

And from year after year these wrongs continue, politicians don't seem to know what to do. Indeed, during the many centuries of the progressive development of mankind, women in particular have been left behind, they were treated very unfairly, ignored by society, and that went on for many centuries.

With politicians who came and went, one after the other they did nothing.

So women remained victims of superstitions, myths and taboos, and were taken for granted, often beaten, and advantageously disadvantaged.

And even from within the law, women have been the victims of injustice more and more.

And that has been so for far too long it has been going on, a condition in life that became the norm, therefore nothing was wrong, and whether or not it was written or unwritten as law, that's how things were done, and accepted by everyone.

And so they were done again and again, although they were wrong, centuries came and went, and so too were many politicians before anything was done to correct the wrongs, which were only done when disorder came along.

And when it came to reasoning, no one would listen to a woman, so she was stuck with her problems without help or assistance, often treated by the law as a nuisance.

And that's why in most cases things took so long to change.

And that was the kind of world human beings were developing as they progressed at each stage, and at every age, problems got worse, or they remained the same.

With women continuously taken for granted and disadvantaged, injustice to them at every moment in time as yesterday's norm was passed on, and so today injustice to women has not disappeared, it has not gone, it is still very common, as a disgraceful failure of politicians.

Yes indeed, and most shamefully, two thousand years after Christ came, and yet today the injustice to women remains a problem and is the cause of resentment; still needing change, which of course is the politicians to blame, too many years without doing anything.

But that is nothing new, it is something everyone got used to, it was happening daily for centuries gradually becoming a male propensity.

Not that men did it deliberately over the years, but century after century and without any change, bit by bit it just happened, injustice to women became normal practice; unfortunately for far too long women tolerated it, so it became a male habit, natural in their characteristic.

But perhaps for women they had no other choice, it was really difficult for them without proper laws.

Laws were hardly ever in the favour of women, and that may be because the laws were made by men.

So in men's favour they were made, and to women's disadvantage.

Indeed, laws were seldom seen to be wise, most of the time they were very unkind.

That is the way the world was developing, with laws that were intimidating.

And it mattered not that they were wrong, again and again that was the way things were done. And yes they were done for far too long, year after year it just went on.

And for very long they carried on, for centuries change never came.

So life went on, right or wrong, whatever was the tradition, that's how things were done.

And perhaps that may be the cause of today's problems, too many wrongs of yesterday are still in the systems today.

A good cleaning up is what they all need, or, as like Mr. George Floyd did plead, we may all one day, just can't breathe.

Not because of the pressure of a policeman's knee, but the greater pressure of the wrongs in societies.

Wrongs which become a part of daily life, and are committed taking advantage of victims, because most of the time there were no consequences.

And as politicians come and go one after the other, with a few changes they made here and there while advancing towards the future.

Most of the time the world wasn't much better, their duty to the people was too often a lost letter.

They failed to deliver on the things that really matter, often criticizing and blaming one another instead of working together for the better.

Yes indeed, it is a very transparent condition, in too many countries daily murders are very common; societies are chaotic and disorderly, gangs with drugs and guns roaming the streets, too many people are destitute, trapped hopelessly in the acid of the gut of poverty.

They can't breathe clean air, a good meal is rare, and law and order are nothing more than living in fear of gangsters everywhere.

Yes, in many places around the world today, people would say that deaths are common on the streets every day, and the murderers get away, not even arrested, in fact the situations were not even investigated, even the police are afraid.

Indeed, the systems are ineffective, too many crimes go unpunished, crimes committed by those in high office, and by the ordinary man on the streets, who commit crimes not to get rich but just to make ends meet.

So the forming of gangs gets very strong, everybody with a gun, and the law goes on the run.

And that becomes an everyday norm, a clear indication of the failures of politicians.

Yes they failed, gangsters with guns on the rampage, drugs an epidemic, and crimes of all sorts endemic.

Yes, with crimes going up right to the top, the police are lame ducks, and governments fail to govern with the required tough punishments.

So yes, failure is theirs, and yet they still want to serve for many more years.

Serving themselves yes, definitely not the public.

Indeed it is a vicious circle, not easy to know what to do, but doing nothing is signaling the wrong message, which is indeed to the criminals advantage.

And that's when crimes go up on the rise, and to no one's surprise, the law enforcement institutions close their eyes.

Yes it is happening day after day, governments' failures are on display.

They are obvious, they are transparent, they are what you see every moment.

In several places in the world that's what is happening, and in some of them it is frightening.

And that is why the world is as it is, with centuries of governments' sluggishness.

Yes they failed and failed again each time after they were elected.

And then the people get very vex and enraged, corruption among politicians is what they blame, and yes indeed that's what it is.

So they respond; striking, protesting, and rioting, doing anything to draw attention to the problems.

Yes indeed the people are fed-up, they want a decent living, they want to be able to pay their bills. But what do they get? More promises and threats, some governments don't even care less, and those who do, they don't even know what to do for the best.

So things continue just as they are, in some places they get a little better, in others crime takes over with corruption and mismanagement embracing each other, and countries left with little progress.

And this is so in several parts of the world, where governments are useless instead of useful.

And with those conditions existing, politicians are afraid to do anything.

Yes indeed, they are afraid for their families, that's how bad things are in some countries.

And law and order remain only in name, corrupted politicians to blame, for years doing nothing, and the situations escalating, only to become a problem too big, too big indeed to be fixed, so the politicians just leave it.

So yes politicians failed in whatever it is, and that is so in their health care systems.

Indeed in many countries health care is a very serious problem, and yet no one could ever deal with the situation, not even in the affluent nations, healthcare it seems is a very big problem.

With everyone asking the same question. Why can't politicians provide a good and efficient national health care system benefiting everyone?

Without paying low wages resulting in staff shortages, long waiting lists, and shortages of beds and whatever else, and of course shortages of medicines and pills, and even shortages of shortages.

It is as if the health care systems themselves are often sick occupying beds.

Leaving many people in pain or to die unnecessary, because they can't get the treatment they need, often waiting for years.

And that is because healthcare services are a very slow process with long waits claiming deaths.

And yet that is the everyday norm, it is a regular custom, politicians don't seem to know what could be done; or maybe perhaps they don't care a damn, year after year ignoring the situations, and the problems get worse, the system can't deliver cure nor care, it cannot deliver what should be there.

Indeed no doubt, bad policies are the cause, with neglect affecting treatment, cure, and recoveries. Every sickness and injury appear to be some sort of lottery, a gamble with death or recovery.

And most regretfully, life is bought and sold like a rugged old ferry, left to sink if nobody comes up with the money, sorry if you are in a hurry, and need treatment urgently, can't help you without the money; that's the system of health care offered in many countries.

So the rich live and the poor die. But who really cares? It is the system we live by.

Who among politicians were ever really concerned about the welfare of the poor?

Then, where are the policies for better healthcare?

When the present systems are models of the past, and still as they were developed over the years.

That is the kind of healthcare system mankind created, and from the past the present inherited, perhaps with some changes, and the installation of modern equipment; but services to the public remain a problem, and that has been the cause of many lives lost, some of which neglect was the cause.

Yes indeed that's how it has always been; nothing was ever free, only the air humans breathe, and that could be temporary, no one knows what the future is likely to be, humans are really crazy, you may have to pay for the air you breathe.

And unless someone comes up with something better, that's how the system will always remain, with either little or no change.

Unjust and unfair, and with politicians who don't even seem to care.

So year after year they do nothing, and that's why the systems never change.

With too many people going early to their grave, when with a good healthcare system their lives could have been saved.

But yes, as it will be expected in many places, they are not all the same, some health care systems are better than others, and perhaps some could be said that they are as good as perfect with very high standards.

But those are for the rich and the privileged, few may be for the working classes.

So the health care systems remain as they are for a very long time before they get better.

During which time they even get worse as standards drop and frustration grows.

Giving way to even more shortages, with systems that don't have enough nurses.

Overworked and underpaid, they left feeling that they were exploited.

But the health care systems are not alone causing concern, due to neglect by politicians, the same could be said about education.

In some places it is free, in others you pay, with debt a necessity, with which students are heavily burdened.

Yes indeed it is so for many students, burdened with debt is an irritating nuisance, it's difficult to sleep, and even to study, the weight is too heavy to carry.

From free education to loan packages, that is called progress some governments have made.

Upon their backs students carry their loads, with debt pressing heavily upon their back bones.

But what else can they do? They don't know which way to turn, can't get an education without a loan, the money is needed for the country's defense, to build bombs to kill millions.

Yes indeed, politics is tricky, making right decisions is not easy.

And it is not difficult to see what sort of a world human beings are living in, the priorities given in decision making, after so many centuries, not one institution is perfect, efficiently serving the public; not health care, education, or defense, not banking, commerce, or housing, nor the judiciary, agriculture, transportation, or fisheries, not anything which will make life easy benefitting everybody.

Everyone is with problems: and are left to cope in the best way they can.

But who really cares? Those are the systems, and the policies of the politicians, good or bad, it makes no difference, as long as things get done, whatever is in their program.

Yes, a university education was free yesterday, but with progress you pay today, tomorrow it may be taken away; and getting even worse still as systems struggle with their bills.

And the same could be said about housing, more and more people on the streets are where they are sleeping, and without hygiene conveniences, and that is because they can't afford rent nor a mortgage.

So with no fixed address they are in a mess, and the politicians say they are making progress.

And this is now seen even in affluent societies, societies that claim to have very strong economies, and yet their social problems appear to have no remedies, poverty is claiming more and more families.

In fact, in very few places social care has been at its best serving the public's interest.

In most places it has always been a mess, and even when it is at its best.

With many people hungry and sleeping on the streets, with numbers daily on the increase.

Queuing for hours for free food hand-outs, a necessity which is transparent daily.

And this is now a fact in affluent societies, poverty everywhere in the world is on the increase.

With prices constantly rising, and the cost of living inflating, no one knows what tomorrow will bring.

And yet still the rich get richer, the more they have they still want more.

What do they do with it? No one is sure.

So unfortunately, this is how it has always been, the survival of the fittest, that is the purpose of the rat race, created within the system of capitalism to assist mankind in his efforts to make a living.

And in doing so the rich get richer with no regards for the poor, whether or not they get poorer.

But then again this is also true, no need to argue, capitalism provides opportunities too, both for the rich and the poor, the opportunities are always there.

But this you must remember, with everything capitalism has to offer, job security is not one of them, capitalism is not so kind.

You can have a job believing it is for life, and tomorrow when you wake up, things just changed overnight, you could no longer see the future, there is no light, your job simply disappeared from your sight.

So now, "what should be done?" Should one turn to crime or depend upon handouts?

Living on handouts from hand to mouth, that's no life at all.

And yet that is how it is for many families trapped in the jaws of poverty.

Trapped without an exit, which develops into a crisis, a crisis that becomes too big to fix; so the politicians just ignore it.

And that is where politicians have failed again, and they have failed miserably.

Some made no attempts, some tried and failed, and poverty has now become an international tragedy embracing billions of human beings.

With millions of people displaced into homelessness, destitute poverty is the condition in which they live.

Driven by bad policies including wars, politicians are the cause of them all.

And this is in the twenty-first century, in this day and age, an age of plenty, and yet the world is as it is, it is indeed a human disgrace.

The extent of poverty with its dehumanizing effect, more and more people everywhere in the world, in destitution is where they are trapped, living in slums alongside rats; with no hygiene, they can't keep clean, and with many degrading problems in between: and that is the reality for many families, many who don't even have a bed on which to sleep.

Not forgetting the problems caused by nature, which were directly or indirectly triggered by the ravaging forces of human beings, forcing many more people into destitution and homelessness.

And yes, even wars, with bombs their homes are destroyed, so from their homelands they are on the run, it is no fun, survival is indeed a very precarious problem for some.

Yes, regretfully but necessary, from their homelands many people are packing their bags and running, taking with them their problems, their children, and just a few things.

Yes, taking their problems to a different land with a few pieces of rags, and their children.

And there they go where most things are different, even the language that is spoken.

And still they go, although they themselves don't know, when they get there what will they do.

But at least they are alive, instead of, with a bomb they are slaughtered, and dumped in a grave on top of others.

So yes indeed it is a very serious crisis, and yet no one seems to know how best to deal with it.

In the places they go the people don't really want them, so they are stuck in overcrowded camps, some don't even have good hygiene standards.

Yes indeed by the thousands in very large crowds people are fleeing their countries, they call them refugees, millions of them on the road to uncertainty; trapped in destitution, trapped in poverty, trapped in the wilderness of uncertainty, and with the doors locked, can't find the key; they are all trapped together in misery both in and out of their country.

Yes indeed it is real, it is with both uncertainty with difficulties, and difficulties with the reality that their life could be much worse than in their own country.

But that is exactly what they don't want to know, as far as they are concerned, they must get up and go.

To somewhere, anywhere, they just felt they must get out from there, regardless of what it would be like elsewhere, at that moment they really don't care.

Yes indeed, many people are on the run from their own countries, running from bad policies.

Yes, that's how bad things are, that's the situation in their homelands everywhere, acute destitution, bombs, death, and destruction, no jobs, no security, it is as hopeless as it could ever be; those are what they are running from, bad policies, bad governments, mismanagement, and destitute situations.

So they take their problems elsewhere with them, to find a better life in some foreign land.

So yes indeed, it is the politicians to blame for whatever situation a country is in.

Too often they failed to do the right things, and that was often because they are corrupted, often ignoring problems, breaking agreements, and their double standards are very common, with results that even lead to wars, then pointing fingers at each other to blame, instead of getting together to find solutions in agreements to solve problems, they pour fuel upon the flames, and then wonder why the fire is spreading.

Yes, politicians are the architects of the world's conditions, whatever the situations the responsibility is always in their hands, unless of course whatever was the disaster it came direct from nature.

Something for which no predictions were engaged, neither were there any preparations made.

So the situations created whatever they are, with the policies of politicians things get worse or they get better.

And as they get worse year after year, people realize they have no future.

And when things get so bad that the people have to run, who else to blame but the politicians.

Because they failed to provide the things they should; good enough systems that are free from erosion, yes indeed, good enough systems serving everyone.

Yes, systems that are functioning and are maintained, providing good reliable services.

Indeed, that is their job, that is their commission, that is the reason why the people elected them.

But instead, most of the systems are in a mess, even those in the West, where they are claimed to be the best.

So when the best is in a mess. What then is left? What is there to expect?

And still the failures continue in so many avenues, all have experienced situations of bad policies which in some way or the other affected businesses and families.

And indeed, like a domino effect, bad policies crumbled one after the other, taking with them whatever.

And the preservation of the forest, clean air and water, humans have polluted the air, lands, and the seas with their bad policies.

Not forgetting the distribution of food, in that too they have failed the world, and perhaps one day, they may even starve the world, right now today things are not looking too good.

And of course, women especially, it is as if politicians have failed them deliberately as a part of their duty, or perhaps a conspiracy, yes indeed, women were always left forgotten, many of their rights were stolen.

Right through the ages they have been disadvantaged, and even today in the twenty-first century despite the changes to treat them fairly, they are still victims of inequality.

So yes indeed, politicians have failed them as they have failed the world in so many things, they have failed again and again, and each time they refused to take the blame.

And what has been very annoying despite their failures, they always wanted to remain, just another term, and another term again.

Yes, after many years in office without much progressive leadership, they always wanted to continue still, to resign is always against their will.

Indeed, they always wanted to carry on, and to carry on for as long as they could.

Disregarding the people's dissatisfaction with their performance, and the overall corruption right at the top in circulation.

Whatever the situation, it never did seem easy to remove a politician.

They put their feet down, firm on the ground, refusing to move on.

And that they did, they held on tight; breaking all the rules is how they fight.

Not going clean nor in disgrace, not until a few more bribes they must take.

To increase the weight of their bank accounts, so that they could continue to live in the lifestyle in which they become very accustomed.

But not only politicians as world leaders were failures.

Institutional bodies too were failures, failing in their duty in some way or the other to prevent wars, to persecute government officials, and to prevent the causes of injustice and disasters that often claimed lives as well as jobs.

And this too has been very common, institutional racism, sexism, and their disparaging attitude towards minorities.

And yes indeed, this also is true of religious institutions where children were abused by the clergy and nuns, which only got exposed many years on.

Indeed, a very disgraceful situation which was covered up for far too long.

Yes, institutions had a part to play, regardless of whatever was the nature of their business, they failed in some way.

And as institutional establishments they harbour wrongs in corruption, sexism, racism, discrimination, and bigotry; indeed, whatever were the wrongs a lot of damage was done operating as the norm for so very long, wrongs which became institutional norms, and so deeply rooted, quietly executed, and without any concern that they were doing wrong.

And because they were regular and common, they were done without fear, no hesitation.

But purposely, as well as habitually, functioning secretly to the disadvantage of minorities.

Yes, in silence were their operations, quietly covering up their crimes, conscious of their wrongs hidden in secrecy, behind closed doors they operated quietly.

And that was true within the corridors of colonization, The European Union, The Arab League of Nations, and the African Union; and the Commonwealth, NATO, The United Nations, The World Health Organisation, and The World Trade Organisation, even religion, the secret services, the police and judiciary, and of course other institutional bodies, in fact any institution that was created by humans.

All of those institutions at some time or the other, how they dealt with some problems was a complete failure.

Take for an example the United Nations, an institution established many years ago with good intentions, to create a better world was their ambition.

But in what matters were they united? Was their unity transparent or hidden?

Because most of the time they spoke with divided voices, and common interest disintegrated through the natural process of metamorphosis, transforming into self-interest with world problems harder to fix.

Indeed, they couldn't even prevent wars which carried on for years, their half-baked efforts were doomed to failures.

And whenever they got directly involved with their troops on the ground to prevent wars, they committed crimes, and as lame ducks they hardly ever cleaned up the mess their rank and file left behind.

Indeed, there were whistleblowers who lost their jobs, and for no other reason but speaking out and exposing criminal offenses committed by those in high places.

So what is the purpose of the institution? What is the purpose of the United Nations?

Yes it is true, some good things they do, the apple is not yet rotten all the way through.

So it is time to listen to whistleblowers, and clean up the mess within its borders.

They are always talking about countries in ruins, and what is done is never sufficient.

And even that which was done, often it was tarnished with corruption.

Yes indeed, many crimes have been reported, committed by UN forces.

And rapes in particular, a common feature among the officers, taking advantage of girls in destitute places.

Indeed, in the world today and even yesterday, not one institution is perfect without blemishes, not even religion, and that is because they were created by humans.

But that does not mean that human beings don't have the ability to be perfect without blemishes, but only that they are more easily drawn to their weaknesses.

Most of their strength appears to be in their muscles, and not much in their principles.

So yes indeed, despite the many years of institutional formation, yet still flaws could be found in their operations.

Especially operations in Third World countries, where foreign institutions interfere in their own interest, not with common laws in the application of justice, but double standards is the norm that usually suffice.

Making matters worse whatever was the disputed situation, and then they disappear to wash their hands.

But then again, they never reasoned with one another, they engaged in arguing to convince the other.

And that's what politicians do quite often, pursuing their own interests with the pretext that they were helping.

And it is this hypocrisy with the selfishness in their policies that always benefit the donor country.

And when they made decisions they created more problems, often worsening bad situations as were transparent in the operations in two of the latest events, one in Iraq, and the other in Afghanistan.

So yes indeed, it has been foreign interference with very bad policies that left those two nations today desperate and very hungry, worse than they were before their invasion by foreign lands.

Engaged in wars for much too long, and yet still they could not correct their many wrongs.

So indeed it is better not to invade nor interfere if you are going to create bigger problems and disappear.

That is a very simple piece of common-sense ideology, and yet you could find politicians who wouldn't agree.

'So what really were the functions of politicians?' 'Why do they execute so many wrongs?' Why do they seem to lack common sense? Creating a reservoir of problems.

When all of them are educated, and yet still too often they are not doing the things which they should be doing.

Dragging their countries into ruins with the pursuit of bad policies, wars, mass murders, slavery, injustice, and exploitation.

Why do politicians allow those things to happen, when they have the power to prevent them?

'What have they done as world leaders, as Emperors, Presidents, Kings, or Dictators?'

After so many centuries with so many leaders, some who claimed to be even gods.

Why did they not use the magic of their godly powers to create a better world if not for themselves, for others?

Instead, what has been more transparent than ever, was their abuse of power in the ruthlessness of their draconian laws.

And that's why the world is as bad as it is, that's why it has developed to be the way it is.

A world divided with each nation big and small, often pursuing their own interest at the expense of others.

Can't trust each other, no integrity whatsoever, world leaders break the very rules they make, or with double standards they operate.

Abusing their powers, applying double standards, and whatever they did, it was for their self-interest they were motivated.

So hardly ever they work together for the common good; self-interest was paramount, and the common good, well, that was never important.

And that is why the world is as it is today, very unjust, very corrupt, very uneven from bottom to top, and with hostile and unjust laws, instead of avoiding, they created wars.

Yes indeed, politicians engaged in wars that lasted for years before they could agree to bring them to an end, taking millions of lives with them.

And not forgetting the widespread destruction, roads, buildings, everything, well, that itself was hell.

Yes indeed it has always been humans' divisions which were the cause of most problems.

So why didn't the politicians work together, embracing a global family in unity?

If they had tried and failed. Why didn't they try harder until they succeed?

After centuries of divisions with so many devastating problems, world unity may yet still take many more centuries to achieve.

Regardless of what they called the United Nations, that is in name only; in the spirit of its formation unity is not a reality.

Indeed, not yet among nations, nor even among religions; despite human beings' existence for centuries, and the problems caused by divisions; for such trust and fraternity, and for global unity, humans are still not quite ready.

There is no sight of it, it is not within vision, it is as if it may never happen, it is not a policy of politicians, nor is it that of religion, they are all quite very happy with divisions, hence, despite the Institution of the United Nations, global unity is not really anyone's intention, nor is it their ambition, it could be indeed an idea fraudulent.

Then why is there no desire for world unity? Is it because disunity has lasted too long with its roots very deep in the ground, and trust is lost among everyone?

Why can't humans unite and live peacefully together, instead of always warring with one another?

That indeed is a politician's job, so many of them came and went, in four figure numbers they could be counted.

More than enough together that could ever be needed to create a perfect world.

And yet today the world is still struggling to correct the effects of social injustice, and to redress the wrongs of yesterday.

Yes, perhaps that is why the world has developed to be as it is.

Something has gone wrong with world leadership, very transparent is the madness of yesterday which still appears to be common among today's new generations.

But just try and ask a politician the question. Why is the world as it is, corrupted everywhere?

And even among the leadership, that's why there is so much injustice.

Indeed his face will bulge with wide open eyes, and maybe looking up into the skies, scratching his head a million times before an answer is given.

He never has an answer, and perhaps that's why he never bothers, can't find a way out to put things right, so problems gather in a pile to be dealt with perhaps once in a while.

Indeed, one never needs magnifying glasses to see at any time the mess in which the world was in. The direction in which it was heading, a better future was not certain.

Too many wars, and still preparing for even more wars, and with weapons with the power to demolish whatever.

Leaving nothing in its path that did not feel the wrath of the aftermath.

Yes indeed, the politicians are the ones who sanction the weapons of mass destruction, and then in fear they hope it will never happen; indeed, the logic is very brilliant, a token of very good common sense, that's the attitude of politicians, those who govern.

Yes, it is the attitude of world leaders, with the common sense of an ass, the common sense that invites problems.

And with the weapons they create, they can't find peace, their minds are troubled with pieces, their nights are restless, they can't sleep.

For wars they prepare, for pieces they fear, they don't know what it will be like, they were never in pieces before, not as it is expected with a nuclear war.

Times were always brutal, something to worry about, fear was always there, nowhere to hide, it could find you day or night, in the darkness or the light, fear has very good eyesight.

But not until humans could find a way to peacefully solve the problems of yesterday, tomorrow things will still be the same.

Indeed, tomorrow will come and go, and so will the politicians too, with things remaining the same, or perhaps with some little change, indeed with some new things.

Not forgetting injustice which has been, and still is an international blight of the human race, it is rampant everywhere; no place is safe from the monster humans create, the devouring jaws of injustice.

And yet it could be said that the politicians are the ones who are the cause of it, they create injustice with the laws they make, and even with those that they did not make, they ignore the situations that allows injustice to dilate; so injustice becomes an everyday norm, with unjust laws the politicians govern, that's the way in which things are done.

And that was what humans did, during their progressive development, injustice became a part of normal life, that's what one had to pay, that was the price, and it still is.

And so too were wrongs as crimes became part of normal life, killing and wounding millions of men, women, and children in wars that dragged on for years.

And if asked Why? What was wrong? What was the cause of so much death and destruction?

The answer that was given from everyone's tongue, in their answer, they blame the politicians.

513

Yes it was in apprehension, in hate, rage and resentment, that was how the answer was given with attitudes enraged against politicians.

Dissatisfaction here, discontentment there, and with tempers boiling, people were protesting everywhere.

And yet politicians don't seem able to get things right, they argue among themselves, sometimes with themselves, or they fight with someone else.

Indeed, it has been witnessed and recorded in history, that there have been many places where bullets fell like rain upon protesters, someone gave the orders; protesting was never easy, there was often an element of insecurity.

Yes, there were often arrests, beatings, and even deaths, those were not only a threat, they were real events.

And yet protesting was the only means to acquire change as quickly as it needed to be.

Indeed, century after century came and disappeared, one by one, year after year, and yet still today in every place people are dissatisfied with how things are, and in places everywhere injustice is running wild.

And that's because the same problems arrive, many are about how to stay alive.

So it is a shame and a human disgrace that in this day and age, after so many centuries of humans' progressive development, the world is as it is, when it could have been different, a much better place.

But that's how the world has been developing everywhere, and it is still the same today.

Politicians never did the jobs for which they were paid, too many things were left neglected.

People everywhere are fed-up, they want things to be better, and they want them now not later, but to get them, there has to be disorder, without it there's never any change whatsoever.

And yet, the answer they got from the politicians, came usually from the barrel of their guns. Forcing the people to retreat with nothing gained but defeat.

And this is why the world is as it is today, it is because of the wrongs committed yesterday, and are still in the systems today.

And at every age it has been the same, despite the many changes again and again.

Too many things are still done in the same old ways, and despite the changes, human beings everywhere are still fighting for justice.

Yes indeed, it is because of the many bad policies, and of course the bad laws that justified so many wrongs which remained in the systems for far too long, and without disorder change never comes, and that's what urges the protesters on.

So until disorder vents its temper wrongs may continue to be ignored forever, despite the injustices the masses suffer.

Politicians indeed seldom implement change, regardless how bad a situation is, not until disorder shows its face angry with hate and rage.

So there again it has been the same the politicians to blame, one after the other they failed, and the things that were wrong remained the same for far too long yet again.

And not until there is change, injustice will be the norm for decades and even for centuries.

With policies implemented by world leaders, repeating the same mistakes as their ancestors.

Policies they said were to keep the peace, but instead, their policies smashed the peace into pieces, and scattered all over beyond man's reach.

And when it did, the problems it created, it would have been better that the policies were never implemented.

Causing chaos and mayhem, that's what the policies brought with them.

Inviting protesters everywhere, and where there were no protesters there was fear, the jails were filled with those who dared.

Indeed, regretfully, at this present day in time, it appears as if the world has entered into a phase of discontentment, with riots here, there, and everywhere, riots wherever you went, you could see, smell, and feel the dissatisfaction, as well as to hear the disgruntled arguments.

With the rise of poverty and destitution, injustice and oppression; just to survive is a very big problem, human beings are forced into crimes.

Fueled mainly by greed, selfishness, corruption, and of course politicians' bad policies.

Indeed, it is clearly obvious today at this very moment in time.

The conditions in the world couldn't be more transparent, with world destitution in a rapid upwards climb.

With homelessness and hunger, no clean water: how much worse it must be before it gets better?

With technology on the move destroying jobs, politicians would have to get their fingers out.

Get them out from wherever they are stuck, and do something quick to prevent tomorrow's rot.

So yes, it is very true and without an excuse, the world has always been with difficulties and tragedies in some place here and there, in fact everywhere, tragedies were always there.

Not hiding, but transparent for all to see the results of bad policies, one too many.

And that had always been so, wherever humans gathered together there was trouble, especially if they were miserable.

And this is because humans were never wise enough to be able to foresee, and hence predict and prevent adversities.

So the streets got overcrowded with people uprising, some were shot dead just for protesting.

Some were wounded, beaten, arrested and jailed, and many more intimidated.

And that was the price the people paid, just for protesting and demanding change.

And that was why change was so very slow; the politicians just didn't want to know.

They preferred to rule, stubborn as mules, and with the same policies as their consistent tools.

Unfortunately, that's how things had been for many centuries, that's how they were witnessed by the eyes of history.

The masses always had no other choice but to fight for their rights that never came overnight, and sadly it was often with lives lost, people were beaten, arrested and locked up in jail for protesting against injustice, that's how it had been in most places, and at every development stage.

Yes indeed, that's just how it had been from century to century, generation after generation, old and young.

It was always the same, those protesting for change were shot at, beaten, arrested, and thrown into jail, and still today in several places it is still the same with little or no change.

And that is true just as it had been, that's how it was yesterday, today, and tomorrow it will.

Nothing was given free, not even the end of slavery, there were always those who believed that wrong was right, and they were ready to defend it with all their might.

And with that belief held dearly, their choice was always to fight to prevent the workers from having rights.

The workers were always seen and treated as a class inferior, 'they got what they deserved, they didn't need better', that was the voice of their employers, the voice of their superiors.

That was the unreserved opinion of the elite, so for centuries they kept the workers under their feet.

And that was just how the world was developing, that's how it was progressing, uncompassionate and ruthless, and with no surprise, discontentment was everywhere steadily on the rise.

Workers were realizing that for their rights they have to fight, there were no free deliveries neither during the day nor during the night, even though no one was on strike.

So with water cannons, rubber bullets, and batons; that was the response from the other side, to disperse the crowds protesting for their rights, protesting for a better life.

Indeed, politicians were failing, not doing the right things, and abusing their powers too often.

There was no reasoning with anyone since reason was dead and gone, and that was the cause of many problems resulting from bad policies affecting economies, which triggered the disturbances on the streets.

So yes, it had always been a struggle, that's how things were, although it was never an ambition nor a dream, to fight for freedom was necessary, as was for justice and equality, and for every bit of basic human rights; it was an urge that was compulsory, no hesitation, one too many, no fights, no rights, that was the norm in daily life; so it was written, so it was done; there was to be no vacillation.

Yes, fighting for survival, fighting for life, fighting for rights, fighting was to be, although an evil, it was an unavoidable necessity forced upon the masses by the elite.

Because rights were never given, they always had to be taken from the ruling elite, the politicians who kept the rights of the working classes trampled under their feet.

Indeed, oppositions were always very strong, there were those who benefitted from the wrongs that were done, and would fight to keep it that way; nothing was to be given away, that's what they repeated how things must stay.

So there was never an end to the fighting, which was always for, or about something.

And that was the cause of the political mess in the world everywhere, and for which the politicians were never wisely prepared, they just dealt with situations as they came, and usually in unorthodox ways.

Making things worse than before, ignoring the cause which were unjust laws, and which, although there had been some changes over the years, whatever was changed still had to be changed again, there was always need for complaint.

And that was because the politicians never got it right, so the protesters continued with more battles to fight.

And that's how the world got a little better during mankind's advancement towards the future.

The masses always had to fight again and again to achieve most of the things that were changed.

Things that were deserving, basic human rights, and yet still to get them the people had to fight.

And that was because the educated seemed to lack common sense, and the law makers, they were something else.

Stubborn and indifferent to workers' rights, to acquire them was always through the engagement in a fight.

So yes indeed, it is not hard to believe, people had to fight for all their rights; from the injustice that was oppressive, and from exploitation with hand to mouth wages, and from the long and exhausting hours in the factories, to the right to vote where it was democratic; all were won after battles at different stages, indeed, even lives were sometimes paid for changes.

Yes indeed that's how it had been, lives were sometimes claimed, some badly wounded, some arrested and locked up in jail, that was the price paid for change.

And regretfully even women were arrested, beaten and locked up in jail, for their crime of demanding change, change from injustice to justice, from exploitation to fair wages.

And as they went on hunger strikes locked up in jail, painfully through their nostrils they were forcefully fed; and that was the sort of everyday injustice with which women were treated over the years.

Indeed nothing was given, all had to be demanded, grabbed or taken, and in the process one could have been badly beaten to death.

No one cared about the working classes, for centuries they were exploited.

Exploited and badly paid, I repeat again, workers had to fight for all the changes that were made. Changes that make life better today and taken for granted by the new generations that came. Indeed, changes did not come easy overnight, nor did they come from the kindness of hearts, whenever they came early or late, you could bet your last dollar that a fight was engaged.

Yes a fight in some way or the other, sometimes orderly, sometimes with disorder.

And yet still without protest and disorder, today many things may not have been better.

So yes indeed many lives were lost, people were beaten and jailed, acquiring basic human rights were never easy to obtain.

And that was the case everywhere, the struggle for rights was with great despair, and it is still so even today, it appears that there is always a price for rights which one must pay.

No lessons have not yet been learned from the systematic struggles of yesterday.

No lessons have not yet been learned so that things could be done in a much better way.

Indeed, no lessons have not yet been learned from the wrongs of yesterday still causing concern.

So yes indeed, and regretfully, after so many painful years with death, blood and tears; everywhere in the world human beings are still fighting for justice, especially the poor, women, and minorities are still fighting for equality, they are still fighting against hate, racism, and bigotry, and against corrupt laws, they are still fighting with the systems, and even sometimes among themselves, and with everybody else; indeed still fighting, and especially to make a living.

So, could anyone predict an end to the fighting, something good to look forward to?

Or would it always be a part of living, something you don't want but have to do?

Creating a world in a mess, despite the many centuries with changes and progress.

Many things that should have been put right are still wrong, and the world is turning upside down.

Changing and changing from wrong to right, and from right to wrong, no one knows for how much longer, whether or not it will go on forever.

And after a long fight weary and exhausted, with most of the time achieving little or nothing, breaking one's back whilst the head is aching.

Humans continue fighting still, not only for their rights but to make a living, because as they came to their senses, they realized that nothing was given, all had to be earned or taken.

And with that attitude for progress, how much has the world changed over the years to the benefit of the masses, after so many troubled years of weary fighting and protesting?

Indeed, changes have been very many, and yet still there is so much in need.

And still to obtain most things it is the same, it is still through protesting and fighting.

So for how much longer human beings will have to continue fighting against those opposing their rights for justice, and for a good living, or for whatever is rightfully theirs?

As human beings, are we not all entitled to the fruits of righteousness, some rightfully given, some to be earned, instead of fighting, to be taken?

Indeed I repeat, humans have existed for several millennia, and during those years the world has changed a great deal for the better.

To this fact there is no doubt that a great deal of changes came about.

Yes indeed, human beings are not as superstitious nor as foolish today as were their early ancestors during the period of medieval years.

Neither are they as brutal and ruthless, with the knowledge they have acquired humans have changed as they progressed over the years.

Taking better ways from the past to the present, introducing them to new generations.

And yet still unfortunately, human beings are not as wise as they should be, despite their experiences acquired from numerous problems and difficulties.

Still, despite however they are, wise or foolish, half of the world today exists in poverty, and the numbers are increasing yearly.

Indeed that is a deplorable reality; year after year the numbers have been increasing, and yet the politicians are doing little or nothing.

Failure is theirs for whatever it is, they are not driven by any incentive to really make the world a better place.

Too many problems are still ignored, until they become a burden upon us all.

And perhaps that too is the reason why after progressive development for so many centuries, the world turned out to be as it is?

Year after year politicians ignored problems while destitution continued on the rise right before their eyes.

With millions of people in countries everywhere living a life in the gutter, with no clean running water, and in conditions degrading in disgusting un-sanitary, unhealthy slums.

Where were their leaders? Where were the politicians? Were they all just having fun?

Traveling first class to meet someone, to embrace, shake hands, joke and laugh in idle discussions, and at the end of the day nothing is done, not even a meaningful agreement.

So millions of people continue living in degrading conditions not fit for humans.

And in that situation a million questions could be asked, and yet politicians never have answers, no solutions whatsoever, they don't know how to han-dle the matter.

Knowing quite well as everyone knows that millions of people are living today perhaps just a little better than their ancestors did centuries ago, when there is so much in the world today, enough for everyone to have their fill, so much so that it is at the brim, it overflows.

Indeed, overflowing into wastage when there are so many lives in need.

But then what is the alternative, how can humans prevent the wastage?

How could they satisfy everybody with at least the things that are necessary?

Perhaps indeed what is needed is the ambition to succeed with good policies.

Policies which will make things better, with no one existing in the gutter.

In a world filled with plenty, and yet so many people in need, in need of a place to sleep instead of on the streets, in need of a daily meal instead of scraps collected from a rubbish heap, in need of clean drinking water instead of that collected running from a sewer.

Yes indeed, there are so many people with no permanent residence, can't afford the rent, so they crouched on the ground in parks, and on pavements, or in leaking shacks where families crouched up against each other on the floor, and in the same dirty clothes which they were wearing three weeks before.

And added to that to make their misery complete, all day long some didn't even have something to eat.

Not even scraps from a rubbish heap where they searched desperately for a little something to eat, scraps which they may only get if they were lucky, and yet barely enough to prevent starvation like a wild pest rumbling in their bellies.

But who really cares about anyone's problems, whether they eat or where they sleep? Who cares about their destitution? indeed maybe charities, but not the politicians, they never seem to have the time on their hands, not even for discussions.

Indeed, the world is filled with conniving vagrants, you help them and from you they steal.

So life goes on as it has developed to be, some without and some with plenty, that's the human reality, that's the politicians' policy.

Yes indeed, some with an abundant excessive amount, much more than what they could ever need or want, whilst families go hungry, their purse empty, not a single penny.

Some have, but hardly enough, struggling just to make ends meet.

Some can't even change from the rags they wear daily, scavenging the streets in bare feet.

Some commit crimes to survive, ruining other people's lives.

Some don't know just what to do, whether they should eat or heat.

And that's how things are, that's how the world has developed to be, so far.

To make a living, some people will do anything, even committing crimes, if that's what it takes for them to survive; like everyone else, they want a good life.

So yes again the politicians have failed on yet another trail, they failed in their duty to the people.

They failed, and failed, and failed again, they failed too often to do the right things.

So life goes on just as before, and those with much more than plenty, this is how extravagantly they spend their money.

Not to help others by giving to charity, nor even to save the life of some-body, or to put some food in a hungry child's belly; but perhaps they do those things already by giving to charity, and yet still they are left with plenty, so some of it they must enjoy spending wastefully.

And that is exactly what they do, so a fleet of cars is what they have, many more than two.

And a house here and everywhere, a house in different countries, many to spare.

And a yacht is what they also have got, upon the oceans riding the waves is our unbridled oligarch.

And they may even have their own transport up in the air, to fly around here and there.

And at the end of the day with a smile on their faces, they are off to the auction houses where fools gather, those who have got plenty of money, to enjoy a spending spree.

Yes indeed, they are off to the auctions where they wastefully spend millions that don't even put a dent in their bank accounts.

Competing with one another for whatever, until it is sold to the highest bidder.

Yes indeed, it is off to the auction houses where they go to lose their senses, although not drunk in the circumstances, bidding for items at exorbitant prices for useless pieces of objects.

Objects that have no usefulness, and are kept locked away in darkness.

Put in a drawer, or in a vault, or in a box up in the loft.

Indeed, it is not difficult to believe that human beings have the ability to waste such large sums of money; like clean water from a burst pipe wastefully gushing down a drain, when others so destitute, can't even get enough to drink.

And it is never spent on things needed, but on otiose objects which have no purpose and yet wanted. And that could be any piece of rubbish with absolutely no usefulness.

Especially if it is a few thousands of years old, and that it came from an imperial household.

And even just a worn piece of garment that once belonged to someone famous, that can fetch millions of pounds from a fool who has too much.

Yes indeed, if that is what someone wants, not what he needs; something to lock up in a vault, and then perhaps throw away the keys.

Yes, something to keep hidden in darkness, in a drawer, a vault, or up in the loft hidden in a suitcase, that's the purpose of the purchase, because it really has no usefulness, but maybe to sell at a profit at a later date.

So for one single item that has no usefulness, and yet millions of pounds is what someone paid for it, that is the measure of human's foolishness.

And that could be because of its history, and not necessarily its quality.

A thousand years old, and from a rich household, that's what puts its value up in gold.

Yes indeed, money that could have been so much better spent, and with greater usefulness, helping destitute children.

But then again, if your tap is connected to the sea, then you will have a lot of water to waste, no one will disagree.

Well, it is the same with money, the more you have the more you waste; whatever is the price, you could purchase, and not even above the sky, is the limit.

But then again who do you blame? That's just how life is, that's how the world has developed to be over many centuries.

That's how humans have created it, and that perhaps is how it may stay, change is not yet on its way.

What is wasted here is wanted elsewhere; and that is how it has always been everywhere.

That's just how things are, humans don't seem to know better, they are more often in a pursuit of pleasure, for other awareness they don't really care.

But then who really cares? Life goes on fair or unfair, and that's how it is everywhere.

And without attempts to put things right, that's how they will remain throughout life, in an uncompassionate and a sinful world.

That's how it was yesterday, that's how it is today, and for tomorrow: Who knows?

So yes indeed it is very sad, the rich waste millions of their dollars on useless trash.

A vase, a bowl, a plate, or a picture painted by a famous artist; any piece of object, it matters not what it is, as long as it is dated with old age.

Yes indeed something dated centuries old, and better still, if it is the only one in the world.

Objects that have no usefulness whatsoever, and make no difference to anyone's life, but maybe perhaps, just a moment of happiness when they bought it at a very exorbitant price.

Happy to know they won the bid for it, happy to know they could afford it, and even happier to know what the hell they will do with it. What is its purpose or usefulness?

So where or what is the sense of it, in the making of such an exorbitant and unnecessary purchase?

Indeed, human values exceed common sense, no one knows where it will end; trash is paid for with large sums of money, when everywhere in the world children are hungry.

But maybe their purchases are investments to make a profit from another fool who is just as rich, and may even pay more for it, despite its uselessness.

And proud to be the owner of a piece of trash which no one else has got.

So yes indeed, it is in auction houses where fools gather to waste their money, large sums of it, on things that have no usefulness.

Wasting such large sums of money when it could be so much better spent.

Helping somebody who is desperately in need, a sick child, and there are so many who may die. And why? only because they have no money, can't pay for health care, can't pay for medicine. So, with a little thought and reason, with a little sense of understanding.

Is it not helping someone in need, money is much better and well spent?

Or are they just useless people, helping them makes no difference, they are better left with their miserable self and with their aggravating problems.

So is that why humans spend so wastefully whenever they have much more than plenty? Is it better to spend that to give, whether or not it is wasted?

With so many children sick in the world, desperate, and weakened with starvation, many in a state of destitution, denied even an education.

Is there no inspiration to give at all, no compassion to fellow mankind?

No sympathy for destitute children?

Are those silly earthly material trash to humans they are more important than to be kind?

Wasting a great deal of money on things which are without usefulness and are unnecessary, and indeed not needed at all, things one could do without.

And at a very high cost, purchasing otiose trash that is completely useless.

When there are so many children in need of whatever you can give, in need of what you are wasting.

If one should have so much to waste, to be blessed with such a privilege; Why not help others who are desperate with generous acts of kindness?

Putting a smile on their faces, and happiness in your heart as storage.

For surely there is happiness in giving, it is indeed most rewarding.

Yes indeed, there are many children you can help who are desperately in need of an operation, children born with certain conditions and have no hope for a better life, just because money is what they don't have.

So will it not be money much better spent, helping someone in such a situation?

Instead of wasted on a piece of material object which could be in a better place; in a museum, there is where such things belong for the public to gaze upon.

Indeed, that is the care home for things with old age, things which have no usefulness, but to lay exposed for all to see with the comfort of their history.

So does keeping them for yourself, and perhaps stored away hidden in darkness.

Is that the only usefulness of your purchase, and perhaps at some later date to sell at a profit?

Just because you are the owner of something that is centuries old, or perhaps it is the only one in the world, or that it is the underpants of a very famous musician.

What does it really matter, with some old useless pieces of trash you are the owner?

In all common sense, is that the best way money could be spent?

Isn't such things better left resting in the brightness of light in a museum exposed for all to see, instead of hidden in darkness and left forgotten, out of sight and memory?

So why not spend your excessive amount to give some destitute children an education, wouldn't that be money much better spent, and indeed, much more rewarding?

Or is generosity something to scorn, something no one should ever take on, it never ever worth the efforts.

Even giving destitute children a future to look forward to, is that another thing nobody should do?

Preferring to purchase something for millions of dollars, something which has no usefulness at all, so it is kept locked up in darkness, and maybe for years, until perhaps you can sell it at a profit, your only moment of happiness.

So yes, Mr. Human Being, why not forget the profit for your useless piece of object and do something worthwhile? On the faces of desperate children put a smile.

Instead of being influenced by forces of egoism and vanity, with value belonging to the realm of stupidity.

What does it matter one way or the other, with a piece of ancient trash you are the owner? Indeed, something which has no usefulness, and yet millions was paid for it, perhaps to be sold at a later date, there is always another fool who will pay more for it.

And with nothing better, nor have you done anyone any good when you could and should.

Competing with one another in a price war, paying millions; and what for.

When those millions could have improved so many lives of children, many who are alive and daily starving, many who need an operation, many who need an education, many who need shelter and a bed to sleep on.

But then again, who do you blame? Humans created the system called capitalism, and that's just the way it is.

And until human beings are wiser and come up with something better, this disparity will continue to be a part of the survival reality, and it may still get worse, most likely.

Yes indeed, that's how it will always be, some with plenty, some with their purse empty, and some with a grumbling belly.

And that is because it is by the capitalist values mankind will continue to live by, you can have much more than enough, a bank full of dollars that are all yours, you don't have to give if you don't want to give, that's your privilege.

Indeed, you don't have to give, it's all yours to spend however you wish, that's the system we all live in, the system we call capitalism.

The system some people make very good use of, those labeled as millionaires.

So if you want to waste just because you got more than enough, it's no shame, it's no disgrace.

As long as whatever you do is within the law, then whatever you do is up to you.

So yes, you can spend it just as you like, like a fool, or like someone wise.

Like a miser or like someone who cares, either buying trash or helping others.

At the end of the day it is yours to spend, to do with it whatever you want.

To give it away, to put on display, or in some bank in a vault locked up it stays.

That is the world mankind has created, that is exactly how it is, that's your freedom, that's your will, to spend as much as you can, however you want, and without ever giving away a penny, not even a cent, if that's your decision.

To spend as you like, to Jupiter, take a flight, however you spend that's your right.

That is how the world has developed to be, it is part of the freedoms in societies, some people with nothing and some with plenty, it's up to you to make use of the opportunities.

A world with a very uneven playing field, where the game is very rough and hard to succeed.

And not until there is change again, that's just how the world will remain.

A world where governments are corrupt, most laws they make are unjust.

With the rich avoiding tax, the poor paying too much, and governments short of cash.

Indeed human beings know how to land on the moon, and they could visit blackholes, and further they can go colonising the Universe, using mathematical equations.

But social problems are more challenging, square roots will not solve them.

Indeed, they are of a more complex nature, requiring a higher level of enlightenment, wisdom instead of intelligence.

And that is why there are so many unsolved social problems, humans are not as wise as they are intelligent.

So yes you may ask once again: what the hell human beings have been doing?

What kind of a world are they creating?

So unfair are so many things, and it does not appear that they will ever change.

Even to create a level playing field is a challenge, and survival indeed is full of problems.

After centuries in developing, yet still there is no clarity of humans' ambitions and their aims.

So the surface of the world remains very rough, every step taken could be dangerous.

A world divided and in a hell of a mess, is what human beings created and said it is their very best.

And passing it on from generation to generation, and each time with many more problems; drifting further away from Utopia, with problems that made it harder to survive, and even worse still to stay alive.

And as the world remains just the same without good reasoning, and with idiocy in control, and uncertainty a threat to the changing world.

It has always been obvious in problems that were numerous, that too many bad decisions were made, and worse still, they were executed.

Yes, it was the bad decisions made and executed that sent many people to an early grave.

And that got worse especially, after it became known to everybody, that reason was assassinated, bad policies escalated.

Indeed it happened throughout the ages, governments had implemented too many bad policies, one after the other they flowed like a stream.

Policies that lacked common sense, policies that lacked reason, policies that were detrimental, policies that released not only a bad smell, but the devastating wrath of hell, and the anger of the people too, rioting is what they do.

And why? Indeed, mankind was no longer getting together to reason with one another.

Instead they were exchanging opinions in arguments which became very common, and were clear and obvious in decisions made that were disastrous, and that included Brexit; the good life took an exit, with new problems especially inflation pushing up prices going right through the ceiling, then through the roof, and upwards much further again, everyday is the same.

And it has been so in numerous other cases, two of the latest were COVID-19, and the invasion of Ukraine where bad policies led to war once again; and with a fool's cap someone was wearing.

Indeed, the consequences were the result of bad policies, so they are always, and so they will be, bad policies will breed catastrophes.

So yes indeed, Covid-19 was a very good example to the world, where arguing instead of reasoning stumbled wildly out of control, as the world was led by policies of fools.

Regretfully, it was a tragedy in which mankind just seemed unable to reason together, so arguing became more popular, and the problems got worse than ever.

Opinions differed everywhere, bombarded with criticisms, and yet still nothing was very clear just how to solve this threat to health care.

Some politicians said, and without good reason, that it was just a simple flu, and for a simple flu, yet still the fools didn't know what to do.

And even worse still, they would not listen to scientific advice, they said that it wasn't wise.

And although the problem was getting worse, with deaths on the rise and hospitals full.

Determined with their decisions as bad as they were, it was their economy they tried to put first.

And as it was in some places, Covid was beginning to be associated with taboos and myths.

Superstitions were creeping in upon the reality of Covid-19.

Yes indeed, people were believing in all sorts of things, some were even saying that Covid-19 didn't really exist, others were searching for the cause and the cure in superstitions, taboos, and myths.

Yes indeed it was laughable, as much as it was frightening and threatening.

Ridiculous opinions were often heard and followed, with the rise in deaths all over the world; criticisms and arguments were well out of control;

whereas intelligence and common sense, into a dark corner they were pushed, and the ideas of fools were the ones listened too.

Indeed, fools are never far away from any event, especially fools in government.

And they often make things worse with their arguments, which are caused by different opinions converging into altercations that often end up in disagreements.

And yes, they seldom listen to reason or good advice, believing they are the ones who are wise; refusing even to compromise.

And whenever they get their own way, make no mistake the damage they do is just too big.

As was the spread of Covid-19 experienced all over the world.

Fools were the cause of most of the problems; refusing to listen to the voice of science.

Unfortunately in the world there are too many fools in high office implementing bad policies, from government institutions, and wherever else you could find them.

They are always there wherever you go, with their big ideas for a worse tomorrow.

And that is exactly what they did with the spread of Covid.

Indeed it could have been less effective, with fewer cases, fewer deaths, fewer disturbances.

But as politicians they failed again with bad policies implemented.

Listening to foolish opinions instead of those which came from science.

And yes, there is still a much greater problem created by humans, the result of years of destruction which today poses a serious threat, which politicians have failed to address.

And this threat from nature, as bad as it is, is the threat known as 'Climate Change.'

It has been building up for years from industrial policies which were encouraged and promoted.

Indeed, deforestation and air pollution were ignored repeatedly in the interest of economies.

Yes indeed, completely ignoring the consequences that may come as cataclysms which may even erupt as Armageddon.

Yes, this has been realized a bit too late, with flimsy attempts to prevent the destruction that maybe, is on its way already.

So leaders of the world gathered together to find a common solution to prevent the disaster threatened by nature, a response to humans' bad behaviour.

But instead, this was what they did; instead of reasoning together to find an answer, they were arguing with one another, self-interest was at the top of the agenda.

Each division as a nation, intransigent with their opinions pursuing their own interest.

And at the end of the day with much time wasted making empty promises, which were in previous cases never got implemented.

The climate change threat, with no agreement how to prevent it, still remains a natural cataclysm by which mankind is threatened.

And yet indeed, although it is already happening, and as transparent as it could be, yet still it is not taken seriously, self-interest is still the priority.

So let me ask this question once more again. How much more stupid could humans be?

Already experiencing some natural disasters, and still not taking the situation seriously enough.

Nobody is reasoning, the assassination of reason is what they blame, they say that reasoning is dead, so everyone is arguing instead.

So perhaps humans are not to blame, there is no one with whom they could reason and come up with some answers without committing treason.

So yes it looks like Armageddon, unless mankind could find some sort of solution, and it is not because of the impact of a meteorite, but an impact created by humans, resulting from bad policies constituted by politicians.

They are always in heated opinions exchanged in arguments which are punctuated with criticisms instead of reasoning together to find solutions.

The very same thing was done with Covid-19, and many other bad policies implemented again and again during the reign of history.

Perhaps maybe that since the assassination of reason, to make decisions as a politician, it is not that easy as it always had been.

So yes again it was the politicians to blame as it was with most things, they failed to find suitable solutions. Failing to convince the entire public of the reality of the deadly Covid.

And of course the dangers of climate change in which humans were recklessly engaged.

Oh yes indeed the politicians failed, and whenever they did too many people suffered the consequences as it often is.

And that was because the decisions they made and were taken, were not the ones scientifically given, and yet those were the ones pursued at will, making many mistakes.

Pushing the world nearer to the edge of the bridge, closer and closer to its grave.

Pushing the world towards armageddon, either by the natural forces of nature, or by the forces from their nuclear bombs.

But not only human lives that were destroyed, with bad policies deployed.

Some had a very devastating effect on wildlife in the natural forests, and fisheries, yes, on species deep down below on the sands of the oceans' seas.

Regretfully, there are many living species humans have already wiped out, and many more graves are already dug.

And yet still human beings continue with their reckless damage, still causing devastating climate change, the seriousness of it has not yet sunk into their brains, they are more concerned with other things.

And adding to it, despite the seriousness, they have also been polluting the oceans, recklessly causing deaths and destruction.

Yes, that's what humans have been doing, polluting the sea, the air, and the land, ravaging nature from the sky above, to the bottom of the oceans' sand.

And yet despite their unrestrained cruelty, destroying nature senselessly.

Nature has co-existed peacefully, trying to live with mankind in harmony.

But then it appeared that things were changing, as mankind provoked nature again and again. And although nature had already delivered some serious warnings, humans were never certain of what they should or should not be doing; or how they could even reason together to find an answer to the problems they caused by provoking nature.

And how to protect themselves from the damages that nature can cause, if it unleashes the full blast of its powers.

But of course that was not much of a concern to humans, not to anyone, that was something they pushed behind them, their economy came first in front, that was always their biggest worry, and doing things in a hurry, mistakes were often one to many.

And yet they continued with their relentless destruction, still not listening to the voices of science, not listening to any voice at all, they were so stubborn, that they were not even listening when nature called.

So yes, it is true and very true that politicians right through the ages from BC into AD times, could have done a great deal more to make the world a much better place; but they were no sages.

Indeed, they could have spent less time in wars fighting with one another, and more of their time in efforts together to find solutions to make the world better.

Yes indeed, that's what they could have done, everyone believed that politicians could have created a better world if only they had tried much harder, a world in which justice and peace together were common factors in law and order.

If only they were enlightened, and were more sensible, dedicated, caring, and responsible, more daring, bold and determined, and as wise as the fox is cunning.

Yes indeed, no one doubted that it was the politicians' responsibility to make the world a much better place for the entire human race, and that is what they should have done, and not from their responsibilities to dodge and run.

Indeed, they could have seen that there was no need for the jostling and bustling marathon rat race, and they should have got rid of it, because it is a race that keeps humans very busy on their toes wherever they go, pushing and shoving to make a living.

There was indeed no need for the hustle and bustle that got so many in serious trouble.

And certainly there was also no need for destitute poverty when there was always plenty enough in the world for everybody.

Yes indeed, so too there was no need for children to go hungry, and living in slums in very unhealthy conditions; with no running water, no sanitation whatsoever, and yet that is the everyday lifestyle for millions of children, in fact for millions of families, destitution is in the air they breathe, breathless is how they feel.

Yes living perhaps as their ancestors did, who had none of today's conveniences.

For it was totally the politicians' responsibility to develop the world as it should be, a sanitary place with sufficient space healthy enough for everyone to live.

So once again, the politicians have failed, and in yet another place.

Too little was done to prevent the slums, and yet still they will not accept the blame, although they did nothing, so as bad as things were, that's how they remain.

And they remain so for as long as it takes, politicians were never in a hurry to make any change, not for the poor, not for the lame, in fact, most things to better the lives of the working classes, politicians were not interested without disorder demanding.

Yes indeed unfortunately, that's how it was, and that's how it is, the present has inherited the past's footprints, and only after riots and disorder comes about change.

And so the world continued to be governed by fools who plunged their countries into ruins. With bad policies that cause catastrophes, both natural and man-made.

And that was because their aim and their purpose were too often for their own benefit, abusing their powers yet again, with results without merit.

Creating wars, implementing draconian laws with policies that led to bad results.

Yes, it was always the same, as it happened again, this time in Ukraine.

Many people lost their life, and many who live lost everything, their life is left in ruins.

And that is why the world today is as it is, reaping the consequences of yesterday's mistakes.

Mistakes that occurred right through the ages, many repeated again and again each time new generations came.

And by governments failing their nations, not doing the things expected of them.

Enforcing equality, preserving an incorruptible judiciary, eliminating injustice, destitution and poverty, and the many other wrongs that became the norm, which was their duty to eradicate effectively.

But instead, those things they ignored, government after government each one was a fraud.

The neglect of politicians to do the things expected of them, was an unavoidable contribution to their failures.

Too much time was spent engaged in wars, either in battle or in making preparations constructing more deadly weapons.

And indeed, most regretfully too much time was spent in arguments, often resulting in a waste of time without conclusive agreements.

And as mankind continues to build and destroy time and time again, in an unpredictable cycle of progressive development and change.

Change often from bad to good, yet sometimes though from good to worse.

And so things were done changing all the time, some perfect, some were very good, some did not turn out to be the way they should.

And as the changes continue to change and change, still what was always needed, it was yet again even still more change.

And that was because human beings never reached the peak of their development; the world was always in need to be ameliorated.

And this was so in both social and material developments, both were always in need of improvements, as humans headed onwards in one direction towards the future with all their requirements.

So yes indeed, this was something very well known that whatever was changed, governments were to take the blame whether they were the wrong or the right things.

And that was because governments were responsible for developments both good and bad, so they always had the trump card.

And yet still, too often there were imperfections with whatever was done, governments did too many things that were wrong, often cutting corners and ignoring what should be done.

So yes it is true they failed everyone, they failed to eliminate too many wrongs, and the laws which justified them.

Yes indeed, time and time again they failed to put their feet firmly on the ground, and stand against what was wrong, so as things were they just carried on.

Wrongs that became a daily norm, scattered out of control in many places around the world.

Wrongs that became too big a problem, that governments couldn't even handle them.

And added to the mess, politicians were often less useful and more useless.

Yes they were useless, failing to clean-up their mess, which was at the heart of many governments and their colluding institutions with too many red tapes to get things done.

Yes, tapes much bigger than a shoelace, and getting in the way blocking progress, slowing things down, which thereafter they never get done.

Yes, that is very common in many government departments, red tape is a nuisance, it hinders progressive development, indeed, it really slows things down.

And not for a moment forgetting governments that commit and cover up crimes, either taking or paying bribes, and they do it all the time, knowing quite well that it is wrong, but believing it must be done, and kept in the closet of confidentiality, or under the carpet hidden secretly; there they hide the evidence of their crimes.

And that is very true in large institutions, as well as in small corporations.

Wherever there is government influence, there is where it could be found, any number of hidden wrongs.

Often there is no need to look carefully, transparent there are so many.

From false accusations, imprisonment and torture, and even death in cold-blood murders.

And in conspiracies of something or the other, regime change, political assassinations, or some plot to destabilize a government.

Yes indeed, all those crimes are secretly covered up, especially by those at the top.

And it gets worse from country to country, with little or no transparency; corruption is the mother of irresponsibility, and the fertilizer of disaster in many countries.

And whoever is responsible for it, they could become a blackmailer's target.

And that is what leads directly to failures, especially when governments don't have a good policy to eliminate the wrongs in societies.

Yes, wrongs of every kind and of every sought, especially the injustices within the laws.

Those wrongs in particular, they seem to last forever.

And that has been the case for centuries one after the other, rulers were corrupt everywhere.

It was the direction taken by them, by Kings and Emperors, Pharaohs and Dictators, Presidents and Prime Ministers; it was with their corrupted laws that order was enforced.

But perhaps it was something they inherited, nonetheless, as bad as it was, they were never anxious to change any laws.

So politicians came and went, many of them, one replaced the other, leaving the world not much better.

And religion too offered nothing new, superstitions they still held to be true.

And yes indeed, they were involved in the mess of a brutal and ruthless past, corruption in religion was nothing less than that of the ruling oligarchs.

Accused as witches; or devil worshipers, religion burnt alive many innocent women, after they were arrested and ruthlessly tortured for the admission of a confession.

So yes, those were the conditions in the world, and as bad as things are today, in the past they were many times worse.

And yet it is that past that shaped the present, with both good and bad, whatever at that time the people had.

So yesterday's sins visited the present, and then towards the future was where they went.

Taking with them millions of people still living in filthy slums, and from decency estranged, despite the many years of change, the numbers are still increasing, and that from the past is what the present has inherited, and it looks like the future may inherit the same with many people living in slums everywhere, and without a good meal and clean water, nor with any hope of a better future; in fact, without any hope whatsoever.

And that's just how many families live, yesterday, today, and tomorrow they will.

And the reason for that, some blame the capitalist for exploiting and cheating the workers.

From hand to mouth, and for years that was how they were paid, regardless of how much work they did, and the fat profits companies made.

But many others think that it was their government to blame for doing nothing, hence failing again. Failing to recognise the root of the problems, and to act to bring it to an end.

By enforcing proper laws to prevent the exploiting and the cheating of the workers.

In fact, in many cases they ignored or supported it, or they turned a blind eye, leaving the workers breathless, consumed by injustice as an illness to live with until they die.

Injustice from which they had no escape, it was as if their governments had turned their backs in their faces.

But it is true to say, and certainly it is, that despite how bad things may be, capitalism provides opportunities, and that is no lie, that of course is what it does, that is its function, that is its purpose, that's what capitalism does for all of us.

So yes, it provides opportunities in all sorts of ways, giving everyone a chance to make a living in whatever way they could benefit, a chance from poverty to escape.

Yes, it provides ways to enslave, to exploit and to cheat, as well as to be honest without deceit.

Ways to commit crimes of every kind, with drugs on the loose, children abused, some kidnapped and sold as sex slaves as objects to be misused. Indeed, unfortunately how sad it could be, what a world it is that these wrongs of yesterday are still very common today.

And they are getting worse, too many people with an empty purse, so crimes are committed for what it's worth.

Yes indeed, after centuries that came and went, and many politicians with them, there is still a lack of benevolence.

Yes, unfortunately as sad as it is, everyday things are getting worse still.

Children are kidnapped from their parents, some are sold by them, some from their homes they run away, to escape the torment day after day.

With drunken husbands beating their wives, heated arguments, neglected babies in wet nappies screaming in tears.

And those considered lucky, by their parents they are sent to beg, so that they may eat a slice of bread.

But who really cared whether destitute children were alive or dead, whether they were beaten or starved to death, or as a slave they were sold for sex?

Yes indeed who really cared that they were in some way or the other misled, or to the vultures they were fed.

Indeed, and most regretfully, thousands of young girls and boys, many with age still in single figures were kidnapped from their parents and sold as slaves for sexual pleasures, that's how they were disparagingly used; as nothing more than objects for the pleasure of perverts around the world.

And many more were often kidnapped and gang raped, in cultures that took it for granted, no consequences, no proper laws implemented, that's how bad it is.

And yes indeed, you can even hear the stories told by rapists themselves without fear, nor shame, but proudly boasting about their savage encounters which they claimed were successful events which they will do again.

And that was because no arrest was made, no charges, no consequences; the pain, shame, and disgrace were all upon the victims, and even from their family they usually receive no sympathy; in fact, they are often made to feel guilty, and are treated as something dirty; and even worse still, sometimes their own family no longer wants them, the disgrace and dishonour are too much for the family to bear; can't face the neighbours, can't face the community, can't face anybody who knows the family; and that's because their daughter was raped.

So young girls are left to go it alone, rejected from their homes, with no friends, no protection, no one to lend them a helping hand.

So yes, they are left in a mess, disadvantaged in places corrupt, heartless, and lawless.

And so it continues, family abuses, and daughters remain at the mercy of their heartless families.

Conformity was more important, and family honour, that was never to be questioned.

So yes indeed, driven by their cultural beliefs, or perhaps a need which may be a little hard to believe. Some daughters were sold into marriages by their parents, regardless of their very young age, most in their early teens, sold to men old enough to be their granddad.

Yes, sold to them to be used for anything, as a wife or a prostitute, a gardener or a maid, a servant, or just someone to do everything, whatever it was demanding.

Suffering abuses within a marriage, where love and respect were both disregarded, and where beatings were common, often for disobedience.

Any chance of a divorce? that never happens unless it was a request of the husband.

And despite this pejorative sexism, from within their culture the idea was inspiring especially by parents, that it was better to be married, with or without respect, love, or romance; to be married was more important.

So children were left enslaved, sold and tightly knotted in bondage as young wives with no escape, and with their frame of mind in their destitute state of survival, was brimming with thoughts that were suicidal.

Afraid to live, afraid to die, from either one they could not hide.

And in this area of forced marriages, sexual abuses, disrespect, and beatings.

As widespread as it is, yet politicians have failed again, most of the time ignoring the crimes doing nothing apart from making puerile bleatings.

And even taking bribes to turn a blind eye to the suffering in human trafficking and forced child marriages.

Yes indeed, those offences are very common today, the sexual trade is big business, thriving illegally with bribes paid for security.

Indeed, the trafficking of boys, girls, and young women, to be used as tools in sexual engagements is protected by corrupted law enforcement, many hands receive payments, and the crimes flourish to the youngster's disadvantage.

Yes indeed, bribes are commonly paid, changing hands as a means to cover up crimes, especially among politicians, and the police is no exception.

And this is very much in practice among drug cartels; they pay bribes in large sums of money to keep their businesses afloat successfully.

Indeed, wherever organized crimes are very successful, corruption is rampant in high places.

And that's when nothing is done to bring them down, so they operate free in fear of no one.

And that is because bribes are paid in large sums to politicians, to judges, and the police.

It is common practice in many countries within the chain of their judiciary.

And that is why those wrongs continue to exist for so very long, they enjoy protection from top to bottom, and with that sense of security they carry on, no need to be afraid of anyone, no need to be on the run, no need to shut down.

Not forgetting the disabled too, it is true, as victims of political failures it is nothing new, just view the world and see how it is; everywhere in the world the disabled are often disadvantaged, they are indeed too often unfairly treated, they too are victims of societies' injuries.

So yes, no one has to guess, it is certain that the failures of politicians have spread far beyond a thousand miles, very far and wide, especially in Third

World countries where the law is often ignored, and order is somewhat mediocre.

And two of the main causes are the politicians' indifference to problems, and their lack of leadership, and of course, and quite often too, their life or their family lives may be threatened.

So they don't want to know, and would not do what they ought to do, so the problems just continue.

More crimes are committed, widespread injustice, and even wars are the result of their failures, failing to prevent the cause, failing to be tough on criminals.

Indeed, it is no secret, all the wrongs in societies are due to politicians' failures in some way or the other, directly or indirectly.

And the worst of all are those which lead to wars, failing to find a peaceful solution for whatever was the problem.

So yes indeed, politicians often fail no matter what it is, and the reasons are often the same.

It is always their indifference and their idiocy, failing in their duty, as was the case in this example that happened just a few years recently, in a matter of the highest conspiracy.

Yes indeed, as it has been recorded, indifference and idiocy led to the assassination of JF Kennedy.

With institutions failing to adhere to warnings and to recognise the threat, and do their duty to prevent and to protect their President from an unnatural death.

Yes they failed terribly, ignoring advice and the signs of a plot and conspiracy; they exposed the President as an easy target for assassination in an open automobile.

Something they knew was inviting as much as it was unsafe, moving at a slow pace.

So yes indeed, there is no doubt that they failed, they failed to persuade the President that danger could be hidden anywhere along the route to be taken, and that his protection was much safer within a bullet-proof enclosure.

It was for sure that their failure was nothing more than gross neglect and inefficiency within the institutions of security, they failed in their duty miserably.

And that's how bad it can get, even when politicians are doing their best.

And each time they failed things got worse, forcing gears into reverse.

And that was one of the reasons why humans' development and progress were slow, what should have been done yesterday was done tomorrow.

And as open eyes shut blind to all sorts of crimes, allowing them to multiply.

Distorting the order of societies by presenting criminals with opportunities.

And as divisions in the systems got wider and wider, expanding as much as they can.

With the rich getting richer and the poor getting poorer, drifting closer and closer into the arms of destitution.

Then the cataclysm of capitalism, much sooner than later, the arrival of its end may be its final solution.

But for now, this is the world humans have created, the world today in which we all live in. A world that has taken several thousands of years to develop to this stage of progress.

And during that time, with their hands human beings have created many things, some very simple, some with excellence, which were a real challenge to their imaginations, and yet they were changed as they were made better still.

Indeed, that's how the world is, that is the world we are all living in, and without any doubt, humans have made astonishing developments and progress, and yet still there are many more better things to come, which will come as humans continue on their journey towards the future; still improving things making them better, acquiring knowledge in science, and using it to make things better all the time.

Indeed, so it will always be, things will change, they will always change, and still change again as long as humans continue to acquire knowledge.

And that is because of new ideas; and not until mankind achieves his very best, he will never rest, tomorrow indeed there will always be progress, because progress is success.

So yes, that's the way how things have developed, both good and bad, they were all the result of humans' efforts.

And yes without any doubt things could still get a great deal better, or even a lot worse, as things keep on changing all the time, no one can predict the final solution, no one could predict the end.

And despite the changes, new generations come and take things for granted, as if the world had always been as it is, never by the new supplanted.

Not knowing how long it took to develop, nor even how long it took to reach at this stage of progress.

Not knowing the difficulties with which human beings were engaged in the development of progress with change.

Not knowing the many lives lost in the fight for justice and human rights, and still today they are compromised.

Especially after the assassination of reason, to voice an opinion no one would listen, and if they did, no one would reason, preferring to argue.

So, decisions were made about whatever it was, some good, some bad, some right some wrong;

And whatever was the decision taken, whether it was right or wrong, that was how things were done. And that was how it always was in the past, and so it is in this present age.

Changes were made and things were done, and when they were done, they were sometimes better as well as different.

Different and confusing, so they changed again, that was the norm, that was how things were done during the years of humans' progressive development.

Yes they did, at every development stage things changed and they changed again, with the times things were always moving, better and better they were getting.

But not always at the same pace, many things remained the same, not everything was always changing.

And those that changed, changed again in a cycle of continuous destruction and progress.

It was towards the future humans were always heading, taking with them whatever they were carrying, things they believed they may need.

And although they were often not quite sure of what they were doing, whether it was for worse or for better.

They still kept on going nonetheless, despite sometimes having regrets when things didn't work out as they did expect.

And as the years pushed ahead with humans still developing, still creating new things all the time progressing from age to age, turning all the time from page to page.

It became their vocation, creating whatever they can to create a better world was always humans' intention, and that's what they have been doing with their new inventions.

Crossing over from one age to the next, stage after stage the challenges were difficult, but they often ended with good results.

And as human beings entered further still into a new age, the age of this present day.

This new age from superstitions to knowledge, from ignorance to intelligence; this age of technology and science could well be indeed humans' biggest challenge.

Yes indeed, after countless years of traveling, and with a heavy load of problems which humans were always carrying from generation to generation, and with the knowledge and experiences which they have gained; the world indeed would never remain the same, there will always be room for new things, hence constant change will always be happening again and again, and yet again.

And it will always be challenging, the more advanced, the more problems, or perhaps less problems with more satisfaction, and probably with more discontentment, more unemployment, indeed, and regretfully, there may even be still more criminal activities.

So yes indeed, it is very difficult to predict, there is no science for it, not even a good voodoo trick.

What will be will be, no one will be able to tell accurately what the future will be.

What kind of a world it is likely to be with the new discoveries in science and technology.

But as it is today, mankind has already entered a very astute age, today's age of science and artificial intelligence.

And those other ages humans left behind there is none to match, this one is a real challenge.

Yes, it is true to say that it is an age that is very challenging, very awakening, with brilliant new ideas unfolding.

Humans are creating things that are very smart, indeed, even smarter than humans.

It is an age so technically advanced that humans are able to create things that are even able to think; and in some cases they are even smarter than humans.

Indeed it is an auspicious challenge which demands that I pop this question.

Could you win a robot in a game of chess?

Without hesitation, on the robot I will place my bet at one thousand to one, and with no regrets.

And although it has taken humans several millennia to reach this age of technology and science.

The progress they are now making, and the speed at which they are developing, things are indeed rapidly changing, can't keep up with anything.

But that is one of the benefits of the technical age, things are no longer very slow to change as they were in the old days.

But that is mainly with material things, whereas the social structures, the injustices and disadvantages are either getting worse or they remain the same, indeed those are the things that are always very slow to change.

But there are still even a lot more challenges yet to come, and they may make a great deal of difference, even with social problems.

And when they come; What will they bring? That no one knows how things would be then; what kind of a world mankind would be living in with the new object's technology frame.

So sorry to say, that is a question without an eye of prediction, or with a clear indication, it is too foggy to see in that direction.

But whatever comes, it will be with more knowledge in science, and it will make a lot of difference, life as it is today may not be the same, it could be much harder to make a living; so beware humans of your reckless changes.

Indeed, the present at this moment in time, it is an entire new world compared with the old, with developments and progress humans have drifted very far away from the past.

From the darkness of superstitions and ignorance, to knowledge in technology and science.

And from the marauding years of BC, and the difficulties and problems of a ruthless AD.

And from all the horrors and fears one dreaded each day when darkness fell.

Not to mention the swift speed of lightning whenever it was traveling, humans dread with thoughts that it came from the gods as a warning.

And of course too, the roar of the heavens, nothing was so frightening, believing that the gods were offended, and fearing what may happen next, should the gods become very vexed.

All of that mankind had feared, during his existence in the medieval years when knowledge was scarce.

So yes indeed, this new age of science and technology, this moment in time where humans have reached; they are now fully awakened from their sleep into the reality of their consciousness, and they are as excited as they could be.

To rise to the challenges of their intelligence, there may be yet no limits to humans' ambitions.

Creating most things both smart and intelligent, with nothing stupid, that is the modern-day challenge.

And still with a very long way to go to reach to the future, anything is possible, with scientific knowledge every door could be open.

So yes indeed in this new age, science and technology are the master key, unlocking new doors, creating new opportunities, inviting humans' expertise.

Changing things which are always better than before, with new problems piling one on top of the other. So what is the future really going to be with all this new technology?

No one ever seems to know what it would be like tomorrow.

Some say there is a possibility, perhaps for holidays on Mars or Mercury, everyone may jet off to go with their family, or on Venus they may jet off for a few days during Christmas.

So yes it could be said and without being misled, that mankind has made astonishing progress over the years, in the dawn of materialism.

Who could have predicted? Not even Nostradamus, that humans one day so successful, would have been loitering at the edge of the universe.

Never mind the very long time it took them to climb such a very steep and rugged mountain.

Upon the mountain is where human beings have reached, and it is from there their ambitions will be achieved.

Indeed, humans have already created some outstanding and amazing things, and still it is just the beginning.

In this new age, and with the tools of science and technology, there are tremendous opportunities which would open the doors to new discoveries.

And as humans unlock them one by one, exploring nature's hidden secrets for their development.

And even investigating still further, because there are so many secrets to unlock, secrets still held by nature, behind her unseen girder.

Secrets hidden in the darkness of invisibility; secrets humans' naked eyes could never see.

But with the eyes of artificial intelligence, nothing could be hidden from the curiosity of humans. So beware mother nature, your secrets are no longer safe.

Mankind is knocking at your door to collect what is his.

For far too long they were hidden under the sun, barricaded in darkness where they did not belong. But now is the time for your secrets to be exposed and given to humans so that they can build a much better world.

Unfortunately my friends, don't yet become too crazy, or be overwhelmed with optimism, because with all its splendour and glory, with all the expectations of a better tomorrow, it is quite obvious for anyone to see what life on earth is likely to be.

The direction in which humans are heading is not at all promising, the brightness appears to be getting dim.

It has drawn a margin for two extremes separating the rich from the poor.

Those with plenty and those with their bellies empty; those who have, and a have not society, that's how the world is looking likely to be, in fact, that is how it is already.

And that division getting wider all the time, that too is on the list of the failures of politicians.

Failing in their duty as their responsibility, to root out poverty from society.

And although the world is already full of opportunities in science and technology, the world is still many miles away, very far indeed from the state in which it should be.

A state of justice, a state of peace, a state in which there is no poverty.

And that may be because the present has inherited too many wrongs from the past, causing it to flabbergast; causing it to be burdened with problems, so the present just passed them on to the next generations.

Yes, the past as dust has settled upon the present, some got blown away, some tightly held on. Creating a sinful world very exposed, affecting humans' body and soul.

And that was for certain the politicians' responsibility to remove the dust from history.

But what did they do? They failed again, failing to take seriously the commitments of their duty, and to do them effectively.

Yes indeed, they failed to do the things that really mattered most, so those same things just got worse.

And still getting worse every other day, with a lot more to come from nature's anger and rage.

So then, with the same question asked so many times.

What type of a world are the politicians developing? Those in charge, are they stupid or mad? They are never able to answer the same questions asked.

Century after century so many came and gone, and so too were even more politicians.

So what in the past have the politicians been doing? What really were their ambitions and their aims?

A question never answered at any point in time, things just moved on or they got left behind.

So yes it could be said, the world has moved on very far away from primitive times, indeed, the progress human beings have made has been superlative and extremely impressive, and yet still the world is as it is, an uneven divide which is getting very wide.

And although the world is very much progressive, and less superstitious as mankind has acquired knowledge.

This is the way the world has been developing, with the politicians making the decisions.

And as the world remains an uneven divide, with an escalation in crimes.

And with the gap between rich and poor stretching outwards further and further, getting wider even more.

With nothing to lose as their excuse, more and more people are turning to crime.

Finding it easy and very exciting, they get carried away and do it again.

And that's how crimes thrive in societies, with less deterrents and more opportunities.

And that too, many see it to be very unfair, and gives credence to the suspicions that the politicians don't really care.

And when they don't care, they don't even try to make decisions that are wise.

Yes, they make decisions creating a mess, and then they say it was their best.

And although it may be true that many do their best, they themselves are often left with something to regret.

And that is dangerous because the public loses trust, which then explodes into chaotic consequences with riots.

So yes it is said that throughout history, politicians made decisions all the time, that's their job, that's their duty, that's why they were elected, to govern responsibly, and with words wisely spoken, some of the decisions of politicians were good, very good, but some were bad, and affected lives.

And despite all their decisions, regardless of whatever was the purpose or their intention, yet still they failed to slam the brakes on the rise in crimes, although it was obvious that they were increasing in numbers all the time.

And yes indeed, so too they failed to eliminate the root causes of injustice, and in the social structures they failed the masses in many ways.

And that has been going on for centuries, with politicians one after the other they came and went, leaving things behind either a little better or in decline.

With both crimes and injustice embracing each other as partners together, delivering their services everywhere.

And that they did right through the ages, and today crime and injustice as partners still, their services like a flourishing good business have widely expanded.

So yes, there is nothing else to be said, to fail is what politicians often did, so the world developed to be as it is, with so many failures, the condition of the world as it is, could not be prevented.

With wrong and right, bad and good, values to follow, and yet the world is not as it should.

Considering the many centuries human beings have already existed, and the many politicians that came and gone, forget the bad ones. What indeed have the good ones done?

Has evil triumphed over good, that's why the world is not as it should?

No doubt indeed, that there have been many opportunities which have been lost.

Opportunities to make the world a much better place without the many problems human beings always face.

Not necessarily opportunities with luxury for everybody, that may be seen as an unnecessary stretch of generosity; but at least living in dignity, and in peace and harmony, and with justice as a fundamental premise.

Indeed, living in peace and not in pieces, living in dignity without any breaches.

Living at least in good sanitary conditions, instead of in slums that are degrading to humans, and where diseases are a constant threat, with frequent visits by the angel of death, even though one had not retired yet.

So with or without luxury, and relaxed instead of being in a hurry, human beings continued daily on their forward journey, the future was still their destiny.

Step after step they kept on going printing their toes in the mud, some heavy, some just scraping the ground, worrying sometimes where they went wrong, looking straight ahead they carried on; with their thoughts and imaginations in conflict sometimes, creating confusion in their minds.

Worrying about what next it should be, and what should they make their priority.

Was it to explore the Moon, Mars, or Mercury, or to go to the sun and return with some energy, or to remain on earth and eliminate wars, crimes and poverty, creating better societies?

Creating systems that were just and fair with laws that were impeccable in every country everywhere.

What are the things humans have not done? After so many centuries, so many things are still very wrong.

Spending billions to reach out into space, in an anxious search to find another human race.

Spending millions on weapons of mass destruction, when so many needed good causes are left forgotten.

Indeed, why are billions spent on those projects when social problems are in a mess?

The same unanswered questions yet again are put to the politicians spending billions on projects that are really of no usefulness.

Yes spending millions on weapons of mass destruction, too many nations are enemies instead of friends.

Can't trust the other, can't come together in harmony and peace with one another.

So yes indeed, what are human beings' priorities?' 'What are their ambitions and their aims?' What kind of a world are they developing?

How many times must the same questions be asked to get some explicit answers?

After century upon century, from the dark ages to that of science and technology, the same questions are asked again, with everyone waiting for science to explain.

What are the things human beings are not doing so that everyone could have a decent living?

Unfortunately it is obvious to see that at this moment in time, and confused in their minds, human beings still don't seem to know in which direction to go.

Whether to stay on earth and clean up their mess, or journey into space in search of somewhere to escape, some other place to contaminate.

But before that is done, humans should know this before it is too late, the universe is not theirs for them to mess with.

Doing things which cannot be undone may lead to consequences far beyond their imaginations.

Yes indeed, in this world of human beings there are still so many things to be done, humans are confused, they don't know where to start, on which one, and they don't even seem to know what is right or wrong with a positive conclusion.

So with each other humans are still fighting, when there are so many wrongs to be corrected.

But no one seems to care, least of all the politicians, they don't seem to have any answers on how to solve the problems.

And that is why despite the developments and progress, the future of the world looks threatened with darkness.

The light is not getting through as bright as it should be, there are too many obstacles, and the politicians seem lost for both ideas and words.

And because of that, there was never a clear answer, so to one of the problems politicians pointed their fingers; climate change was what they blamed, and yet still they continue to do the same, yes they talked a lot, with fear and threats in their spoken words, predicting a future that doesn't look too good.

And yet still provoking nature, although they are fully aware of the dangers of climate change appearing everywhere, stubbornly they continue as if they didn't care.

And now as it is getting a bit late with the damage to nature badly ravaged, they are trying to put their act together, fearing a devastating attack from nature.

After creating several species' extinction one after the other, many plants and animal life already disappeared; disrupting the delicate balance of nature.

And that they did as if they really didn't know that it was reckless to do so.

Or, maybe it was that they just didn't really care, or in their honesty, they didn't realize it was so severe.

Or perhaps just maybe, humans may like to engage in a war with nature, humans always like a good challenge, anxious maybe to use their nuclear weapons so as to gain the experience of the taste of a devastating cataclysm.

Yes humans often like to confront danger, in some way or the other, it makes them feel better.

Fortunately for human beings, the idea appeared in their heads, and then they realized that the destructive forces of nature combined with that of a nuclear war were really something to dread; something which they don't really want to experience, for it could be something even worse than catastrophic, something which could be devastatingly horrific.

Indeed, the ravages of nature have been going on for far too long, especially after the assassination of reason, that's when they exploded doing damages like the effects of a bomb, with large areas destroyed within seconds.

Yes, humans appeared to have lost common sense, no debating, no reasoning; criticisms and arguments were the voices heard at every meeting, dominated with matters of self-interest, regardless of the importance of whatever was the purpose of the business.

And that indeed only made matters worse, much worse, because nobody was reasoning, they were all arguing, shouting at each other at the top of their voices, everybody seeking their own interest, the common good was just another boring subject, not something to be bothered with.

So yes, the things politicians were doing after their confrontations in heated arguments were only sliding the world into ruins.

Ravaging nature again and again, whilst at the same time developing weapons of mass destruction, with nation provoking nations, and with a readiness to use their weapons.

With chaos and destruction always on their minds, either from nature or their own kind, peace was becoming very hard to find, it was as though the politicians were becoming partially blind, searching for peace in the wrong direction.

But no one dared to be the first to unleash such a horrendous curse with their weapons of mass destruction, fearing retaliation could be worse, and it was that fear for many years right until now which kept the peace, and indeed, the world was able to peacefully sleep.

So instead, and still with the urge for excitement, deep down into the hollowness of uncertainty, there is where humans took their curiosity.

Still searching for knowledge they carried on as far as they could reach, above the heavens, or even in hell deep down beneath.

Invading the boundaries of outer space, and lying to themselves that they were doing it for the benefit of the human race.

When the reality was, that there was always so much to do in their unjust world, with millions of people at all times were without a proper education, and living in unhealthy slums and privation; indeed, their conditions were beyond destitution.

Human beings whose abilities were completely wasted, and only because they were not educated.

And despite that, health care was unaffordable for many, death cut short their life too early as they waited many years for surgery.

Indeed, it was a disgrace when their lives could have been saved, but because they could not pay, for years they had to wait, and when an opportunity came it was too late.

And still scattered in many places, there are numerous cases, where thousands of children go hungry. Yes, in this day and age it is happening daily, this indignity is even spreading in affluent societies, and with bad policies operating daily, there could be food shortages, and a lot of wastages, with many more people going hungry.

And yes it is true, this is nothing new, in many places around the world many children go to work instead of going to school, transformed from children into factory tools, with no safety or proper rules, no law enforcement to prevent them from being abused.

And that's their predicament, a side effect of the failures of politicians.

Indeed, all those atrocities of yesterday are still happening today in many places, and yet they are never exposed in any way, so they continue from day to day.

They just continue to be a necessity, an essential part of economies.

So say the politicians turning a blind eye, doing nothing to prevent this callous crime, the exploitation of children, in fact, the pernicious abuse of the young generation.

But what can the world do if anything? When the politicians themselves are confused, and the wheels of production are successfully turning around by the forces of exploitation, and effectively contributing to the economy, so child labour they say is necessary.

And yes, during all this child exploitation, and the many more civil wrongs, governments stockpile weapons of mass destruction, for the purpose of killing people by the thousands, or perhaps by the millions.

Spending extravagantly on their military, with no real benefit to their country.

And even spending millions more to reach Mars and Mercury, when on Earth there is so much destitution and poverty.

But that is never a priority, to eradicate poverty there is no policy, money is better spent on a strong military, there is always an enemy, either real or imaginary.

So poverty remains constantly on the rise with nowhere for anyone to hide, and with the biggest single problem, how to stay alive.

Yes indeed, those are the policies, they are never in the favour of those in need, especially those who are destitute, their lives are without value, no one cares a damn about their existence, no need to be concerned about them, they are of no importance.

And that indeed is the attitude, that is the response, it is another failure of the politicians.

So yes indeed, truth is very real, it is all in this book for you to read, and from over the years there were some real facts now brought to you in white and black, where the politicians of the world have let things get too slack.

They have failed to prevent the spread of sin, when all the time that's how the world was developing; creating a sinful world with no peace, or justice; life went on without them as if to mankind peace and justice were of no importance.

And yes, despite those irritating problems, politicians failed their nations in health care and education, in housing, transport, and social structures; a lot of disasters were due to their failures. Things which for years were left ignored, expanding all the time until they explode.

Not forgetting the system of law and order, there is where they have failed more than ever; their failures are something much more than deplorable, they are worse than abominable.

Failing to deliver justice whenever needed, failing to prevent injustice from spreading.

Failing to prevent the double standards in law, one for the rich, one for the poor.

And within the institutions of International order, double standards are rife more than ever.

Failing to crush the roots of corruption, this capitalist virus that affects every nation.

Taking a tight hold on politicians, with effects that are often damaging, which give rise to double standards that become common practice among world leaders.

Indeed, an effect of corruption, not hidden but transparent, and yet nothing is ever done to eradicate that addiction affecting politicians, it appears that the alcohol is too strong, and that no cure has yet been found.

So they break or bend the rules, some nations are supported, some are ridiculed and condemned, and for the very same offense.

Yes indeed that's how it is, that's how double standards are operated.

Creating the mess the world is in, and pointing fingers at someone else to blame.

Indeed, when there is no international clarity on world policies, and no unanimous voice deciding wrong from right, and the very nation accused could veto other ideas.

Then how could the world ever be a better place? How indeed could it ever deliver justice?

When the leaders of the world can't agree on anything, self-interest is their favourite, in fact the very rules they put in place are often idiotic, hence, there is hardly any wisdom in some decisions they make.

Yes indeed politicians may try to do good, that is understood, but too often they try with policies that are useless instead of useful.

And towards their own interest many of them break the rules, some abuse the rules, and some are innocent victims of the rules.

And this quandary created by world leaders executing double standards to suit their purpose.

How indeed could the world ever be at peace with itself when nincompoops are world leaders?

Yes indeed, there are still too many of them, and that's the reason for bad policies creating wars, and opening doors for the spread of corruption.

When it is by fools the world is governed like this, "How could it ever be a better place?"

So yes again politicians have failed, and this time their cowardice has us all derailed.

Failing to condemn what is wrong, and the only reason why, the wrong which was done was done by an ally, and there is where support lies, it is often more important than wrong or right.

And yes, as I continue to expose the failures of world leaders, again I have repeated this, that for many centuries and in every country, disgracefully politicians have failed women especially.

It was always as if they had forgotten them, or simply that they just couldn't care a damn, except of course at election times, that's when they used their charms.

And soon after the elections were over women were forgotten, just as things were that's how they continued.

Denying them their rights of equality, denying them education, protection and security, their right to vote and equal pay, which they are still denied in some places today, yes, they are denied all sorts of rights, and are even abused as a wife.

Not to mention the daily abuses and harassment which they encounter in public places wherever they went, often raped and murdered, and yet still again and again politicians do nothing but to wash their hands clean.

Failing to implement the laws to prevent the daily abuses of women, and to execute proper punishments upon the cowards who offend them.

Failing even to take their complaints seriously, institutional sexism is very common among the police, so the offending culprits escape scot free, not enough evidence is the excuse given, and even without a proper investigation.

And yes, this has been so in racism too, opportunities were denied if you were not white; for justice and equality one always had to fight, and with no other but the ruling elite; they caused problems to ignite with their bad policies they believed to be right.

So yes indeed, if you didn't already know, this is something you could believe.

Politicians have failed once, then again and again, they have failed in a lot of things, one after the other, too many wrongs they have endorsed or ignored, allowing them over time to become the norm.

Oh yes indeed, most regretfully they have failed to guarantee financial security and certitude in the safety of the welfare of every family, in that they failed miserably.

And they have failed to discipline institutions which implement policies that become institutional norms to the disadvantage of minorities, racism, and sexism; despite it has been happening for a very long time, and yet nothing was ever done, that's why it lasted so long.

And yes they have also failed to sustain full employment, and the rise in poverty to prevent, they have failed even not to fail, in weakness they prevail.

And they also failed young innocent children, no one should forget them, exploited in every form.

And the results of their failures have been damages which led to the world as it is with a dangerous surface and rough edges.

Oh yes my goodness, it was humans' recklessness that led to the development of the world into the condition as it is today, and that was so at every stage of development, in every age that was how it was progressing.

A world that has been quite progressive in many ways, but the many years it took, too many people have been killed and wounded during each development stage: in wars humans created, always engaged, because to prevent them the politicians failed.

And that was for real because of bad policies, callous indifference, general neglect by politicians, and of course their persistent arguments and disagreements, blaming each other all the time.

So yes unfortunately, those were the forces that created the world as it is today, both constructive and destructive.

Destruction caused by too many wars, wars created when they could have been avoided; if only the politicians were less intransigent, more co-operative and sensitive, more willing and determined.

Wars which could have been avoided and lives saved, with disputes settled in better ways.

But war was what politicians often chose, and often with powers they abused.

And although this was something the politicians knew; that the art of politics is in convincing the masses.

That they often did either to confuse, or to exploit, and to take advantage to their benefit.

And that happened wherever they went, especially whenever there was an election.

To get elected they convinced the masses during their campaign, they convinced them that they will do all sorts of things, yes indeed even better wages, and a better standard of living.

As miracle workers, things will not be the same, they will only get better again and again.

And after they got elected their promises simply vanished, into thin air they disappeared invisible above everyone's head, so most things remained the same; some changed for better or for worse, either filling or emptying someone's purse, with prices going up, when at the same time earnings got stuck, and what is on offer is never enough, times indeed are getting tough.

Yet nothing was ever done, nothing came with a guarantee whatever politicians promised, that's just what they did to get elected; yes promising the world, an arm, and a leg, and even a crown upon your head.

Promising what they had no intention to deliver, jobs, and bread with peanut butter, but as they already knew, they were all only useless promises, so it didn't really matter if they didn't deliver.

And that was how when policies were delivered, many bad policies were implemented within the systems, supported by the masses with good intentions.

And when the masses found out just how bad it is, the policies had already done a great deal of damage.

As was the cause of wars, many people lost their jobs with their livelihood lost.

Some policies created the systems of serfdom, ethnic cleansing and fascism; slavery, apartheid, segregation and communism; whatever they created they were oppressively implemented.

Some just made existing things worse, as it was exposed during Covid-19 and Brexit.

Oh yes indeed, human beings everywhere were often misguided with bad policies, one of which was the cause of Covid-19 rapidly and easily spreading.

Indeed Covid-19 has been a good example of how governments dealt with problems yesterday, today, and even tomorrow, regardless of the size, the weight, or whatever was the measure of the seriousness.

The institutions of world politics sadly they appear to be places brimming with corruption; and hypocrisy, double standards, self-interest, and callousness, so with that bundle of dirty linen, and with no one ever cleaning, that is why the world is as it is, it's like a dustbin mixed with clean and dirty linen.

So yes it is true if you didn't already know that in most cases it has always been so, in politics strength dominates, not wisdom nor weakness, not even common sense or good intentions.

It is those with devastating bombs, weapons of mass destruction, and strong economies; those are the ones who are respected, those are the ones with the influence, those are the ones who make the decisions, those are the ones who give the orders.

And that is why the world is as it is, judge for yourself, it is obvious there is nothing else.

In most places governments are corrupt, the world is in a mess, too many people are desperate, and those are the results of years of politicians' failures.

Too many problems were ignored, despite the fact that they were getting worse over the years.

Perhaps there was not much governments could have done, but not even trying, that was very wrong.

Yes indeed, confused and agitated, that was often politicians' mood, and instead of working for the common good by reasoning together towards an outcome that could be fruitful.

Engaged in arguments and criticisms is what politicians do all the time in voices with different opinions; all with selfishness seeking their own interest.

And often pointing their fingers at someone else to blame, criticizing instead of doing the right things, hence, accusing China of developing a Covid-19 factory; instead of encouraging face masks, and vaccines.

Yes indeed, and very true to say that it is customary, the blame game is what politicians always play, it is their favourite; it has no rules, but if you are weak, you are sure to lose.

And for Brexit, that's just it. What will happen? It is still too early to predict; although some signs are showing darkness, maybe that may change with the click of a switch.

So yes indeed it could have been, that governments throughout the centuries should have done much better working harder together to create a better world.

That has always been their duty and responsibility, it is their commission, their mandatory vocation, in fact, it is their one and only priority, to govern in the interest of the people.

Indeed, they had so much time on their hands, and that's what is so difficult to understand.

Why didn't they work harder together for the better? Instead of always criticizing one another, with hardly ever any agreement whatsoever.

Indeed, and most regretfully, the international confusion during Covid-19, has been a very good example of governments' policies, how they deal with situations, and how they handle problems, during Covid-19 that was very transparent.

So it is true that they could have done much better, there were always so-lutions, good opinions, but they always got lost in political arguments.

Yes. always competing with one another instead of working together, espe-cially in the preparation for war, each wanting their weapons to be deadlier than the other, victory is in who killed many more.

And that was just how it was during the Covid-19 confusion, everyone in an argument voicing a different opinion without a meaningful agreement on how to deal with the situation.

Everyone with their own opinion, each claiming to be better than the other, can't put them together, no agreement whatsoever.

So they carried on engaged in the marathon rat race, pushing and shoving always in a haste with nothing in its proper place.

So the marathon led to both destinations, it was either into hell or into heaven.

Created by the forces of capitalism, with obstacles throughout from begin-ning to end.

Racing towards the future, to heaven, or to hell, to somewhere anywhere, somewhere with a bed. To capture their dreams as they rest their heads, some never woke up; they were dead.

And that was the tragedy of Covid-19, many died from the result of bad policies.

And those who woke up just kept on pushing towards wherever they were heading.

Afraid that they may never get there, so they hustled on their journey with-out much care.

And that was because they had nowhere else to go, except of course, six feet down below.

And so things were year after year for better or for worse, however they were, they were the inspirations of the rulers of the world.

The Kings, Pharaohs, Emperors, Dictators, and Presidents were the ones who made the decisions, shaping the world in whatever way they could.

Shaping the world to make it a great place, or to make it more divided and corrupted.

With hate and suspicions common norms, affecting the prudence of world leaders.

Creating still more divisions with more problems, no one could tell whether it would ever end.

Shaping the world sometimes for better or for worse, making themselves either useless or useful.

And to shape the world was exactly what they did, into a world submerged in sin, and yet progressively successful with an abundance of material things.

Which, when they were divided, some were without because of shortages.

And as leaders of the world responsible to keep the peace, what they some-times did, although they were seen, they were indeed very hard to believe.

Yes what they did, they smashed the peace into pieces with unjust draco-nian policies, causing resentful protesters everywhere.

And as the rulers of the world got agitated and confused, whatever powers they used they abused.

So without reasoning they engaged in hasty thinking, which led directly to a bad policy, shooting indiscriminately.

Killing and wounding, beating and arresting was the brutality harshly exe-cuted time and time again upon the protesting masses.

But that was the norm, that's what governments often did, and today all over the world they are still doing it, no lessons were learned from yesterday, so they can't yet find a better way.

Yes indeed, in some countries you could even get killed when protesting, some government's policies are very oppressive.

They have no ideas, they have no skills; they don't know how to deal with protesters in better ways.

Protesters who are usually protesting against injustice, to raise concerns so that politicians would get down to the root cause of it.

But it never always works, and protesters are still left with the same burden of injustice.

A burden which they carry sometimes for far too long, before disorder steps in and gets things done.

Indeed, it cannot be doubted that human beings have travelled a very long way to reach at this point of their journey in the twenty-first century where they are today, and it had been a journey with many tragedies, and greater still were the difficulties.

This I have repeated so that it may not be forgotten, just how long the journey has taken.

From their humble birth in the density of a wild forest, humans traveled out from the darkness many centuries ago.

And from their nakedness to clothing, indeed humans were making efforts progressing, and that they did.

So from caves they moved into houses which they built with tools they invented, and gradually equipped with domestic conveniences over a period of many centuries, and from the skill of riding horses to that of automobiles, and that too was developed gradually stretching over many centuries, yes indeed all were achieved as humans journeyed through different centuries, and at different development stages, improving all the time on what they had already invented as they acquired more knowledge, making them better with new ideas.

But progress indeed was extremely slow, there was still a lack of knowledge, with too many things which humans still didn't know.

And yes, although human beings have been very courageous, reaching this point in time has been nothing but miraculous.

Indeed, it is in the 21st century AD where humans have now reached after a very long and perilous journey, and through desperate times without knowledge, it was indeed ruthlessly intimidating, very tough to survive.

A journey which had been nothing but, fraught with dangers both natural and superstitious, with fear a constant companion generated by forces of intimidation.

And yet today humans are still travelling because they still have a very long way to go, unfortunately, they could be travelling still for many tomorrows, and that is because no one knows how much further to reach the future they still have to go.

So yes it is right, humans have travelled through darkness and light, up and down hills, turning left and right, most of the time without knowledge, most of the time scared and in fright, scared of the supernatural and the darkness of the night, scared of sounds, and no one in sight.

And yet still, despite their fears, despite the darkness in which they dwelled, humans were always on the path towards the future, and always with the desire for things to be better, changing and changing all the time, that's what progress meant to humans.

Not many things were perfect whatever they invented, so they always changed, then changed again, with new ideas they created better things.

Yes, leaving things behind, those which were redundant, those which were replaced by new inventions.

And as human beings continued forwards straight ahead, still developing and progressing, advancing from age to age, step by step, day after day.

Into a new age they have now entered, a new technological age with challenges in need of addressing, challenges that are very demanding.

Yes, challenges that would change the world, but no one was certain if they would do any good.

Indeed, this is the age of science and technology, this part of their journey where human beings have now reached, and everyone knows that it is a new age of enlightenment, new skills and developments, and yes excitement with new discoveries, the age of the twenty-first century, the age with a mirror view of how the future could be.

And from this age there is no going back, humans can't reverse on this track.

So yes, human beings are now creating things that are smarter than themselves, and doing the jobs they need to earn a living.

There is no doubt that these are very challenging years, and with acquired knowledge humans are creating some very smart things which are pinching jobs more than what foreigners did.

And despite this, humans are still making things to be as smart as they can, for them it is a dignified challenge, compelling, and even intimidating.

And that is what human beings are doing over and over again with the things they are creating, still making them smarter all the time with jobs for humans on the decline.

And as they were doing so, what they failed to realize and to know, was that the side effects were real, causing a very serious threat. But what could be done? Humans didn't know yet, not even how to combat the threat.

So the side effects continue to be the cause of the loss of many jobs, and at the same time a rise in crimes; both together were the result of science, with its advantages and disadvantages not separated and kept in check, but with both functioning at the same time, with the disadvantages transparent in crimes.

Indeed, science is bringing with it a lot of changes, including an unprecedented wave of new crimes, crimes committed online.

Crimes that were never committed before, bank accounts are now disappearing more and more.

And who was the culprit? Who was to blame? Who was the scapegoat in this criminal escapade?

Yes indeed it was Artificial Intelligence, that's what everybody blames.

This new discovery in science has become criminals' new beloved companion and friend.

A discovery in which everyone is engaged, regardless of their age.

Yes indeed, a discovery causing havoc every day, and yet most of the criminals get away.

It is a discovery causing a lot of headaches, perhaps its invention is a mistake, but indeed it has tremendous advantages which are too great to be left to disintegrate.

So now with another question no one ever asked.

With all this science and technology with new advantages and disadvantages, just what kind of a world is the future likely to be with more and more sophisticated crimes daily on the rise?

Could science and technology be ever used to eradicate crime, catching the criminals all the time? With certainty of no escape, no door, no window, not even a gate.

Making the world a safer and a much better place, with crimes de-escalating tumbling down upon its face.

And what could it do for those in poverty? How could they be helped with Science and Technology?

From one age to the next humans have progressed, and now into this modern new age of science, it is indeed an imponderable challenge.

A challenge that is so sophisticated, which can't be dealt with if you are not educated.

So would this be an age of new opportunities? The age in which nature's secrets are seen in all their glory, assisting human beings in all their needs.

After an exhausting very long journey, into the brightness of this new age, humans can now widely exploit their abilities with their knowledge, experiences, and skills.

Indeed, it may be an age of more successes and less failures, and even assisting the police to catch lawbreakers, reducing crimes to much fewer numbers with no escape for criminals.

So yes indeed, this is a very momentous human need, an age which could be safe and secure, with justice delivered as it had never been before.

This new age of science and technology, it could be human beings' golden age of prosperity, indeed, an age of healthy longevity with new cures and remedies capable of preventing diseases.

Or it could even be flooded with all sorts of new crimes, an age aided by the science of artificial intelligence, it could really be very exciting and desperate times, no one could predict the outcome of science.

Yes indeed, the world could be brimming with criminal activities, and at the very same time with poverty and prosperity, both at the extreme, some with very plenty, some with their purse completely empty as it is happening already.

So yes indeed it could even be a world with more complex problems because criminals feel much more secure, they don't have to be on the scene of their crimes as they did before, robots may even be used to commit murder, who can tell what will be on offer.

Just as criminals are already robbing banks from any distance, thanks to their newfound friend artificial intelligence.

Yes for sure, crimes are now committed with no criminals on site, and courageously bold in broad daylight, they are committed day and night with artificial intelligence behaving spooky online, and they don't even have to hide.

So yes indeed it is very tempting to come out of retirement, and become a criminal once again, even if it meant doing just a few hours part time.

Artificial Intelligence has made it so easy, it has even bamboozled the police.

Oh my goodness, just the thoughts of it, indeed it is very tempting, and already happening, and it could even be worse still.

So yes indeed, it is not that hard to believe that it is very real, human beings are still heading towards an uncertain future, and still at this moment they don't know when they will get there.

Neither do they know what it will be like tomorrow, it is too foggy for them to see, so they can't tell with certainty what it is likely to be, what are the possibilities.

Passing through ages from one to the next, and still with fear, despite their progress.

Hoping still as difficult as it is, to reach a future without corruption and injustice, and well maintained by wise leadership in whom trust is.

A leadership without wars nor the enforcement of draconian laws, yes, a leadership that is determined to make the world a much better place where everyone can live peacefully, and with some dignity.

No more Kings, Pharaohs, Emperors or dictators; no more individuals with absolute powers, but elected by the people are democratic rulers.

Or, will it still be humans' destiny for them to continue on the same rugged journey?

With the same rights and wrongs, the same pros and cons, the same injustices, humans' weaknesses, and the same abuses of power and corruption.

For there is no certainty nor a guarantee, that the world would be better with democracy, and that everything would be as good as it should be, just because it is not a monarchy.

But after so many centuries living in dismal conditions, the world should not be waiting any longer to put right those which are wrong.

And yes indeed, regretfully, it has always been clearly seen, that after so many centuries of humans' existence one after the other, and in places everywhere, not for one single year the world has never yet been a paradise, human beings have never been that wise.

Yes, for the corrupted rulers maybe, for the Kings, Emperors, Pharaohs, and Dictators, their lives maybe were in paradise, but never for the masses, that's no lie.

And it was transparent as well as obvious for all to see, one simply had to open their eyes.

Whoever was a leader, was not necessarily clever, neither was he incorrupt implementing policies that were fair and just.

Most leaders were like everyone else, none were gods, most perhaps were demons, and were in politics for themselves.

So the world carried on in the same direction, with unjust laws and unnecessary wars with human beings mercilessly slaughtering one another to fulfill the ambitions of the leaders.

And with the people protesting for change whenever it becomes overbearing, that scenario remains the same, they were shot at yet again.

But who was to blame, when the politicians together could not find an answer.

They carried on arguing in their own interest time and time again, everybody hearing whatever was said, but no one listening, and day after day they achieved nothing.

And that may be because of the accusations, the denials, and the criticisms, all bundled together in heated arguments, instead of constructive and sensible debating with good reasoning.

And not only hearing, but listening and understanding what the others were saying were important.

Yes, listening to opinions with a good sense of comprehension, without inviting altercations.

But that was exactly what was not happening since reason was assassinated; arguments became commonplace, so wise decisions were seldom made.

There were more arguments with one another instead of reasoning together in search for a wise answer.

Indeed, humans argue all the time, and still they don't realize that it is never wise, in arguments there are no answers.

And that maybe was the reason over the years for so many political failures, and which was very obvious, in the confusion of the Covid virus, searching for an answer in arguments, when indeed there were none to be found.

And because there was no reasoning there were a lot of mistakes, a lot of criticisms and arguments, so Covid-19 just kept on spreading instead of receding.

But that was no surprise, that's how politicians make decisions all the time.

And the results of their decisions were often the same, too many bad policies yet again.

So it may be, and quite necessary with urgency, for reason to be resurrected and brought back to life again: so that mankind will be wisely reasoning together, understanding each other, and making wise decisions with agreements from the wisdom of different opinions.

Yes, making and implementing wise decisions, hence, preventing further developments of unnecessary problems.

And especially the savagery of wars, there should be nothing to justify its cause, yes indeed, it is time that wars should be banned completely so that the world could sleep peacefully.

So yes it is time to bin the arguments and return to reasoning, so that the world could get back on track again.

But then again, and this is true as it is certain, the world could only be, and it will always be whatever human beings make it to be.

Yes it is theirs to develop or destroy, humans have but only one choice.

So again I repeat. What kind of a world are human beings creating? What is it likely to be?

Into the future could anyone see?

For at this moment in time there seems to be no clear indication.

It appears to be a world with an unsavoury mix of affluence, poverty, superstitions, crimes, technology and science.

So what is it going to be something much better or something worse, a blessing or a curse?

Unfortunately no one knows.

However the world may turn out to be, rest assured that it is the politicians responsibility.

They will be the ones to take the credit or blame, whether or not they failed again.

So as politicians they should be wise and create a paradise.

A world in which everyone is happy to live, because the world is no longer a sinful place.

Indeed, there is no doubt that humans have the ability, the wisdom and integrity, so what is now required is for humans to use them sensibly.

And it is only then there would be a much better world, with each person doing the best they could.

Doing what is right and despising wrong, because on earth there is heaven, and that is because everyone is again reasoning together instead of arguing, so wise decisions are made, and are implemented, hence the world a much better place.

Indeed, during the past centuries, during human beings' exhausted journey, they have developed a very corrupt and sinful world, this has been known.

But they were always with hope that things would be better, and that was because they could.

So now, and very truthfully to say, with humans' acquired knowledge in science and technology, the world could now be as good as it should be.

This is the hour to make it better, this is the time to make the changeover.

And that is because it is not too late, humans have arrived at heaven's gate, all they have to do now is to enter, and do the things to make the world better.

So now you have finished reading this book right to its last page and the last word.

You should now be wiser and looking younger, because the facts in it should have awakened your hibernating consciousness to both the darkness of sin, and the brightness of humans' successes; in both of these realms humans have dwell experiencing the joys of heaven and the torments of hell. Yes indeed, it should have unlocked your awareness to the reality of human beings' capabilities, capturing every breath of their imagination, whatever humans could imagine. And at this very moment you have entered heaven's gate; for what it is worth reading this book you should have gained some knowledge.

And with that knowledge you should have changed with efforts to make the world a better place.

Yes indeed, working together with everyone else, with each individual doing their best.

No more corruption especially from the top, to acquire a better world it has to stop.

But after two days if you feel no change, it is advised that you should read the book again, because it will be certain that you did not absorb everything.

God bless you my friend, and thank you for reading.

For I am certain that at least some knowledge you have gained about the ethics of human beings; whether a beggar or a king, humans' weaknesses are the same.

And with that knowledge you should have the courage to always fight for justice.

Creating a better world for both young and old, without disparities affecting livelihoods.

Creating a better world for everyone, regardless of their sex, their race, or religion.

Yes indeed creating a better world, one which is not selfish and sinful.

Contents